THE BURGHS AND PARLIAMENT IN SCOTLAND,
c. 1550–1651

To Janet

THE BURGHS AND PARLIAMENT IN SCOTLAND,
c. 1550–1651

ALAN R. MACDONALD
University of Dundee, UK

Research for this book supported by the

Arts & Humanities
Research Council

ASHGATE

Published by
Ashgate Publishing Limited
Gower House
Croft Road
Aldershot
Hampshire GU11 3HR
England

Ashgate Publishing Company
Suite 420
101 Cherry Street
Burlington, VT 05401-4405
USA

Ashgate website: http://www.ashgate.com

British Library Cataloguing in Publication Data
MacDonald, Alan R., 1969–
The burghs and parliament in Scotland, c.1550–1651
    1.Boroughs – Scotland – History – 16th century 2.Boroughs – Scotland – History –
    17th century 3.Scotland – Politics and government – 16th century 4.Scotland – Politics
    and government – 17th century
    I.Title
    328.4'11'09031

Library of Congress Cataloging-in-Publication Data
MacDonald, Alan R., 1969-
The burghs and parliament in Scotland, c. 1550–1651 / by Alan R. MacDonald.
    p. cm.
Includes bibliographical references and index.
    1. Municipal government–Scotland–History. 2. Boroughs–Scotland–History. 3. Convention of Royal Burghs (Scotland)–History. 4. Representative government and representation–Scotland–History. 5. Scotland–Politics and government–1371-1707. 6. Scotland. Parliament–History. I. Title.

JS4123.M33 2007
328.411009'031–dc22

2006020596

ISBN 978-0-7546-5328-8

Printed and bound in Great Britain by MPG Books Ltd, Bodmin, Cornwall.

Contents

List of Illustrations

Acknowledgements

Although the writing of books like this is ostensibly the ploughing of a lone furrow, whatever its flaws it would be much the poorer had it not been for the input and support of many people. Some were acutely aware of their involvement, possibly to the extent of groaning internally every time I raised the issue, while others were unwitting helpers. To all I should like simultaneously to express my thanks and ask their forgiveness. Keith Brown, Michael Lynch and Charles McKean read parts of the text and I owe them much more than a free copy in return for their comments, corrections, references and suggestions. Many others shared thoughts, lent books, responded to queries, provided references, tips on making graphs and help with an application for funded research leave. In the most egalitarian order (allowing no room for processing *ad seniores or ad juniores*) I thank Callum Brown, Helen Carmichael, Steve Connolly, Mark Cornwall, Judith Cripps, Mark Godfrey, Julian Goodare, Bob Harris, Richard Hunter, Billy Kenefick, John McGavin, Allan Macinnes, Gillian MacIntosh, Alastair Mann, Rosalind Marshall, Derek Patrick, Roy Pinkerton, Miri Rubin, Hamish Scott, Marion Stavert, Laura Stewart, Chris Storrs, Roland Tanner, Martine Van Ittersum and Eila Williamson.

The almost universally helpful and courteous staff of the archives and libraries in which this research was carried out made the process of gathering the data a happy one. To all staff at the following institutions, I give my thanks: Aberdeen City Archives, Angus Archives, Ayrshire Archives Centre, Dumfries Archives Centre, Dundee City Archives and Record Centre, Dundee University Archives, Dundee University Library, Dundee University Law Library, Edinburgh City Archives, Edinburgh Central Library, Fife Council Archives Centre, Glasgow City Archives, the National Archives of Scotland, the National Library of Scotland, Perth and Kinross Council Archives, Perth Guildry Incorporation, the Royal Commission on the Ancient and Historical Monuments of Scotland, Stirling Council Archives, and St Andrews University Library Department of Manuscripts and Muniments. I should also like to thank the earl of Dalhousie for permission to quote from his family papers, on deposit at the NAS.

The University of Dundee granted me sabbatical leave over one semester and the Arts and Humanities Research Council's Research Leave Scheme allowed me to add a second semester, without which this book would never have been written. The Carnegie Trust for the Universities of Scotland was generous in providing financial support for research trips to archives all over Scotland and I am grateful to the Department of History at the University of Dundee for similar support. The Strathmartine Trust provided generous help in defraying the costs of copy-editing, a task which was expertly carried out by Alison Duncan, to whom I am deeply indebted for saving me from an attack of subjunctivitis, *inter alia*.

My family bore a greater burden than any others and I should like to apologise to them for spending most of 2005 in the dining room and putting it out of action as a social space. David, Johnnie and Elsie deserve thanks for accepting (most of the time) that, even though I was at home, I could not always play with them and for not asking to play pinball on my laptop too often. It remains a mystery to me that minor details of burgh commissioners' expenses are not universally fascinating and Janet has patiently borne a series of excited outbursts on that and other obscure aspects of early modern urban parliamentary activities. Her eye for the incomprehensible sentence has rescued me from many pitfalls: all the incomprehensible sentences which remain are there in spite of her numerous pleas for clarity. In return for her solid support in every possible way, the dedication is a small token of thanks.

Alan MacDonald
January 2006.

Conventions and Abbreviations

Dates

Before 1 January 1600, the year began on 25 March but all dates are given in post-1600 style, therefore 5 January 1569 is 1569, not 1570.

Language and terminology

The letters *u*, *v* and *w* were interchangeable in the period and have been regularised according to modern usage, as have *i* and *j*. The letters 'yogh' and 'thorn' have been given as *y* and *th* respectively. The spelling *quh* was equivalent to English *wh*, so quhair = where, quhilk = which. In Scots, plurals and possessives were formed using '-is', past participles using '-it', and present participles using '-and'. Except where they appear in quotes, proper names have been modernised. The word 'bill', meaning a legislative proposal, was not current in Scotland until the middle of the seventeenth century. A draft could be called an 'article' but it was also common to call it an 'act'. The committee which drafted the acts was called 'the committee of the articles', 'the lords of the articles' or sometimes just 'the articles'. Less familiar words in quotations are explained in the text or in footnotes. Where no explanation is given and the meaning remains unclear, readers are referred to the dictionaries cited in the bibliography.

Currency

All money is expressed in £ Scots, unless otherwise stated. Between the middle of the sixteenth century and 1603, the value of the £ Scots in relation to the £ sterling declined from about 4:1 to 12:1. The latter was then fixed as the exchange rate in perpetuity. The merk was commonly used in accounting and was worth two-thirds of a pound (13s 4d). For the benefit of those unfamiliar with pre-decimal currency, there were 12 pence in a shilling and 20 shillings in a pound.

Citation

In citing manuscripts, three forms have been used: where a manuscript is foliated, folio numbers (f.) are specified; if the manuscript is paginated, the citation uses only numbers; where there is no foliation or pagination, the date is given.

The following abbreviations have been used in footnotes:

AA	Angus Archives, Restenneth, Forfar.
AAC	Ayrshire Archives Centre, Ayr.
Aberdeen Letters	L. B. Taylor (ed.), *Aberdeen Council Letters*, 6 vols (Oxford, 1942–61).
Aberd. Recs.	J. Stuart (ed.), *Extracts from the Council Register of the Burgh of Aberdeen*, 4 vols (Aberdeen, 1844–72).
ACA	Aberdeen City Archives.
Adv. MS	Advocates' Manuscripts, National Library of Scotland.
APS	T. Thomson and C. Innes (eds), *Acts of the Parliaments of Scotland*, 12 vols (Edinburgh, 1814–75).
Ayr Burgh Accounts	G. S. Pryde (ed.), *Ayr Burgh Accounts 1534–1624* (Edinburgh, 1937).
Baillie, *Letters and Journals*	D. Laing (ed.), *The Letters and Journals of Robert Baillie, A.M. Principal of the University of Glasgow, 1637–1662*, 3 vols (Edinburgh, 1841–2).
Balfour, *Works*	J. Haig (ed.), *The Historical Works of Sir James Balfour*, 4 vols (Edinburgh, 1824).
Balfour Paul, *Scots Peerage*	J. Balfour Paul (ed.), *The Scots Peerage*, 9 vols (Edinburgh, 1904–14).
Birrel, 'Diary'	'The Diarey of Robert Birrel, Burges of Edinburghe Containing Divers Passages of Staite and Uthers Memorable Accidents', in J. G. Dalyell (ed.), *Fragments of Scottish History* (Edinburgh, 1798).
BOEC	*Book of the Old Edinburgh Club.*

Calderwood, *History*	David Calderwood, *History of the Kirk of Scotland*, 8 vols, T. Thomson and D. Laing (eds), (Edinburgh, 1843–9).
CSP Scot.	J. Bain et al. (eds), *Calendar of the State Papers Relating to Scotland and Mary Queen of Scots, 1547–1603*, 13 vols (London, 1898–1969).
DAC	Dumfries Archives Centre.
DCA	Dundee City Archives and Records Centre.
Diurnal of Occurrents	*A Diurnal of Remarkable Occurrents That Have Passed Within the Country of Scotland Since the Death of King James the Fourth Till the Year MDLXXV*, T. Thomson (ed.), (Edinburgh, 1833).
ECA	Edinburgh City Archives.
Ecclesiastical Letters	B. Botfield (ed.), *Original Letters Relating to the Ecclesiastical Affairs of Scotland*, 2 vols (Edinburgh, 1851).
Edin. Recs.	J. D. Marwick et al. (eds), *Extracts from the Records of the Burgh of Edinburgh*, 13 vols (Edinburgh, 1869–1967).
EHR	*English Historical Review.*
ER	*The Exchequer Rolls of Scotland*, J. Stuart et al. (eds), 23 vols (Edinburgh, 1878–).
FCAC	Fife Council Archives Centre, Markinch.
GCA	Glasgow City Archives.
Glasg. Recs.	J. D. Marwick et al. (eds), *Extracts from the Records of the Burgh of Glasgow*, 11 vols (Glasgow, 1876–1916).
Kirkcud. Recs.	John, IV Marquis of Bute and C. M. Armet (eds), *Kirkcudbright Town Council Records 1606–1658*, 2 vols (Edinburgh, 1958).

Moysie, *Memoirs*

David Moysie, *Memoirs of the Affairs of Scotland, 1577–1603*, J. Dennistoun (ed.), (Edinburgh, 1830).

NAS

National Archives of Scotland, Edinburgh.

NLS

National Library of Scotland, Edinburgh.

PER

Parliaments, Estates and Representation.

PH

Parliamentary History.

PKCA

Perth and Kinross Council Archives, Perth.

Pryde, *The Burghs of Scotland*

G. S. Pryde, *The Burghs of Scotland: A Critical List* (Oxford, 1965).

Rait, *The Parliaments of Scotland*

R. S. Rait, *The Parliaments of Scotland* (Glasgow, 1924).

RCRBS

J. D. Marwick and T. Hunter (eds), *Records of the Convention of the Royal Burghs of Scotland*, 7 vols (Edinburgh, 1866–1918).

RMS

Registrum magni sigilli regum scotorum, Register of the Great Seal of Scotland, 11 vols, J. Thomson et al. (eds), (Edinburgh, 1882–1914).

RPC

J. H. Burton et al. (eds), *Register of the Privy Council of Scotland*, 37 vols (Edinburgh, 1877–).

RSS

Registrum secreti sigilli regum scotorum, Register of the Privy Seal of Scotland, 8 vols, M. Livingstone et al. (eds), (Edinburgh, 1908–82).

SAUL

St Andrews University Library.

SCA

Stirling Council Archives.

SHR

Scottish Historical Review.

TA   *Accounts of the Lord High Treasurer of Scotland*, T. Dickson and J. Balfour Paul (eds), 13 vols (Edinburgh, 1877–).

Young, *The Parliaments of Scotland*   M. Young (ed.), *The Parliaments of Scotland: Burgh and Shire Commissioners*, 2 vols (Edinburgh, 1992).

Introduction

Happily, the Scottish parliamentary historian no longer needs to lament the dearth of recent scholarship. Since the 1980s, work on parliament in particular and national government in general has been carried out on a scale unknown in Scotland since the first quarter of the twentieth century.[1] The connection with the rising demand for political autonomy in Scotland during the last quarter of the twentieth century cannot be ignored, although it would be dangerously simplistic to link them too directly. The Scottish Parliament Project at the University of St Andrews was initially funded by a government which opposed the establishment of a new parliament for Scotland, determined to demonstrate that an interest in the old parliament did not necessarily denote a desire for a new one. The work at St Andrews to create a digital edition of the records of the Scottish parliament between the thirteenth century and 1707, nearly complete at the time of writing, has served to provide another boost to parliamentary historiography. This book had its origins in that project, which has also led to a number of other new works on Scotland's parliament.[2] It was born out of a realisation that parliament tended to be understood and portrayed primarily as a political assembly, dominated by the peerage and the monarchy, with relatively little attention given to its legislative function and its relationship with the nation at large. The burghs in particular have not featured prominently in the revival of Scottish parliamentary historiography.[3] Similarly, Scotland's urban history, which has also

---

[1]   Some of it remains as unpublished theses but much is in print: I. E. O'Brien, 'The Scottish Parliament in the 15th and 16th Centuries' (Glasgow PhD, 1980); J. Goodare, 'Parliament and Society in Scotland, 1560–1603' (Edinburgh PhD, 1989); J. Goodare, *State and Society in Early Modern Scotland* (Oxford, 1999); J. Goodare, *The Government of Scotland 1560–1625* (Oxford, 2004); J. R. Young, *The Scottish Parliament 1639–1661: A Political and Constitutional Analysis* (Edinburgh, 1996); R. Tanner, *The Late Medieval Scottish Parliament: Politics and the Three Estates, 1424–1488* (East Linton, 2001). For an overview of Scottish parliamentary historiography, see K. M. Brown, 'Parliament, Crown and Nobility in Late Medieval and Early Modern Scotland', in *Rapprasentanze e Territori. Parlamento Friulano e Istituzioni Rappresentative Territoriali nell'Europa Moderna* (Udine, 2003), 119–39.

[2]   K. M. Brown and R. J. Tanner (eds), *The History of the Scottish Parliament, Volume 1: Parliament and Politics in Scotland, 1235–1560* (Edinburgh, 2004); K. M. Brown and A. J. Mann (eds), *The History of the Scottish Parliament, Volume 2: Parliament and Politics in Scotland 1567–1707* (Edinburgh, 2005); A. A. B. McQueen, 'The Origins and Development of the Scottish Parliament, 1249–1329' (St Andrews PhD, 2002); G. MacIntosh, 'The Scottish Parliament in the Restoration Era, 1660–1681' (St Andrews PhD, 2002); D. J. Patrick, 'People and Parliament in Scotland 1689–1702' (St Andrews PhD, 2002).

[3]   Some early twentieth-century works, notably J. D. Mackie and G. S. Pryde, *The Estate of the Burgesses in the Scots Parliament and its relation to the Convention of Royal Burghs* (St Andrews, 1923), as well as a few journal articles did look at this issue. The works of Julian Goodare have incorporated the burghs into the wider picture of government and society, while

recently undergone a healthy revival, has tended not to give much consideration to parliament, albeit that a number of works have considered the burghs' relationship with central government and their role in national politics.[4] The parliamentary life of the burghs fell between these two stools and this book picks it up.

Partly because of the new political context, partly as a result of other changing historiographical fashions, Scotland's parliament tends now to be looked at without the prejudices of previous generations which measured it against the English parliament and found it wanting.[5] Early twentieth-century historians followed a long tradition, with its origins in the eighteenth century, which gloried in Great Britain and its empire and denigrated institutions which seemed not to form a part of that story.[6] The Anglo-British parliament at Westminster took a leading role and because the Scottish parliament looked very different from it, the inevitable conclusion was that it was sub-standard. Robert Rait, whose work remains useful to this day, provided a more positive impression of the Scottish parliament than was adopted by some of his contemporaries, but he still concluded that 'defects and ... impotence' were its most salient features, encapsulating its inferiority to the English parliament in its failure to 'give to the world that example of, and inspiration to, representative government which is perhaps the greatest English contribution to the development of civilization'.[7] Even if that were true of Westminster, which is doubtful, to dismiss another parliament for failing to set a trend for the world would be to condemn as inadequate every other representative assembly that had ever existed.

Representative assemblies need to be understood within their social, political and geographical contexts, not in relation to some abstract notion of an ideal parliament. In taking this approach, a better understanding of the form, role and function of these institutions can be achieved. It is just such an approach that characterises most modern parliamentary historiography, and is particularly exemplified in the output of the journals *Parliamentary History* and *Parliaments, Estates and Representation*.

---

my own '"Tedius to rehers"? Parliament and Locality in Scotland *c.*1500–1651: the Burghs of North-East Fife', in *PER*, 20 (2000), 31–58, made some tentative steps towards this detailed study.

[4]   M. Lynch, M. Spearman and G. Stell (eds), *The Scottish Medieval Town* (Edinburgh, 1988); M. Lynch (ed.), *The Early Modern Town in Scotland* (London, 1987), and E. Ewan, *Townlife in Fourteenth-Century Scotland* (Edinburgh, 1990) provide an impression of the breadth of work on towns. Studies of individual burghs include M. Lynch, *Edinburgh and the Reformation* (Edinburgh, 1981); E. P. Dennison, D. Ditchburn and M. Lynch (eds), *Aberdeen Before 1800: A New History* (East Linton, 2002); T. M. Devine and G. Jackson (eds), *Glasgow Volume 1: Beginnings to 1830* (Manchester, 1995).

[5]   C. S. Terry, *The Scottish Parliament: Its Constitution and Procedure* (Glasgow, 1905); R. S. Rait, *The Scottish Parliament Before the Union of the Crowns* (London, 1901); R. S. Rait, *The Parliaments of Scotland (G*lasgow, 1924).

[6]   K. M. Brown and A. J. Mann, 'Introduction: *Parliament and Politics in Scotland, 1567–1707*', in Brown and Mann (eds), *Parliament and Politics in Scotland*, 1–56, which provides an overview of historians' views of the Scottish parliament at 5–10.

[7]   Rait, *The Parliaments of Scotland*, 125–6, although see J. D. Mackie's review of Rait in *EHR*, 40 (1925), 425–7, where Mackie praises Rait's work for moving away from old Anglo-centric paradigms.

Yet there remains in some quarters a tendency to see parliamentary history primarily from the point of view of those at the centre of political power, which serves to present parliaments, and government in general, in a rather two-dimensional way. Old-fashioned 'whiggish notions of success and failure' of assemblies and their role in the advance or decline of 'liberty' in any given state remain prominent.[8] Early modern representative assemblies, because they were meetings of members of the political elites from all over a state with the ruler of that state, or at least the ruler's representative, were more than just a 'point of contact' between central government and the nation at large.[9] Parliaments did serve that purpose, but 'point of contact' gives too bi-polar an impression of how early modern states worked: it can be applied more appropriately to central law-courts, the monarch's privy council or the royal court but, even in those contexts, it can draw too stark a distinction between central government and the rest of the political nation. In the Scottish context, the work of Julian Goodare has broken new ground by examining who actually wielded power, how government worked with the resources it had, what it was trying to achieve and how the governed and the government interacted; parliament plays a prominent role in that story.[10] In examining what 'the state' actually was, what central government was trying to do and how successful it was in its efforts, he has prompted historians to re-examine existing assumptions.

A parliament was a representative assembly, not a confrontational setting in which two entities faced up to one another in an adversarial manner, nor one in which two groups of people, those at the 'centre' and those from the 'localities', met.[11] This study seeks to address this issue by examining the distribution of power, the utility and effectiveness of statute, and perceptions of central institutions in the localities. The power to admit a burgh to parliament, discussed in chapter one, provides insights into the degree to which royal authority was mediated through other bodies, while the examination of the theory and practice of representation in chapter two reveals ways in which power was understood, wielded and transferred. Chapters three and four explore, in different contexts, how parliament actually worked for the burghs, both collectively and individually, by looking at how they interacted with it, what they sought from it, what they got from it and how much store they set by it. Edinburgh is given special attention because it had a peculiar relationship with central government and with parliament. By looking at Edinburgh's unique role in relation to the convention of burghs and parliament, chapter five adds another dimension to the story. It also acts as a bridge between an assessment of the burghs' use of parliament and an exploration of another aspect of their relationship with

---

[8]   Brown and Mann, 'Introduction', 1–5, which provides an overview of current parliamentary historiography for the early modern period.

[9]   G. R. Elton, 'Tudor Government: The Points of Contact I, The Parliament', in *Transactions of the Royal Historical Society*, fifth series, 24 (1974), 183–200; R. Tittler, 'Elizabethan Towns and the "Points of Contact": Parliament', in PH, 8 (1989), 275–88.

[10]   Goodare's ideas have their full expression in his *State and Society* and *The Government of Scotland* (which begins by making clear the importance of parliament's role and emphasises that it is a study of how institutions of government 'were *used* by the political classes'). See also his numerous articles cited in the bibliography.

[11]   Goodare, *The Government of Scotland*, 114–18.

the legislature, their role in the staging of parliamentary meetings. This, in turn, opens up the question of how parliament was understood by the political nation through an exploration of perceptions of the political significance of parliamentary venues. Finally, chapter seven's study of the ceremonial side of parliament enables the investigation of another aspect of how parliament was perceived, for it provided the most important public setting in which the status of the individuals and burghs entitled to attend were projected and affirmed.

High politics plays only a limited role in this story. As far as the burghs were concerned, that was not what parliament was for. Indeed, parliamentary historiography in general has a tendency to concentrate too much on high politics.[12] In a recent collection of essays on the English parliament, its editors argued that the tendency of English historians to look at 'parliamentary politics in isolation and only in relation to the centre of government' stifled the subject's true potential, leaving 'many important questions that would have explained parliament's importance to contemporaries unasked or, if asked, were asked in such a way as to provide only limited perspectives'.[13] This cogent critique could be applied to much that has been written on the Scottish parliament and it strongly informs this study. Most of the business of most sessions of most parliaments did not relate to high politics and this business has received less attention than it merits. The bulk of it involved the passage of measures to benefit the common weal: regulations to ensure the proper conduct of the law-courts; measures to preserve game; statutes to regulate trade, both domestic and foreign; the establishment of commissions to reform the coinage or to visit the universities; acts which made new criminal offences and sought the enforcement of existing criminal laws; acts regulating inheritance, and a whole host of acts ratifying the rights, privileges and properties of individuals and corporations. For all but a few Scots and for the vast majority of commissioners sent to parliament by the burghs, this was what mattered.

Burgh commissioners came with urban concerns on their minds. For most of early modern Europe, a study of these people and their parliamentary activities would be understood in the context of 'parliament and locality'.[14] It would look

---

[12]   D. L. Smith, *The Stuart Parliaments 1603–1689* (London, 1999), which maintains a traditional focus on high politics, procedure and structures. Even the recent overview by M. A. R. Graves, *The Parliaments of Early Modern Europe* (London, 2001), has much more to say about power politics than legislation.

[13]   D. M. Dean and N. L. Jones, 'Introduction: Representation, Ideology and Action in the Elizabethan Parliaments', in D. M. Dean and N. L. Jones (eds), *The Parliaments of Elizabethan England* (Oxford, 1990), 1–13, at 1.

[14]   This is an idea which has become prominent in recent English work, particularly that of David Dean: see D. M. Dean, 'Parliament and Locality', in Dean and Jones (eds), *The Parliaments of Elizabethan England*, 139–62; D. Dean and C. Jones (eds), *Parliament and Locality, 1660–1939* (Edinburgh, 1998); R. Tittler, 'Elizabethan Towns and the "Points of Contact": Parliament', in PH, 8 (1989), 275–88; K. Sharpe, 'Crown, Parliament and Locality: Government and Communication in Early Stuart England', in *EHR*, 101 (1986), 321–50; A. Cosgrove and J. I. McGuire (eds), *Parliament and Community* (Belfast, 1983). It has also been explored in a number of European states: see P. Sanz, 'The Cities in the Aragonese Cortes in the Medieval and Early Modern Periods', in *PER*, 14 (1994), 95–108; I. A. A.

at how individual local communities, or at least the politically dominant elites in those communities, interacted with the national representative assembly. This is a relatively new approach in parliamentary historiography and it is drawn upon here, with particular regard to English comparisons. In the Scottish context, however, the concept of 'parliament and locality' is only a part of the story because Scotland's parliamentary towns had their own national representative assembly, the convention of burghs. Individual burghs were not alone in their interactions with central institutions because they had at their disposal the support and resources of an assembly of their peers which met regularly, regardless of whether a parliament was called by the monarch. The records of the convention of burghs allow a perspective on parliamentary history which is not available for any other estate in Scotland, possibly not for any other estate in Europe and certainly not for any other urban estate. Although most early modern representative assemblies consisted of estates, which represented different social groups, historians have paid relatively little attention to the activities of individual estates *per se*. Parliamentary estates rarely had a corporate existence outwith the representative assemblies in which they participated. The only possible exception is the estate of clergy but, although provincial councils and national ecclesiastical synods met all over Europe, they consisted of a much wider group than ever represented the Church in parliaments. The convention of burghs was, effectively, the parliamentary estate of burghs meeting independently of parliament.

To understand the operation of the convention of burghs and its relationship with parliament during the sixteenth and seventeenth centuries, it would be useful to know something of its evolution. In spite of the efforts of a number of historians, the precise details of its origins and early development remain elusive, but the reasons for its emergence are easier to pinpoint.[15] From their foundations by the crown in the twelfth century, the trading towns of Scotland were bound together by a single set of laws and regulations, the *leges burgorum*, possibly based on English and French models, closely related to those of Newcastle-upon-Tyne in north-east England, and developed to suit Scottish circumstances.[16] This legal uniformity was the essential prerequisite for many later developments for it locked existing and later foundations

---

Thompson, 'Cortes, cities and procuradores in Castile', in his collected essays *Crown and Cortes: Government, Institutions and Representation in Early-Modern Castile* (Aldershot, 1993); B. Kümin and A. Würgler, 'Petitions, *Gravamina* and the Early Modern State: Local Influence on Central Legislation in England and Germany (Hesse)', in PER, 17 (1997), 39–60; J. H. Grever, 'The Impact of the City Councils of Holland on Foreign Policy Decisions (1660–1668)', in *PER*, 14 (1994), 31–46.

[15]   T. Pagan, *The Convention of the Royal Burghs of Scotland* (Glasgow, 1926), ch.1; T. Keith, 'The Origin of the Convention of the Royal Burghs of Scotland, with a Note on the Connection of the Chamberlain with the Burghs', in *SHR*, 10 (1913), 384–402; G. S. Pryde, 'The Burgh Courts and Allied Jurisdictions', in G. H. Campbell and H. Paton (eds), *An Introduction to Scottish Legal History* (Edinburgh, 1958), 384–95; R. J. Tanner, *The Late Medieval Scottish Parliament: Politics and the Three Estates, 1424–1488* (East Linton, 2001), 25.

[16]   H. L. MacQueen and W. J. Windram, 'Laws and Courts in the Burghs', in Lynch et al. (eds), *The Scottish Medieval Town*, 208–27.

into a single legal structure: because the *leges burgorum* applied to all burghs, later statutes which built on their foundations did the same. It was thus logical for national bodies to emerge with jurisdiction over incorporated towns, the most notable and enduring of which was the convention of burghs. By the end of the thirteenth century, there was a 'court of the four burghs'.[17] It was presided over by the king's chamberlain and, by the middle of the fourteenth century, it oversaw the enforcement of the burgh laws, arbitrated in disputes between towns and merchants, and heard appeals from burgh courts and from decisions made by the chamberlain on his annual justice ayre around the burghs. It also acquired powers over the regulation of weights and measures. Until at least the end of the fourteenth century, it consisted only of representatives from the four principal burghs (Roxburgh, Berwick, Edinburgh and Stirling until 1368 when the first two, which had fallen into English hands, were replaced by Linlithgow and Lanark).[18]

During the fifteenth century it appears that this court became more broadly representative, but the confusing nature of the surviving evidence makes it impossible to pin down the chronology and nature of this development, which was crucial to the emergence of the convention of burghs. References survive to bodies variously described as the 'court of the four burghs', the 'parliament of the four burghs' and even 'the court of the parliament of the four burghs' but their laconic nature makes it impossible to discern whether they were different bodies with different compositions and functions or the same body as it evolved from a court of law into a representative assembly. Another impetus behind the development of the court of the four burghs into a national representative assembly was the establishment of the estate of burgesses in parliament during the fourteenth century. The burghs' prominence in payment of taxation under Robert I (1306–1329) and David II (1329–1371) meant that, from the outset, they required to meet separately as an estate during sessions of parliament to discuss their collective response to the crown's requests for money. They took advantage of such occasions to undertake other collective action, particularly relating to trade: in the 1340s '*toutes les ... grosses villes du royaume d'Escoce*' negotiated independently with Middelburg and Bruges, while in 1387, the duke of Burgundy received a supplication from the '*marchans du Royaulme d'Escoce*'.[19] This collective action in parliamentary and extra-parliamentary affairs continued and evidence for it increases during the fifteenth century.[20] Parliament brought the towns' commissioners together in a context in which the promotion of mutual self-interest naturally emerged. The advent of the estate of burghs in parliament must thus have played a significant role in the emergence of the convention of burghs. There was much business to be handled at parliaments which would have made it difficult for the burgesses to concentrate on their own affairs, so their representatives gravitated towards the court of the four burghs. Thus, during the fifteenth century, a body which

---

[17] Most of this paragraph is based on Pagan, *The Convention of the Royal Burghs*, ch.1.

[18] Pagan, *The Convention of the Royal Burghs*, 11; *RCRBS*, vol. 2, 482–4. Had the court been a general assembly of burgh representatives in 1368, there would have been no need to make specific replacements.

[19] Pagan, *The Convention of the Royal Burghs*, 17.

[20] Pryde, 'The Burgh Courts and Allied Jurisdictions', 394.

had been established as a royal court to oversee the burgh laws and which consisted of an officer of the king (the chamberlain) and a few representatives from four towns evolved into one in which all the towns subject to it were represented. As well as the impetus provided by the emergence of the parliamentary estate, it would have been in the interests of all burghs to send representatives to meetings of the court of the four burghs, since they would all have had an interest in its decisions. The next logical step would then be to incorporate them into the constitution of the court.

When the convention of burghs begins to emerge from relative obscurity in the 1550s, the king's chamberlain is nowhere to be seen. Indeed, the decline of that office may be another piece of the explanation for the emergence of the convention of burghs as a quasi-independent assembly. The chamberlain's job was to collect all the king's revenues, which theoretically involved an annual ayre, a tour of the royal estates and the king's burghs, although ayres may not have been as frequent in practice. In the fifteenth century, his jurisdiction became confined to the burghs when James I appointed a treasurer and comptroller to oversee royal finances. The last chamberlain ayre was recorded at Edinburgh in 1517, although it was not part of a tour, the last of those having occurred in 1511–1512 when at least Cupar, Dundee, Perth and Aberdeen were visited.[21] Perhaps the turmoil of the minority of James V was responsible for the demise of the chamberlain's role but, whatever the cause, it was formally ended in 1535 when the burghs were ordered to submit their accounts annually for audit by the exchequer. It may even have been at around the same time that the legal role of the chamberlain finally disappeared with the increasing authority and competence of the court of session, formally constituted as the college of justice in 1532.[22] It acquired jurisdiction over most of the judicial business which had previously come before the court of the four burghs and its formal constitution may have been, along with the chamberlain's loss of financial powers, a decisive event in the emergence of the convention of burghs as a representative assembly.

Long before this time, however, representative assemblies of burghs had met, although there is no evidence that they did so regularly. Before the end of the fifteenth century, burgh commissioners met 'for the gude of merchandice', in other words, they were not just convened by the crown to deal with a specific issue.[23] The only reason that the official minutes of the convention begin in 1552 is that these were the earliest available when, in the 1580s, the convention ordered the compilation of an official record. Although the passage of an act in 1552 that the burghs should meet annually makes it look like the beginning of something, a similar resolution had been adopted by a meeting of burghs in 1533, while fifteenth-century statutes also sought to establish annual conventions.[24] Records referred to as 'the auld statutes in the conventiounis of burrowis' were consulted in 1574, suggesting the existence then of records from before the 1550s.[25] As early as 1405, the court of the four burghs

---

[21]   Keith, 'The Origin of the Convention of Royal Burghs', 398; A. Murray, 'The Last Chamberlain Ayre', *SHR*, 39 (1960), 85.

[22]   Keith, 'The Origin of the Convention of Royal Burghs', 402.

[23]   ACA, Council Records, CR1/7, 865.

[24]   *RCRBS*, vol. 1, 2; *APS*, vol. 2, 179; Pagan, *The Convention of the Royal Burghs*, 25.

[25]   *RCRBS*, vol. 1, 30–31.

ordered that two or three commissioners from each royal burgh south of the River Spey should attend its annual meeting.[26] There are good grounds for believing that it began to evolve into a representative assembly during the fifteenth century. A statute of 1487 described something which sounds very like the convention of burghs of the later sixteenth century. It stipulated that commissioners from all burghs should meet annually at Inverkeithing to 'comoune and trete apoune the welefare of merchandis ... for the commoun proffit of borowis and to provide for remede apoun scaith ... sustenit within burrowis'.[27] It made no reference to the chamberlain or the court of the four burghs, although providing 'remede apoun scaith' sounds like a judicial function. This might even be the statutory recognition of the evolution of a court into a representative assembly.

References to the court, or 'parliament', of the four burghs do continue into the early sixteenth century and it was at about this time that the direct relationship between the annual meeting of burgh commissioners and the crown began to disappear, as the chamberlain ceased to convene conventions.[28] Some time between 1507, the last recorded 'court' or 'parliament' of burghs, and 1552, when its surviving records begin, the convention of burghs assumed the form it was to take for the rest of the period. There were certainly meetings of burgh commissioners in 1526, 1529, 1530, and 1532, and in 1533 commissioners from five burghs amended the statute of 1487 to the effect that the annual convention would meet at Edinburgh. There were further meetings in 1539 and 1541 and the next recorded convention is that with which the official records commence.[29] Most recorded meetings before 1552 resulted from summonses issued by the crown: Mary of Guise, regent in the 1550s, continued to summon some of their meetings but the convention's own records show that the burghs fixed the date and place of the next meeting themselves.[30] Only two conventions of burghs were summoned by James VI (in 1590 and 1592), and they were for consultation on specific matters of interest to the crown. A statute of 1581 confirmed the convention's already long-standing practice of choosing the date and place of its own meetings.[31] Not until the 1580s does something approaching a full record of conventions survive, with each annual general convention setting the date and place of the next, as well as scheduling meetings of commissioners from selected burghs to deal with specific issues.[32] In the intervening months, *ad hoc* conventions normally met for matters arising (including parliaments). From 1597, the burghs' own records distinguish between 'general' conventions which met early in July at a different burgh each year, and 'particular' conventions, which usually met at Edinburgh.

---

[26] C. Innes (ed.), *Ancient Laws and Customs of the Burghs of Scotland*, vol. 1 (Edinburgh, 1868), 156; Pryde, 'The Burgh Courts and Allied Jurisdictions', 394.

[27] *APS*, vol. 2, 179: remede upoun scaith – redress for harm done.

[28] Pagan, *The Convention of the Royal Burghs*, 13.

[29] Ibid., 13–14, 19–21, 24; *RCRBS*, vol. 1, 517; *APS*, vol. 2, 315.

[30] *RCRBS*, vol. 1, 10.

[31] ECA, Edinburgh Council Minutes 1558–1561, SL1/1/3, f. 39r; *RCRBS*, vol. 2, 521, 525–6; Mackie and Pryde, *The Estate of the Burgesses in the Scots Parliament*, 2–3; *APS*, vol. 3, 224–5.

[32] *RCRBS*, vol. 1, 108.

Many of the functions exercised by the convention of burghs, and the fundamental significance of that assembly, will become apparent in the pages which follow. Its records provide invaluable insights into the relationship between the parliamentary burghs collectively and the government of Scotland, the relationships between the burghs themselves, and their individual interactions with central government. Just as the records of the convention of burghs come into their own in the later sixteenth century, so too do the local records. From the middle of the sixteenth century onwards, an increasing number of the financial and administrative records of Scotland's parliamentary towns survive in local and national archives. Few have such splendid collections as Aberdeen, whose surviving council minutes begin in the 1390s, but most have some records dating from all or part of the period of this study, the starting-point of which was largely determined by the survival of these manuscripts and of the records of the convention of burghs. The Cromwellian conquest of Scotland saw the temporary eclipse of the Scottish parliament and marked a tidy point at which to stop, the only other obvious candidate being 1707, but the research required to cover the period between 1661 and 1707 would have taken many more years. The story of the burghs in parliament in its last 46 years, if it is to be written, must be left to another book and another scholar.

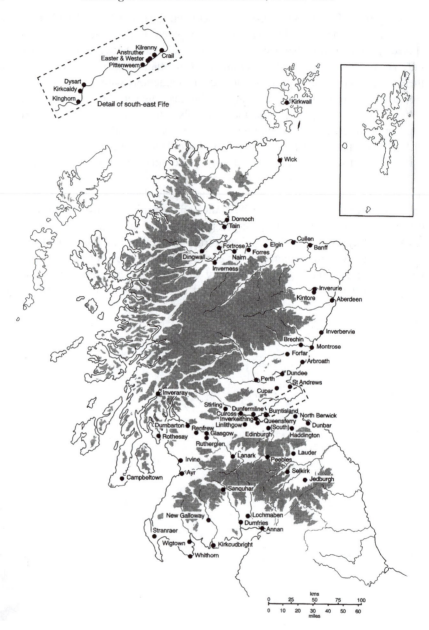

Figure 1   Parliamentary burghs before 1707. Note: Campbeltown, Cromarty, Fortrose/Rosemarkie, Inveraray, Inverbervie, Kirkwall, Stranraer and Wick were not represented until after 1660. Reproduced by permission of the Trustees of the Conference of Scottish Medievalists from P. G. B. McNeill and H. L. MacQueen (eds), *Atlas of Scottish History to 1707* (Edinburgh, 1996) and with permission of P. G. B. McNeill, the author of the map.

Chapter 1

Erection and Enrolment:
Gaining Entry to Parliament

Origins and development

The absence of a clear distinction between royal and other burghs before the middle of the fifteenth century makes it hard to define in the abstract which burghs could be summoned to parliaments and general councils (in the medieval period) or parliaments and conventions of the estates (from the sixteenth century onwards). However, none of the burghs which sent commissioners to parliament or paid tax during the fourteenth and fifteenth centuries was dependent on a secular superior other than the king. The only parliamentary burghs which were not dependent on the crown before the sixteenth century were subject to bishops. Thus most parliamentary burghs were royal burghs, although the two are often regarded as synonymous.[1]

In some ways, the situation in Scotland was akin to that in the many European states where only towns on the royal demesne were entitled to representation which thus remained firmly based on feudal principle.[2] However, there were significant differences: royal burghs were free-standing tenants of the crown, rarely situated on royal estates. Many were surrounded by the estates of landowners to whom they had once been feudally subject. Some royal burghs, Falkland in Fife for example, were on crown land, but Falkland did not become a royal burgh until 1458 and was never represented in parliament.[3] In the absence of concrete evidence, a royal precept of summons was probably the key factor in a burgh gaining entry to parliament before the sixteenth century: if it was called to parliament by the king, then it was represented, if not, it was not. In this sense, there were similarities with the Aragonese, Castilian and English systems, where the monarch chose which towns to summon.[4] As a result, there was considerable variation in which towns sat from one session to another in

---

[1]   K. M. Brown, *Kingdom or Province? Scotland and the Regal Union, 1603–1707* (London, 1992), 15.

[2]   A. Marongiu, *Medieval Parliaments: A Comparative Study* (London, 1968), 140, 154, 164–5, 227; K. J. Dillon, *King and Estates in the Bohemian Lands 1526–1564* (Brussels, 1976), 10–11; I. A. A. Thompson, 'Cortes, Cities and *Procuradores*', in idem, *Crown and Cortes: Government, Institutions and Representation in Early Modern Castile* (Aldershot, 1993), part 8, 1–2.

[3]   Pryde, *The Burghs of Scotland*, no. 51.

[4]   P. Sanz, 'The Cities in the Aragonese Cortes in the Medieval and Early Modern Periods', in *PER*, 14 (1994), 95–108, at 103–5; Thompson, 'Cortes, Cities and *Procuradores*', 5; A. D. Hawkyard, 'The Enfranchisement of Constituencies 1509–1558', in *PH*, 10 (1991), 1–25, at 14.

those states before the sixteenth century. Yet there is no evidence that Scottish kings could do this; once a burgh had obtained the right to parliamentary representation, it was summoned whenever a parliament met.

Not until the later sixteenth century do records become sufficiently detailed to enable an assessment of the process by which a burgh gained a place in parliament. Still, some things are considerably clearer for Scotland than for England, where dates of enfranchisement are uncertain due to the patchy survival of local records and the lack of central registers of crown grants. Scottish local records are similarly patchy but this is offset by the existence of codex registers of crown grants issued under the privy seal and the great seal, containing copies of the charters by which new burghs received privileges.[5] It is thus easy to pinpoint the date at which a Scottish town became a royal burgh. However, becoming a royal burgh was not the same as gaining entry to parliament. In England, royal charters explicitly included parliamentary rights but this was not the case in Scotland until the reign of Charles I.[6] Before 1625, the privileges granted to new royal burghs related only to trade, self-government and the administration of justice. Charters contained only a general statement that the burgh would have the same rights as all royal burghs, not an explicit grant of parliamentary representation. Under Charles I, the new phrase '*cum potestate commissionarios pro parliamentis eligendi*' appeared in charters, perhaps indicating an anglicisation of practice combined with the controlling instincts of a king who was keen to extend his prerogative.[7]

Some royal burghs never sent commissioners to parliament and not every burgh which was represented in parliament was a royal burgh. The first list of burghs at a general council in 1357 comprises 16 royal burghs and St Andrews which was dependent on its bishop. They were present because of their wealth rather than their legal status; many royal burghs were absent. For the next 200 years the number of parliamentary burghs grew until, by *c*.1550, there were 35. The incomplete nature of central and local records means that it is not clear how, why or even when a burgh was first summoned to parliament, but the key factor was probably taxation: the burghs which paid a share of taxes levied by the crown with the consent of the estates were entitled to parliamentary representation, on the *quod omnes tangit, debet ab omnibus approbari* principle. The seven ecclesiastical burghs which were taxed along with 35 royal burghs in the earliest extant national burgh tax roll of 1535 were all represented in parliament (St Andrews, Glasgow, Arbroath, Brechin, Dunfermline, Kirkcaldy and Dysart), and at least four of them were taxed in 1483.[8] Yet some of them paid

---

[5]   For problems with English sources, see Hawkyard, 'The Enfranchisement of Constituencies', at 3. Scottish charters are calendared in *RMS* and *RSS*, while the full MS registers are held in NAS.

[6]   Hawkyard, 'The Enfranchisement of Constituencies'.

[7]   Ibid., 11–12. For a typical crown charter of the sixteenth century see *RMS*, vol. 3, no. 2292 (Pittenweem, 1541) and for one specifically granting the right to parliamentary representation, see *RMS*, vol. 8, nos 1289 and 1346 (Dornoch, 1628, and New Galloway, 1630): the phrase can be translated as 'with power to elect commissioners for parliaments'.

[8]   *RCRBS*, vol. 1, 514, 543. The list from 1483 includes only burghs 'north of the Forth', so Glasgow would have been excluded, even if it had been liable for taxation. The Latin means 'That which affects all should be approved by all.' For discussion of the relationship between

tax long before they were represented in parliament. St Andrews was represented from the fourteenth century and Brechin first sent a commissioner in 1479, yet Glasgow's first commissioner appeared in 1546, Arbroath's in 1579, Kirkcaldy's in 1585, Dysart's in 1600 and Dunfermline's not until 1604.[9] Five of the royal burghs on the 1535 tax roll (Whithorn, Nairn, Tain, Lauder and Cullen) were also late in joining parliament. Perhaps they had the right to attend (they may have received summonses) but simply chose not to. None of those on the tax roll, with the exception of Tain, whose entry was opposed by Inverness, encountered any difficulty in being recognised as parliamentary burghs.[10] Thus inclusion in the tax roll appears to have been a crucial factor. Elsewhere in Britain and Europe, it was common for provincial capitals or county towns to be represented and most Scottish 'head burghs' of shires were parliamentary burghs, although some were not.[11] Although a clear set of rules to explain why a burgh was represented could be sought, none is satisfactory.

Some burghs which sent commissioners to parliament did not become royal burghs until many years after they had entered parliament, while others never became royal burghs, and some royal burghs never sent commissioners to parliament.[12] It would thus be better to describe those which were represented as 'parliamentary burghs'. The reasons for the lack of clarity about the qualifications for a parliamentary burgh can be traced to the emergence of the urban estate during the fourteenth century, perhaps even to the origins of the burghs themselves. They were latecomers to a body which began as an assembly of churchmen and lay tenants-in-chief. By the early fourteenth century, when the first signs of the participation of burghs can be traced, a number of other assemblies, notably those in the Iberian peninsula, already included representatives of towns, that of Leon having led the way with an urban component in the later twelfth century.[13] Yet the advent of the burghs was not exceptionally late;

---

taxation and representation, see R. S. Rait, 'Parliamentary Representation in Scotland', in *SHR*, 12 (1914), 115–34, at 128–9.

[9]   Pryde, *The Burghs of Scotland*, section 1. Dysart and Dunfermline were summoned to a convention of estates in 1594, but their first appearances at parliament were in 1600 and 1604 respectively (*RCRBS*, vol. 2, 93, 172). The first recorded election of a commissioner by Dunfermline was in 1608 (NAS, Dunfermline Burgh Court Book, B20/10/3, ff. 92v and 125r).

[10]   Tain rarely sent commissioners to conventions of burghs and this lack of commitment raised questions about its right to exercise the privileges of a free burgh. See *RCRBS*, vol. 1, 115–16, 163, 283.

[11]   The cities in the Castilian cortes were provincial capitals: Thompson, 'Cortes, Cities and *Procuradores*', 2. Welsh parliamentary boroughs were shire towns, while in England (as in Scotland) not all shire towns were represented: see Hawkyard, 'The Enfranchisement of Constituencies', 12; Pryde, *The Burghs of Scotland*, nos 213, 218, 230. Clackmannan, Kinross and Kincardine were head burghs without parliamentary representation; when Stonehaven became head burgh of Kincardineshire in 1607, it was not made a royal burgh: see *APS*, vol. 4, 374–5.

[12]   Rait, *The Parliaments of Scotland*, 250, 255; T. Pagan, *The Convention of the Royal Burghs of Scotland* (Glasgow, 1926), 27–8.

[13]   M. A. R. Graves, *The Parliaments of Early Modern Europe* (London, 2001), 10, 14–16; Marongiu, *Medieval Parliaments*, 62–72, 87–90; J. F. O'Callaghan, 'The Beginnings of the Cortes of Leon-Castile', in *The American Historical Review*, 74 (1969), 1503–37.

towns were not represented in England until the late thirteenth century and were not a regular feature until after 1320, nor did Aragon's cities figure prominently until the same period.[14] The twelfth and thirteenth centuries witnessed significant urban growth across Europe, accentuated in Scotland by the lack of pre-existing urban settlements. Alongside this came a growth of 'community consciousness', expressed in Scotland in the use of the phrase 'the community of the realm' to underpin political action during interregna and war with England. This extended the understanding of the political community beyond the relationship between monarchs and individual vassals to include corporate bodies, especially towns, which, because of the density of their populations, were quick to develop distinctive community identities.[15] A growing awareness of the difference between urban and rural society, combined with the fact that most early Scottish burghs were tenants-in-chief of the crown, meant that towns were soon seen as a separate group, socially and politically. A collective community identity developed as society began to understand itself as divided into 'estates'.[16] The first manifestation of this occurred in 1296 when six burgh seals were attached to the ratification of a Franco-Scottish treaty which had required 'the communities of the towns' to contribute to war against England. The phrase is French, indicating that the initiative came from France, where the participation of the *bonnes villes* in matters of national importance was already established.[17] There must have been urban involvement at whatever assembly ratified the treaty, but there is no evidence that it was a parliament.[18]

Burgesses petitioned parliaments in the 1310s and may have sat in a parliament in 1326, although there was considerable debate over this in the early twentieth century. The grant of a tax of an annual tenth to Robert I (1306–1328) listed the communities of the burghs as present 'while a parliament was being held': on this basis, Robert Rait argued that burgesses were not truly part of parliament. Balfour Melville countered that the phrase in question, '*tenente plenum parliamentum*', had previously been used in other parliamentary contexts, so did not merit Rait's narrow interpretation.[19] One of the earliest parliamentary summonses (from 1328) sought 'six suitable people from each of the communities of the burghs', a long-winded

---

[14] Sanz, 'The Cities in the Aragonese Cortes', 97; E. W. M. Balfour Melville, 'Burgh Representation in Early Scottish Parliaments', in *EHR*, 59 (1944), 79–87, at 86–7.

[15] A. R. Myers, *Parliaments and Estates in Europe to 1789* (London, 1975), 19–22; G. W. S. Barrow, *Robert Bruce and the Community of the Realm of Scotland*, 3rd edn (Edinburgh, 1988).

[16] S. E. Finer, *The History of Government*, 3 vols (Oxford, 1997), vol. 2, *The Intermediate Ages*, 1027–9.

[17] Marongiu, *Medieval Parliaments*, 95. The Latin phrase is '*communitates villarum*' (communities of the towns); Scots would have used '*communitates burgorum*' (communities of the burghs).

[18] A. A. M. Duncan, 'The Early Parliaments of Scotland', in *SHR*, 45 (1966), 36–58, at 51; N. A. T. Macdougall, *An Antidote to the English: The Auld Alliance, 1295–1560* (East Linton, 2001), 19–20; Ewan, *Townlife*, 147: the six were Aberdeen, Perth, Stirling, Edinburgh, Roxburgh and Berwick.

[19] Ewan, *Townlife*, 148–9; Rait, *The Parliaments of Scotland*, 240–41; Balfour Melville, 'Burgh Representation in Early Scottish Parliaments'; A. A. M. Duncan (ed.), *Regesta Regum*

phrase suggesting that no customary form for summoning the burgesses was yet established.[20] Robert I's parliament of 1328 was another false start, for no burghs were summoned in 1331.[21] Their participation in 1326 and 1328 can be linked to grants of taxation and it was the need for consent to further taxation which secured their place under David II (1328–1371): burgh representatives are recorded at parliaments which granted taxes in 1340 and 1341.[22] Although not possessing the wealth of the nobility or the Church, and relatively small and poor compared to their European counterparts, the merchants of Scotland's burghs were the main source of specie which was especially useful for payment of David II's ransom from the English. In the early fifteenth century, when James I (1406–1437) was also in English captivity, the burghs raised the first instalment of a tax for his ransom.[23]

The survival of only two summonses from the fourteenth century complicates the task of pinpointing when the burghs became an established component of parliament. The starting point for regular attendance is usually given as 1357, yet no parliament met in that year. General councils, predecessors of conventions of the estates, which met in January and September, might have been attended by burgesses and they were 'almost certainly' at another in November.[24] Rait tentatively posited 1367 as 'the first Parliament of Three Estates' but a precise starting point is illusory. Burgesses attended parliaments before 1367 and probably continued to appear irregularly thereafter.[25] Unlike the prelates and magnates, burgh commissioners were often described as having been summoned '*ad hoc ex causa*' (for a specific reason). However, Archie Duncan persuasively argued that the record usually stated that the burgesses had been '*summonitis et vocatis more et solito*' (summoned and called in due and accustomed manner) and that the record 'makes no distinction in this respect between the other groups and the burgesses' as early as 1366. So, although the burgesses were last described as being present '*ad hoc ex causa*' in 1401, in every instance for which there is evidence after 1365, burgesses were listed as present.[26] Between the 1320s and the 1360s, their place in parliament was becoming established; thereafter they became an increasingly normal part of parliament and the uniformity of designation from 1401 was a tardy recognition of that.

Scottorum [*RRS*], vol. 5, *Robert I* (Edinburgh, 1988), nos 300 and 335; Duncan, 'Early Parliaments', 51–3.

[20]   *RRS*, vol. 5, no. 563. The phrase summoning everyone else is shorter than that for the burgesses. See ch. 2 for a fuller discussion of this summons.

[21]   *RRS*, vol. 6, no. 480.

[22]   Balfour Melville, 'Burgh Representation', 85–6; Duncan, 'Early Parliaments', 52; Ewan, *Townlife*, 149; *ER*, vol. 1, clxii, clxv–vi, 501–3, 513.

[23]   *APS*, vol. 2, 6. They used contacts with Flemish money-lenders to borrow the cash: see R. Tanner, *The Late Medieval Scottish Parliament: Politics and the Three Estates, 1424–1488* (East Linton, 2001), 11.

[24]   Rait, *The Parliaments of Scotland*, 242–3.

[25]   Ibid., 246; Duncan, 'Early Parliaments', 52.

[26]   Ibid., 53; Rait, *The Parliaments of Scotland*, 247; *APS*, vol. 1, 498, 503–6, 547.

The expansion of the estate, 1550–1651

The period under examination saw a significant expansion in the number of royal burghs. Between 1550 and 1600, nine new royal burghs were created, more than in any century, let alone half-century, since 1200. Moreover, there were 25 creations across the period 1500–1650, compared to only 20 in the preceding 300 years.[27] There was also a significant increase in the proportion of burghs sending commissioners to parliament.[28] So what were the reasons for this explosion of creations and interest in parliament? The latter can be attributed to a number of factors. Parliament was taking on more and more business, passing legislation on a growing range of matters.[29] One aspect of this was the increasing prominence of ratifications or confirmations by which new and long-standing privileges were endorsed. The need to ensure that one's rights were not undermined by others' ratifications provided a considerable spur to regular attendance. Coupled with this was an increased collective impetus among the parliamentary burghs. The records of the convention of burghs reveal a growing level of interest in parliament, manifested in strategies to encourage participation, promote favourable legislation and improve the burghs' chances of prevailing against the other estates.[30]

It is more difficult, however, to be clear about the reasons for the startling growth in the number of royal burghs. Burgh records rarely survive from the period before they joined the ranks of the free burghs and charters of erection are laconic regarding the reasons for having been granted. Economic reasons must, however, have been significant.[31] Fiscal considerations on the part of the crown might have had a role but, since the burghs paid one-sixth of any tax voted by the estates, increasing the number of tax-paying burghs did not necessarily bring in more to the crown's coffers. However, both the level and frequency of taxes increased in this period, so the existing tax-paying burghs might well have welcomed others to share the burden, albeit with some reluctance since newcomers were simultaneously an economic threat to neighbouring burghs.[32] There was an inevitable tension between the growth of the estate on the one hand and its dilution by the addition of new members on the other. The convention of burghs was not sure how to respond. In 1574, aware of the rise of some baronial burghs in Fife, it decided to discuss 'giff for releiff of the decayit burrowis, the unfrie townis upoun the coist side [i.e. the south coast of Fife] salbe ressavit into the society of fre burrowis, to beir burding with thame or not'.

---

[27] Pryde, *The Burghs of Scotland*, section 1. The figure of 25 excludes St Andrews and Brechin: although erected as royal burghs after 1500, they were already parliamentary burghs.

[28] See Appendix 4.

[29] This phenomenon is extensively discussed by Julian Goodare. See, e.g., *The Government of Scotland* (Oxford, 2004), ch. 12.

[30] See ch. 3 for details.

[31] But see Goodare, 'Parliament and Society in Scotland, 1560–1603' (Edinburgh PhD, 1989), 288–9, where it is argued that the elevation of some burghs was 'probably for political rather than economic reasons'.

[32] J. Goodare, 'Parliamentary Taxation in Scotland, 1560–1603', *SHR*, 68 (1989), 23–52.

Eight years later, the convention resolved to ensure that those burghs which 'usurpis the liberty and privilege of frie burrowis' should be investigated so that those with crown charters 'may be compellit to ... beir all maner of ... charges with the remanent frie burrowis'. Thus the convention was asserting its right to oversee the free burghs and see to their fulfilment of their obligations. In 1584, however, it was agreed that 'gif it salhappin ony toune to be erected in ane frie burgh within the ... libertie of ane uther frie burgh, the haill burrowis sall interpone thair poweris in contrair thairof'.[33] Since every new burgh inevitably lay within the liberties of an existing free burgh, this was a blanket stipulation. In practice, newly erected burghs were treated on a case-by-case basis.

The most significant factor in the expansion of the number of parliamentary burghs was Scotland's economic growth from the middle of the sixteenth century. As a proportion of the population, the towns grew more than four-fold.[34] The parliamentary burghs' trading privileges were increasingly lucrative, and although the rights of burghs of barony were limited, considerable illegal trade must have been conducted by their inhabitants. The free burghs, acutely aware of the problem of maintaining their privileges in the face of a rapid expansion of unfree burghs, regularly took legal action to maintain those privileges, both individually and collectively, through the courts and in parliament.[35] It was thus in the interests of an ambitious burgh of barony to seek elevation to the status of royal burgh, rather than risk the prospect of a long and expensive case before the lords of session.

In most cases, the landed superior of a baronial burgh sought its erection as a royal burgh–the magistrates and council could hardly obtain a royal charter without the consent of their landlord. James Beaton of Balfour was instrumental in obtaining the admission of Kilrenny to the convention of burghs and parliament, and in 1596 the convention noted with alarm that 'the erectioun of the willageis of Stranrawer and Ballanclath in fre brughis' had been obtained by the lairds of Kinhilt and Park respectively. Yet this was not like 'the clamour for enfranchisement' coming from the English gentry, for whom a seat in parliament was the prize.[36] The lairds' main motivation was economic: as a burgess, a royal burgh's former feudal superior would have access to an enhanced market, so might acquire imported goods legally and more conveniently. Whatever pressure there was from the lairds (untitled nobles) for a place in parliament was relieved by the introduction of elected shire commissioners after 1587 and no former feudal superior entered parliament as a commissioner for 'his' burgh.[37] Political influence was a possible motive, but it was not overtly

---

[33] *RCRBS*, vol. 1, 35, 137, 197.

[34] I. D. Whyte, *Scotland Before the Industrial Revolution: An Economic and Social History, c.1050–c.1750* (Harlow, 1995), 172–5. For a general assessment of the economy with particular reference to towns and trade see chs. 10, 11 and 15.

[35] *RCRBS*, vol. 1, 68, 137, 197, 482–3, vol. 2, 89, 129, 235–6, 373, 424; Whyte, *Scotland Before the Industrial Revolution*, 180–81.

[36] *RCRBS*, vol. 1, 149, 483. Other examples can be found in vol. 2, e.g. 204; R. Tittler, 'Elizabethan Towns and the "Points of Contact": Parliament', in *PH*, 8 (1989), 275–88, at 275.

[37] J. Goodare, 'The Admission of Lairds to the Scottish Parliament', in *EHR*, 116 (2001), 1103–33.

exercised; it would have been foolish for a burgh's commissioners to act against the interests of a powerful landed neighbour and useful to support him. With only one exception, the new parliamentary burghs were not erected at the instance of a major political figure, whereas English nobles and courtiers obtained the enfranchisement of boroughs to secure seats for clients and relatives.[38] In Scotland, this did not happen for a number of reasons. A parliamentary burgh had to be a real trading town, so there were no 'rotten' burghs. Roxburgh was one of the four great burghs before *c.*1300, but its position on the border, continual Anglo-Scottish warfare in the fourteenth and fifteenth centuries, and its frequent occupation by the English meant that, by the time it was finally recovered in 1460, there was nothing left. As a result, no commissioner could represent it in parliament.[39] The role of the convention of burghs in admitting new members dates from the middle of the sixteenth century, so cannot explain this state of affairs. Roxburgh's story demonstrates that the Scots' understanding of urban representation differed considerably from that of the English.

Another reason for the non-existence of 'rotten' burghs in Scotland is the nature of the power of the Scottish nobility. Unlike their English counterparts, they were able to wield sufficient political influence without having to resort to the creation of pocket burghs. The only possible instance of this phenomenon is the erection of Inveraray in January 1648. The leading noble in the Covenanting regime was Archibald Campbell, first marquis of Argyll, on whose estates Inveraray lay. It would therefore be reasonable to suppose that he obtained its erection for political reasons. However, the burgh did not send a commissioner to parliament until 1661. This would suggest that, in common with other landlords who sought the erection of their burghs, Argyll was expecting commercial advantage and prestige rather than political capital.[40]

One of the ostensible reasons for the erection of Inveraray was the lack of royal burghs in Argyll. The crown had long desired to establish towns in the Highlands as part of a 'civilising' policy: in 1597, parliament had proposed three new burghs for the region, one in Argyll, one in Lochaber and one on Lewis. However, in spite of attempts to found a burgh at Stornoway in the later 1620s, Inveraray was the first and only success.[41] English parliamentary historians have debated the reasons for the new enfranchisements there in the sixteenth and seventeenth centuries, some arguing that political patronage was the key, others favouring the view that there were efforts to provide MPs for hitherto under-represented parts of the country. The former position is more convincing, since the over-representation of poor and

---

[38] L. Stone, *The Crisis of the Aristocracy, 1558–1641* (Oxford, 1965), 446; Hawkyard, 'The Enfranchisement of Constituencies', 1, 19–20; N. Ball, 'Representation in the English House of Commons: The New Boroughs, 1485–1640', in *PER*, 15 (1995), 117–24.

[39] Pryde, *The Burghs of Scotland*, no. 2.

[40] RMS, vol. 9, no. 1901, 707–8; *RCRBS*, vol. 3, 345–6. For further discussion of Inveraray, see Rait, 'Parliamentary Representation in Scotland', 130.

[41] M. Lynch, 'James VI and the "Highland Problem"', in J. Goodare and M. Lynch (eds), *The Reign of James VI* (East Linton, 2000), 208–27; J. Goodare, *State and Society in Early Modern Scotland* (Oxford, 1999), ch. 8; A. I. Macinnes, *Clanship, Commerce and the House of Stewart, 1603–1788* (East Linton, 1996), 68; C. Kidd, *British Identities Before Nationalism: Ethnicity and Nationhood in the Atlantic World* (Cambridge, 1999), 126–7; *APS*, vol. 4, 139.

sparsely-populated Cornwall was intensified (the duchy of Cornwall belonged to the crown and the enfranchisement of boroughs there was politically useful). Similarly, although there were enfranchisements in the grossly under-represented north, these too were largely on crown lands, this time those of the duchy of Lancaster.[42] By the sixteenth century, the idea that Scottish parliamentary burghs had to be real trading towns was so entrenched that the crown could not create new burghs for its own political advantage. The distribution of parliamentary burghs also suggests a response to economic development, rather than an economic policy. Nearly half were situated on the Firth of Forth, and all but five were on or near the east coast, which dominated Scotland's overseas trade. The greatest concentration of new parliamentary burghs was on the south coast of Fife and can be linked to the fact that the tax contribution of the Fife burghs quadrupled between 1535 and 1600.[43] One consequence was that the imbalance of the distribution of parliamentary burghs intensified. Between 1579 and 1612, the number of parliamentary burghs in Fife rose from five to 13, while Stirlingshire remained with only one and there was none across a huge swathe of the north and west.[44]

The only burghs whose arrival in parliament might have been on the initiative of the crown were those which were on royal estates. That such burghs were not automatically admitted to parliament is demonstrated by the Act of Annexation by which former ecclesiastical lands came to the crown in 1587.[45] Many dependent burghs of monasteries and cathedrals fell into crown hands, yet they did not immediately qualify as parliamentary burghs. The picture is confused because, in 1587, some ecclesiastical burghs were long-standing royal burghs, while they and some others already sent commissioners to parliament, or at least to the convention of burghs, and were taxed with the parliamentary burghs.[46] Only Culross and Anstruther Wester entered parliament as a consequence, but only an indirect one, of the Act of Annexation. In the case of Culross, the initiative came from the burgh itself. One of its bailies, George Bruce, had 'at the speciall command of the ... beilleis, counsall and cummunitie, advancit and debursit greit sowmes of money in procuring the said toun of Culros to be erectit in ane frie burght royall', by which they expected it to be 'greitlie inrychit and agmentit to the profeit and behuif of the present inhabitantes ... and thair posteritie for ever'.[47] He had spent £1,000 over and above an unspecified sum that he had previously received to secure this and, because the council could not repay him, they gave him the rents and duties of the burgh's saltpans 'to provyd him ane convenient and ressonable annuel and yeirlie dewtie' until the principal sum could be repaid. He already had substantial interests in coalmining and salt-

---

[42] Hawkyard, 'The Enfranchisement of Constituencies'; Ball, 'Representation in the English House of Commons'; Smith, *The Stuart Parliaments*, 23; Stone, *The Crisis of the Aristocracy*, 446.

[43] See Appendix 2; Whyte, *Scotland Before the Industrial Revolution*, 175.

[44] A. G. Muir, 'The Covenanters in Fife, *c.*1610–1689' (St Andrews PhD, 2001), 41–2.

[45] *APS*, vol. 3, 431–7.

[46] See Appendix 2 and *RCRBS*, vol. 1, 514. They were St Andrews, Brechin, Glasgow, Arbroath, Pittenweem, Kirkcaldy, Whithorn and Burntisland.

[47] FCAC, Culross Town Council Minute Book, B/CUL1/1/1, 50.

making, so this was wholly appropriate.[48] Bruce was on good terms with the king, but there is no evidence to suggest that the burgh's erection was the king's idea. Only the erection of Anstruther Wester might have occurred on the initiative of the crown. Its great seal charter noted that it had grown since its erection as a burgh of barony in 1541 and specifically mentioned that it had fallen to the crown as part of the annexation of ecclesiastical lands in 1587 and was thus being erected as a royal burgh.[49] It is just as likely however, that, as with Culross, the bailies and council had sought its erection. So, even when an opportunity like the annexation of Church lands presented itself, the crown was not interested in the wholesale creation of new burghs for parliamentary advantage, unlike in Ireland, where 1613 saw the arrival of MPs from 84 new boroughs deliberately created to overturn the 'longstanding catholic Anglo-Irish majority' in Ireland's House of Commons.[50] It might be argued that such tactics were unnecessary in Scotland because of the crown's control of the royal burghs, as has recently been implied, but their behaviour in the political sphere would indicate otherwise.[51]

Admission to parliament

Whatever had been the mechanism for gaining access to parliament before the middle of the sixteenth century, it was transformed thereafter as a result of the emergence of the convention of burghs as a quasi-autonomous national assembly of burghs. Another possible factor was the increasingly bureaucratic tendency in government, where royal grants had to proceed through a number of stages before coming into effect.[52] From the 1550s, although occasionally summoned by the monarch or a regent during a royal minority to discuss specific matters, the convention met without royal summons and quickly acquired authority in a number of spheres, including the admission of new burghs. Although known from the later seventeenth century as the 'convention of royal burghs', it referred to itself in the period of this study simply as the 'convention of burghs', possibly because its members knew that not all of them were royal burghs; it consisted, more or less, of commissioners from all parliamentary burghs.[53]

In 1590, when Culross was celebrating the attainment of royal burgh status, it had crossed only the first hurdle, albeit the most expensive one, of obtaining a royal signature by which the king agreed that it could become a royal burgh. It had to wait until 1592 for a crown charter, and it was 1593 before its commissioner

---

[48]   R. A. Houston, 'Bruce, Sir George (c.1550–1625)', *Oxford Dictionary of National Biography* (Oxford, 2004) [http://oxforddnb.com/view/article/47923, accessed 21 April 2005].

[49]   *RMS*, vol. 5, no. 1396, 480–81.

[50]   Graves, *The Parliaments of Early Modern Europe*, 175.

[51]   Ibid., 164 described royal burghs as 'directly under royal control'.

[52]   P. Gouldesbrough, *Formulary of Old Scots Legal Documents*, Stair Society (Edinburgh, 1985), 39–40.

[53]   See *RCRBS*, vols 1–4, *passim*.

sat in parliament.[54] None of the new burghs gained entry to parliament as a direct consequence of receiving a crown charter, in contrast with England where it was one of the 'traditional rights of the monarch' to enfranchise a borough, which led directly to admission to parliament and could not be blocked by a third party.[55] In 1563, Mr Peter Strang, commissioner from Pittenweem in Fife, appeared before the convention of burghs with a great seal charter of James V, issued in 1541, 'contenyng the erecting of thair said toun in fre burch'. He came as a supplicant, asking for Pittenweem 'to have thair placis [sic] amangis uther fre burrois, and offerit to sustein taxtis, stenttis and uther portable charges amangis the remanent burrois'.[56] This is the first record of such a request; perhaps similar ones had been made before but the fragmentary nature of the early records of the convention means that it is impossible to be sure. Between 1563 and 1707, a succession of recently-erected burghs came to the convention requesting enrolment. It was no mere court of registration. Indeed, in the early 1630s, it:

> declaired that the priviledges granted be ... parliament to the free royall burrowis is only competent to the said burrowis quho ar subject to his majesties taxatiounes and ar inrolled with the rest, and no utheris to have power to exerce the saidis liberties notwithstanding of quhatsumevir giftis granted or to be granted to thame.[57]

At about the same time a burgh which was going through the process of erection sought the advice of the lord advocate, Sir Thomas Hope (the crown's chief legal officer) regarding the necessity of enrolment by the convention. Lesser advocates had been consulted and their opinion was that enrolment was necessary to make 'ane frie burght'. It was hoped that the lord advocate's answer would be different, but he agreed that enrolment by the convention of burghs was necessary to ensure a newly-erected burgh's status.[58]

Of the 24 burghs which first sent commissioners to parliament in the period under examination, at least 17 (possibly 18) were enrolled by the convention before sitting in parliament.[59] Various reasons explain the six anomalies. Tain and Nairn had appeared on the 1535 tax roll and can thus be understood as having been accepted by their peers already. Theodora Pagan noted that the burghs on the 1535 tax roll which subsequently entered parliament were admitted to the convention without formal enrolment, in contrast with other newcomers.[60] Yet Kintore, South Queensferry, Dingwall and Inverurie were not on the 1535 tax roll and all sent commissioners to parliament before being enrolled. The three northern burghs of Kintore, Inverurie and Dingwall had obtained their charters between *c.*1190 and 1227, yet none sent

---

[54] *RMS*, vol 5, no. 2093; Pryde, *The Burghs of Scotland*, no. 65.

[55] Hawkyard, 'The Enfranchisement of Constituencies', 3.

[56] *RCRBS*, vol. 1, 531.

[57] ACA, Acts of Convention, CRB vol. 2, f. 395v. The paper, from 1631, contains a list of acts of parliament in favour of the burghs and a number of matters for which parliamentary ratification would be sought.

[58] ECA, Queensferry Council Minutes 1634–61, SL59/1/1/1, ff. 12v, 13r.

[59] See Appendix 2. The eighteenth is Dornoch, whose date of enrolment is unknown.

[60] Pagan, *The Convention of the Royal Burghs*, 28.

commissioners to parliament until the reign of James VI. Even then, representatives from each turned up only two or three times before 1660: Kintore's in 1579, 1617 and 1621, Inverurie's in 1612, 1617 and 1621 and Dingwall's in 1587 and 1593.[61] It is thus debatable whether they were genuinely active parliamentary burghs until the later seventeenth century. Local reasons may explain their brief bursts of parliamentary activity but it is hard to pin these down, although Dingwall's appearance in 1587 did coincide with a ratification obtained by Andrew Keith, Lord Dingwall, of his title and lands. It would not be surprising if a local landowner had encouraged or even helped a neighbouring burgh to send a commissioner to support his cause.[62] As for the other instances, although no acts were secured for Dingwall, Kintore or Inverurie, that does not mean that they were not hoping for one. The proximity of Kintore and Inverurie (they are only four miles apart) and the occurrence of five of their six appearances between 1612 and 1621 might indicate external manipulation of the membership of parliament, but none of their records survive, so this must remain conjectural. Suspicions are also aroused by the fact that Kintore's commissioner in 1579 was an Aberdonian lawyer.[63] Perhaps the convention of burghs would have paid more attention to their activities had they exercised a more frequent interest in parliament but, since they did not, their irregular attendance (in both senses) did not trouble the others.

That leaves only South Queensferry. Linlithgow opposed its erection from 1635 onwards, lobbying at court, in the exchequer and working through the convention of burghs. Initially it was successful, but Queensferry received a charter of erection in October 1636. Lengthy negotiations ensued involving representatives of both burghs and the crown until, in 1641, an agreement was reached by which Linlithgow's merchants would have rights in Queensferry which were not reciprocated.[64] Although the records of the convention of burghs for this period are lost, a royal letter to the convention in 1638 reveals that Queensferry tried to follow customary procedure but was thwarted.[65] Linlithgow had blocked Queensferry's petition for enrolment in 1637

[61]   Pryde, *The Burghs of Scotland*, nos 26 and 30; Young, *The Parliaments of Scotland*, vol. 2, 772, 779–80.

[62]   *APS*, vol. 3, 637; Balfour Paul, *Scots Peerage*, vol. 3, 115–16: Keith was an illegitimate great-nephew of George, fifth Earl Marischal. See also Rait, 'Parliamentary Representation in Scotland', 129–30, which discusses Dingwall.

[63]   *APS*, vol. 3, 125, 428, vol. 4, 7, 467, 468, 526, 528, 594, 596. Young, *The Parliaments of Scotland*, vol. 2, 501.

[64]   NAS, Linlithgow Town Council Minute Book 1620–40, B48/9/1, 339–40, 353, 355, 360–61, 365–70, 375; Linlithgow Town Council Minute Book 1640–59, B48/9/2, 22–5; *RMS*, vol. 9, no. 603, 216–17 (n.b., Pryde, *The Burghs of Scotland*, no. 76, follows a misdating of November in *APS*, vol. 5, 571: the printed *RMS* did not cover the 1630s when Pryde conducted his research); ECA, Queensferry Council Minutes 1634–61, SL59/1/1/1, ff. 12v, 13r, 15–16, 24–5, 55v, 57v, 59r, 67r, 67v, 68r, 81v.

[65]   NAS, Charles I to the Royal Burghs of Scotland, 25 July 1638, Dalhousie Papers, GD45/1/38. Oddly, South Queensferry's charter did not specify the right to send commissioners to parliament, as those of Dornoch and New Galloway did. Had it done so, enrolment after admission to parliament might have been less puzzling: *RMS*, vol. 9, no. 603; ECA, Queensferry Council Minutes 1634–61, SL59/1/1/1, f. 43v, 47r.

but Charles I pointed out that the exchequer had already approved Queensferry's erection in spite of Linlithgow's objections. The convention still refused to enrol it. Linlithgow prevented Queensferry's enrolment again in 1639 and 1641 and protested against its presence in parliament in 1640. It was not enrolled until 1642.[66] This episode has the superficial appearance of a tussle between the crown and the burghs at the time of a revolution, with Queensferry defying the convention of burghs by sending a commissioner to parliament in 1639 in what could have been a gesture of loyalty to the king. However, its active participation in the Covenanting movement makes this unlikely.[67] It is more probable that Linlithgow simply used the collapse of royal authority to its own advantage to minimise the impact of a new erection nearby, although it was successful only in delaying the process.

The arrival of a commissioner from a recently-erected burgh always caused a stir. The trading rights of burghs over broad hinterlands meant that new erections technically infringed their liberties.[68] Objections and delaying tactics therefore usually ensued, and the affected burghs went to some lengths to exclude upstart neighbours. Pittenweem's request for enrolment in 1563 was opposed by Crail, within whose liberties Pittenweem lay, on the grounds that it would prejudice Crail's case against Pittenweem's 'pretendit privelege and libertie' before the court of session. This delayed Pittenweem's admission, but its commissioners attended conventions from 1575, and in 1579 its name was added to the burghs' tax roll months before it sent commissioners to parliament, with Crail still protesting.[69] Crail felt threatened: its tiny harbour was awkwardly positioned and could not be developed, and it was faced with the emergence of four new parliamentary burghs within its liberties (Pittenweem, Anstruther Wester, Anstruther Easter and Kilrenny). It sought to exclude them all. In 1584, it blocked the enrolment of Anstruther Easter, which had first applied in 1575. However, in November 1587, in spite of another case before the court of session, the convention of burghs, 'Craill onlie except', voted to admit Anstruther Easter.[70] What seems to have won the day for Anstruther Easter was the ratification of its erection 'in the twa last parliaments'. The first, in 1585, had contained the proviso that it would not be 'prejudiciall to the burgh of Craill thair rychtis and actioun ... aganis the toun of Anstruther tuiching thair privilegis befoir the lordis of counsall and sessioun'. The act of 1587 contained only a vague reservation of the 'rychtis of uther baronis [sic, burghs]'. In parliament, Crail's parliamentary commissioner had protested and obtained a counter-ratification of his burgh's privileges, including its liberties stretching inland along 25 miles of coastline.[71] Strictly speaking, this ought to have nullified any rights that Anstruther Easter had obtained. It can only be assumed that, by this ratification, Crail affirmed its trading liberty except within the

[66] NAS, Linlithgow Town Council Minute Book 1640–59, B48/9/2, 1; *RCRBS*, vol. 4, 547.

[67] Young, *The Parliaments of Scotland*, vol. 1, 180–81.

[68] For the development of 'liberties' see E. P. Dennison and G. G. Simpson, 'Scotland', in D. M. Palliser (ed.), *The Cambridge Urban History of Britain: Volume I, 600–1540* (Cambridge, 2000), 715–37, at 721–4.

[69] *RCRBS*, vol. 1, 47, 72, 74, 79, 80, 531.

[70] Ibid., 44, 47, 189, 250–51; NAS, Court of Session General Minute Book, CS8/4, f. 147r, 25 Jan 1587/88.

[71] *APS*, vol. 3, 421, 507.

bounds of the new burgh which would thus have had no hinterland, its liberties being coterminous with the burgh and any common lands which lay adjacent.

Crail continued to protest against the enrolling of Anstruther Easter and it put up similarly unsuccessful resistance to Anstruther Wester and Kilrenny.[72] Its failure to exclude Kilrenny is surprising because of the anomalous nature of the latter's claim to be a free burgh. Its entry to parliament demonstrates the crucial role played by the convention of burghs but also suggests that parliamentary ratification could carry considerable weight. It was never erected as a royal burgh but was enrolled by the convention in 1592 and sent its first commissioner to parliament in 1612. The strange course of its admission began in 1582 when its feudal superior, John Beaton of Balfour, submitted to the convention a charter of 1578 granted by the archbishop of St Andrews, a ratification of that charter under the privy seal and a parliamentary ratification of 1579 recognising Kilrenny as a burgh of regality under Beaton.[73] The convention failed to distinguish between two similar Latin terms, thus the charter's *regalitatem* (in regality) was mistakenly interpreted as *regalem* (royal) and Kilrenny was duly enrolled. The convention of burghs thought that Kilrenny had been made a royal burgh and had obtained a parliamentary ratification of that status, even though neither had actually happened. Insofar as Kilrenny now paid a share of parliamentary taxations, could send commissioners to parliament and conventions of burghs and indulge in foreign trade, the convention had made it a royal burgh. In 1672, it finally admitted the deception in an attempt to be removed from the list of royal burghs. Parliament acceded to the request but only on condition that all arrears of taxation were cleared. Fifteen years later, having failed in this regard, it resorted to the convention of burghs, 'craving to be expunged out of the borrow rolls' and claiming that, without financial help, it would 'not be able to continow as a royall burgh'. The burghs, 'out of great kyndnes and tendernes' agreed to pay half its tax arrears and cancel the dues it owed the convention. Kilrenny agreed and remained a royal burgh, while Cromarty and Anstruther Wester, which really had been royal burghs, were successful in their attempts to demit.[74]

The story of Kilrenny might indicate that there was a significant role for parliament, although it is clear that it could not confer parliamentary status on a burgh, as happened for some boroughs in sixteenth-century England and Wales.[75] A pilot study which examined the seven parliamentary burghs of north-east Fife

---

[72]   *RCRBS*, vol. 1, 188–9, 236, 250–51, 275, 295, 364.

[73]   Ibid., 149, 188, 371; *APS*, vol. 3, 167–9. Its title, 'Confirmation of the infeftment of the heavin of Kilrynne to Johnne Betoun of Balfour', proves it was not being made a royal burgh. Regality status exempted heritable property from the jurisdiction of the king's courts, even in the four royal pleas of murder, rape, fire-raising and robbery with violence (reserved to the crown in grants '*in baroniam*', the normal status of a non-royal burgh). It did not confer self-governing status.

[74]   *APS*, vol. 8, 68–9, 77–8; *RCRBS*, vol. 4, 70, 77; A. R. MacDonald, '"Tedious to rehers"? Parliament and Locality in Scotland *c.*1500–1651: The Burghs of North-East Fife', in *PER*, 20 (2000), 31–58, at 38; Pryde, *The Burghs of Scotland*, no. 66; Pagan, *The Convention of the Royal Burghs of Scotland*, 31–2.

[75]   Hawkyard, 'The Enfranchisement of Constituencies', 7–8; C. G. Cruickshank, 'Parliamentary Representation of Tournai', in *EHR*, 83 (1968), 775–6.

suggested that parliament did have such a role: three of the four new parliamentary burghs from that region obtained parliamentary ratifications before enrolment by the convention of burghs and entry to parliament.[76] However, an examination of all new parliamentary burghs reveals this to have been misleading. Of the 24 burghs which first sent commissioners to parliament in the period of this study, only five obtained a ratification beforehand, the three from north-east Fife plus Culross and Burntisland. Thus, a prominent role for parliament has to be dismissed.

Although Crail's neighbours were successful in overcoming its challenges and gaining entry to the convention and parliament, it took each of them many years. Some had to wait decades. In 1596, the laird of Kinhilt had overcome the first hurdle in the erection of Stranraer, eventually obtaining a royal charter in 1617, in spite of opposition from neighbouring Wigtown.[77] Undaunted, Wigtown continued to oppose Stranraer's erection, with the support of the convention of burghs which promised £550 towards its legal expenses in 1618. In 1629, Wigtown obtained a decree from the court of session suspending Stranraer's erection. Not until 1683 was it enrolled by the convention, 66 years after its royal charter and 87 years after the process had begun.[78] Although Wigtown failed to prevent the erection of Stranraer and ultimately its enrolment, others were stopped outright. In 1590, David Strachan appeared before the convention of burghs as commissioner from Earlsferry, to the west of Pittenweem in Fife. Like the two Anstruthers, it had recently obtained a charter of erection and Strachan must have been optimistic that the prosperity of the Fife coast would guarantee admission. He produced a royal charter of 1589 and 'ane suplicatioun ... desiring to be admittit and enrollit' but he was turned down 'in respect of thair knawledge of the inhabilitye of the said toun', the admission of which 'suld be veray prejudiciall to the haill estait of frye burrowes'. The issue was taken so seriously that the commissioner from Burntisland, another recent arrival and therefore unaware of his gaffe, was fined 'for making of ane bal [i.e. celebration] to the commissioner of the unfrie toun of Erlisferrye'.[79] He had to learn the need for solidarity in the face of encroachments. No more was heard from Earlsferry. This is the only record of the explicit rejection of a newly chartered burgh, yet others never realised their status in sending commissioners to parliament or the convention of burghs.[80] There is no record of action against them by other burghs, so their failure to be represented may have been due to economic weakness. Nevertheless it demonstrates that the king could not create parliamentary burghs at will. In 1632, the convention of burghs recorded legal proceedings to prevent Newburgh, a royal

---

[76] MacDonald, 'Parliament and Locality in Scotland', 37.

[77] *RCRBS*, vol. 1, 483.

[78] *RCRBS*, vol. 3, 32, 67, 70, 87, 94, 296–7, vol. 4, 39; NAS, Court of Session General Minute Book Jan 1629–March 1632, CS8/19, 10 and 11 Feb 1629, proving that the case was being heard. The judgement was not traced.

[79] *RCRBS*, vol. 1, 326; G. Law, 'The Earl's Ferry', *SHR*, 2 (1905), 14–29, at 25–6.

[80] Falkland (erected 1458), Auchtermuchty (1517), Hamilton (1549), Rattray (1564) and Newburgh (1631) were never represented in parliament or the convention of burghs. See Pryde, *The Burghs of Scotland*, part 1.

burgh, 'frome usurping the liberties of the frie royall borrowes'.[81] In the eyes of the convention, there was a difference between a free and an unfree burgh, royal or otherwise, and it was confident of its role as gatekeeper.

Some would-be royal burghs were stopped at an even earlier stage. In 1596, the commissioners from Wigtown also informed the convention that Ballinclach was seeking erection. Although the convention decided that it could not intervene so early in the process, it promised its 'assistance and fortificatioun' and no more was heard of Ballinclach. Similarly, Aberdeen prevented the erection of Peterhead in 1633 and continued to place the blocking of new royal burghs in Aberdeenshire high up its parliamentary agenda thereafter.[82] In spite of their reluctance to get involved in the case of Ballinclach, the burghs mounted a sustained collective effort against attempts to erect a royal burgh at Stornoway on Lewis in the 1620s. Although requested by the earl of Seaforth, whose estates included Lewis, the proposed erection of Stornoway was also part of an integrationist crown policy which sought to bring the peripheries of the kingdom more fully within the Scottish polity. Stornoway also presented an ideal site for a fishing port, the establishment of which close to the fishing grounds in the north-west might boost the lucrative Scottish fisheries and help to restrict the activities of already more successful Dutch competitors.[83] It had proved difficult to monitor the northern fishing grounds because the whole coast from Rothesay in the west to Tain in the east was devoid of established royal burghs. However, the burghs' fishing fleets were already active in the area and they feared that the creation of a purpose-built fishing port at Stornoway, with the settlement of expert foreign fishermen, would threaten their interests. In 1628, a convention of burghs first discussed 'the mater of the erectioun of the burght of Seyfort [Stornoway] in a frie burght royall'. A list of reasons was compiled to prove that it would be 'prejudiciall ... to the borrowis nixt adjacent, to the whole borrowis and ... to this whole realme', and word was sent to John Hay, their agent at court, to lobby against it.[84] Their campaign against the erection of Stornoway provides a rare insight into the early stages of the process by which a royal burgh was made in the reign of Charles I. By June 1628, Seaforth had obtained a 'signature' (an authorisation under the royal sign manual) approving the erection. Hay reported to the convention of burghs at Perth in July that this had been passed to the lords of exchequer for approval, so they turned their attention to that body to prevent the issuing of a charter under one of the seals. By January 1629, a royal letter had been obtained 'staying the signature granted to the earl of Seaforth'. Lobbying at court in London and before the privy council in

---

[81]   ACA, Acts of Convention, CRB vol. 2, f. 441r. There is no evidence that Newburgh sought enrolment.

[82]   *RCRBS*, vol. 1, 483; Pryde, *The Burghs of Scotland*, no. 171; ACA, Aberdeen Council Minutes, CR1/52/1, 116; *Aberdeen Letters*, vol. 3, 116: on this and other occasions, Aberdeen's commissioner was told to oppose new erections within Aberdeenshire, in spite of the absence of any specific threatened erection.

[83]   Goodare, *The Government of Scotland*, 230; Pagan, *The Convention of Burghs*, 215–27.

[84]   SCA, Stirling Council Minutes 1619–58, B66/20/4, 6 June 1628; *RCRBS*, vol. 3, 257–62. The notion of 'adjacent' burghs is absurd: it was over 200 miles by sea to the nearest parliamentary burgh.

Edinburgh by Seaforth and the burghs continued until, in August 1630, Hay reported that 'his Majestie wes gratiouslie pleased to cancell the signature ... for erecting the burgh of Stornway in the Yle of the Lewes in ane burgh of royall'.[85] The burghs had convinced the king and his Edinburgh government that they could adequately develop Scotland's fisheries. This might have been in the interests of the existing burghs but their identification of their own interests with those of the 'whole realme' would not have been universally shared.

Although the representation of the ecclesiastical burghs was perhaps anomalous, this was rectified for most of them during the period of this study. In 1599 Arbroath obtained a charter and in 1611 Glasgow followed, as did St Andrews in 1620, Brechin in 1641 and Kirkcaldy in 1644.[86] The only exceptions were Dunfermline and Dysart which both lay within the regality of Dunfermline, the property of the Benedictine abbey of Dunfermline until the Reformation. The regality passed through a number of hands until, in March 1594, it was granted to Queen Anne. This did not make the burghs within the regality tenants of the crown but tenants of the queen as a private individual, so none automatically became a royal, let alone a parliamentary, burgh.[87] Dunfermline's story is complicated: although founded by the monarch in the early twelfth century, it belonged to the abbey by 1300. In spite of this, it contributed to national taxation as early as 1424 and sent a commissioner to the convention of burghs from at least 1555. Although summoned to a convention of the estates in 1594, it did not send a commissioner to parliament until 1604.[88] Dysart was also on the 1535 tax roll. It sent commissioners to the convention of burghs from 1578 without requesting enrolment; like Dunfermline its commissioner was invited to a convention of estates in 1594, and it first sent a commissioner to parliament in 1600.[89] The crucial factor appears to be taxation. Just as St Andrews was included among the parliamentary burghs in the middle of the fourteenth century, the convention of burghs admitted Dunfermline, Dysart and Kirkcaldy because they were economically strong enough to pay a share of taxation and, had they not been admitted, they might have been powerful enough to threaten the trading privileges of the other free burghs. Until their erection as royal burghs, all the burghs within the regality of Dunfermline remained technically subject to its jurisdiction, demonstrated by heirs to property being served by a brieve from the 'chapell of Dunfermling', rather than the royal chancery.[90]

The evidence presented here suggests that it would not be 'going too far' to suggest that 'the burghs themselves controlled their attendance in Parliament'.[91] This view, expressed in the 1920s, seems to stem from an instinctive reluctance to acknowledge the practical limitations on the power of the crown. Those who

---

[85] *RCRBS*, vol. 3, 265–6, 276, 279, 281, 291, 300, 302–4, 308–9, 318, 321–3.

[86] Pryde, *The Burghs of Scotland*, nos 69, 70, 72, 77, 78.

[87] Dunfermline, Dysart, Kirkcaldy, South Queensferry and Musselburgh all lay within the regality of Dunfermline.

[88] Pryde, *The Burghs of Scotland*, no. 3; *RCRBS*, vol. 2, 172.

[89] Pryde, *The Burghs of Scotland*, no. 67; *RCRBS*, vol. 2, 93.

[90] See, e.g., FCAC, Kirkcaldy Burgh Court Book 1590–95, 1/06/03 f. 42v; NAS, Dunfermline Burgh Court Book 1606–13, B20/10/3, f. 37v.

[91] J. D. Mackie and G. S. Pryde, *The Estate of the Burgesses in the Scots Parliament and its relation to the Convention of Royal Burghs* (St Andrews, 1923), 5.

expressed it could not quite bring themselves to admit the only conclusion which the evidence allows. One unanswered question, however, relates to the parliamentary summons. If the convention of burghs had the final say on which burghs were admitted to the society of the free burghs, how was this reflected in the crown's behaviour? Unlike their English counterparts, Scottish parliamentary burghs received individual precepts of summons.[92] However, copies of these were not kept centrally and the financial records of the crown which record the sending of messengers to various parts of the country simply list the counties which each messenger was to cover, without specifying to which burghs he should go.[93] There was no need to do so: the messenger had only to take each summons to the burgh named on the precept. So it is impossible to be sure when a burgh was first summoned, even if it is known when it first sent commissioners. So how did the crown know which burghs to summon? There is no evidence for the mechanism by which it found out when a burgh had been enrolled by the convention, if that was indeed what triggered the issuing of a summons. There is another approach to the problem which, although it does not provide an exact match, can serve as a surrogate for establishing the point at which the crown understood a burgh to have been admitted by its peers. Every year, the royal burghs sent to the exchequer their 'maills' (the rent owed to the crown as their landlord) and a summary account of their common good (income from petty customs, properties and harbour dues, and expenditure on salaries, municipal works and commissioners to national assemblies).[94] These accounts, along with receipts of burgh maills, give an impression of which burghs were reckoned to be royal burghs and provide further evidence that a burgh was not understood to have become fully fledged until enrolled by the convention. Although payments were theoretically due from Burntisland, Anstruther Easter, Anstruther Wester and Culross from the year of their erection, none of them paid until after they had been enrolled by the convention of burghs.[95] Moreover, the royal burghs which were not represented in parliament or the convention of burghs did not render their accounts to the exchequer. Instead, their rents were recorded in the accounts of the crown's bailies ad extra (the ordinary rent-collectors for crown lands).[96] So, although the date of erection by royal charter was important, it was activated retrospectively after enrolment by the convention of burghs.

Conclusion

The process of a burgh gaining parliamentary status highlights the sharing of power between the crown and the burghs. Only the king could issue a charter of erection creating a new royal burgh, but that did not admit a burgh to parliament, or to the

---

[92]   Hawkyard, 'The Enfranchisement of Constituencies', 22.

[93]   *TA*, vol. 13, 201–2, 279; NAS, Treasurer's Accounts 1587–8, E21/66.

[94]   NAS, Burgh Common Good Accounts, E82. This was a real audit which might disallow items of expenditure and revise accounts accordingly.

[95]   *ER*, vol. 22, 338–9, 429, vol. 23, 125.

[96]   See, e.g., *ER*, vol. 23, 300–310, 303 for Auchtermuchty and Falkland.

convention of burghs, or to the economic and legal privileges which supposedly came with royal status. This chapter has also sustained the previously acknowledged fact that not all burghs which sent commissioners to parliament and the convention of burghs were royal burghs. Thus the supposed uniformity and distinctiveness of the royal burghs is undermined. Consequently, it might be concluded that the Scottish parliamentary burghs were more eclectic than has been assumed, perhaps more like their English counterparts. However, a number of factors make such a conclusion unsound. The enfranchisement of an English borough made no automatic difference to its status in terms of tenure, internal administration or payment of tax. In Scotland, new burghs were accepted by the other burghs because of their economic strength, their ability to contribute to taxes and the likelihood that, if they were not brought within the incorporation of free burghs, they would pose an economic threat. Also, once a burgh, royal or otherwise, had been enrolled by the convention, added to the burghs' tax roll and admitted to parliament, it automatically gained a set of privileges common to all parliamentary burghs and became subject to the same laws and regulations. Furthermore, through membership of the convention of burghs, every parliamentary burgh was drawn into an organisation which was acutely conscious of these common privileges and determined to maintain and defend them. Any economically ambitious burgh, before the Cromwellian conquest, knew that the only legally secure route to greater prosperity lay in being enrolled by the convention of burghs.

The story after 1660 is less clear-cut. The Restoration period saw the erosion of the royal burghs' international trading monopoly and the economic advance of many baronial burghs. A knowledge of the period before 1650 would suggest that this ought to have led to a further increase in the size of the estate of burghs. Yet circumstances were different. The nobility, terrified of the challenges to the natural order which had resulted from the Covenanting revolution, colluded with the monarchy in a conservative reaction after 1660. One consequence was that they were able to flout the royal burghs' economic privileges without fearing the legal challenges which had occurred in the past, so they did not seek the erection of new royal burghs. On the other hand, the convention of burghs did itself no favours. Although it allowed the admission of burghs which had obtained royal charters before the Cromwellian occupation, it did not seek to embrace the newly-prosperous baronial burghs, a move which would have preserved the free burghs' economic privileges and helped them to strengthen their vote in parliament in the face of a growing nobility and an increasing number of shire commissioners. Instead, it put up an increasingly futile resistance to the rising baronial burghs, demanding that they pay a share of taxation without seeking their admission to parliament. The union of 1707 may have been responsible for the arrested development of Scotland's representative system, yet the parallels with England suggest wider reasons for the failure of the urban component of parliament to develop. The pattern of the admission of new burghs in Scotland was similar to that in England, although on a smaller scale. In England, the number of urban seats in 1603 was nearly 70 per cent greater than it had been in 1485 (372 compared to 219) but only 45 further seats were created before 1640 and only four more by 1690; thereafter there were no more until 1832.[97] In Scotland, the number of parliamentary burghs grew from 34 in 1500 to 49 by 1600, an increase of 44 per cent. A further ten began to attend between 1600 and 1641; in 1661, there was an influx of burghs which had been erected before 1651 but which had not been enrolled by the convention or admitted to parliament. Thereafter, only four more began to send commissioners to parliament. A direct comparison between Scotland and England is complicated by the fact that the date of a burgh's erection and the date of its first appearance in parliament were so divergent. If the dates of erection are factored in, all but Campbeltown disappear from the list of post-1660 arrivals.[98] Scottish urban representation at Westminster was frozen in 1707 and so it remained until 1832.[99] In both countries, long before the creation of the British parliament the link between commercial power and political representation had been broken, although it had never been strong in England. After the union, the transfer of power to Westminster meant that the piecemeal assimilation of new burghs by the convention was no longer possible, and its inability to respond to the developments of the post-union period led ultimately to its eclipse as a politically and economically significant body.[100]

---

[97]   Smith, *The Stuart Parliaments*, 22; A. Dyer, 'Small market towns, 1540–1700', in Clark (ed.), *The Cambridge Urban History of Britain*, Vol. 2, 425–50, at 445.

[98]   See Appendix 2; Pryde, *The Burghs of Scotland*, part 1.

[99]   W. Ferguson, 'The Reform Act (Scotland) of 1832: Intention and Effect', in *SHR*, 45 (1966), 105–14, at 105–6.

[100]   Pagan, *The Convention of Burghs*, 257–8, discusses this in the context of the later eighteenth century, but the convention's problems had their origins in the third quarter of the seventeenth century.

Chapter 2

Representation

Recent work on elections to the English House of Commons has shown that disputed elections became increasingly common from 1640, marking the beginnings of ideological electoral politics, based on a broadening franchise.[1] Although a case study suggested that this can be detected in the 1620s, it does not undermine the conclusion that contested elections became more familiar.[2] The traditional system, even where voters were numerous, involved a narrow elite presenting candidates for election by acclamation; Mark Kishlansky called this 'selection' to distinguish it from 'election', in which voters chose between opposing candidates. Since 'elect' simply means 'choose', this is an anachronistic distinction: Scottish burgh representatives were normally said to have been 'electit', not in an attempt to mislead, merely to describe what had happened.[3] The transformation which occurred in seventeenth-century England is barely apparent in Scotland because of the nature of its urban political system. Although not as bewilderingly various as those in France, England's parliamentary boroughs exhibited a broad array of electoral systems, ranging from all male householders having the vote to restricted franchises incorporating a small number of proprietors, occasionally even placing the franchise in the hands of one individual.[4] In English terms, Scottish burghs were all 'corporate': the governing bodies were usually the electors. This was a characteristic they shared with the Italian states, the Netherlands, some states of the Empire and Castile, where *procuradores* were chosen by city councils.[5]

---

[1]   M. Kishlansky, *Parliamentary Selection: Social and Political Choice in Early Modern England* (Cambridge, 1986); D. Hirst, *The Representative of the People? Voters and Voting in England under the Early Stuarts* (Cambridge, 1975).

[2]   R. Cust, 'Parliamentary Elections in the 1620s: The Case of Great Yarmouth', in *PER*, 11 (1992), 179–91.

[3]   Kishlansky, *Parliamentary Selection*, 12; S. E. Finer, *The History of Government*, 3 vols (Oxford, 1997), vol. 2, 1035; M. A. R. Graves, *The Parliaments of Early Modern Europe* (London, 2001), 171–3.

[4]   Hirst, *The Representative of the People?*, ch. 5; Smith, *The Stuart Parliaments, 1603–1689* (London, 1999), ch. 2; N. Ball, 'Representation in the English House of Commons: The New Boroughs, 1485–1640', in *PER*, 15 (1995), 117–24; H. G. Koenigsberger, 'The Powers of Deputies in Sixteenth-Century Assemblies' in idem, *Estates and Revolutions: Essays in Early Modern European History* (New York, 1971), 176–210, at 179.

[5]   I. A. A. Thompson, *Crown and Cortes: Government, Institutions and Representation in Early-Modern Castile* (Aldershot, 1993), part 10, 'Cortes, Cities and *Procuradores* in Castile', 1–72, at 5–6; Graves, *The Parliaments of Early Modern Europe*, 171–2; B. Kümin and A. Würgler, 'Petitions, *Gravamina* and the Early Modern State: Local Influence on Central Legislation in England and Germany (Hesse)', in *PER*, 17 (1997), 39–60, at 41;

Parliamentary elections

The earliest reference to parliamentary elections comes from Aberdeen where, in 1437, the council resolved that 'Commissioners to parliament and general councils of the king should be elected by the whole common council'.[6] In Linlithgow in 1540, it was 'the counsall and courte' which chose the commissioners. The typical phrase declared that the magistrates and council had 'electit and choisin' their commissioners.[7] In 1594, Kirkcaldy's council 'nominated' its commissioner 'after consultation' (among councillors) while Edinburgh's commissioners were variously 'constituted and ordained', 'chosen named and constituted', 'voted and nominated', 'made, created and constituted' and 'elected': all these describe the same process.[8] Yet sometimes more than just the council were involved. Occasionally the previous year's councillors joined in and, in many burghs, craft deacons participated; one later sixteenth-century commentator believed this to be normal.[9] Another variation involved putting candidates in 'leets', the one (or more) with the most votes being elected – 26 such elections have been identified in eight burghs. There is no indication in any case as to why this method was used, although a desire on the part of more than one person to be elected or a genuine division of opinion are the most likely reasons. The earliest record of such an election comes from Haddington in 1604, while all but one of the others occurred after the revolution of 1637.[10] Perhaps, on a

J. H. Grever, 'The Municipal Level of Decision-Making in Holland (1660–1668)', in *PER*, 13 (1993), 17–27.

[6]   *Aberd. Recs.*, vol. 1, 394.

[7]   NAS, Linlithgow Burgh Court Book, 1528–65, B48/7/1, 184; Linlithgow Town Council Minute Book, 1620–40, B48/9/1, 264.

[8]   ECA, Edinburgh Council Minutes, SL1/1 *passim* (the quotations are modernised).

[9]   Aberdeen: ACA, Aberdeen Council Minutes, CR1/48, 102; Edinburgh: ECA, Edinburgh Council Minutes, SL1/1/15, f. 190r–v; Haddington: NAS, Haddington Burgh Registers, Council Book 1554–80, B30/13/1, ff. 30v, 106r; Cupar: SAUL, Cupar Court and Council Records 1640–53, B13/10/3, 27 Nov 1648; Dundee: DCA, Dundee Council Minute Book, vol. 3, 1597/8–1613, f. 88r; Perth: PKCA, Register of Acts of the Council June 1601–Feb 1622, B59/16/1, f. 76v; Edinburgh: *Edin.* Recs., 1573–89, 339; Lord Lindsay, *Lives of the Lindsays*, 3 vols (London, 1858), vol. 1, 487–8: a draft act of 1587 for the representation of freeholders below the peerage via elected shire commissioners. One argument put forward in the draft was that lairds should elect commissioners, since even 'every mean craftsman' was represented 'in a manner', which probably refers to the participation of craft deacons in parliamentary elections and was not a claim that every craftsman might vote. For a different view, see J. Goodare, 'The Admission of Lairds to the Scottish Parliament', in *EHR*, 116 (2001), 1103–33, at 1116, n.67; Rait, *The Parliaments of Scotland*, 265–8.

[10]   NAS, Haddington Burgh Registers, Council Book 1603–16, B30/13/3, ff. 17v, 42v; NAS, Dysart Burgh Registers, Court Book, 1623–45, B21/10/1, ff. 34v, 38v, 40v; NAS, Burntisland Council Minutes Aug 1646–Jan 1653, B9/12/9, 20; GCA, Glasgow Council Minutes May 1636–September 1642, C1/1/10, 10 Nov 1640, 2 Jan 1641; AA, Montrose Council Minutes M1/1/2 1634–73, 28 Feb 1650; NAS, Burgh of Peebles, Council Record Dec 1604–May 1652, B58/13/1, 27 May 1633, 16 Nov 1640; NAS, Linlithgow Town Council Minute Book 1640–59, B48/9/2, 127, 240, 278; SAUL, Liber Sessione et Concilii de Pettinwem 1629–1727, B60/6/1, ff. 13v–14r. 'Leet' is current Scots usage for shortlist.

much smaller scale than in England, this is evidence of the emergence of contested elections, although it would require detailed local studies to verify this.

Aberdeen provides the only unambiguous evidence of regular popular involvement, although Perth's election in 1560 appears to have been opened up to the burgesses.[11] Until the 1590s almost all of Aberdeen's commissioners were chosen after 'the haill toun' had been summoned by the ringing of a hand-bell through the streets.[12] This should not be taken literally; all inhabitants were neither summoned nor expected. Since those who came could fit into the council chamber, probably only burgesses were summoned, perhaps just merchants, and even they cannot all have responded.[13] The record described them as 'representand the haill toune', indicating a desire to give their commissioners a broadly-based mandate.[14] However, this did not result in the election of commissioners who differed significantly from those elected elsewhere, nor were votes ever divided between rival candidates. This chimes with Kishlansky's findings for England before the 1640s, where voters endorsed the choices of governing elites in a consensual process which affirmed hierarchy.[15] In 1592, the council of Aberdeen elected a commissioner, then 'Ordanit ... the haill town to be warnit' for his name to be 'notefeit and devulgat to thame'.[16] This may have been an indirect result of a ruling by the court of session in 1591 forbidding popular involvement in Aberdeen's municipal elections. Simply announcing the commissioner's name indicates a reduced role for the community and thereafter, in spite of protests from discontented groups, Aberdeen resorted to election by the council alone.[17] The system used at Aberdeen until the 1590s may have once been more widespread. Other burghs occasionally paid lip-service to the 'community' in commissions, the written mandates carried by their commissioners. Most instances of this merely stated that the magistrates and council acted on behalf of the community, although a seventeenth-century commission from Crail and another from Lauder

---

[11] M. Lynch, 'From Privy Kirk to Burgh Church: An Alternative View of the Process of Protestantisation', in N. Macdougall (ed.), *Church, Politics and Society: Scotland 1408–1929* (Edinburgh, 1983), 85–96, at 88.

[12] ACA, Aberdeen Council Minutes, CR 1/4, 119; Rait, *The Parliaments of Scotland*, 267, downplayed the significance of this, for he knew of only two such instances (1515 and 1530) because he used only the printed records of Aberdeen; W. C. Dickinson, 'Burgh Commissioners to Parliament', in *SHR*, 34 (1955), 92–5 gives another sceptical view based on limited evidence.

[13] E. P. Dennison, 'Power to the People? The Myth of the Medieval Burgh Community', in S. Foster, A. Macinnes and R. MacInnes (eds), *Scottish Power Centres* (Glasgow, 1998), 100–131, discusses the narrow understanding of 'community' at 112.

[14] ACA, Aberdeen Council Minutes, CR 1/10, 90, CR 1/29, 800.

[15] Kishlansky, *Parliamentary Selection*, ch. 1, distinguishes between 'voice' and 'vote' (at 10), suggesting that the former denotes acclamation, the latter a division of opinion: in Scotland the words were interchangeable. The limited evidence for Scottish shire elections suggests the same there: see Goodare, 'The Admission of Lairds', 1121–2.

[16] ACA, Aberdeen Council Minutes, CR 1/34/1, 338.

[17] See A. White, 'The Menzies Era: Sixteenth-Century Politics', in E. P. Dennison et al. (eds), *Aberdeen Before 1800: A New History* (East Linton, 2002), 224–37, at 234–6; *RCRBS*, vol. 1, 312–37, 354–60.

claimed that the election had been conducted with the community's 'consent', suggesting acclamation. In Lauder's next surviving commission the magistrates and council took upon themselves the burden on behalf of the community.[18] Any symbolic role the community played was a thing of the past in most burghs before the seventeenth century, as the burghs became more uniform through their own self-regulation.

Burgh councils

Since the magistrates and councillors were usually the electorate, it would be useful to establish who they were. Councils, elected annually in late September or early October, were typically headed by a provost. Beneath him were between two and four bailies who presided over the burgh's court. Each council also had a treasurer and, in many cases, a dean of guild, head of the merchant guild. There were usually between 12 and 24 councillors who were predominantly merchants; some burghs had craft councillors but only in Perth, Stirling and Glasgow was there an even balance of merchants and craftsmen.[19] Councils were not representative of the people, but no early modern organ of government was. Councils represented burghs just as parliament 'represent[ed] the haill body of the common-weal'.[20] Until 1469, there was some popular involvement in municipal elections. In that year, in line with European developments, parliament ruled that outgoing councillors would choose their successors; once this was done, the old and new councils, with a representative from each craft guild, would elect the magistrates. This sought to avoid the 'gret truble and contensione ... throw multitud and clamor of commonis sympil personis' at elections.[21] Similar sentiments justified such changes in England, and in Castile where restrictions were tighter, with life tenure for councillors, as was the case in

---

[18]   NAS, Parliamentary Commissions, PA7/25/46/2 (Crail, 1641), PA7/25/53/1 (Dumbarton, 1639), PA7/25/54/1 (Dumfries, 1567), PA25/55/1 (Dunbar, 1639), PA7/25/65/1 (Haddington, 1639), PA7/25/79/1 and 2 (Lauder, 1639, 1640), PA7/25/92/1 (Rutherglen, 1639), PA7/25/95/1 and 2 (Selkirk, 1639, 1641), PA7/25/98/1 (Tain, 1612); SAUL, B60/6/1 Liber Sessione et Concilii de Pettinwem 1629–1727, f. 17r–v. Only nine commissions survive from before 1639 in the official register, so analysis of developments is difficult.

[19]   For the origins and composition of burgh councils see W. M. MacKenzie, *The Scottish Burghs* (Edinburgh, 1949), chs 7 and 8; Dennison, 'Power to the People?'; M. Verschuur, 'Merchants and Craftsmen in Sixteenth-Century Perth', in M. Lynch (ed.), *The Early Modern Town in Scotland* (London, 1987), 36–53; M. Lynch, *Edinburgh and the Reformation* (Edinburgh, 1981), appendix i; SCA, Burgh of Stirling, Fragmentary Records 1561–97, B66/15/5, f. 26v; GCA, Liber Actorum Burgi et Civitas Glasguensis 1609–13, C1/1/7, ff. 13v, 98r–v.

[20]   R. Tittler, 'Elizabethan Towns and the "Points of Contact": Parliament', in PH, 8 (1989), 275–88, at 275; A. Cowan, *Urban Europe 1500–1700* (London, 1998), chs 2 and 3; A. R. Myers, *Parliaments and Estates in Europe to 1789* (London, 1975), 24–5; A. H. Birch, *Representation* (London, 1971), chs 1–3; J. Goodare, *The Government of Scotland, 1560–1625* (Oxford, 2004), 60; Lindsay, *Lives of the Lindsays*, vol. 1, 487–8.

[21]   *APS*, vol. 2, 95; T. Keith, 'Municipal Elections in the Royal Burghs of Scotland: I. Prior to the Union', in *SHR*, 13 (1915-16), 111–25.

the province of Holland.[22] The maintenance of order rather than the narrowing of power may have been the true motive, for it is easy to assume a narrowing of power when evidence for who held it before is lacking, and historians are divided over this issue.[23] However, attempts by Charles I to create closed councils in Scotland, akin to those in Castile, indicates that political control must have been one of the motivations for constitutional change.[24]

Although not all burghs immediately implemented the act of 1469, by the time that urban records become numerous in the middle of the sixteenth century, it was broadly applied. In Aberdeen, Dumfries, Inverurie, Kirkcudbright, Montrose, Peebles and South Queensferry, however, some of the openness of the earlier period persisted, with little 'contensione' in evidence. In Montrose in 1618, 92 votes were cast for the provost, all but two going to one candidate. Not until 1638 did Montrose conform to the law, two years after the convention of burghs insisted that only the old and new councils could participate.[25] In spite of this, 'the communitie of the toune' of Kirkcudbright continued to elect a merchant 'to vote for thame in electioune of the magistratis', a symbolic process to affirm consensus.[26] It remains a mystery how some burghs retained popular participation so long after others had given it up, particularly since the convention of burghs took an increasing interest in electoral procedures. These examples do, however, serve as a reminder that blanket descriptions of 'normality' can mask more diverse realities.

There was considerable continuity of personnel on councils because outgoing magistrates became councillors, while only some ordinary councillors demitted office each year. Although few burghs have been studied in detail, some patterns can be cautiously identified. Only one-quarter of the 357 merchants recorded in Edinburgh in 1565 were ever councillors; only 14 of the poorer 50 per cent ever served, and the dominance of the wealthy intensified over time. Municipal service was time-consuming, so unless one had the sort of business that did not require constant personal attention, it was difficult to share in the direction of municipal affairs. Some magistrates received an annual fee but it was a nominal sum.[27] Similar

---

[22]   Thompson, 'Cortes, Cities and *Procuradores*', 5; Rait, *The Parliaments of Scotland*, 266; Grever, 'The Municipal Level of Decision-Making in Holland', 18.

[23]   C. R. Friedrichs, *Urban Politics in Early Modern Europe* (London, 2000), 19–20, argues that the narrowing of power is only an assumption; Cowan, *Urban Europe*, ch. 2 accepts it as a reality.

[24]   ACA, Copies of Convention of Burghs minutes, CRB, vol. 2, f. 511r–v; D. Stevenson, *The Scottish Revolution, 1637–1644: The Triumph of the Covenanters* (Newton Abbot, 1973), 51.

[25]   NAS, Peebles Court Book and Council Record 1554–65, B58/8/2, f. 84r; DAC, Dumfries Burgh Court and Council Book 1569–74, WC4/10/3, 633; NAS, Inverurie Burgh Court Book 1612–20, B36/6/2, 30 Sept 1617; ECA, Queensferry Council Minute Book, 1634–61, SL59/1/1/1, f. 11r; AA, Montrose Council Minutes 1617–39, M1/1/1, 1 Oct 1618, 4 Oct 1627, 26 Sept 1638; T. Pagan, *The Convention of the Royal Burghs of Scotland* (Glasgow, 1926), 77.

[26]   Kirkcud. Recs., vol. 2, *passim*.

[27]   Lynch, *Edinburgh and the Reformation*, 15–16; Cowan, *Urban Europe*, 37–8. For payments, see NAS, Burgh Common Good Accounts, E82. In the 1570s, Perth's provost

patterns are repeated elsewhere, although in some places, kin connections were more important than wealth; for much of the sixteenth century, Aberdeen was controlled by a dynasty of 'merchant-lairds' who were not its wealthiest merchants.[28] Over half of burghs had fewer than 1,500 inhabitants, so merchant communities of well under 100 would have been common, allowing little difference between oligarchy and openness.[29]

The constitutions in a few parliamentary burghs permitted external interference. As was the case in many episcopal towns in Europe, Glasgow's archbishops had rights over the appointment of its magistrates.[30] The outgoing magistrates and council presented leets to the archbishop from which he chose new magistrates. This persisted even after Glasgow became a royal burgh in 1611.[31] The prior of Pittenweem and his post-Reformation successors retained rights of appointment which still existed in 1598 but which had lapsed by the 1630s.[32] A similar situation possibly prevailed in Brechin and Arbroath, which had belonged to a bishop and an abbot respectively, but no council records survive. By the seventeenth century, the council of St Andrews was not under archiepiscopal jurisdiction, nor was Dunfermline controlled by its abbot's successors.[33]

The involvement of outsiders was not restricted to ecclesiastical burghs. It is a commonplace that the nobility (peers and lairds) controlled royal burghs to gain 'power, wealth or both', although Michael Lynch has suggested that this was not normal.[34] In some places, peers did muscle in, notably the earls of Huntly in Aberdeen, yet they never secured control and their approaches were often resisted.[35] By the end of the sixteenth century, Huntly's intervention led to one faction looking to the Earl Marischal for protection. Thus burghs, and groups within them, used neighbouring nobles for their own ends and played one off against another, a pattern

---

received £20 and the four bailies each got £5 (E82/46/1) while Kirkcudbright's provost and bailies each got only £2 (E82/58/1).

[28]   White, 'The Menzies Era', 224–37.

[29]   M. Lynch, 'Continuity and Change in Urban Society, 1500–1700', in R. A. Houston and I. D. Whyte (eds), *Scottish Society, 1500–1800* (Cambridge, 1989), 85–117, at 101–5. Even a medium-sized burgh like Burntisland had only 140 taxpayers (including 22 women who could not be councillors) by the 1640s, while Montrose had fewer than 100: NAS, Burntisland Council Minutes 1639–42, B9/12/7, f. 140r–v; AA, Montrose Council Minutes 1617–39, M1/1/1, 1 Oct 1618. Small burghs must have had under 50 burgesses.

[30]   Friedrichs, *Urban Politics in Early Modern Europe*, 22–3.

[31]   Pryde, *The Burghs of Scotland*, 31; GCA, Act Book of the Burgh and City of Glasgow 1573–81, C1/1/1, *passim*, Council Minutes 1648–54, C1/1/12, 3 June 1648; A. S. W. Pearce, 'John Spottiswoode, Jacobean Archbishop and Statesman' (Stirling PhD, 1998), ch. 4.

[32]   *RPC*, first series, vol. 5, 487–9; SAUL, Liber Sessione et Concilii de Pettinwem 1629–1727, B60/6/1, *passim*.

[33]   *RPC*, first series, vol. 9, 277, 287, 635; NAS, Dunfermline Burgh Court Book 1606–13, B20/10/3, *passim*.

[34]   Verschuur, 'Merchants and Craftsmen', 39; Stevenson, *The Scottish Revolution*, 27; M. Lynch, 'The Crown and the Burghs, 1500–1625', in idem (ed.), *The Early Modern Town*, 55–80, at 56.

[35]   White, 'The Menzies Era', 226–7, 232, 235.

familiar elsewhere in Europe.[36] It is helpful to see the relationship in terms of patron and client only if that is understood as one of mutual benefit: there was no 'slavish obedience to over-mighty magnates'.[37] Although Perth's relationship with the Ruthven family looks like dominance by a peer, Perth was no helpless victim. In the 1540s it compelled William, Lord Ruthven, to agree never to enter its muniment room nor touch its documents while he was provost: he could be provost as long as he behaved himself.[38] An ally at court was a valuable asset: a judgement in favour of Perth in a dispute with Dundee in 1582 was secured because its provost was the king's treasurer.[39] Yet, when the Ruthvens fell from grace, in 1583 and 1600, Perth quickly dropped them, turning to Sir David Murray of Gospertie, a local laird and courtier who, as Lord Scone, rose to prominence in government.[40] Some burghs maintained an association with a peer without making him provost; in Linlithgow, Peebles and Cupar their noble patrons' names head the annual list of magistrates and councillors, indicating an acknowledgement of the deference due to a man of pedigree, not dependence.[41]

What was in it for the nobles? Status was one obvious benefit. In 1580, William Ruthven could boast of being earl of Gowrie, treasurer of Scotland and provost of Perth: it was another feather in his cap. In 1594, in the dying days of Ruthven power, the council agreed to elect Gowrie as provost during an indefinite absence from Scotland; he wanted to be able to say, while abroad, that he was provost of Perth.[42] Simple one-upmanship was a prominent motivator among the acutely status-conscious nobility. A burgh could have only one provost, so when one obtained that office another might be trumped, while a bond with a burgh strengthened a nobleman's political power in the locality. The Ruthvens' involvement in Perth began as part of a tussle with Lord Gray, while the Earl Marischal's rivalry with Huntly was a factor in Aberdonian politics in the 1590s. There were also economic benefits. Nobles became honorary burgesses, cementing an alliance and encouraging a wealthy neighbour to bring lucrative custom to the burgh by providing favoured access to its market. The reluctance with which some burghs relinquished noble provosts is testament to the mutual benefit of the arrangements. In 1609, parliament outlawed the election of non-residents, yet Perth wanted to retain Lord Scone and he, in turn, undertook 'to releve thame of all inconvenientis, paines and unlawes

---

[36]   Friedrichs, *Urban Politics in Early Modern Europe*, 36.

[37]   K. M. Brown, 'Burghs, Lords and Feuds in Jacobean Scotland', in Lynch (ed.), *The Early Modern Town*, 102–24, at 103, which also discusses the Maxwells' relationship with Dumfries, at 103–4, which was valued by both parties; Dennison, 'Power to the People?', 111, stops short of suggesting that burghs 'actively sought' landed patrons.

[38]   PKCA, Court and Council Minute Book, B59/12/2, f. 8v.

[39]   See ch. 7 for details.

[40]   PKCA, Perth Court and Council Minute Book, B59/12/2, ff. 34r, 63v; Register of Acts of the Council, 1601–22, B59/16/1, f. 12r.

[41]   NAS, Linlithgow Town Council Minute Book 1620–40, B48/9/1; NAS, Burgh of Peebles, Council Record 1604–52, B58/13/1; SAUL, Cupar Court and Council Records 1626–39, B13/10/2.

[42]   PKCA, Court and Council Minute Book, B59/12/2, f. 59r.

[fines]' that might result.[43] He remained provost until 1628, in spite of repeated attempts by the convention of burghs and the privy council to enforce the law.[44] A good relationship with a prominent courtier could only be beneficial, and this was replicated elsewhere, albeit not so overtly.

Perth was exceptional in having a peer as provost for most of the period between 1530 and 1630. For others they were an occasional feature, but many provosts were lairds and the benefits to the burgh would be similar, although perhaps less lucrative. Yet there were two distinct types of landed provost. In Aberdeen, Dumfries and Kirkcudbright, for example, they were active provosts: their origins were urban, many having bought into land with mercantile wealth; they regularly attended council meetings and were engaged in trade. Others held urban office purely for political and social reasons. The most striking thing about the latter is the rarity with which they participated in burgh affairs. When Perth wanted Gowrie's signature, a messenger was sent to Edinburgh, and similar tactics were needed to keep in touch with Scone, who was also given gifts by the burgh to retain his patronage.[45] Perth's courtier provosts attended so rarely that a moderator was appointed to chair the council.[46] This typifies the relationship between many burghs and their landed provosts: often they did not even attend annual elections, so a letter was sent requesting their acceptance of office.

Burntisland provides an instructive case-study of such a relationship.[47] Its provost in 1598 was Robert Melville, son of Sir Robert Melville of Murdocairnie, a neighbouring laird, privy councillor, treasurer depute and an extraordinary lord of session.[48] In spite of the obvious advantages of maintaining good relations with a well-placed neighbour, by the time the younger Robert had been knighted and admitted to the privy council in 1600, he had been replaced as provost by the king's comptroller, Sir George Hume of Spott, who, as earl of Dunbar, would soon be the most powerful man in government. The Melvilles had sought too much, demanding that Burntisland be thirled to their mills, so Melville was demoted to an ordinary councillor. He was elected provost again in 1604 but only 'provyding he will accept ... frielie and absolutlie but [i.e. without] conditioun'.[49] His two-year return to office suggests agreement but in 1606 the council 'understanding that the Earle of Dumbare hes done sindrie gud offices to this burgh And bearis yit ane greit gud will to this same, thinkis him maist meit to bruik the office of Provistrie'.[50] He was on his way

---

[43]   *APS*, vol. 4, 435–6; *RPC*, first series, vol. 8, 356, 597; PKCA, Register of Acts of the Council 1601–22, B59/16/1, f. 202r.

[44]   *RCRBS*, vol. 2, 411–12, 445, 455, vol. 3, 4, 18–19, 21, 36, 57, 79, 103; *RPC*, first series, vol. 12, 120–21, 142–3. Linlithgow and Banff were also reluctant to give up their noble provosts.

[45]   M.L. Stavert (ed.), *The Perth Guildry Book, 1452–1601* (Edinburgh, 1993), 328–9; PKCA, Register of Acts of the Council 1601–22, B59/16/1, ff. 130r–v, 127r, 131r–v, 147r–v.

[46]   Ibid., ff. 62r, 151r, 242v.

[47]   NAS, Burntisland Court Books, B9/10/1–2; Burntisland Council Minutes, B9/12/1–6.

[48]   Young, *The Parliaments of Scotland*, vol. 2, 486.

[49]   NAS, Burntisland Court Book 1602–12, B9/10/2, f. 35v. Thirlage: an obligation to grind cereals at a particular mill, with a proportion taken by the owner.

[50]   NAS, Burntisland Council Minutes, B9/12/1, f. 82v.

to court, so a messenger chased him to Berwick; he accepted and remained provost until his death in 1611, being called upon occasionally to further the burgh's interests in London and Edinburgh. He never set foot in Burntisland but could add 'provost of Burntisland' to an impressive list of titles, and he may have trumped a rival at court in the acquisition of a client. After his death, the office reverted to the Melvilles, who were elevated to the peerage in 1616. They continued to argue over the mills but eventually the burgh took them on a tack (lease). Burntisland drove a hard bargain: in 1625, Lord Melville unsuccessfully sought an increase in the rent.[51]

In 1633, two years before Melville's death, Burntisland dispensed with provosts, falling into line with Culross, Kirkcaldy, Pittenweem and Dysart, all on the south coast of Fife. In Kirkcaldy in June 1587,

> the haill counsall ... all in ane voce dissasentis that ane provest be chosin ... Bot to retene thame selff with thair auld ancient maner of baillyerie and na uther wayes, because thay understand the chesing of ane provest will be hurtfull and prejudiciall to thair antient liberties.[52]

It is not clear where the suggestion, or the perceived threat, had come from, or why it was so alarming: perhaps they feared the incursions of powerful neighbours or the dominance of a faction within the burgh. Yet almost all parliamentary burghs had provosts; most were merchant burgesses and those who were prominent outsiders tended not to interfere.

The crown was a more frequent meddler than the nobility, or at least less subtle, lacking local kin networks. Legally, it was on surer ground than any noble, being the feudal superior of every royal burgh. Intervention had many goals: to bolster those in power at times of crisis or transition; to enforce the law; to resolve local disputes. The second and third were the crown's duty, although disputes provided an opportunity to ensure amenable magistrates. The first is most pertinent since it concerns the extent to which burghs were under central control. Although it was the intervention of James V in 1528 which instigated the Ruthvens' long reign in Perth, it became a valuable partnership for the burgh: most crown impositions rarely lasted longer than the crisis which lay behind them.[53] The last of the short-lived regimes of the minority of James VI, led by James Stewart, earl of Arran, imposed provosts on nine of the 12 wealthiest burghs in 1583–1585. This was 'interference on an unprecedented scale', indicating a regime fearful of its grip on power and therefore using blunt instruments.[54] At Michaelmas 1584, Haddington was ordered to elect 16 named magistrates and councillors. But this was no purge: the previous year's provost and a bailie remained as councillors; two of the old councillors became a bailie and

---

[51]   NAS, Burntisland Council Minutes, B9/12/5, f. 35v.

[52]   FCAC, Kirkcaldy Burgh Court Book, 1/06/02, f. 36r.

[53]   Verschuur, 'Merchants and Craftsmen', 40–41.

[54]   Lynch, 'The Crown and the Burghs', 56–8, identified seven (Edinburgh, Dundee, Perth, Glasgow, Stirling, Dumfries and Cupar) to which can be added Haddington (NAS, B30/13/2, f. 18v) and Ayr (AAC, B6/11/1/2, f. 228v). For the ecclesiastical policy of the Arran regime, see A. R. MacDonald, 'The Subscription Crisis and Church–State Relations, 1584–1586', in *Records of the Scottish Church History Society*, 25 (1994), 222–55.

the treasurer; three more continued in office. The new provost, Francis Stewart, earl of Bothwell, although a prominent courtier, lived nearby and was already a burgess. In common with other noble provosts, he almost never showed face and got in touch only to borrow money. In spite of being nominated by the crown only once again and in spite of the council's declaration that they would never again relinquish 'the accustumat maner of electioun ... to the greit ... prejudice of this burght and [its] auntient liberteis', he remained provost until 1591, when he fell from royal favour, lost his value to the burgh and was dropped.[55]

Interference in 1584–1585 was a brief episode of authoritarianism, and the early years of the personal rule of James VI were marked by conciliation.[56] He did intervene occasionally although never with the intensity of Arran. Provosts were imposed on Perth in 1588 and 1589, on Dumfries and Montrose in 1599 and on Ayr in 1611.[57] Not every burgh enthusiastically accepted the nominee. In 1584 and 1585, Ayr reluctantly acquiesced, formally protesting on both occasions. In 1587, when charged once again to receive Sir William Stewart of Monkton, it refused: although the councillors were 'all of ane mynd to gif thair faythfull and trew obedience' to the king, they were determined 'to resist all oppressionis that the said Sir William may onywyis infer [*sic*] upoun thame with thair lyfes and guidis'. Commissioners were sent 'to mein the matter to the kingis majestie', who was persuaded to relent.[58] A burgh would not have a provost who abused his position. Unlike in many other European states, it was the exception rather than the rule, even in most larger burghs, for the crown to nominate magistrates.[59]

Edinburgh was different: as well as being the seat of government, it was by far the wealthiest burgh.[60] It was normal for its provost, sometimes its other magistrates or even the whole council, to be appointed by the crown. During the Reformation crisis of 1559–1560, the opposing sides in the brief civil war effected purge and counter-purge whenever they occupied the burgh, a story repeated during the Marian civil war of 1568–1573, while incumbents came and went with monotonous regularity during the series of factional governments between 1578 and 1585.[61] Control of the capital provided surer control of the realm and, after the fall of Arran in November 1585, the crown continued to interfere. Yet even here, by the beginning of the

---

[55] NAS, Haddington Burgh Registers, Council Book 1581–1602, B30/13/2, ff. 18v, 36v, 43v, 50v, 58v, 66v.

[56] A. R. MacDonald, *The Jacobean Kirk 1567–1625: Sovereignty, Polity and Liturgy* (Aldershot, 1998), ch. 2; J. Goodare, 'Scottish Politics in the Reign of James VI', in Goodare and Lynch (eds), *The Reign of James VI*, 32–54, at 37–8.

[57] PKCA, Court Books and Council Minute Books, B59/12/2, ff. 39r–v, 49r; *RPC*, first series, vol. 6, 34, 39, vol. 9, 252–3.

[58] AAC, Ayr Court and Council Records, B6/11/1/2, ff. 228v, 297v–298r; Ayr Court and Council Records, B6/11/1/3, ff. 445v–449v. The nature of the 'oppressionis' is unclear.

[59] P. Sanz, 'The Cities in the Aragonese Cortes in the Medieval and Early Modern Periods', in *PER*, 14 (1994), 95–108, at 100; Cowan, *Urban Europe*, 46, erroneously suggests that Scotland conformed to this pattern, portraying provosts as 'officers' of the crown, 'appointed ... to oversee matters in royal burghs'.

[60] Lynch, 'Continuity and Change'.

[61] Lynch, *Edinburgh and the Reformation*, part 2 and appendix i.

seventeenth century, intervention declined and, having spent the previous century foisting landed outsiders on burghs, the crown performed a *volte face*, placing an act before parliament in 1609 banning non-residents from holding office, a move which contrasted with the increased crown intervention in Castile and Aragon, where courtiers and royal officials bought municipal offices from the crown. Perhaps the act of 1609 was part of what Julian Goodare portrays as James's desire to reduce the independent power of the nobility.[62] Michael Lynch posits persistent opposition to attempts by the crown to impose a provost on Dundee as an explanation, but his suggestion that the nobility were losing interest in urban office in this period is more likely, for they would have put up an almighty fight in parliament otherwise.[63] The privy council subsequently supported the convention of burghs in its relentless pursuit of Perth, Linlithgow and Banff until their noble provosts were forced to take their urban feathers from their caps.[64] In an attempt to enforce some controversial religious legislation in 1621, James VI tried to compel burghs to elect only those who would 'in all pointis conforme', but faced stiff resistance.[65] Charles I, no fan of noble power, maintained his father's policy and, in a few burghs, interfered merely to replace one resident burgess with another. In the 1630s, he floated the idea of 'constant councils' to secure greater stability by doing away with annual elections but he left it too late: revolution broke out in 1637 just as the burghs were beginning to discuss it.[66]

During the 1640s, central intervention reached unprecedented levels.[67] The Michaelmas elections of 1645 came immediately after the defeat of a royalist rising under the marquis of Montrose. In that year and again in 1646 the committee of estates ordered that none could 'be magistratts or ... [on] the counsell ... wha have complyed with the rebels' and in December 1646, supporters of the uprising were banned from public office.[68] Similar actions were carried out by the royalist Engager regime in the summer of 1648. In Glasgow, those who had supported Montrose

---

[62] J. Goodare, 'The Nobility and the Absolutist State in Scotland, 1584–1638' in *History*, 78 (1993), 161–82. It is a theme of his *State and Society in Early Modern Scotland* (Oxford, 1999) and *The Government of Scotland*.

[63] Lynch, 'The Crown and the Burghs', 64–5; APS, vol. 4, 435–6; Thompson, 'Cortes, Cities and *Procuradores*', 51–6; Graves, *The Parliaments of Early Modern Europe*, 174.

[64] *RPC*, first series, vol. 12, 120–21, 130–31, 142–3, 152–3; RCRBS, vol. 2, 411–12, 445, 455, vol. 3, 4, 18–19, 21, 36, 57, 79, 103.

[65] A. G. Muir, 'The Covenanters in Fife, *c.*1610–1689', (St Andrews PhD, 2001), 71.

[66] *RPC*, second series, vol. 6, 172–5; ACA, Copies of Convention of Burghs minutes, CRB, vol. 2, f. 511r–v; GCA, Council Minutes 1636–42, C1/1/10, 24 June 1637; G. DesBrisay, '"The Civill Warrs did overrun all": Aberdeen, 1630–1690', in Dennison et al. (eds), *Aberdeen Before 1800*, 238–66, at 241; D. Stevenson, 'The Burghs and the Scottish Revolution', in Lynch (ed.), *The Early Modern Town*, 167–91, at 175–6; M. Lee, *The Road to Revolution: Scotland under Charles I, 1625–1637* (Urbana, 1985), 133, 142–3, 175.

[67] Stevenson, 'The Burghs and the Scottish Revolution', 173, 181–2, 185–6.

[68] GCA, Glasgow Council Minutes 1642–48, C1/1/11, 30 Sept 1645, 6 Oct 1646, 25 Jan 1647; NAS, Burntisland Council Minutes 1643–46, B9/12/8, f. 58v; ACA, Aberdeen Council Minutes, CR1/53/1, 79–80, 85–6, 96; ECA, Edinburgh Council Minutes, SL1/1/16, f. 133r–v; APS, vol. 6, part 1, 503–5.

under duress in 1645 were reinstated, only to be ousted four months later when the Engagers fell.[69] All over Scotland, an unprecedented purge took place, based on the Act of Classes which excluded people from office for various lengths of time depending on the level of their involvement with the Engagers.[70] The committee of estates commanded burghs to elect nobody who had been party to the ousted regime and to submit proof that elections had been carried out accordingly.[71]

There is no direct evidence that monarchs interfered in the election of commissioners to parliament, in contrast with Sicily, for example, where urban representatives were usually chosen by a viceroy.[72] Only two occasions have been identified when a courtier was involved in the election of a burgh commissioner. In 1609 and 1612, Perth experienced the highly unusual presence of its provost, David Murray, Lord Scone, when its commissioners to parliament were elected. Yet the commissioner in 1612, Andrew Grant, had just been ousted as provost by Scone and was later to complain to the privy council that Scone held the office illegally.[73] Scone, also present for the election of commissioners to the general assembly of the Church in 1618, was probably acting off his own bat; there is no record of other outsider provosts attending the elections of parliamentary commissioners. There is, however, strong evidence of crown interference in the election of representatives from the shires. In 1612, James VI recommended named lairds to the shires of Moray and Linlithgow. This has been dismissed as evidence of significant intervention on the basis of the evidence for Moray alone, but the discovery of a letter to the shire of Linlithgow strengthens the suspicion. That it was written at Grafton on 26 August 1612, the same day as the letter to Moray, suggests the production of a letter for every shire. To argue that a royal recommendation was not a command credits the king with too much magnanimity: he was not offering to relieve the electors of a tricky or tedious task. There was also royal interference in the shire elections before the parliament of 1633.[74] The survival of evidence for even limited interference in shire

[69]   GCA, Council Minutes 1648–54, C1/1/12, 13–14 June 1648, 3 Oct 1648; D. Stevenson, *Revolution and Counter-Revolution, 1644–1651* (Edinburgh, 2003), ch. 3.

[70]   *APS*, vol. 6, part 2, 143–8.

[71]   ACA, Aberdeen Council Minutes, CR1/53/1, 186–9, 193; DAC, Royal Burgh of Dumfries Town Council Minutes 1643–50, WA2/1, ff. 99r, 118r; NAS, Linlithgow Town Council Minute Book 1640–59, B48/9/2, 274, 277, 278; SCA, Stirling Council Minutes 1619–58, B66/20/4, 9 Oct 1648, 28 Nov 1648; SAUL, Liber Sessione et Concilii de Pettinwem 1629–1727, B60/6/1, f. 51r–v; ECA, Edinburgh Council Minutes 1648–53, SL1/1/17, ff. 48v–49r, 50r, 54r–55r.

[72]   Graves, *The Parliaments of Early Modern Europe*, 174; J. M. Hayden, 'Deputies and Qualities: The Estates General of 1614', in *French Historical Studies*, 3 (1964), 507–24, at 517–23.

[73]   PKCA, Register of Acts of the Council 1601–22, B59/16/1, ff. 185v, 201r–v, 332r; *RPC*, second series, vol. 2, 213.

[74]   NAS, Commissions to Parliament, Moray, PA7/25/23/1/1; NAS, Dundas of Dundas Muniments, GD75/604; Rait, *The Parliaments of Scotland*, 302–4; J. Goodare, 'The Admission of Lairds to the Scottish Parliament', in *EHR*, 116 (2001), 1103–33, at 1122; J. R. Young, 'Charles I and the 1633 Parliament', in K. M. Brown and A. Mann (eds), *The History of the Scottish Parliament, Volume 2: Parliament and Politics in Scotland, 1567–1707* (Edinburgh,

elections is significant because their records are so scanty. That nothing survives for the burghs whose records are infinitely better suggests an absence of central interference: councils which recorded the crown's nomination of magistrates and councillors would have recorded similar intervention in parliamentary elections. It might be argued that the crown had no need to interfere because it already controlled burgh councils.[75] There are two problems with this: the first is the rarity of central interference in the election of magistrates and councillors; the second is that there is no evidence that burgh commissioners were particularly amenable to the king's wishes. In 1621, the crown, after strenuous efforts, managed to force through parliament some highly controversial religious legislation: the burgesses were the only estate to reject it.[76]

Only after the fall of the Engagement regime in 1648 was there central interference in burghs' parliamentary elections. Determined to ensure that none associated with the Engagers could sit, the committee of estates specified the types of people 'incapable of being elected or having place ... in parliament'. The burghs were commanded to submit a note of their commissioners' names so that their suitability could be verified.[77] When summonses were issued in 1649 and 1650, burghs were reminded of the restrictions on who could be elected and a parliamentary committee was appointed to 'visit' all commissions to 'see quho is fitt to sitt ... and quho is not'.[78]

Commissioners' qualifications

The parliamentary ban on non-resident magistrates in 1609 should not be taken to indicate that they were common; it would be perverse to assume that something prevailed just because it was outlawed. Had the burghs been dominated by outsiders, their conventions would hardly have sought to ensure that every urban office-holder was 'ane merchand traffiquer'.[79] As well as supporting the efforts of the crown to exclude outsiders, the burghs consistently sought to enforce similar regulations for commissioners to parliaments, conventions of estates and conventions of burghs. Again, they would not have passed and reiterated these had the majority of burghs

---

2005), 101–37, at 103–14. Survival of evidence from shires is also a problem in England: see Hirst, *Representative of the People?*, 163.

[75]   This is asserted in Rait, *The Parliaments of Scotland*, 302, and implied in Graves, *The Parliaments of Early Modern Europe*, 164.

[76]   Calderwood, *History*, vol. 7, 499–501; J. Goodare, 'The Scottish Parliament of 1621', in *The Historical Journal*, 38 (1995), 29–51, at 36–8 and 50–51; Rait, *The Parliaments of Scotland*, 303.

[77]   NAS, Burntisland Council Minutes 1646–53, B9/12/9, 140–41; SAUL, Cupar Court and Council Records 1640–53, B13/10/3, 27 Nov 1648; Liber Sessione et Concilii de Pettinwem 1629–1727, B60/6/1, f. 51r–v; NAS, Linlithgow Town Council Minute Book 1640–59, B48/9/2, 273.

[78]   DCA, Council Minute Book, vol. 4, 1613–53, ff. 212v, 222r; NAS, Burntisland Council Minutes 1646–53, B9/12/9, 187–8; Balfour, *Works*, vol. 4, 52.

[79]   *RCRBS*, vol. 2, 411.

not supported them. It was the strength of the convention of burghs in this regard which made it hard for 'foreigners' to represent burghs in Scotland, compared to their frequency in England, Castile and elsewhere.[80] When this became more common, in the later seventeenth century, the power of the convention of burghs was waning and it was less able to enforce its own regulations.

The convention of burghs first defined the qualifications for commissioners in 1574: they were to be 'merchantis and traffiquaris, haifand thair remanyng and dwelling within burgh, and beris burdene with the nychtbouris and inhabitantis thairof'.[81] Only three months later, Haddington's commissioner, a craftsman, was refused admission.[82] The rule was not applied only to craftsmen; in 1579, Dundee was fined for sending a laird who was 'nocht ... a merchant trafficquar'.[83] In 1587, parliament ruled that 'Na ... persoun sall tak upoun him the functioun, office or place of all ... thrie estaitis or of tua of thame Bot sall only occupie the place of that ... estait quhairin he commounlie professis him self to leif'.[84] Some did ignore the regulations: in 1598 the convention fulminated against

> certane burghis quha of lait hes derectit thair commissioneris to parliamentis and conventioun of estaittis ... furth of sic rankis of persounis quha haid littill skeill or experience of thair effairis, and als litill cair and guid will to the standing thairof, haifand na regaird to the actis and constitutiouns maid of before anent the directioun of commissioneris to parliamentis, conventiounis of estaittis and conventioun of burrowis.[85]

Acts relating to the qualifications of commissioners were confirmed, with the further stipulation that none 'above the rank and degre of ane merchand, traffikquer, indweller within the burgh, and beiring burding with the samyn' could be elected. This was to be intimated to burgh councils and proof that this had been done was to be brought to the next convention of burghs. In July 1599, only ten failed to do this and were ordered to comply at the next general convention: all but four did.[86] A few continued to flout the rules. In 1600, Dunbar's commissioner was ordered to explain his burgh's failure to comply, having sent to a convention of estates an unqualified person who voted against agreed burgh policy.[87] Further enactments were made in 1601 and 1603 and, by 1606, only Inverness had failed to acknowledge the acts and was fined accordingly.[88] Religious qualifications were also adopted, although

---

[80]   Smith, *The Stuart Parliaments*, 25–9; Thompson, 'Cortes, Cities and Procuradores', 55–7; Graves, *The Parliaments of Early Modern Europe*, 173–5.

[81]   *RCRBS*, vol. 1, 25–6.

[82]   Ibid., 75.

[83]   Ibid., 80–81.

[84]   *APS*, vol. 4, 443.

[85]   *RCRBS*, vol. 2, 31–2.

[86]   Ibid., 45, 74, leaving only Stirling, Dysart, Renfrew and Dumbarton.

[87]   Ibid., 74–5.

[88]   Ibid., 102–3, 130–31, 156–7, 174, 196, 212–13. Inverness escaped its fine by registering the act in 1607, W. MacKay and H. C. Boyd (eds), *Records of Inverness*, 2 vols (Aberdeen, 1911–24), vol. 2, 55. For examples of more timeous intimation, see DCA, Dundee Council Minute Book, vol. 3, f. 50r; NAS, Dysart Burgh Registers, Court Book 1603–10, B21/8/7, f. 5v; PKCA, Register of Acts of the Council 1601–22, B59/16/1, f. 54r.

surprisingly not until 1602 when it was declared that all commissioners should be 'of the trew religoun', while in 1638, the burghs agreed that commissioners must have subscribed the National Covenant.[89]

Challenging the then accepted view that lairds began to take over the urban estate in the later seventeenth century, Robert Rait asserted that it 'began a century earlier, and ... was almost universally successful', while the burghs' efforts to prevent it 'failed to secure obedience'.[90] Some who represented burghs were lairds, but that fails to distinguish between those ready to 'tyne or win' with the burghs, and disengaged outsiders.[91] There were lairds at the convention of burghs in 1599 which confirmed an act on the qualification of commissioners, yet none was expelled because they were active members of the merchant communities they represented. The act of parliament of 1587 did not ban lairds from representing burghs any more than it banned burgesses from representing shires, for burgesses could be lairds and vice versa. It was saying that, because there was a separate estate for lairds, they would have to choose which to represent. Between 1587 and 1651, the act was breached by only five lairds who sat in both estates. This can be contrasted with the period after 1660, when 21 did so.[92] These later instances are exemplified by Sir Alexander Home of Castlemains who represented Kirkwall, the most northerly burgh, and Berwickshire, one of the most southerly shires; a native of Berwickshire, he had no meaningful connection with Orkney. Sir Patrick Murray of Saltcoats was elected for three different burghs between 1669 and 1701, as well as the county of Fife in 1702. One could represent different shires by virtue of dispersed estates, but it was impossible to be a 'trafficking burgess' in more than one burgh. In contrast to England, where many MPs represented different boroughs during a parliamentary career, only six ever sat for different burghs in Scotland, and only two did so before 1651.[93] The maintenance of residential qualifications can be contrasted with English efforts to abolish them in 1571. In spite of the widespread flouting of the existing law, the bill failed amidst a wave of what Geoffrey Elton called 'humbug and pomposity' about the necessity of resident MPs: only greater boroughs like London and Norwich and a few lesser ones, such as Great Yarmouth, elected residents exclusively.[94] It was

---

[89]   *RCRBS*, vol. 2, 145, vol. 4, 543.

[90]   R. S. Rait, 'Parliamentary Representation in Scotland', in *SHR*, 12 (1914), 115–34, at 123–4.

[91]   *RCRBS*, vol. 2, 156–7. Tyne = lose.

[92]   Figures based on Young, *The Parliaments of Scotland*. Although there are problems with Young's work, its breadth of coverage and biographical detail mean that it provides a good basis for comparison. The commissioners can be found in vol. 1, 42, 68, 87, 89, 119, 127, 142, 181, 228, 310, 349, 352, and vol. 2, 456, 458, 460–61, 470, 485, 495–6, 523, 530–31, 615, 622, 628, 631, 672–3, 713–14. For its shortcomings see J. Goodare, 'Who was the Scottish Parliament?', in *PH*, 14 (1995), 173–8.

[93]   Young, *The Parliaments of Scotland*, vol. 1, 21, 76, 107, 174–5, 349, 383, vol. 2, 530–31; Smith, *The Stuart Parliaments*, 25.

[94]   G. R. Elton, *The Parliament of England 1559–1581* (Cambridge, 1986), 227–8; Cust, 'Parliamentary Elections in the 1620s', 181; D. M. Dean, 'Parliament and Locality', in D. M. Dean and N. L. Jones (eds), *The Parliaments of Elizabethan England* (Oxford, 1990), 139–62, at 141–3.

a similar picture elsewhere in Europe, with outsiders increasingly dominating by the seventeenth century.[95]

The figures weaken Rait's case for a sixteenth-century lairds' takeover, but he could have made other arguments. Some may have chosen to represent burghs because it provided access to parliament without election by their peers. Yet most landowners representing burghs were active burgesses: of the 137 who sat for burghs between 1550 and 1651, at least 84 had a commitment to the burgh that they represented and most of them also sat in conventions of burghs.[96] If they had no real interest in urban affairs, they would not have wasted time discussing weights and measures and the conduct of the conservator of Scottish privileges at Veere if a seat in parliament was what they really wanted. The most significant thing about the 53 landowners with no obvious urban interests is that they constituted a mere 7.5 per cent of burgh commissioners between 1550 and 1651.[97] Burghs almost always adhered to the law by electing genuine merchants.

The figures above exclude members of landed families who never themselves became landowners. The growth of towns, in Scotland as elsewhere, was largely due to the influx of rural people from across the social spectrum. Younger sons of lairds were apprenticed to merchants and craftsmen, while intermarriage meant that most lairds had an interest in urban affairs and most prominent merchants an interest in the land.[98] Although they were similar people, their economic interests could differ considerably: if the burgess estate had been dominated by people who thought of themselves as landowners rather than merchants, it would not have objected to the virtual doubling of shire votes in 1640.[99] Nor would it have sought to exclude commissioners from the stewartry of Kirkcudbright on the grounds that it was part of Wigtownshire.[100] English borough MPs may have merited the epithet 'so-called burgesses' by 1600, as only 25 per cent were residents. The same cannot be said for their Scottish counterparts: even the 50 lairds and three nobles who sat for burghs without a meaningful urban interest lived in the same county as the burghs they

---

[95]   Graves, *The Parliaments of Europe*, 173–4; Thompson, 'Cortes, Cities and *Procuradores*', 55–7.

[96]   Figures based on Young, *The Parliaments of Scotland*. Commitment is indicated by combinations of: at least two attendances at conventions of burghs other than those preceding a parliament; service as a bailie; service as clerk or treasurer; service as an ordinary councillor; evidence of mercantile or craft activity. Some of the 53 others may also have had unrecorded urban connections.

[97]   Figures based on Young, *The Parliaments of Scotland*: 708 people served as burgh commissioners between 1550 and 1651.

[98]   Young, *The Parliaments of Scotland*, vol. 1, 62, 402, vol. 2, 664–5, 692.

[99]   Stevenson, 'The Burghs and the Scottish Revolution', 169–70. Although in 1640 there were 51 burghs (with 52 commissioners), they would have been outvoted by 36 nobles and 23 shires, *APS*, vol. 5, 258–9.

[100]   *APS*, vol. 6, part 1, 286, 614; Balfour, Works, vol. 3, 247–8. The burghs were on shaky ground: the stewartry of Kirkcudbright had sent commissioners since 1612 (see Young, *The Parliaments of Scotland*, 795–6) so this was not 'giving the lairds two extra votes', Stevenson, 'The Burghs and the Scottish Revolution', 170.

represented; in later sixteenth-century England, 41 per cent of borough MPs did not.[101] Even after 1660, most commissioners were merchants and the convention of burghs continued to enforce the occupational and residency qualifications. Objections were raised against ineligible commissioners and some were disqualified.[102] Only after 1690 did the burghs cease to press for the maintenance of residency qualifications.[103] So why did lairds not use the burghs to get into parliament? Short sessions meant that parliament did not become a route to political advancement, unlike in England. Instead, service to the crown and kin connections with a great noble or courtier were the ways to get on. A study carried out in the 1920s showed a huge overlap between commissioners at conventions of burghs and the parliamentary estate of burgesses.[104] The effectiveness of the convention of burghs in ensuring adherence to residency qualifications meant that the representatives of Scotland's towns were overwhelmingly resident burgesses, in contrast with their counterparts in England, Ireland and in many parts of Europe.[105]

It is hard to characterise burgh commissioners, although they were drawn from a narrow section of urban society. Over 80 per cent were merchant burgesses, although some from Edinburgh were craftsmen. Magistrates were frequently elected but parliamentary experience often overrode office-holding. Patrick Grieve attended six parliaments for Burntisland but only twice as a magistrate.[106] In 1633, Kirkcudbright elected William Glendinning, a bailie; in 1639, he sat as provost; he was elected again in 1641, although just an ordinary councillor.[107] Sometimes commissioners were not even councillors. Graduates featured prominently, many of whom were lawyers, an increasingly significant urban group, although they did not come to dominate Scotland's towns as they did elsewhere.[108] Burgh clerks were often notaries and some represented burghs in parliament, notably the Wedderburn dynasty of Dundee, clerks from the middle of the sixteenth to the middle of the seventeenth century.[109] But graduates and lawyers constituted less than ten per cent of burgh commissioners. When it comes to crown office-holding, the figures are

---

[101] Smith, *The Stuart Parliaments*, 22, 29–30: under Elizabeth, 25 per cent were residents, 34 per cent neighbouring gentry and 41 per cent lived outwith the county; between 1603 and 1640, the figures were 23 per cent, 50 per cent and 27 per cent respectively.

[102] Rait, 'Parliamentary Representation in Scotland', 124–5.

[103] *RCRBS*, vol. 4, 281–2, 305, 341.

[104] J. D. Mackie and G. S. Pryde, *The Estate of the Burgesses in the Scots Parliament and its Relation to the Convention of Royal Burghs* (St Andrews, 1923).

[105] Thompson, 'Cortes, Cities and *Procuradores*', 42–3, 55–7; Graves, *The Parliaments of Early Modern Europe*, 173–5.

[106] NAS, Burntisland Council Minutes, B9/12/1, ff. 50r, 79r; Burntisland Council Minutes, B9/12/2, ff. 12v, 42v; Burntisland Council Minutes, 1611–15, B9/12/3, f. 28v; Young, *The Parliaments of Scotland*, vol. 1, 303. In Sweden, one of the representatives had to be a burgomaster: M. Roberts (ed.), *Sweden as a Great Power, 1611–1697: Government, Society, Foreign Policy* (London, 1968), 25.

[107] *Kirkcud. Recs.*, vol. 2, 471, 602, 634, 644, 736, 758, 783, 802, 820.

[108] Cowan, *Urban Europe*, 40–41.

[109] Young, *The Parliaments of Scotland*, vol. 2, 722–4; Lynch, 'Continuity and Change', 87.

unimpressive: 59 commissioners (8.3 per cent) held any crown office when elected and most held minor posts such as customers, justices of the peace and sheriff clerks, only 19 holding prominent positions such as privy councillors, lords of session, and sheriffs-depute.[110] This contrasts with the English House of Commons and the third estate in the French Estates General, where around 90 per cent of members held crown offices, although, as in Scotland, most held minor positions. In the Italian states, in Castile and in Sweden, it was also common for royal officials to represent towns.[111] Again, in terms of the truly urban nature of the representatives and their independence from the crown, Scotland seems distinctive. In England, merchants in parliament were an ever-shrinking minority but it was not until the later seventeenth century that the solidly mercantile nature of the urban estate in Scotland even began to be eroded.

Delegates or free agents?[112]

There was tension between what the crown wanted from those who came to parliament and what the burghs wanted from their commissioners. In Castile, the Habsburgs struggled to secure *poder cumplido* (full power) for cities' *procuradores* (eventually achieving this in 1632) and brought similar pressures to bear on the towns of the States General of the Netherlands. However, after their break with Spain, the States General operated on a strongly delegate principle.[113] It has been argued that *plena potestas* indicates strong central authority, while limited mandates suggest central weakness. The evidence for England and Scotland, where *plena potestas* existed in theory but was significantly modified in practice, and for Castile and Aragon, where Philip II, hardly a weak monarch, was unable to secure it in spite of strenuous efforts, would counsel against adopting this analysis. It also renders redundant many discussions of the significance of the ostensible powers of representatives: how they behaved and how they were expected to behave is a better guide to the nature of representation than an examination of their written mandates.[114]

---

[110] See Young, *The Parliaments of Scotland.* Customers collected import and export duties; sheriff clerks served in county courts; sheriffs-depute were the judges in those courts, sheriffs often being hereditary; lords of session were judges in the central civil court.

[111] Smith, *The Stuart Parliaments*, 22–30; Graves, *The Parliaments of Early Modern Europe*, 168, 174; Thompson, 'Cortes, Cities and Procuradores', 12–15, 51–2; Cowan, *Urban Europe*, 47; Hayden, 'Deputies and Qualities', 520; G. Rystad, 'The Estates of the Realm, the Monarchy, and Empire, 1611–1718', in M. Metcalf (ed.), *The Riksdag: A History of the Swedish Parliament* (New York, 1987), 61–108, at 93–4.

[112] Birch, *Representation, and Finer, The History of Government*, vol. 2, *The Intermediate Ages*, 1032–6, provide some simplistic models of these concepts, but none matches reality.

[113] Graves, *The Parliaments of Early Modern Europe*, 177; Thompson, 'Cortes, Cities and *Procuradores*', 20–37, 63; Koenigsberger, 'The Powers of Deputies'; G. Griffiths, *Representative Government in Western Europe in the Sixteenth Century* (Oxford, 1968), 2, 3, 81, 124, 298–303, 312, 533; J. H. Grever, 'The Municipal Level of Decision-Making in Holland (1660–1668)', in *PER*, 13 (1993), 17–29, at 18, 26–7.

[114] Hirst, *Representative of the People?*, ch. 8; Smith, *The Stuart Parliaments*, 29–30; Myers, *Parliaments and Estates in Europe*, 57; Griffiths, *Representative Government in*

Royal precepts expected *plena potestas*; Aberdeen's council minutes recorded precepts requiring commissioners with 'full power' in 1579 and 1606. Burghs always granted 'full powar and auctoritie for us and in our names and upone our behalffis ... to ressoun, treat, voit and conclude' in all matters. Magistrates and councils promised to 'hald firme and stable' (accept without question) everything done in their name, a phrase used in the same context in thirteenth-century France.[115] Just as in England, commissioners had no right to consult their councils before voting and the brevity parliaments before the 1640s meant that this was impracticable anyway. The British parliaments differed from a number of European assemblies in which representatives could assent to measures only conditionally before referring back to those who had sent them.[116] Scottish commissions did include phrases which clearly indicate limitations. This circumscribed *plena potestas* is linked to the direct election of representatives by councils and has also been observed in some Italian states.[117] Commissioners were to do whatever 'we micht do ... our selffes and [i.e. if] we war personallie present'.[118] Some commissions provided detailed descriptions of the sorts of things commissioners were expected to do.[119] Early commissions from Aberdeen even refer to specific issues, one instructing commissioners to see 'how the multitude of vyle salaris may be repressit'.[120] Many emphasised the need for urban solidarity, authorising commissioners to meet 'with the remanent commissioneris of the borrowis' to deal with matters 'tuiching the cuntrie, commoun weill and estait of burrowis in generall or particulare'.[121] So, although explicit restrictions disappeared during the sixteenth century, commissioners were reminded of their duty to their burgh and to all burghs, as well as to king and common weal. A burgh commissioner did not, however, have to vote 'the way the burgh council wanted him to'.[122] Commissions reveal that commissioners were delegates with interests to defend and maintain but also free agents, expected to vote according to their own judgement. These ostensibly contradictory roles operated in different contexts. If the interests of the burgh were at stake, commissioners should do their utmost to defend

---

Western Europe, 2 n.1; Finer, *The History of Government*, vol. 2, 1035, 1037; Sanz, 'The Cities in the Aragonese Cortes', 104.

[115] PKCA, Register of Acts of the Council 1601–22, B59/16/1, f. 201r–v (the central register of commissions has numerous other examples, NAS, PA7/25); ACA, Council Records, CR1/29, 800, CR1/42, 733; A. Marongiu, *Medieval Parliaments: A Comparative Study* (London, 1986), 230.

[116] Ibid., 224–32.

[117] Ibid., 229.

[118] NAS, PA7/25/37/1 (Anstruther Easter, 1607).

[119] NAS, PA7/25/38/2 (Anstruther Wester, 1649), PA7/25/49/1 (Culross, 1639), PA7/25/57/1 (Dunfermline, 1639).

[120] ACA, Aberdeen Council Minutes, CR1/13, 105–6. The 'vile sailors' were presumably unfree traders.

[121] NAS, PA7/25/43/1 (Brechin, 1633), PA7/25/44/1 (Burntisland, 1639), PA7/25/54/1 (Dumfries, 1567).

[122] A shire commission was rejected for containing 'limitations and restrictions ... contrary to the order and practice of this kingdom', quoted in Rait, *The Parliaments of Scotland*, 309; Goodare, 'Who was the Scottish Parliament', 178.

them; they were also to toe any line previously agreed by the burghs, although 'every commissionar [would] haif the frie libertie according to his conscience to ... vote, exceptand it be concludit befoir be the haill that ane sall speik and vote for all'.[123]

There were undoubtedly similarities between English MPs and Scottish commissioners and, in terms of how they might behave in parliament, the differences can be exaggerated.[124] The power of the two parliaments to make binding legislation was unusual in Europe.[125] Yet there were significant differences between Scottish and English theories of representation. Most significant was the collective voice of the convention of burghs, an institution unique in Europe and, although groups of English boroughs occasionally banded together, there was no unified urban interest there.[126] The lack of a collective voice in England made borough MPs free agents to a much greater extent than their Scottish counterparts, providing more scope for political advancement, which made being an MP a more tempting prize for politically ambitious gentry. Other distinctions also merit attention. While the number of MPs any English town could elect was fixed (most sent two but some only one), many Scottish burghs elected two or more commissioners, even though, with the possible exception of Edinburgh, each had only one vote and, from 1621 onwards, only one could sit at any time. Before 1621, multiple members were elected 'conjunctlie and severallie', one being able to exercise full powers in the absence of the others. As well as permitting flexibility, multiple commissioners could emphasise a burgh's status, might satisfy divisions within a burgh and could lobby more effectively before and during sessions. Larger delegations came from wealthier burghs but even smaller ones occasionally sent two. This practice originated in the early fourteenth century: the earliest surviving parliamentary summons, from 1328, sought 'six suitable people from each of the communities of the burghs', which could have led to the attendance of up to 192 burgesses.[127] Six was the maximum a burgh could send; some would send only one or two, others none. All prelates, barons and freeholders were summoned but not all were expected. In the middle of the fifteenth century, burghs were asked

---

[123] *RCRBS*, vol. 1, 25.

[124] Stevenson, *The Scottish Revolution*, 27, draws the contrast too sharply.

[125] Koenigsberger, 'The powers of deputies', 178–9; X. Gil, 'Parliamentary Life in the Crown of Aragon: Cortes, Juntas de Brazos, and Other Corporate Bodies', in *Journal of Early Modern History*, 6 (2002), 362–95, at 371–2; Myers, *Parliaments and Estates in Europe*, 30.

[126] P. Glennie and I. Whyte, 'Towns in an Agrarian Economy, 1540–1700' in P. Clark (ed.), *The Cambridge Urban History of Britain, Volume 2, 1540–1580* (Cambridge, 2000), 167–93, at 170; J. Miller, 'Representatives and Represented in England 1660–1698', in *PER*, 15 (1995), 125–32, at 126.

[127] *RRS*, v, no.563. The Latin is '*sex personas sufficientes de singulis communitatibus burgorum*'. Geoffrey Barrow translated it as 'six sufficient persons of the various burgh communities' allowing a total of six to be understood, as in 1296 when six burgh seals were appended to a Franco-Scottish treaty: G. W. S. Barrow, *Robert Bruce and the Community of the Realm of Scotland* (Edinburgh, 1988), 300. Yet 'singulis' cannot permit that translation; it also meant 'each' in twelfth-century Leonese urban representation: J. F. O'Callaghan, 'The Beginnings of the Cortes of Leon-Castile', in *The American Historical Review*, 74 (1969), 1503–37, at 1514; P. McNeill and R. Nicholson, *An Historical Atlas of Scotland c.400–c.1600* (St Andrews, 1975); map 30. I am grateful to Roy Pinkerton for help with the Latin.

for three or four and similar numbers were requested from English, Aragonese, Leonese and Sicilian cities in the medieval period.[128] In 1504, a remarkable ten were sent by Aberdeen which also commissioned six, four, three and two at other times. By the middle of the sixteenth century, it usually sent three and this continued until 1579, after which two became normal, although in that year, royal precepts were still seeking 'thre or four sufficient burgessis' from each burgh.[129] There is thus nothing remarkable about Aberdeen's three commissioners at the Reformation parliament in 1560. They may have represented the range of religious opinion in the burgh, but two of them were also experienced parliamentarians.[130] At least 22 burghs sent more than one commissioner at least once before 1621.[131] Most usually sent only one but a special occasion might inspire more to do so: in 1617, when James VI made his first visit since 1603, 18 sent two.[132]

In 1621, a new pattern is discernible: two commissioners from Edinburgh and one from each of the others. As the capital and by far the wealthiest burgh, this was analogous to London's four MPs or Zaragoza's four *procuradores* in the Aragonese *cortes*.[133] The reasons for the timing of this change are obscure. It ought to have aroused some discussion, considering how many had sent more than one commissioner as recently as 1617, yet no act of parliament, privy council or convention of burghs established this new system.[134] Increasing crown control was clearly on the agenda but if this had been the reason for restricting the number of commissioners, an outcry from those whose privileges were being undermined might be expected. There is a tradition which dates the decision to a convention of burghs in 1619, but no such act is extant in the records of the convention.[135] An act of the burghs relating to the

---

[128] APS, vol. 1, 104; Rait, *Parliaments of Scotland*, 269–70, 272; K. Mackenzie, *The English Parliament* (Harmondsworth, 1950), 17, n.1; O'Callaghan, 'The Beginnings of the Cortes of Leon-Castile', 1530; Sanz, 'The Cities in the Aragonese Cortes', 104; Marongiu, *Medieval Parliaments*, 164–5.

[129] ACA, Aberdeen Council Minutes, CR1/8, 324; CR1/9, 418, 467; CR1/10, 90; CR1/11, 470; CR1/12, 63, 388–9; CR1/13, 431; CR1/18, 6, 291; CR1/21, 126–7, 651; CR1/22, 60–61, 301, 674–5; CR1/23, 55, 319; CR1/25, 520; CR1/26, 100, 359, 452; CR1/29, 800. The word 'sufficient' in 1579 demonstrates continuities with 1328. In 1609, plural commissioners were still sought: *RPC*, first series, vol. 8, 578–9.

[130] ACA, Aberdeen Council Minutes, CR1/22, 674–5; CR1/23, 55, 319; Lynch, 'The Crown and the Burghs', 55, nor is there anything odd about Edinburgh's four in 1560.

[131] See *APS*, vols 2–4, *passim*. The lack of sederunts (attendance lists) between 1592 and 1612 (save for 1593) and the tendency to record only one name even if more were sent means that figures given are minima.

[132] *APS*, vol. 4, 525–6 (Stirling sent two, although only 'Jhonne Williamesoun' is in the sederunt. See SCA, Stirling Council Minutes, B66/20/1, 26 May 1617).

[133] *APS*, vol. 4, 593–4; Rait, *Parliaments*, 272–3; Graves, *Parliaments of Early Modern Europe*, 172; Sanz, 'The Cities in the Aragonese Cortes', 104.

[134] But cf. Mackie and Pryde, *The Estate of the Burgesses*, 7–8, which argues that the act of 1578 (see below) was applied to parliament by the burghs.

[135] *RCRBS*, vol. 3. The supposed act of 1619 is referred to in the preface to APS, vol. 1, 18 (from 1815). It is also mentioned in undated MS notes in NAS, Cosmo Innes Transcripts, vol. 2, RH2/2/14, no. 36, 'Notes on Burghs'. See also Rait, The Parliaments of Scotland, 272, and Mackie and Pryde, The Estate of the Burgesses, 6–7.

number of commissioners was passed in 1625 but it makes no reference to an act of 1619, so must be regarded as the first unequivocal statement that Edinburgh was to send two while the others should send only one.[136]

The lack of division lists makes it unclear whether Edinburgh's commissioners could vote separately.[137] Others certainly had only one vote. By the fifteenth century, each English MP could vote and most boroughs sent two (a few sent only one and London sent four).[138] On the basis of an act of parliament of 1578 relating to the convention of burghs, Edinburgh claimed two votes and in 1583 the burghs accepted that this applied to parliament. In a dispute over the tax roll Edinburgh claimed two votes 'according to the act of parliament and thair auld use'. Its right to two votes was not disputed, except that 'in this cais of alteratioun of the extentt roll' only one of its commissioners was elected to the sub-committee so could exercise only one vote, although three years later, Edinburgh was given two votes on another commission to apportion a tax among the burghs. In 1611, it was agreed that only one commissioner from each burgh might sit *and vote* at the convention's table, with the exception of Edinburgh 'quhilk has ordinnarlie tua commissionars'.[139] Before 1640, each shire had one vote but in that year, every shire commissioner was granted a vote, almost doubling the strength of their estate. In protesting against this on behalf of the burghs, Edinburgh made no claim for a vote to be granted to each of its commissioners, suggesting that they already voted separately. However, the inclusion of nine burgesses (two from Edinburgh) on the committee of articles in 1633, when each estate had only eight votes, confuses the issue.[140] A decreet arbitral of 1583, ruling that Edinburgh would send one merchant and one craftsman to parliaments, ostensibly explains why it sent two commissioners, yet its claim to two votes dates from no later than 1578.[141] Other burghs had experienced pressure from the crafts; in Dundee in 1563, they had even claimed that it was customary for the burgh to send a craftsman and a merchant to parliament.[142] Only in Edinburgh, perhaps because it had the right to two votes, were the crafts successful in securing a place.

---

[136]   *RCRBS*, vol. 3, 193.

[137]   The only division list is an unofficial one from 1621 (Calderwood, *History*, vol. 7, 498–501). It lists only one commissioner voting for Edinburgh, possibly indicating that he exercised the burgh's single vote, or that his colleague abstained. For further details see *Ecclesiastical Letters*, vol. 2, 658–62; *RPC*, first series, vol. 12, 557–9n; Goodare, 'The Scottish Parliament of 1621', 48–51.

[138]   Ball, 'Representation in the English House of Commons', 118; Miller, 'Representatives and Represented in England', 133.

[139]   *APS*, vol. 3, 102; *RCRBS*, vol. 1, 172, 207, vol. 2, 315. In this context 'two commissioners' appears to mean 'two votes'.

[140]   *APS*, vol. 5, 9–10; Stevenson, 'The Burghs and the Scottish Revolution', 172, shows that eight votes were exercised by the burgesses on the committee.

[141]   A decreet arbitral – a judgement reached by arbitration, in this case resolving a dispute between merchants and craftsmen; see Lynch, *Edinburgh and the Reformation*, 54–5, 63–4, 161.

[142]   DCA, Council Minute Book, vol. 1, 76–7; A. Maxwell, *The History of Old Dundee* (Dundee, 1884), 184–5.

The system which first appeared in 1621 and was confirmed by the burghs in 1625 was not universally respected: some sent two or more in 1633, but their commissions were rejected. One of Burntisland's commissioners hurried home to intimate 'That thair will not be ane commissione acceptit ... quhilk containis any ma [more] commissionaris namis bot one ... And that sundrie burrowis hes causit reforme thair commissiones quha had mea commissionaris names nor [i.e. than] ane'. The council chose one and ordered 'the commissione to be alterit and writtin over agane'.[143] Aberdeen's commission also contained two names, Paul Menzies and Patrick Leslie. Menzies sat on the first day and served on the articles but was absent on the last day, being replaced by Leslie, who aroused the king's ire by voting against key crown legislation.[144] That one commissioner could replace another during a session of parliament might have struck an outsider, particularly one from England, as bizarre. However, in August 1633, the convention of burghs explicitly recognised the burghs' right to send with their commissioners 'assessores ... that ... sall have voat in the commissioners absence', while in 1640, burghs were reminded that a commission should 'conteine bot on persoun' although they were to 'direct moe if you pleas, as assessouris ... to have voice in absence of your commissioner'.[145] Since commissioners were elected 'cunjunctlie and severallie', the burgh was represented whoever was sitting. Only Edinburgh's council minutes and commissions almost never used the phrase, lending further weight to the view that it had two votes.[146] There was a corporate understanding of representation: the commissioner was a delegate. The burgh had the right to be represented and in this respect the Scottish commissioner was more akin to his European counterparts than to an English MP.[147] That commissioners were seen primarily as delegates was emphasised in 1594 when the convention of burghs ruled that no commissioner could raise a matter at the convention without 'ane speciall and severall commissioun of his burgh'.[148]

Across Europe, monarchs sought greater control over the representation of towns by attempting to prevent the change of members during sessions.[149] In Scotland this was not achieved until after 1660, although there was an abortive attempt to prevent changes of commissioners in 1647: none was to be changed until 'thair be ane generall rule set doune theranent' but such a rule did not materialise and burgh commissioners continued to sit in turns.[150] Changing commissioners during a session was rare before 1639 but became common thereafter. This may have originated in the drawn-out process of the establishment of the revolutionary government in 1637–1638. In that period, the 'tables' (representatives of nobles, lairds, burghs

---

[143] NAS, Burntisland Council Minutes 1631–37, B9/12/6, ff. 54v–55r.

[144] DesBrisay, 'Aberdeen 1630–1690', 240–41; Lee, *The Road to Revolution*, 133.

[145] ACA, Acts of Convention, CRB vol. 2, f. 445v; ACA, Aberdeen Council Records, CR1/52/1, 591–2.

[146] Only in 1555 and 1617 is the phrase used in Edinburgh's council minutes or parliamentary commissions: ECA, Council Minutes Oct 1551–July 1558, SL1/1/2, f. 49r; NAS, Commissions to Parliament, Edinburgh, PA7/25/59.

[147] Birch, *Representation*, 46.

[148] *RCRBS*, vol. 1, 447.

[149] Marongiu, *Medieval Parliaments*, 144–5.

[150] *APS*, vol. 6, part 1, 677, vol. 7, 396.

and clergy) sat in Edinburgh as a provisional government. Their sessions were too long for individual commissioners to be able to remain permanently, so to avoid prolonged absences, commissions named two or more people who were to sit '*per vices*' (by turns).[151] It would be easy to dismiss such expedient adaptations as devoid of principle and thus of no use in understanding the thinking of those who introduced them. However, it was the burghs' corporate rather than personal understanding of representation and the fact that their commissioners were active merchants that compelled them to envisage such a solution. In 1641, Linlithgow's commissioners were to attend 'weik about'; in 1650, Dysart elected three and 'ordayned ilkane [i.e. each] ... to attend ... tuentie dayis *per vices*'.[152] Another device was to elect an 'assessor' along with a single commissioner, to give advice and take his place in case of his absence.[153] This entrenched the principle of the burgh's right to be represented, not the representative's right to sit as was the case in England and Castile.[154]

Another indicator of the nature of Scottish urban representation is the relationship between commissioners and the councils which elected them. English historians disagree about the interaction between MPs and boroughs. Derek Hirst argued that it was normal for MPs to receive instructions throughout the early modern period, while a case-study of Great Yarmouth revealed a borough which actively sought to direct its representatives.[155] Others have argued that MPs merely invoked duty to their constituents as a rhetorical device in debates.[156] David Smith, although acknowledging a degree of interaction, suggested that representation of local interests was informal, except at 'turbulent times'.[157] The conditions under which Scottish commissioners were sent are less ambiguous. As with those elsewhere in Europe, limited mandates and specific instructions were common, whether times were peaceful or turbulent, although Scottish commissioners may not have carried instructions as detailed as French *cahiers de doleances*.[158] In spite of the laconic

---

[151] DAC, Commissioune for Dumfreis [7 July 1638], RD3/5.

[152] SAUL, Liber Sessione et Concilii de Pettinwem 1629–1727, B60/6/1, f. 17r–v; NAS, Linlithgow Town Council Minute Book 1640–59, B48/9/2, 21; FCAC, Dysart Council Minute Book, 1/02/01, 25 Feb 1650. Similar examples can be found for most burghs. There is limited evidence for European parallels but see Marongiu, *Medieval Parliaments*, 144–5.

[153] NAS, Commissions to Parliament, Aberdeen PA7/25/3.

[154] Thompson, 'Cortes, Cities and *Procuradores*', 7: the *procuración* in Castile could even be inherited.

[155] Hirst, *The Representative of the People?*, ch. 8 and see ch. 9 on reports from MPs; Cust, 'Parliamentary Elections in the 1620s', 182–3; L. F. Brown, 'Ideas of Representation from Elizabeth to Charles II', in *The Journal of Modern History*, 11 (1939), 23–40, at 24, 25.

[156] Ball, 'Representation in the English House of Commons', 123.

[157] Smith, *The Stuart Parliaments*, 30, 177.

[158] Koenigsberger, 'The Powers of Deputies'; Sanz, 'The Cities in the Aragonese Cortes', 104; Graves, *The Parliaments of Early Modern Europe*, 177; Marongiu, *Medieval Parliaments*, 229; Myers, *Parliaments and Estates in Europe*, 57; Thompson, 'Cortes, Cities and Procuradores', 20–37; Griffiths, *Representative Government*, 124, 298–303, 305–6, 312; Birch, *Representation*, 46; O. Ulph, 'The Mandate System and Representation to the Estates General under the Old Regime', in *The Journal of Modern History*, 23 (1951), 225–31, at 227–8.

nature of the records, it is clear that it was common for burghs to issue instructions, communicate with commissioners and receive and approve reports of their conduct. Ayr seldom recorded the issuing of instructions but they must have been normal; in 1584, because its commissioner was already in Edinburgh, he was sent 'ane missive concerning the effaires of the toun'.[159] Burntisland's note in 1604 that its commissioner had 'ressavit his injunctiounis and directiounis' has the ring of normality, while detailed instructions survive for Aberdeen's commissioners from 1633 onwards.[160] Edinburgh's council even appointed committees to prepare petitions and draft acts, and sometimes continued to meet during sessions of parliament.[161]

In the 1640s, evidence for the issuing of instructions burgeons. This may be the result of the highly-charged political atmosphere but, since local concerns still predominated, it is probably due to the increasing intensity of central government and the better survival of records.[162] Before the 1640s, communication was tricky, given the brevity of sessions and the distances involved, yet it was not unknown.[163] The longer sessions of the 1640s meant that regular communication was essential if commissioners were to carry out councils' wishes. Burgh accounts contain numerous references to letters and messengers passing to and from parliament, although few of these survive.[164] In 1646, Dysart's commissioner was ordered to send weekly reports.[165] This modified the long-standing practice of commissioners reporting on their return on parliamentary proceedings in general and on specific instructions which they had been given. The instructions for Aberdeen's commissioners in 1633 were issued so that the 'commissionares may report thair diligence accordinglie' and only after approval of the reports were representatives formally discharged of their commissions.[166] Such reports were neither required nor customary in England

---

[159]   AAC, Ayr Court and Council Records, B6/11/1/2, f. 200v.

[160]   NAS, Burntisland Council Minutes, B9/12/1, f. 51v; see also NAS, Haddington Burgh Registers, Council Book 1603–16, B30/13/3, f. 42v; *Aberdeen Letters*, vol. 1, no. 351, vol. 2, no. 228, vol. 3, nos 116, 127, 136, 152, 166; J. Stuart (ed.), *The Miscellany of the Spalding Club*, vol. 5 (Aberdeen, 1852), 378–9.

[161]   See ch. 5.

[162]   See for example: *Records of Inverness*, vol. 2, 188–9; DCA, Dundee Council Minute Book vol. 4, ff. 173r, 177v; GCA, Glasgow Council Minutes 1636–42, C1/1/10, 30 Nov 1640; ACA, Aberdeen Council Minutes, CR1/52/1, 593.

[163]   NAS, Burntisland Burgh Court Book 1596–1602, B9/10/1, f. 113v; Burntisland Council Minutes 1617–23, B9/12/4, ff. 89v–90r. For other examples see GCA, Glasgow Council Act Book 1605–10, C1/1/6, f. 83v; ACA, Aberdeen Dean of Guild Accounts 1453–1650, DGA1, accounts for 1605–6, 1609–10, 1616–17.

[164]   DCA, Dundee Council Minute Book vol. 4, f. 216v; NAS, Linlithgow Burgh Accounts, B48/13/5, account for 1640–41; NAS, Burgh of Peebles Accounts 1623–50, B58/14/2, accounts for 1638–9, 1639–40, 1649–50; AA, Montrose Council Minutes 1634–73, M1/1/2, 24 Aug 1641; PKCA, Perth Accounts Charge and Discharge, B59/25/4/1/4A, accounts for 1639–40, 1645–6. For copies of letters to and from the council of Aberdeen, see Aberdeen Letters, vols 1–3, *passim*.

[165]   FCAC, Dysart Council Minute Book, 1/02/01, 30 Oct 1646.

[166]   ACA, Aberdeen Council Minutes, CR1/52/1, 109; NAS, Linlithgow Town Council Minute Book 1620–40, B48/9/1, 267; NAS, Burntisland Council Minutes, B9/12/1, f. 51v, B9/12/2, ff. 13r, 43v, B9/12/6, ff. 59v–60r.

or Castile, although they were sometimes submitted, often in writing rather than in person.[167] In Scotland, approval was normal but not guaranteed: in 1646, the council of Inverness ruled that Mr Walter Ross 'hes not dischairged the office and dewtie of ane trustie and dilligent Commissioner', having acted 'without the consellis consent'. He was fined 100 merks (£66 13s 6d) and ordered to 'com in the presens of the hail consell and thair confess his error and crave thame all pardoun'.[168] It would be hard to find a clearer indication of how seriously burghs understood the delegate nature of parliamentary representation.

Conclusion

'That two men, perhaps men who had bought their offices and knew nothing of the city, had no affection for it, and whose interests did not necessarily coincide with the good of the community, should be able to obligate the cities and their provinces without even consulting them and without being accountable, seemed to the *regidores* to be intolerable.'[169] This description of the representatives of Castilian cities in the 1630s could not apply to Scotland before 1651 and remained exceptional thereafter. The burghs' commissioners genuinely represented the councils which elected them. They were not truly representative of their communities but that did not distinguish them from parliament as a whole which, although claiming to represent the whole kingdom, did so only indirectly. Such virtual representation was normal in early modern Europe. What was distinctive about Scotland was that the vast majority of urban representatives remained genuinely urban people, sharing the interests of the merchant communities from which they were drawn and able to articulate those interests in parliament. The gentrification of the burgess estate was limited and late compared to England where it had occurred during the fifteenth century and persisted thereafter.[170] The estate of burgesses in Scotland remained a national mercantile interest group, bound by the convention of burghs. It is hard to escape the conclusion that the vigorous advocacy of the merchant interest in parliament and the general maintenance of residential qualifications were linked and that the chain which linked them was the convention of burghs.

---

[167] Smith, *The Stuart Parliaments*, 29–30; Thompson, 'Cortes, Cities and *Procuradores*', 20.

[168] *Records of Inverness*, vol. 2, 191–2.

[169] Thompson, 'Cortes, Cities and *Procuradores*', 66–7. Regidores were city councillors.

[170] M. A. R. Graves, *The Tudor Parliaments: Crown, Lords and Commons* (London, 1985), 73.

Chapter 3

The Convention of Burghs, the Burgess Estate and Parliament

The fog which obscures the development of the convention of burghs before the later sixteenth century makes it hard to discern parliament's role in its evolution, although burgh commissioners did co-operate actively in parliament from the outset.[1] The activities of the urban estate were thus akin to those of its counterparts elsewhere, yet the convention of burghs engendered significant differences. In England there was no coherent urban voice. Borough MPs occasionally met separately until, in the fourteenth century, parliament's bicameral structure solidified. Groups of boroughs might also promote mutually beneficial legislation but not through formal mechanisms, except in the case of the Cinque Ports of Kent.[2] In France, although each estate consolidated its *cahiers de doleance*, there was no urban estate, the third estate representing rural and urban communities, a common European pattern.[3] In the French Estates General and in many other European states, even where subjects could submit grievances, the absence of legislative powers meant that estates would be disinclined to collective action since it could achieve little to advance or protect their privileges.[4] In the law-making Aragonese cortes, representatives of towns

---

[1]   Rait, *The Parliaments of Scotland*, 402–3; R. J. Tanner, 'The Political Role of the Three Estates in Parliament and General Council in Scotland' (St Andrews PhD, 1999), 18, 34–5; R. Tanner, *The Late Medieval Scottish Parliament:Politics and the Three Estates, 1424–1488* (East Linton, 2001), 24–5, 110, 158.

[2]   M. Prestwich, 'Parliament and Community of the Realm in Fourteenth Century England', in A. Cosgrove and J. I. McGuire (eds), *Parliament and Community* (Belfast, 1983), 5–24, at 8–9, 14; D. M. Dean, 'Parliament and Locality', in D. M. Dean and N. L. Jones, *The Parliaments of Elizabethan England* (Oxford, 1990), 139–62, at 156; G. R. Elton, *The Parliament of England 1559–1581* (Cambridge, 1986), 259; B. Kümin and A. Würgler, 'Petitions, Gravamina and the Early Modern State: Local Influence on Central Legislation in England and Germany (Hesse)', in *PER*, 17 (1997), 39–60, at 50; but see P. Glennie and I. Whyte, 'Towns in an Agrarian Economy, 1540–1700', in P. Clark (ed.), *The Cambridge Urban History of Britain, Volume II 1540–1840* (Cambridge, 2000), 167–94, at 170, which notes 'a general atmosphere of urban self-interest' in the House of Commons.

[3]   O. Ulph, 'The Mandate System and Representation to the Estates General under the Old Regime', in *The Journal of Modern History*, 23 (1951), 225–31, at 227–8; J. Russell Major, 'The Third Estate in the Estates General of Pontoise, 1561', in Speculum, 28 (1954), 460–476, at 464–5; A. Marongiu, *Medieval Parliaments: A Comparative Study* (London, 1968), 92–3, 139, 157, 160, 202.

[4]   M. A. R. Graves, *The Parliaments of Early Modern Europe* (London, 2001), 195–200.

sat in two estates, hindering a unified urban voice.[5] Where there was deliberation by separate estates and where there was a properly urban estate, collective action would have been possible. In Bohemia, 'urban leagues' were sometimes formed in the fifteenth century but all independent assemblies were banned in the early sixteenth.[6] In Sweden, as in Scotland, all towns were subject to the same laws and Swedish kings sometimes met with individual estates rather than holding a general *Riksdag*. However, although this gave towns occasional opportunities to speak with a collective voice, meetings were rare and convened only by royal summons, so nothing like the convention of burghs emerged outside Scotland.[7]

The English nobility have been described as uniquely 'conscious of belonging to a social formation that transcended local boundaries and embraced the nation'.[8] In Scotland, two social groups possessed that level of self-perception. As in England, the nobility operated self-consciously at the national level but so too did the merchant community and the most important factor binding them together was the convention of burghs. Its regular meetings allowed merchants to develop a group-consciousness which was especially strong among the wealthier burghs. This was enhanced in the later sixteenth century as trade became increasingly concentrated on Leith and, to a lesser extent, Dundee, drawing merchants from other burghs to these ports.[9]

Parliamentary strategies

The merchants' group-consciousness provided opportunities to enhance their parliamentary activities. Foremost among their strategies was the holding of extraordinary conventions before and during parliaments. In 1554, Aberdeen expected its parliamentary commissioner to 'consult with the remanent commissionaris of the burrowis'. The first explicit record of a special meeting at the time of parliament dates from 1555 and there were at least 22 further meetings between 1555 and

---

    [5]   P. Sanz, 'The Cities in the Aragonese Cortes in the Medieval and Early Modern Periods', in *PER*, 14 (1994), 95–108, at 98, 103.

    [6]   W. Eberhard, 'The Political System and the Intellectual Traditions of the Bohemian Ständestaat from the Thirteenth to the Sixteenth Century', in R. J. W. Evans and T. V. Thomas (eds), *Crown, Church and Estates: Central European Politics in the Sixteenth and Seventeenth Centuries* (London, 1991), 23–47, at 28, 39.

    [7]   H. Schück, 'Sweden's Early Parliamentary Institutions from the Thirteenth Century to 1611', in M. F. Metcalf (ed.), *The Riksdag: A History of the Swedish Parliament* (New York, 1987), 5–60, at 26, 40–59; M. Roberts (ed.), Sweden as a Great Power 1611–1697: Government, society, foreign policy (London, 1968), 11–13; Graves, *The Parliaments of Early Modern Europe*, 197; A. R. Myers, *Parliaments and Estates in Europe to 1789* (London, 1975), 19–22.

    [8]   B. Manning, 'Parliament, "Party" and "Community" during the English Civil War, 1642–1646', in Cosgrove and McGuire (eds), *Parliament and Community*, 97–119, at 115.

    [9]   M. Lynch, 'Continuity and Change in Urban Society, 1500–1700', in R. A. Houston and I. Whyte (eds), *Scottish Society 1500–1800* (Cambridge, 1998), 85–117, at 92.

1633.[10] After 1639, when parliamentary sessions burgeoned, conventions of burghs met even more frequently before and during parliaments.[11]

In the later 1570s, the convention of burghs sought to formalise these preparatory meetings: those gathered for the parliament at Stirling in 1578 resolved that, in future, the provost of the burgh hosting parliament should convene the burgh commissioners before the session. In the following November, this was reiterated with the addition that the same should apply to conventions of the estates.[12] At the end of the burghs' conventions, when the date of the next was being fixed, it became normal to add that an extraordinary convention should meet if 'thair happinis to intervine ane parliament'.[13] This desire to co-ordinate their parliamentary activities was maintained in 1579 in the decision that they should meet five days before the next parliament, and similar acts were passed in succeeding years.[14] Mackie and Pryde argued that these meetings were held for reasons of 'economy', taking advantage of a parliament to hold a convention of burghs.[15] Parliaments did provide an opportunity to deal with non-parliamentary matters but the reasons given by the convention of burghs are a surer guide to why they met. In 1585, a meeting immediately before parliament at Linlithgow ruled that it could not consider a complaint from Dumfries about its customs because the burghs were 'alanerlie [i.e. only] cum and convenitt to entreitt upon the effaires of parliament'.[16] Preparatory meetings were held to 'reasoun, entreitt and conclude be thame selves, befoir thair inpassing [to parliament] upoun sic thingis as salbe proponit to thame to determine, or resave knowledge of to be entreittit thairatt'.[17] The same commissioners were sent to both meetings, cementing the link between convention and parliamentary estate; those who met to draw up the burghs' agenda went on to press for its adoption.[18] It was cheaper to send the

---

[10] *RCRBS*, vol. 1, 9; ACA, Aberdeen Council Records, CR1/21, 651. See appendix 3. The convention's records are patchy until *c.*1580 and evidence for three parliamentary meetings (1560, 1563, 1564) comes from other sources: ACA, Aberdeen Council Minutes, CR1/23, 319; ECA, Edinburgh Council Minutes, 1558–61, SL1/1/3, f. 39r, SL1/1/4, f. 115r; DAC, Dumfries Burgh Court and Council Book, WC4/9/2, f. 187v; DCA, Dundee Council Minutes, vol. 1, 1553–88, 75; J. D. Mackie and G. S. Pryde, *The Estate of the Burgesses in the Scots Parliament and its Relation to the Convention of Royal Burghs* (St Andrews, 1923), 17; J. Goodare, 'The Scottish Political Community and the Parliament of 1563', in Albion, 35 (2003), 373–97, at 385, 389.

[11] The records of the convention of burghs are largely missing between 1636 and 1649, so it is impossible to provide an exhaustive list for that period.

[12] *RCRBS*, vol. 1, 54, 70.

[13] Ibid., 108.

[14] Ibid., 108, 120, 205–6, 209.

[15] Mackie and Pryde, *The Estate of the Burgesses*, 13.

[16] *RCRBS*, vol. 1, 204.

[17] Ibid., 209: in other words, things proposed by the burghs themselves, or matters which they discovered were to be raised by the crown or the other estates.

[18] See, for example, ACA, Aberdeen Council Records, CR1/23, 319; AAC, Ayr Court and Council Records 1596–1606, B6/11/3, f. 573; SAUL, Cupar Court and Council Records 1640–53, B13/10/3, 24 Jan 1644.

same people but, since some sent more than one commissioner to both meetings, 'economy' cannot have been the primary concern.[19]

Preparatory conventions are not recorded before six sessions of parliament after 1580.[20] Meetings were probably held on some of those occasions, however. In 1592 and 1594, conventions of the estates held immediately before parliament might have got in the way, while in 1617, a convention of burghs was planned for early May to precede parliament, which was rescheduled to June. The convention of burghs was shifted accordingly, yet no meeting is recorded in the convention's minutes.[21] Possibly when there was no convention of burghs immediately before a parliament or convention of estates, it was because there were no pressing issues on which the burghs felt deliberation was required. This is highlighted in the special measures taken in January 1600 when the burghs noted that a convention of estates in March would discuss certain issues 'quhilk mey impoirt ane grit prejudice to the estait of burrowis'.[22] Fearing that the king might deal with those matters with only a few selected burgh commissioners, they decided that every burgh should send commissioners to advise those chosen by the king. This practice was also applied to the two conventions of estates that met in the personal reign of Charles I and it has been described as 'nothing less than a direct infringement of the prerogative of the crown', although there is no record of anyone in government objecting to it.[23] This provides another example of the distinction between parliaments and conventions of the estates: it was normal for the burghs to meet before parliaments which might deal with matters of concern to the burghs, while they met only occasionally before conventions of the estates summoned for specific matters of concern to the crown.

Burgh commissioners were not unique in staging meetings immediately before parliament. Evidence in the form of articles submitted by 'the barons' suggests that shire commissioners did this too, while the general assembly held extraordinary meetings before parliaments until the mid-1590s.[24] However, the convention of burghs differed fundamentally from both of these. It met more than once every year, whether or not a parliament or convention of estates was summoned, while shire commissioners could meet only at these times. In 1599 and 1639, they petitioned parliament for the right to have annual conventions but were unsuccessful and thus

---

[19]   Mackie and Pryde, *The Estate of the Burgesses*, 13, argues that 'economy' was a significant factor in combining meetings of the estates and the burghs; see AA, Montrose Council Minutes 1617–39, M1/1/1, 22 May 1633, recording that four were commissioned to parliament, with the principal commissioner to meet with the burghs too.

[20]   1581, 1584 (two sessions), 1592, 1594 and 1617.

[21]   A. R. MacDonald, 'The Parliament of 1592: A Crisis Averted?', in K. M. Brown and A. J. Mann (eds), *Parliament and Politics in Scotland, 1567–1707* (Edinburgh, 2005), 57–81, at 59; CSP Scot, vol. 10, 676–7, vol. 11, 343–4; AAC, Ayr Court and Council Records, B6/11/4, 15 April 1617; SCA, Stirling Council Minutes 1597–1619, B66/20/1, 26 May 1617.

[22]   *RCRBS*, vol. 2, 66–7.

[23]   *RCRBS*, vol. 3, 208, 321; Mackie and Pryde, *The Estate of the Burgesses*, 20. No record of this convention of estates survives.

[24]   *APS*, vol. 3, 586; A. R. MacDonald, *The Jacobean Kirk 1567–1625: Sovereignty, Polity and Liturgy* (Aldershot, 1998), chs 1–3.

never developed the same level of common purpose.[25] As for the general assembly, although it met annually (except between 1602 and 1638), it could only ever lobby. It produced a list of requests, not the agenda for an estate. Some of its members (bishops, nobles, lairds and burgesses) were also members of parliament, but most were not.

The burgh commissioners also met during parliamentary sessions, as did every estate as part of the deliberative process.[26] In 1590, it was decided that, with regard to taxation, they must 'ernistlye ressone and conclude thairupoun togidder', which could often be done only once the crown's request for supply had been submitted to parliament. In 1600, those elected to the committee of the articles were instructed 'to seik the consultatioun of the burrowis in all matteris of consequence … afoir the samyn be concludit'.[27] No such discussions are to be found in the minutes of conventions of burghs, but they did happen.[28] They were not recorded in the convention's minutes because they were the proceedings of a parliamentary estate. In July 1593, what looks like parliamentary business was discussed after the session had begun but on closer inspection it proves to be nothing of the sort. Aberdeen was given leave to seek parliament's permission to levy a toll to repair the bridge over the Don.[29] Once this was done, the matter was parliament's business. Similarly, in 1600, after parliament had formally begun, the burghs decided to procure a copy of David II's 'generall chairter concerning the libertie of the burrowis' for its confirmation in parliament. Again, this was not the meeting of the parliamentary estate to discuss parliamentary business but the convention of burghs agreeing to submit something to parliament.[30]

The absence of parliamentary deliberations in the convention's minutes is telling, although not in the way that was once believed. Mackie and Pryde, assuming that most of parliament was excluded from the deliberative process, suggested that the burgh commissioners who were not on the articles met only to conduct the business of the

---

[25]   *APS*, vol. 3, 586; J. Goodare, *The Government of Scotland, 1560–1625* (Oxford, 2004), 58; D. Stevenson, 'The Burghs and the Scottish Revolution', in M. Lynch (ed.), *The Early Modern Town in Scotland* (London, 1987), 167–91, at 169.

[26]   A. R. MacDonald, 'Deliberative Processes in Parliament, *c.*1567–1639: Multicameralism and the Lords of the Articles', in *SHR*, 81 (2002), 23–51, at 31–8. For evidence that this also happened in conventions of estates, at least by 1630, see NAS, Cunningham Grahame Manuscripts, GD22/1/518, a contemporary account of a convention.

[27]   *RCRBS*, vol. 1, 339, vol. 2, 94. The whole membership's role in parliamentary deliberations is discussed in MacDonald, 'Deliberative Processes'.

[28]   T. Hamilton, 'Memoriall anent the progres and conclusion of the parliament haldin at Edinburgh in October 1612', in J. Dennistoun and A. Macdonald (eds), *Miscellany of the Maitland Club*, vol. III, part 1 (Edinburgh, 1843), 112–18, at 116, which describes the individual estates discussing the taxation 'severallie be thame selfis' on 16 October, yet the records of the convention of burghs record nothing between 14 and 23 October, *RCRBS*, vol. 2, 378.

[29]   *RCRBS*, vol. 1, 425.

[30]   *RCRBS*, vol. 2, 94.

convention of burghs.[31] But the convention of burghs rarely met during parliamentary sessions: in 1609, to take a typical example, the full parliament sat on 17 and 24 June, with the convention of burghs meeting only once between those dates.[32] A few opportunities arose, rarely more than one or two, for the burgh commissioners to convene as the convention of burghs during a parliamentary session and those are recorded in the convention's minutes. For the rest of the time they were engaged on parliamentary business so their discussions were not part of the proceedings of the convention of burghs.[33] In the 1640s, separate meetings of the estates became a more formal part of proceedings: hours of meeting were assigned to committees, the 'several bodies' (individual estates) and the full house, and a few papers which were produced by individual estates do survive.[34] The burghs' deliberations were sometimes articulated to parliament through a 'speaker', usually the provost of Edinburgh, a practice also adopted by the shire commissioners and one which had been used in the sixteenth century.[35] Regular meetings of burgh commissioners permitted the development of other parliamentary strategies. The convention successfully sought to ensure that only active trading towns were admitted to parliament and that only genuine merchants might represent them.[36] Maintaining merchant domination of the estate made it peculiarly inclined to the pursuit of common goals and the defence of common interests. Although the qualifications were not universally observed, breaches were rare. In 1600, the convention of burghs fined Dunbar £40 for having sent an unqualified commissioner who had 'be his voitt direcle opponnit him[self] to the rest of the commissioneris' at a convention of estates.[37]

One reason given for the acts regarding the qualifications of commissioners was that sending unqualified people had led to 'difference of opinionis'.[38] The convention of burghs required unanimity on its parliamentary agenda; even those who dissented in the convention were bound to vote with the majority in parliament. Although superficially reminiscent of the *nemine discrepante* rule in the Aragonese *cortes*, where unanimity was theoretically required for any measure to pass, the unanimity of Scottish burgh commissioners was self-imposed and applied only to

---

[31]   Mackie and Pryde, *The Estate of the Burgesses*, 28–9. The same sentiment is found in *RPC*, first series, vol. 11, xxix (editor's preface) and in G. Donaldson, *Scotland: The Shaping of a Nation* (Newton Abbot, 1974), ch. 4.

[32]   Mackie and Pryde, *The Estate of the Burgesses*, 31–3, gives numerous examples.

[33]   Ibid., 33–4.

[34]   *APS*, vol. 5, 333, 625–6, 647; Aberdeen Letters, vol. 2, nos 112, 112A; ECA, 'Overture to Charles I and Parliament, 27 Sept 1641', Moses Bundles, Bundle 24, no. 989; NAS, 'Opinion of the Burghs and Barons on the Matter of the Reward to Assint', 30 May 1650, in Supplementary Parliamentary Papers, PA7/23/2/69/7; J. Scally, 'The Rise and Fall of the Covenanter Parliaments, 1639–51', in Brown and Mann (eds), *The History of the Scottish Parliament, volume 2*, 138–62, at 146, 149; NAS, Marquis of Hamilton's parliamentary diary, 1648, MS 8482, contains brief accounts of the nobles' meetings.

[35]   Balfour, *Works*, vol. 3, 177, 277, 253, 422–3.

[36]   See chs 1 and 2 for discussion of these issues.

[37]   *RCRBS*, vol. 2, 72, 74–5.

[38]   *RCRBS*, vol. 1, 209–10.

certain matters.[39] The need to work for the common good of burghs was expressed in most parliamentary commissions: even before the convention of burghs sought to enjoin unanimity, the idea was embedded in the minds of burgh councils. In 1540, Linlithgow's commissioners were instructed 'to appoynt [i.e. agree] with the laif of the burrowss' in parliament, while in 1557, Aberdeen's commissioners were 'to conclude upoun all thingis necessary and neidfull for the commound weill of burrowis'.[40] Its formalisation was another facet of the development of the convention of burghs in the later sixteenth century as it became increasingly concerned with the promotion of the mercantile interest in parliament. In 1574, the burghs recognised the need for unanimity on specific issues when it was agreed that a commissioner could vote 'according to his conscience' unless it had been 'concludit befoir be the haill that ane sall speik and vote for all'.[41] In 1586, this was restated, with the convention seeking to ensure that 'thair voitis be nochtt different or disaggreand as heirtofoir, bot sua uniforme and aggreand all in ane, as, butt discrepance and divisionis, the samyn may accord with resoune'.[42] Four years later, taxation was explicitly noted as an issue requiring unanimity, although the burghs had previously successfully blocked or reduced the crown's demands and would continue to do so in concert with the other estates.[43] In 1595, the parliamentary discipline of the burgesses was tightened even further: 'na burges of ony brugh' would be permitted to 'gif in ony maner of artikle to parliament or conventioun ... of the estaittis without thai first comunicat the [samyn] to the commissioneris of burrowis than convenit and obtene thair speciall awyse and consent'.[44] There was some concern that individual burghs might be securing rights that infringed those of others or of the burghs in general and this was a means to prevent that.

The need for unanimity was reiterated periodically and in August 1633 the burghs lamented their 'inlaike of lauchfull and uniforme concurrence' at the recent parliament. No culprits were named but the gravity of the problem is encapsulated in their stated need to maintain 'mutuall harmonie in all thinges, and impeding the renting of the body whiche so long by thair mutuall concurrence ... hes bene preserved inteir'.[45] The reaction was so strong that, when combined with Covenanting zeal during the 1640s, the desire for unanimity was taken too far. In 1640, burghs were asked to send commissioners 'who will abyid consteintlie at all suche conclusiones as sall be maid be the most pairt of the burrowes' and in 1646 they passed 'ane act concerning the unanimous votteing of the haill burrowes in parliament and committee of esteat in relation to thes things that concerns the burrows'. This was 'mistaken and interpret to ane sinistrous sense' by some, as if unanimity were required in every

---

[39]   P. Sanz, 'The Cities in the Aragonese Cortes in the Medieval and Early Modern Periods', in *PER*, 14 (1994), 95–108, at 99.

[40]   NAS, Linlithgow Burgh Court Book, 1528–65, B48/7/1, 184; ACA, Aberdeen Council Records, CR1/22, 674–5.

[41]   *RCRBS*, vol. 1, 25.

[42]   Ibid., 209.

[43]   Ibid., 339; J. Goodare, 'Parliamentary Taxation in Scotland, 1560–1603', *SHR*, 68 (1989), 23–52.

[44]   *RCRBS*, vol. 1, 469.

[45]   ACA, Acts of Convention, CRB, vol. 2, 1610–36, f. 445r–v; *RCRBS*, vol. 2, 262.

vote, indicating incidentally that the burghs took their self-imposed rules seriously. The general convention of burghs in 1647 therefore declared that 'unanimitie of voicing was and is onlie meanit in matteris concerning the priviledge and liberties of burrowis, not limiting anie ... in the friedome of thair voice conforme to thair conscience and knowledge in any uther publict or private busines'.[46]

Preparatory meetings did not always involve the whole estate, suggesting that a smaller group of wealthier burghs provided the driving force behind the convention in general and the burghs' parliamentary agenda in particular. Yet, when the convention appointed a select group to handle an issue, the smaller, poorer burghs were happy to vote to leave it in the hands of those with the wealth which bestowed both influence and spare time. In 1582, ten burghs were accorded a special status when it was agreed that no decision could be made by a convention of burghs unless six of the ten were present.[47] The convention often handed responsibility for individual items of business to some of those burghs, with the occasional inclusion of others if the issue being dealt with was particularly relevant to them.[48] In 1597, Edinburgh sent letters to 'the aucht burrowes' to meet there on 1 December to discuss the 'effaires of the burrowes concerning the parliament', while in 1612, Perth anticipated that 'the tuelff burrowis' would meet before parliament.[49] In both instances, however, these numbers are misleading. In 1597, ten burghs met, rather than eight, while others probably joined them, as councils expected their commissioners to meet with each other, as well as attend parliament.[50] In 1612, 47 burghs, not 12, met 'before the parliament'.[51] In 1621 and 1628, similar provisions were made for select groups to meet but the preparatory meeting in 1621 consisted of commissioners from 48 burghs.[52] Planned meetings of a smaller group indicate that, although an inner core of towns dominated the agenda, they never sought to exclude the others. By the later 1590s, they were commissioned to convene if 'spedy deliberatioun' were required on matters arising and a similar group was given responsibility to advise the burghs' representatives on the commission to negotiate Anglo-Scottish union in 1604.[53]

It was all very well to prepare for parliament, to ensure that commissioners were genuine merchants and to promote block-voting on matters of mutual interest, but without good attendance, these efforts would have been of little avail. In December 1585, the convention of burghs allowed all those who had not been elected to the

---

[46]   ACA, Aberdeen Council Records, CR1/52/1, 591–2; NAS, Burntisland Council Minutes, B9/12/9, 78–9; Stevenson, 'The Burghs and the Scottish Revolution', 168.

[47]   *RCRBS*, vol. 1, 137: Edinburgh, Perth, Stirling, Dundee, Aberdeen, St Andrews, Ayr, Glasgow, Linlithgow and Cupar.

[48]   For example, see *RCRBS*, vol. 2, 105, 106, the latter of which includes some of the smaller burghs on the Fife coast because it particularly related to shipping.

[49]   Ibid., 19–21; ECA, Edinburgh Council Minutes, 1594–1600, SL1/1/10, ff. 155v, 157v; PKCA, Register of Acts of the Council of Perth, 1601–22, f. 201r–v.

[50]   *RCRBS*, vol. 2, 21–2; NAS, Burntisland Burgh Court Book, 1596–1602, B9/10/1, f. 66r–v.

[51]   *RCRBS*, vol. 2, 377–8.

[52]   *RCRBS*, vol. 3, 115–16, 275, 277.

[53]   The burghs were: Edinburgh, Perth, Dundee, Aberdeen, Glasgow, Ayr, Stirling and St Andrews. *RCRBS*, vol. 2, 15, 32, 58; DCA, Dundee Council Minutes, vol. 3, f. 24v.

committee of the articles to return home, giving full power to those remaining to act in their names.[54] Apart from raising questions about the nature of voting at the end of the session, this runs counter to the burghs' normal policy for, in the following year, the convention sought to ensure that all burghs sent commissioners to parliaments. The concession in 1585 was made after parliament's agenda was known (once the committee of the articles had begun their deliberations). This parliament met soon after the collapse of the last regime of the minority of James VI; its main business was to put the seal on this transition and only four of its acts related specifically to the burghs.[55] The burgh commissioners were thus given an exceptional dispensation to leave, having secured agreement on an act relating to the sale of fish.[56] They were usually enjoined to remain during parliamentary sessions to promote the burghs' interests and this is the only known instance of their being permitted to leave early.[57]

Not until 1607 were concerns expressed about absenteeism. Three years previously, commissioners from 35 burghs had attended parliament, with 16 absentees listed: a relatively good turnout.[58] In 1607, however, there were 26 absentees and it was probably this which prompted those present to put absenteeism on the agenda for the next convention.[59] Meeting at Selkirk in July 1608, it found that 'thair estait is hevele prejudget be certane burrowis quha repairis nocht to parliamentis ... and depairtis before dissolving thairof, seing that materis ... are borne away be pluralitie of voittis'. Absentees were to be fined £40.[60] This confirms that it was normal for the whole of parliament to vote on the legislation at the end of the session. It also demonstrates a belief, at least among the 38 burghs represented, in the importance of parliament and the need to maximise attendance. It appears to have worked, for at the next parliament, at Edinburgh in 1609, commissioners from 40 burghs attended (the largest number to date). The 13 absentees, all economically weak or far from Edinburgh, were fined. The act was soon reiterated and those attending the next convention of burghs were to bring proof that it had been intimated to their councils: this was done without exception. In 1612 only six burghs sent no commissioner and were fined accordingly.[61] Further evidence that the burghs were placing an increasingly high priority on parliamentary attendance is found in exemptions from attending conventions of burghs. These were not an innovation in themselves, the poorer burghs and those more distant from the usual venues of conventions having

---

[54]   *RCRBS*, vol. 1, 205.

[55]   J. Goodare, 'Scottish Politics in the Reign of James VI', in J. Goodare and M. Lynch (eds), The Reign of James VI (East Linton, 2000), 32–54, at 37; MacDonald, The Jacobean Kirk, 30.

[56]   APS, vol. 3, 378–9, 398, 421; *RCRBS*, vol. 1, 191–2, 204–5; NAS, Petition of the burgesses on the north side of the Forth, and Extract Minute of the Commissioners of burghs, Pittenweem Writs, GD62/10–11.

[57]   *RCRBS*, vol. 2, 66–7, 94, 171, 182–3.

[58]   Ibid., 171–2.

[59]   Ibid., 246–7.

[60]   Ibid., 262.

[61]   Ibid., 269–70, 289, 377–9.

received them before. The difference from 1610 onwards was that they were explicitly 'not to be extendit to parliaments and conventions of estais'.[62]

A high level of attendance was sustained until after the Covenanting revolution of 1637. Thereafter, there were fluctuations due to the wars of the 1640s. In the summer of 1641, over 90 per cent of burghs sent commissioners to parliament. The convention of estates which met during 1644 was more poorly attended, never including commissioners from more than half of the burghs. The parliamentary sessions of June 1644 and January 1645 averaged around three-quarters of burghs, a decline in attendance mirrored in the other two estates.[63] A sharp dip in burgess attendance in the parliamentary sessions of 1645, when parliament met at Stirling, Perth and St Andrews, was also matched across the estates and can be attributed to a combination of civil war (a royalist rising under the marquis of Montrose) and a widespread outbreak of plague.[64] As disease and internal unrest abated in the later 1640s, attendance recovered to the levels of the early part of the decade. With the return of unrest after the collapse of the Anglo-Scottish alliance in 1649, renewed civil war in Scotland and English invasion under Cromwell in 1650, parliamentary attendance collapsed, with only about one-third of burghs sending commissioners to the last two sessions of parliament before its dissolution.[65]

Lobbying and legislation

Attention to the strategies adopted by the convention of burghs should not obscure the fact that they were intended to achieve something: the passage of favourable legislation and the protection of the burghs' interests. They pursued a predictable range of goals, most related to the regulation of trade, both international and internal, to the economy, to the privileges of the burghs in general and to the maintenance of public order. Burghs expected their commissioners to act together for the good of the merchant community: the convention meeting before parliament in 1560 was expected to 'gif in artiklis for the commoune weill of borrowis and mentening of thair privelegis'.[66] They made more requests for general confirmations of their privileges than for anything else. The first such ratification dates from 1535 and there were at least 17 more before 1651.[67] Their success rate in this respect was

---

[62]   Ibid., 295–6.

[63]   J. R. Young, The Scottish Parliament 1639–1661: A Political and Constitutional Analysis (Edinburgh, 1996), 90, 113.

[64]   Young, The Scottish Parliament 1639–1661, 122, 124–5, 136.

[65]   See appendix 4; Young, The Scottish Parliament 1639–1661, 247, 249–50, 266, 275, 283. Young wrote of 'deficiencies' in some sederunts (attendance lists) but he was describing the tendency to list every shire and burgh, with names beside only those with commissioners present. Thus his 'minima' are actual attendances.

[66]   ACA, Aberdeen Council Records, CR1/23, 319.

[67]   APS, vol. 2, 348, 375, 497, 543–4, vol. 3, 33, 59, 102, 145–6, 354, 578, vol. 4, 28, 71, 288, 375, 500, vol. 5, 42, vol. 6, part 1, 171–2, 797. The parliament of 1560 may also have ratified the burghs' privileges, for it was on their agenda: see ECA, Edinburgh Council Minutes, SL1/1/3, f. 42r–v.

high, although repeated attempts to secure the explicit ratification of David II's 1364 charter of liberties to all Scottish burgesses never succeeded, probably because its stipulations were too sweeping and the compromise of a general ratification of urban privileges was more acceptable to the crown and the rest of the political community.[68] The techniques they used to smooth the passage of more important legislation are almost entirely unrecorded. In at least two instances, when key ratifications of burgh privileges were secured, money did change hands. In 1607, the convention authorised the borrowing of £100 for 'thair effaires in parliament', while in August 1633, having obtained the most explicit confirmation of their privileges ever, the burghs commended 'the favour and kyndnes done be thair friendes at the last parliament', and borrowed 1,000 merks (£666 13s 4d), to be given 'with the borrowes good will' to their anonymous helpers.[69]

In relation to trade, the priorities of the convention of burghs largely related to the maintenance of privileges which were not explicitly encompassed within general ratifications. Many articles sought to reinforce laws restricting trade in most commodities to the burgesses of parliamentary burghs: an act of parliament of November 1579 which ratified the exclusive rights of burgesses of the free burghs to buy and sell fish resulted from a decision by the convention of burghs to ensure recognition of these rights.[70] The parliamentary burghs were largely self-governing, with almost no permanent resident representatives of the crown, so external interference was resented and suspected. A number of their complaints and requests to parliament related to the activities of 'searchers', customs officers who monitored merchandise and intercepted forbidden goods. There was a strong feeling among merchants that searchers accepted bribes, imposed bogus duties and pocketed the money for themselves, so in 1586 the burghs demanded that searchers submit regular accounts. The wheels of the state turned slowly but in 1593 parliament passed an act requiring them to make an annual report to the exchequer; those who were found to have abused their position would lose it.[71] The burghs obtained a quicker response to their complaints against Francis Stewart, earl of Bothwell, the king's admiral. In 1590, they claimed that he was taking 'sindrie new exactiounis' and usurping their judicial rights. Fortunately for them, Bothwell spectacularly fell from royal favour between the summer of 1590 and the next parliament in 1592, which forfeited him. An act of the same parliament, after noting that 'the haill burrowis of this realme' had complained about his abuse of the admiralty, restored the admiral's jurisdiction

---

[68] B. Webster (ed.), Regesta Regum Scotorum Volume VI: The Acts of David II, King of Scots 1239–1371 (Edinburgh, 1982), no. 316; *RCRBS*, vol. 2, 94, 129, 156, 169–70; ACA, Acts of Convention, CRB, vol. 2, ff. 395v, 396–7.

[69] *RCRBS*, vol. 2, 246; ACA, Acts of Convention, CRB, vol. 2, f. 447r; see also NAS, Burgh Common Good Accounts, Haddington, E82/27/10, recording a payment of over £200 as its share of expenses including money spent in 'the comoun caussis belonging to the haill burrowis'.

[70] *RCRBS*, vol. 1, 751; *APS*, vol. 3, 146.

[71] *RCRBS*, vol. 1, 75–6, 212; *APS*, vol. 4, 18.

to what it had been under James V, returning to the burghs those privileges which Bothwell had 'usurpit'.[72]

Although the interests of the commissioners of burghs were primarily those of the merchants, they might support the crafts against outsiders. In 1592, an act which had its origins in a request from the burghs in 1581 gave magistrates powers over unfree craftsmen in suburbs.[73] Although ostensibly not in the merchants' interests, the convention of burghs was also prominent in pushing for export bans on wool and coal. With both they were successful: in February 1579, the convention agreed to submit an article to the next parliament seeking a ban on the export of wool and butter. Although butter remained a free commodity, a sumptuary law of 1581 banned wool exports. It contains a tell-tale sign that the burghs had secured an amendment to that effect: exports were banned so that 'the pure may be the bettir haldin to werk', echoing the burghs' view that the ban would prevent 'vagabund wemen to pas ydill ... for laik of woll'.[74] Merchants might profit from exporting wool but the unemployed were increasingly pressing on the minds of magistrates, who dominated the burgess estate in parliament.[75] The free burghs' exclusive rights in finishing raw cloth provided another motivation to retain wool in Scotland.[76]

It has been argued that the initiative for export bans probably came from the crown but, in the case of wool, the burghs' lobbying suggests otherwise.[77] The same might also be said for coal, although the reasons for seeking to ban its export were different, for mine-owners were permitted to export it independently, bypassing the royal burghs. The concern of the convention of burghs was that scarcity and inflation would result from exporting coal, with detrimental effects on urban life. Many craft manufactures required coal and magistrates were also worried because expensive coal meant expensive bread and ale, undermining their ability to fix the prices of these staples and threatening order within burghs. Magistrates were also responsible for the poor whose numbers would grow if coal prices rose. Although it is not clear who instigated the ban, first passed in 1563, the burghs remained committed to it, frequently requesting its ratification and repeatedly seeking its enforcement.[78] The crown sold licences for export to individuals, illustrating the tension between the ban and the legitimate desire of mine-owners to sell their coal, and the tension between the crown's desire to preserve reserves and bring in revenue. In 1608, James VI joined the burghs in urging the enforcement of the ban, resulting in an order by

---

[72]   *RCRBS*, vol. 1, 339–40; *APS*, vol. 3, 580; Goodare, *The Government of Scotland*, 53, 166.

[73]   *APS*, vol. 3, 579; *RCRBS*, vol. 1, 116.

[74]   Ibid., 75, 76; *APS*, vol. 3, 220–21.

[75]   I. D. Whyte, *Scotland Before the Industrial Revolution: An Economic and Social History, c.1050–c.1750* (London, 1995), 112.

[76]   T. C. Smout, *Scottish Trade on the Eve of Union 1660–1707* (Edinburgh, 1963), 16.

[77]   J. Goodare, 'Parliament and Society in Scotland, 1560–1603' (Edinburgh PhD, 1989), 317–18, sees the initiative coming from the government; K. M. Brown, *Noble Society in Scotland: Wealth, Family and Culture, from Reformation to Revolution* (Edinburgh, 2000), 60, sees it coming from the burghs.

[78]   *RCRBS*, vol. 1, 102–3, 240–41, 445, vol. 2, 28, 77, 89, vol. 3, 132, vol. 4, 549.

a convention of estates to republish existing legislation.[79] The privy council was being squeezed between the king and the burghs on the one hand and the mine-owners (usually nobles) on the other, who complained that they had coal which they could not sell. James's characteristically blunt reaction was that it was shameful that their private gain should override the good of the kingdom. He accused mine-owners of stupidity in talking about surpluses because coal does not grow: the ban on exports was intended to ensure a good supply of fuel and to reduce the pressure on native wood.[80] Some lairds with coalmines vigorously lobbied the convention of burghs in 1612, preventing parliamentary ratification of the ban by promising to make 'sic ressonibill offeris as suld tend to the weill of the brughis upoun the sey coasts of this realme' but nothing came of these negotiations.[81] Although the legislation remained in place, large quantities of coal were exported under licence by the 1620s, when Charles I requested (in vain) a duty on foreign boats exporting coal in order to promote Scottish shipbuilding for the good of the realm in time of war.[82] As historians have argued, the crown was actually more concerned with raising revenue from the sale of export licences than preserving coal reserves.[83] In 1649, having repeatedly failed to secure the ban and aware of the value of the trade, the burghs tried another tack, attempting, without success, to have coal classed as a staple commodity which would have compelled the mine-owners to trade through the royal burghs.[84]

As well as granting licences to allow individuals to circumvent export bans, other actions of the crown undermined some of the parliamentary burghs' legal rights. The key strength of the merchants was their monopoly on overseas trade and on all trade in staple goods (wool, skins and hides). By the early seventeenth century, however, the crown was increasingly selling monopolies and patents, particularly to promote manufactures.[85] These gave the holder sole rights to trade in certain commodities, cutting out the merchants of the free burghs, except for the few who betrayed their estate by having the vision to enter into partnerships with entrepreneurial landlords.[86] The convention of burghs lobbied fiercely against them.[87] Although it failed to stamp them out, it did secure the suspension of monopolies in soap and tobacco, its main priorities in the 1620s. Thereafter the rate of creation of monopolies declined, although the burghs continued to seek their eradication, banning merchants from

---

[79]   *RPC*, first series, vol. 8, 517–18, 547; *APS*, vol. 4, 408.

[80]   *RPC*, first series, vol. 8, 568–9, 575–6.

[81]   *RCRBS*, vol. 2, 270.

[82]   NLS, King Charles Letter to the Commissione [sic] of the quholl estaits haldin at Edinburgh in Anno 1625, Denmilne Papers, Adv MS 33.7.11, f. 47v.

[83]   Goodare, *The Government of Scotland*, 267; Brown, *Noble Society*, 59–60.

[84]   *RCRBS*, vol. 3, 353–4.

[85]   See, for example, *RPC*, first series, vol. 12, 91, 106, 189–93, 258, 277, 458–60, 751–2, 771, 772; Smout, Scottish Trade on the Eve of Union, 16.

[86]   Brown, *Noble Society*, 61; J. J. Brown, 'Merchant Princes and Mercantile Investment in Early Seventeenth-Century Scotland', in Lynch (ed.), The Early Modern Town, 125–46, demonstrates that most investment was concentrated in shipping and financial services, although a few merchants were involved in manufacturing partnerships.

[87]   *RCRBS*, vol. 3, 141–2, 161, 163–4, 168, 177–8, 211, 225, 246, 255, 268, 302.

being party to them in 1632 and enacting that a promise to adhere to the ban should be added to the burgess oath.[88] Their exclusive rights to import and export did not enable them to challenge people with royal licences: monopolies were granted under the royal prerogative as part of the system of patronage, one reason why landlords, with their court connections, were better placed to obtain them than merchants. When the king lost control of Scotland after 1637 the burghs took advantage of the situation, securing a complete ban on monopolies in 1641.[89] Even when they were in force, virtually all international trade still remained with the merchants of the free burghs.

While the merchants were keen to stamp out monopolies, they were not really interested in manufactures. They agreed to participate in a project to promote the domestic textile industry in 1601 but their hearts were not in it. They wanted to ensure a good flow of cheap raw cloth by enforcing the ban on wool exports and were initially enthusiastic about importing Flemish craftsmen. But there was little co-ordination of the enterprise and the burghs were threatened with the loss of their rights in the project. When given first refusal of a second attempt to promote cloth manufacture in 1605, they replied that it was not appropriate to them since weaving was a predominantly 'landward' trade. The convention continued to support various manufacturing projects in principle into the 1640s, but the merchant community was not sufficiently enthusiastic.[90] As Keith Brown has demonstrated, economic dynamism was to be found among landowners because there were natural resources (such as coal and metal ores) on their estates which could be exploited, another reason why they received more monopolies and patents than burgesses.[91] Although few of their projects enjoyed success, the die was cast as the merchant community's actions made it clear that it was not going to be the driving force behind economic expansion and diversification. In the first half of the seventeenth century, merchant privileges had been eroded but not seriously undermined. During the later seventeenth century, as a result of the battering which they took during the 1640s and 1650s and because of the huge growth in burghs of barony, they found it impossible to resist the effective end of their own monopolies in foreign and domestic trade. Underlying these changes, however, the inherently conservative mindset of the merchants, bolstered by numerous restrictions imposed upon themselves, significantly reduced the adaptability of the parliamentary burghs, just as had happened to their counterparts in Bohemia more than 100 years before.[92]

Since many burgh commissioners were magistrates, much of what they sought was intended to ease their lives as local governors, a significant motivation for their

---

[88]   See indices of *RPC*, second series, vols 1–5, under 'monopolies' and 'patents'; ACA, Acts of Convention, CRB, vol. 2, 1610–36, f. 405r.

[89]   *APS*, vol. 5, 411; Brown, *Noble Society*, 61–2.

[90]   *RPC*, first series, vol. 6, 123–4, 250, 269–70, vol. 7, 56; *RCRBS*, vol. 2, 75, 89, 98, 106–9, 202–3; Pagan, *The Convention of Burghs*, 208–12; Lynch, 'Continuity and Change', 110–11.

[91]   Brown, *Noble Society*, ch. 2, esp. 57–63.

[92]   Smout, Scottish Trade on the Eve of Union, 16–18; J. Pánek, 'The Religious Question and the Political System of Bohemia before and after the Battle of the White Mountain', in Evans and Thomas (eds), Crown, Church and Estates, 129–49, at 134.

concerns about coal and wool exports as discussed above. They petitioned parliament successfully regarding the confirmation of testaments, to ensure the smooth transfer of property from one generation to another.[93] They asked for enforcement of a ban on carrying firearms in burghs and the lords of the articles took their draft act and turned it into a general statute covering rural as well as urban Scotland. They forgot to change its title, however, which had to be corrected by the clerk after it was copied into the official record: 'For executing of the act of parliament maid anent bering wering and schuting of culveringis and daggis within burrowis'.[94] They successfully got the regulation of burghs' common good funds tightened to reduce their need to seek relief from the others when they had wasted their money.[95] And in a number of other ways, they sought to bolster the powers of urban magistrates in the exercise of their offices.[96]

An 'astonishing' number of acts resulted from successful lobbying by the urban estate, but many supplications and articles never found their way onto the statute book.[97] The wish-list agreed at Dundee in July 1587 can serve as an example: of the nine items which the convention wanted parliament to consider, three resulted in statutes, only one of which, an act against 'regraters and forestallers', was passed in the next parliament.[98] It was not a bad rate of return and compares favourably with the miserable success rate of the general assembly's lobbying. In spite of being able to turn only one request into an act in 1587, the commissioners of burghs would not have left downhearted, for other beneficial acts were passed, including one confirming their share of direct taxes at one-sixth. This parliament annexed to the crown all lands which had belonged to the Church before the Reformation and which had been liable for half of all direct taxes. Many of them had already fallen into the hands of the nobility who paid one-third of direct taxation, so the burgh commissioners would have been relieved to obtain confirmation that no redistribution would occur as a result.[99]

They had less luck when the crown's fiscal policy related more directly to them. Although 'petty customs', small levies on local trade, were retained by burgh councils, the 'great customs' on exports were collected by officers of the crown called customers. Just as direct taxation rose in the later sixteenth century, so did indirect taxation which consisted largely of customs.[100] In the 1580s, the burghs took a tack (lease) of the customs from the crown in return for a proposed rise in duties being shelved, but they failed to collect enough to pay the agreed sum and had to tax themselves to make up the difference. In the middle of the 1590s, financial crisis

---

[93] *RCRBS*, vol. 1, 22, 240; *APS*, vol. 3, 105.

[94] *RCRBS*, vol. 1, 76; *APS*, vol. 3, 146.

[95] *RCRBS*, vol. 1, 415; *APS*, vol. 4, 30–31.

[96] *RCRBS*, vol. 1, 468–9; *APS*, vol. 4, 288–9.

[97] Mackie and Pryde, *The Estate of the Burgesses*, 1, n.1.

[98] *RCRBS*, vol. 1, 238, 240–41; *APS*, vol. 3, 452. Regrating – buying for immediate resale at a higher price; forestalling – buying goods before the market opens.

[99] *APS*, vol. 3, 434, 498.

[100] For details on customs and state finance in general in this period, see J. Goodare, *State and Society in Early Modern Scotland* (Oxford, 1999), ch. 5, and his *Government of Scotland*, 190, 207–8.

hit the crown as never before and John Skene, the clerk register, was commissioned to review crown income. One of his conclusions was that 'Thair is na rent of his hienes propirtie quhairin his hienes is sa far prejugit as in the abuis of his hienes gret custumes.'[101] A wholesale increase in rates and the introduction of import duties on a range of goods was proposed and the burghs complained that they had been promised in 1592 that this would not happen. However, the promise had been on condition that they 'salbe advanceris and furtheraris of his [majesties] commoditie and proffeit' and they could not demonstrate that they had fulfilled their side of the bargain.[102] The crown sought negotiation but the burghs foolishly refused: as 'the meynest of the Estaitts', they could not 'transact in any mater quhairin the haill Estaitts ... hes speciall and grittest interest'. They requested that the customs should stand as they were until the next parliament.[103] A convention of estates in March 1597 appointed a commission to meet representatives of the major burghs and report to parliament. This got nowhere, so another convention of estates in May commissioned the exchequer and the privy council (with no burghs involved) to raise export duties and set out import duties in an alphabetical list ('ane A, B, C'), provoking furious mercantile protests. The burghs resolved to lobby the crown 'to obteyne redres at the nixt parliament', and to 'travell with the lords, erles, barouns and gentilmen, quha hes na les entres in this mater'. The 'aucht burrowes' were to meet in advance of parliament and, in December, they empowered their representatives on the articles to agree to quadruple the export duties set down in 1567 if the reforms were dropped.[104] Their mistake was to expect support from the peers and lairds. Landowners might have had 'no les entres' than merchants since new duties would hit the consumer through price inflation (the burghs must have told them that). However, the rug was pulled from under the merchants' feet when the crown agreed to add this clause to the act of the convention of estates: 'Provyding this act be nocht extendit to erlis, lordis, barronis and friehalderis' who could 'send thair gudis beyond see' and 'bring within this realme wynis, claythis and uther furnessingis for thair awin particular use'.[105] In 1611–1612 there was another across-the-board rise in rates, in spite of a considerable increase in revenue since 1597 and in the face of further objections from the burghs, including direct lobbying of the king.[106] Having already set the customs in tack at the new rates, the crown could claim that the burghs' dispute lay with the tacksmen of the

---

[101]   Quoted in A. L. Murray (ed.), 'A Memorandum on the Customs, 1597', in *Miscellany of the Scottish History Society*, Vol. XIII (Edinburgh, 2005), 66–82, at 66: see also 66–76 for a general discussion of customs; Goodare, *State and Society*, 114–15; Goodare, *The Government of Scotland*, 54.

[102]   NAS, North Berwick Burgh Records, Copy Answer of the Privy Council to the Commissioners of the Burghs with reference to two articles regarding the customs, 30 Dec 1592, B56/16/6; Goodare, *State and Society*, 115.

[103]   *RCRBS*, vol. 1, 497.

[104]   *APS*, vol. 4, 113–14, 118; *RCRBS*, vol. 2, 19–22; ECA, Edinburgh Council Minutes, 1594–1600, SL1/1/10, f. 155v.

[105]   *APS*, vol. 4, 135–6.

[106]   *RCRBS*, vol. 2, 329–31, 340, 360–61, 372–3, 374–5; *RPC*, first series, vol. 9, 728, 729, 743.

customs, although it magnanimously volunteered to arbitrate.[107] The merchants were unhappy but, from the crown's viewpoint, raising revenue this way was preferable to reforming direct taxation and coming into conflict with the nobility.

The defeat over the customs is said to have revealed the burghs' ability to lobby to be 'dismayingly ineffectual', yet alongside this failure there was a modest success.[108] In 1592, a statute claimed that most burghs ought to pay their rent to the crown, their annual 'maills', in sterling but that, through 'oversicht and negligence', they had been paid in pounds Scots for many years. Burghs were to bring their charters to the exchequer for verification, failing which they would have to pay in sterling.[109] The dubious justification was that feu ferm charters had first been granted to burghs in the fourteenth century when Scottish and English money had been of equal value. It was absurd to suggest that burghs of more recent vintage should pay sterling, for their charters specified no currency, had been issued long after the values of the currencies had diverged, and they had never been asked to pay in sterling.[110] Moreover, the crown had been happily collecting burgh maills in pounds Scots for as long as anyone could remember, so it was chancing its arm in claiming what would have been a twelve-fold increase by 1600.[111] The burghs' response was to ignore the statute of 1592 but, as part of the reorganisation of royal finances in the later 1590s, the claim was renewed.[112] The burghs marshalled some impressive arguments based on both principle and precedent. In 1600, the crown sought to negotiate but the burghs would 'nocht be astrikit [i.e. bound] to pay ony uther soumeis for thair burrow maleis bot current money of the realme ... as thei have bene in use to pay thir dyverssis yeiris bygane'.[113] The crown drafted a statute for parliament in November, and the burghs agreed that their commissioners on the articles should 'oppone thame selffis cairfullie to the matter of the Sterling money': no act was passed.[114] Negotiations with individual burghs resulted and some took the opportunity to have existing privileges confirmed and enhanced in return for raising their maills, some

[107] Goodare, *The Government of Scotland*, 208; *RCRBS*, vol. 2, 425.

[108] Goodare, *The Government of Scotland*, 54.

[109] *APS*, vol. 3, 561.

[110] *RSS*, vol. 7, no. 1669 (Anstruther Easter's charter, specifying the rent as 6s 8d, without stating the currency which must therefore be assumed to be Scots); *ER*, vol. 20, 68–9, vol. 22, 338–9 (Anstruther Easter's first maills in July 1593 in pounds Scots), 429, vol. 23, 125 (which record burgh maills of recently-created burghs being paid in pounds Scots); for diverging values of the currencies see M. Lynch, Scotland: A New History (London, 1991), 183.

[111] NAS, Burgh Common Good Accounts, E82.

[112] *RCRBS*, vol. 2, 69, 71.

[113] Ibid., 572–3; Aberdeen Letters, vol. 1, no. 59, pointed out that the exchequer had always used current money for its accounting and cited cases in which courts, including the court of session, had judged that current money, not sterling, was the proper currency for payment.

[114] NAS, Burntisland Burgh Court Book, 1596–1602, B9/10/1, f. 113v; *RCRBS*, vol. 2, 94.

paid lump sums to have charters reissued confirming their maills in Scots money but most continued to pay at the old rate.[115]

The weakness of the burghs in the face of a united effort by the crown and the landed members of parliament was never more stark than in the debacle over the customs in 1597, but they had long been aware of their vulnerability. In 1586, they agreed to submit an article to parliament or a convention of estates 'to crave redres of the greitt abuse usitt ... be the uther twa estaitis concluding actis thairatt, by [i.e. without] the voitt and consentt of the burrowis', albeit that the acts stated that they were 'universallie concludit be the thre Estaitis consentis'.[116] They wanted constitutional reform so that, like some continental assemblies, for a measure to pass it must be approved by each estate. Not surprisingly, nobody else was interested. Yet the same proposal was advanced in 1604 when the burghs asked that 'na thing be concludit in ... parliamentis bot be the adwyse of ... [the] grittest number of ilk estait'.[117] It met with the same result. When constitutional change did come, in the 1640s, it further disadvantaged the burghs. With the abolition of the episcopate, the burgh commissioners could almost outvote the nobles and shires combined. The granting of one vote to each shire commissioner significantly weakened the burghs' position and, although separate deliberation by each estate became a formal part of parliament's proceedings, acts still stood or fell by a simple majority of the full house.[118]

The implications for the burghs were unwelcome, particularly when it came to financial affairs at the time of a thorough restructuring of state finance. A levy of 1639 based on all sources of income revealed that the burghs possessed only one-twelfth of the kingdom's wealth. Their share of national taxation had been adjusted downwards in the later middle ages from one-fifth to one-sixth, but that was not repeated and they continued to pay their traditional one sixth of direct taxes.[119] To add to the merchants' woes, excise duties were introduced by a convention of estates in 1644. Despite 'great debaitt and contest', it was passed 'be maniest voitis and ...

---

[115] PKCA, Charter by James VI to Perth, 15 Nov 1600, B59/23/27, which confirmed and enhanced Perth's privileges in return for a substantial increase in maills to £80 sterling (£960 Scots) but the money was diverted to Perth's own hospital; ACA, Aberdeen Treasury Records 1559–1692, TA1/1, Treasurer's Accounts 1600–1601 and Aberdeen Council Registers, CR1/39, 158, 628, 634, 636–8, 761, CR1/40, 44–6, 126, 128, 148: Aberdeen secured a confirmation of its maills at £213 6s 8d Scots in return for a new charter for a one-off payment of 3,000 merks (£2,000); NAS, Burgh Common Good Accounts, Arbroath 1621, E82/5/1, Dumfries 1612–13, E82/17/2, Haddington, 1557–58 and 1606–1607, E82/27/1, E82/27/8: the maill of Dumfries in 1613 was £20 0s 12d Scots, while that of Arbroath in 1621 was 40s Scots, too small to have been recently increased, yet that of Haddington rose from £10 Scots to £130 Scots; Lynch, 'The Crown and the Burghs', 66.

[116] *RCRBS*, vol. 1, 210.

[117] *RCRBS*, vol. 2, 190.

[118] Young, 'The Scottish Parliament and the Covenanting Revolution', 166–7. Young wildly exaggerated the voting powers of the lairds by erroneously giving two votes to each shire commissioner, rather than each shire.

[119] W. M. MacKenzie, The Scottish Burghs (Edinburgh, 1949), 76; D. Stevenson, 'The Financing of the Cause of the Covenants, 1638–1651', in *SHR*, 51 (1972), 89–123, at 90–93.

the burrowis culd nawayis geatt the said resistit'.[120] Further clashes arose 'betuix the burrowes and the uther two estaits' over finance during the 1640s: in 1645 the burgesses 'disassented from the rest of the housse' over measures to finance the army by monthly payments of 'maintenance', but to no avail, while in 1649, they unsuccessfully resisted a reduction in interest rates from 8 to 6 per cent.[121] Scotland's richest merchants acted as its bankers and many were owed huge sums of money by the state and by individual landowners, so any reduction in interest rates would hit them hard.[122] Again, 'ther fell out a grate debait', with the other estates supporting the reduction. The provost of Edinburgh, Sir James Stewart, himself a moneylender, protested in the name of the burgh commissioners who 'arrosse and depairted the housse' to try to thwart its passage. The other estates proceeded to a vote, the earl of Cassilis saying that 'since they wer gone, they wold vote the acte, for they might als well doe it without them, as they had done maney more of grater consequence bot [i.e. without] a King or his commissioner'.[123] Under the pre-1640 system, with 52 commissioners against 18 nobles and 28 shires, the burghs would probably have outvoted the other two estates. Under the new system, however, even had they stayed they would have been decisively voted down by 18 nobles and 49 shire commissioners. With the increased scope of customs duties after 1597 and a tax on interest payments from 1621, the burghs' real fiscal share was increasing when their proportion of national wealth was apparently shrinking.[124] Added to this in the 1640s were forced loans which came disproportionately from merchants; excise which was specifically aimed at retail trade; monthly maintenance for the army, and quartering of soldiers in lieu of maintenance which also disproportionately hit the burghs. They must have been groaning under a share of fiscal exactions which was greater than ever before and certainly far greater than they could afford in such dire economic circumstances.

It was not all bad during the 1640s, though. Most legislation that they sought aroused no opposition from the other estates. Although the records of the convention of burghs for the period are largely missing, other sources make it clear that, in the sphere of trade regulation in particular, the burgesses continued to enjoy a satisfactory success rate. Even with regard to finance, the traffic was not all one way, as Balfour of Denmilne's account of the parliamentary session of July 1644 demonstrates.[125] Parliament recognised the burghs' contribution to the success of the revolution by agreeing to divert some of the excise back into the burghs to pay off large sums owed to merchants for the purchase of arms and ammunition. Money from the 'brotherly assistance' (pledged by the English parliament in return for Scottish support against

---

[120] DCA, Dundee Council Minutes, vol. 4, 1613–53, ff. 173v–174r; NAS, Burntisland Council Mintues 1643–46, B9/12/8, f. 11v; Stevenson, 'The Burghs and the Scottish Revolution', 170.

[121] Balfour, *Works*, vol. 3, 305, 422–3; Stevenson, 'The Burghs and the Scottish Revolution', 170–71.

[122] Brown, *Noble Society*, ch. 4, esp. 93–4.

[123] Balfour, *Works*, vol. 3, 422–3; *APS*, vol. 5, 258–9; *APS*, vol. 6, part 2, 377–8, 537; Young, *Parliaments of Scotland*, vol. 2, 664–5.

[124] For the tax on interest payments, see *APS*, vol. 4, 597.

[125] Balfour, *Works*, vol. 3, 203–4, 225, 226, 229.

the king) was also promised to the burghs to offset their shipping losses. The burghs also occasionally combined with the lairds against the nobles. In 1644, they proposed to increase each estate's power over the nomination of its representatives on parliamentary committees: an estate might add, but not remove, names on another estate's lists. The act passed in spite of the nobles' fulminations that it was 'ane directe violatione of the liberties of parliament'.[126] It may not have amounted to the emergence of a 'Scottish commons' but there are sufficient examples of co-operation between the burgh and shire estates to suggest that the lairds were not always aligned with a landed interest.[127]

Enforcing statute

The burghs' concern with statute did not end with its passage, for one of its self-appointed roles was its implementation. Some acts even gave rights of enforcement to the convention of burghs. In 1593, the 'Act for the better executioun of decreittis and actis in burrowis' laid down that the court of session should issue letters of horning (outlawry) if urban magistrates applied for them in any case involving those subject to their jurisdiction.[128] The 1607 'Act in favouris of the frie burrowis regall aganis unfremen', first mooted at the convention of burghs at Dumbarton in July, was a real coup. It ordered that the court of session should issue hornings 'upoun all actis and decreittis of burrowis gevin at thair Conventionis betuix burgh and burgh and burgesses of frie burrowes'.[129] Judgements of the convention of burghs were to receive automatic support from the central civil court. This restored to the convention of burghs some of the rights it had possessed as a court under the chamberlain until the early sixteenth century. It was considered of such significance that an extract was obtained and inserted into the minute book of the convention of burghs '*ad futuram rei memoriam*', to make it easier for individual burghs to obtain copies to facilitate its prosecution.[130] In 1612, Haddington raised letters against unfree traders on the strength of that statute and Sanquhar did the same, charging 'ane greit number of unfrie trafiqueris to find cautioun to desist and ceis fra useing of mercheandice': legislation brought results.[131] However, when Forfar did the same against unfree traders in Kirriemuir it was thwarted by William, earl of Angus, who used his

---

[126] Ibid., 238.

[127] Young, 'The Scottish Parliament and the Covenanting Revolution', puts forward a reasonable argument based on the burghs' and lairds' higher level of commitment to the Covenants than that of the nobles, but presents little positive evidence of organised co-operation; Balfour, *Works*, vol. 3, 127, 277, vol. 4, 281.

[128] *APS*, vol. 4, 28.

[129] Ibid., 375; *RCRBS*, vol. 2, 235–6.

[130] Ibid., 291–2; the phrase means 'for future reference'.

[131] NAS, Haddington Burgh Registers, Council Book 1603–16, B30/13/3, f. 89r; NAS, Burgh Common Good Accounts, Sanquhar, 1612–13, E82/53/1 (records the expense of executing the letters). See also NAS, Court of Session, Register of Acts and Decreets, Hay's Office, 9 June 1601–13 Jan 1602, CS7/198, ff. 35r–38r for an earlier example of similar action.

influence at court to have the letters suspended.[132] Social position and influence at court brought results too.

The acts which the burghs most frequently sought, most frequently obtained and most frequently tried to enforce were those which guaranteed their exclusive privileges in internal and international trade. As early as November 1500, the 'Court of the Parliament of the Four Burghs' sent a copy of an act of parliament against craftsmen 'usand merchandice' to every burgh for implementation.[133] The frequency with which such acts were obtained and the persistence with which they were sought to stem 'the grit and daylie incres of the burghis of baronie usurping thair liberties, to thair ruine and overthraw' might indicate a losing battle was being fought.[134] Some ratifications were brief and did not specify which privileges were being confirmed, but others were more detailed: the act of 1607 bestowed real legal benefits, while that of 1633 cited and confirmed individual statutes from 1466 onwards, stating that the burghs' rights and privileges were 'only proper and competent to the frie borrowes royall that have vote in parliament and bear burdein with the rest'.[135] The details of the act derived from a list of statutes drawn up by the burghs in 1631, in preparation for the long-awaited parliament. As in 1607, the act of 1633 was copied into the minutes of the convention of burghs and, in the following year, the convention was seeking to execute it through the courts.[136] Yet, in 1647, the burghs were again lamenting the lack of enforcement of acts against unfree traders.[137] They were never going to stamp out illicit trading in burghs of barony and elsewhere any more than regularly prosecuting people for assault and murder would eradicate those crimes. However, the persistent raising of letters of horning at the court of session and the encouragement of individual burghs to implement the laws indicate that the convention remained vigilant and determined to maintain the burghs' exclusive rights. It was not until after the Restoration that, in a very different political climate, the burghs were no longer able to stem the tide of unfree trading.

Alongside its concern for applying laws against unfree traders, the convention of burghs sought to enforce a range of statutes. Its determination to ensure that (with the exception of one of Edinburgh's representatives) all burgh commissioners were merchants serves as an example of the mechanism by which the convention ensured that its acts, and acts of parliament, reached burgh councils whose responsibility it was to enforce them. Commissioners returning to their burghs were charged to intimate acts to their councils and each commissioner was to bring proof to the next convention of burghs that this had been done.[138] Moves were also made to enforce acts on a range of matters including poor relief, banning Sunday markets, restricting imports and exports, electing burgh magistrates, and controlling the conservator of

---

[132] Goodare, *The Government of Scotland*, 162.

[133] *RCRBS*, vol. 1, 505–6: this copy comes from Edinburgh but the survival of another at Dumfries suggests that they were sent to all burghs: DAC, Act of the Parliament of the Four Burghs, RG2/2/4A.

[134] *RCRBS*, vol. 3, 115–16.

[135] *APS*, vol. 5, 42.

[136] ACA, Acts of Convention, CRB, vol. 2, 1610–36, ff. 395r, 444r–445r, 478v–479r.

[137] NAS, Burntisland Council Minutes, B9/12/9, 69–70 (act no. 15).

[138] See ch. 2 for details.

the Scottish staple port in the Netherlands.[139] The convention took a leading role in seeking to ensure that uniform weights and measures were used. This was one function of the chamberlain that had fallen to the convention of burghs: the four standard measures (of length, weight, dry and liquid volume) were held by four burghs (Edinburgh, Lanark, Linlithgow and Stirling respectively) from which others had to obtain copies.[140] Setting and adjusting standards was done on the initiative of the crown, although parliamentary commissions for this purpose always included burgh representation.[141] After commissions reported, the convention of burghs implemented their resolutions: it endorsed statutes, ordered their adoption, organised the distribution of standards, and investigated their application.[142] In this context, and arguably in all contexts in which it was implementing statute, the convention of burghs acted as an arm of the state. Yet the concept of the state in early modern Scotland remains rather hard to pin down.[143] Numerous agencies enforced statute and carried the decisions of parliament, the court of session, the exchequer and the privy council into the localities. The convention of burghs was one of the foremost of these. With the exception of laws relating to weights and measures, the crown rarely commanded it to do this, yet it often did. It was a voluntary arm of the state, occasionally enforcing statute in response to commands, but usually doing so independently, in the knowledge that if it did not, nobody else would, for most statutes which it sought to implement had been obtained at its own initiative. Indeed, more than once, the privy council had to rein in the convention's enthusiasm for independent action when it was deemed to have overstepped its jurisdiction. In 1580, the burghs introduced a levy on shipping to provide recompense for losses as a result of piracy. Ship-owners complained to the privy council which declared it a 'usurpation of his Majesteis authoritie'. The convention also clashed with the crown when it passed an act in support of statutory bans on exporting wool and importing English cloth: the crown wanted to suspend the bans, and told the burghs that they had 'usurpit upoun thame the royall power of his majestie and his estaitis in setting doun of lawis'.[144] The convention of burghs was a willing participant in

---

[139] *RCRBS*, vol. 1, 69, 102–3, 115, 413, 445, 447, vol. 2, 28, 77, 264–5, vol. 3, 132, vol. 4, 549; ECA, Edinburgh Council Minutes 1636–44, SL1/1/15, f. 353v.

[140] R. D. Connor and A. D. C. Simpson, *Weights and Measures in Scotland: A European Perspective* (Edinburgh and East Linton, 2004), 53–5, 77–8, 320. That these were the members of the court of the four burghs from the fourteenth century is no coincidence.

[141] *APS*, vol. 3, 521–2, vol. 4, 585–9; Connor and Simpson, *Weights and Measures in Scotland*, appendix A and see index under 'assize legislation'.

[142] *RCRBS*, vol. 3, 79–80; *RPC*, first series, vol. 9, 374–5, 527; Connor and Simpson, *Weights and Measures in Scotland*, 47, 76, 242–3, 321–3, 330; NLS, Minutes of Convention of Burghs 1555, Fort Augustus MSS, Acc.11218/5.

[143] Julian Goodare has reflected in depth on the nature of the state in early modern Scotland: see his *State and Society* and *The Government of Scotland* and, although I am more cautious about the extent to which central power grew, Goodare's overall conclusion that it did is sound.

[144] *RPC*, first series, vol. 5, 477, vol. 6, 32–3, 77; J. Goodare, 'The Scottish Parliament and its Early Modern "Rivals"', *PER*, 24 (2004), 147–72.

the process by which statute became supreme and central authority was enhanced, in some instances, a more willing one than the crown.

The enthusiasm of the convention for the implementation of statute was made manifest in its application of pressure upwards on the crown as well as downwards on individual burghs. From the decision to complain about 'certane wrangis allegeit downe to the ... borrowis contrair the acts of parliament' in 1578 to specific requests about implementing the new poor law in 1581 and preventing the export of coal in 1608, the privy council was the recipient of regular admonitions from the convention.[145] The grievance about the poor law also hints at the superior ability of the burghs to implement legislation: the complaint was that, because the act was ignored in rural areas, the burghs were 'oppressit with ane greit and infinit nomber of strang and extraordinar beggeris' from the countryside.[146] In 1611, the convention even asked the privy council for a warrant to put into effect an act of 1581 against foreign shipping operating in the northern and western isles.[147] Although unsuccessful, it demonstrates the convention's faith in statute and its enthusiastic desire to see it enforced. The appeal regarding poor relief shows how the convention of burghs provided Scottish towns with a forum through which they could express common grievances and direct them towards other sources of authority, whether parliament was meeting or not. At every meeting of the convention of burghs, legislative proposals could be discussed, while separate representations could be made to the king and privy council, the exchequer, and the court of session on a whole range of issues. The burgess estate in Scotland collectively interacted with all the principal organs of the state, something which its European counterparts could not do.

Regarding high politics, there is little to be said: as had been the case in the fifteenth century, the burghs rarely took what could be described as collective political actions.[148] The convention made it clear that individual commissioners were free to vote according to their consciences on all matters that were not collectively decided by the burghs and such binding decisions almost never related to high politics.[149] In 1560, however, they did endorse religious change in advance of the Reformation parliament, submitting articles to the estates 'conforme and aggreing with Goddis trew ordinance for the manteinance of the trew religioun'.[150] To be sure, when the convention of burghs met in July, the Lords of the Congregation had already triumphed and Reformation seemed inevitable. Still, the enthusiasm of many burghs for religious change meant that the convention took the unusual step of supporting legislation not directly related to mercantile interests. Religion was again to the fore in the later 1630s: although the records of the convention of burghs from the time of the revolution against Charles I are missing, it clearly played a prominent role

---

[145] *RCRBS*, vol. 1, 101–3, 115, 477–8, vol. 2, 497; *RPC*, first series, vol. 8, 517–18.

[146] *RCRBS*, vol. 1, 101–2; Goodare, *The Government of Scotland*, 190–91, on the greater effectiveness of urban government in general; R. Mitchison, *The Old Poor Law in Scotland: The Experience of Poverty, 1574–1845* (Edinburgh, 2000), ch. 1, which doubts even the burghs' effectiveness.

[147] *RCRBS*, vol. 2, 323.

[148] Tanner, *The Late Medieval Scottish Parliament*, 231–2, 268–9.

[149] See ch. 2 for discussion of this.

[150] ECA, Edinburgh Council Minutes 1558–61, SL1/1/3, f. 42r–v.

in promoting the revolution. David Stevenson has provided ample explanation for why the burghs were unhappy and although their main grievances were, with good cause, 'economic and financial', religion was a significant factor.[151] In November 1637, an extraordinary convention of burghs met at Edinburgh, 'anent certaine important effairis concerning the whole burrowes', and it was undoubtedly there that a petition against the service book was drawn up to be submitted to the privy council.[152] Individual burghs were reluctant to speak out against the prayer book when its use was commanded in the summer but collectively they enthusiastically supported the revolution. In the following summer, the general convention of burghs at Stirling endorsed the National Covenant of February 1638 and imposed it as a test, enacting that 'none be admitted burgesses, commissioners, magistrats, and counsellors of burghs but these that hes taken the Covenant'.[153] Subsequently, the convention of burghs wrote to Aberdeen to urge subscription of the Covenant.[154] Their enthusiasm for constitutional revolution was clear when the parliament of 1639 came to elect the lords of the articles. Although the lairds joined their protest against the election of the committee by the nobles and the king's commissioner, the burghs added their own calls for free speech and the subordination of drafting committees to the full membership of parliament.[155] These were not immediately adopted but were enshrined in the radical reforms later passed by that parliament. After this initial surge of constitutional radicalism, while the burghs remained consistent supporters of the Covenants, there is little evidence for collective political activity, although the loss of the records of the convention of burghs for most of the period makes a definitive judgement impossible. The one surviving full minute (from 1647) and a summary of acts compiled in the later seventeenth century would suggest that they continued to avoid collective political stances.[156]

The only other major political situation in which the convention of burghs took a direct interest was the plan of James VI for a more 'perfyt' (i.e. complete) Anglo-Scottish union after he became king of England in 1603. In July 1603, the convention of burghs was troubled by the prospect of 'the halding of ane parliament of baith the realmis'.[157] Moreover, it is not clear that by 'a parliament of both the realms' it meant parliamentary union, for the later union negotiations between English

---

[151] Stevenson, 'The Burghs and the Scottish Revolution', 176–7.

[152] ACA, Aberdeen Council Records, CR1/52/1, 311; *RPC*, second series, vol. 6, 554.

[153] *RCRBS*, vol. 4, 543.

[154] ACA, Aberdeen Council Records, CR1/52/1, 385; John Spalding, *The History of the Troubles and Memorable Transactions in Scotland and England from 1624–1645*, J. Stuart (ed.), 2 vols (Edinburgh, 1828–9), vol. 1, 54.

[155] J. Robertson and G. Grubb (eds), *History of Scots Affairs, from MDCXXXVII to MDCXLI, by James Gordon, parson of Rothiemay*, 3 vols (Aberdeen, 1841), vol. 3, 64; Spalding, *History of the Troubles*, J. Stuart (ed.), vol. 1, 169; D. Stevenson, *The Scottish Revolution, 1637–1644: The Triumph of the Covenanters* (Newton Abbot, 1973), 170–75.

[156] NAS, Burntisland Council Minutes, B9/12/9, 64–87; ECA, *Convention of Royal Burghs, Acts and Statutes Concerning the Burghs of Scotland, 1552–1700*, SL30/8/14, 134–82; ACA, Convention of Burghs minutes, CRB, vol. 3, abstracts, 1552–1669; *RCRBS*, vol. 4, 525–58.

[157] *RCRBS*, vol. 2, 163.

and Scottish commissioners were also described as 'the generall parliament to be hauldin at Londoun'.[158] When James's desire for closer union became apparent in 1604, the burghs took a close interest, in spite of this being ignored by historians.[159] In parliament, they were prominent in pushing for a guarantee that ecclesiastical union would be explicitly excluded from the negotiations and, although this was not inserted into the union commission, a separate act was passed which stipulated that 'the commissionaris nominat ... for treating upoun the unioun ... sall have na power ... to do ony thing that ... may be hurtfull or prejudiciall to the Religioun presentlie professit in Scotland'.[160] During the parliament, they appointed representatives from selected burghs to draw up 'heidis, artickleis, and instructiounis' for their representatives on the commission.[161] When they met, at Haddington in August, the maintenance of Scots law headed their list, followed by the privileges of burghs and Scotland's special trading rights in France. The next article was 'That we reteyne the prevelege of halding of Parliamentis within the realm'.[162] Most of the other articles related to specific trading issues but the prospect of an absentee monarch was also a concern. They anticipated 'lois sustenit be Scottis men be his majesteis absence' and instructed their commissioners 'to desyre at [i.e. that] his majestie may remayne in Scotland yeirlie ane quarter of the yeir'.[163] The convention of burghs remained opposed to parliamentary union, resisting it in 1660 and again in 1706.[164]

Conclusion

Although the tactics of the burghs were not always successful, their unity and organisational abilities sent a message to the other estates that, in matters of mercantile interest, they were determined and usually united in their resolve to secure and advance their privileges. This was rarely controversial because these interests seldom clashed with those of the other estates. When they did, the burghs usually came off worse but were they 'increasingly unsuccessful' lobbyists during this period?[165] The parliamentary record demonstrates that, as the weight of legislation grew, so did the number of acts passed in favour of the burghs. Some of their privileges may have been eroded, but the most important ones remained, at least until after 1660.

---

[158] NAS, Burntisland Council Minutes, B9/12/1, f. 51v.

[159] W. Ferguson, *Scotland's Relations with England: A Survey to 1707* (Edinburgh, 1977), ch. 6; B. Galloway, *The Union of England and Scotland 1603–1608* (Edinburgh, 1986); B. Galloway and B. P. Levack (eds), *The Jacobean Union: Six Tracts of 1604* (Edinburgh, 1985), xii, xxviii, xl–xli, liv, lxxii.

[160] *APS*, vol. 4, 264.

[161] *RCRBS*, vol. 2, 184.

[162] Ibid., 189–91, the only known instructions to the union commissioners.

[163] Ibid., 190; but see Goodare, *The Government of Scotland*, 109–10, 141–4, for discussion of 'absentee monarchy' which downplays the significance of the 'absence' of the king.

[164] A. R. MacDonald, 'Parliament and the Burghs', in K. M. Brown and A. R. MacDonald (eds), *The History of the Scottish Parliament, Volume 3: The Scottish Parliament, A Thematic History* (Edinburgh, forthcoming).

[165] Goodare, *The Government of Scotland*, 36, 54.

When the burghs lost out, in failing to prevent customs reform in 1597 and in their fiscal defeats during the 1640s, they were facing the same problem they had faced in 1586 when they sought a fully multicameral parliament: lack of strength in numbers in a parliament increasingly dominated by landed wealth. Their relative political and economic weakness compared to the other estates and to their counterparts abroad meant that, without the convention of burghs, they would have achieved significantly less, for they would have been much more vulnerable to division and infiltration by landed outsiders. Moreover, since it is impossible to have more than the vaguest idea of what legislation the other estates sought in all but a few instances, it would be dangerous to conclude that the burghs were peculiarly unsuccessful. They were certainly better lobbyists than the general assembly. Before the end of the sixteenth century, the latter frequently found itself in an adversarial relationship with the crown and with prominent nobles who held former ecclesiastical properties and differing religious opinions. It regularly submitted requests to parliament which were refused. From the later 1590s, it ceased to function as an independent lobbying tool of the church, as it fell under tighter crown control. Only in the 1640s, with the reforming religious agenda of the Covenanters giving the church an influential role, did the general assembly develop into an effective parliamentary lobby, although it possessed firm influence for only about 18 months, between 1648 and 1650.[166] Furthermore, it is only by inference and through oblique references to such things as the crown's intention to secure an act relating to the burgh maills in 1600, that it is possible to identify instances of the burghs successfully blocking legislation which they did not want. There may have been many more unrecorded successes.

---

[166] MacDonald, *The Jacobean Kirk*, chs 1–3; J. R. Young, 'Scottish Covenanting Radicalism, the Commission of the Kirk and the Establishment of the Parliamentary Radical Regime of 1648–49', in *Records of the Scottish Church History Society*, 25 (1995), 342–75; Goodare, 'The Scottish Political Community and the Parliament of 1563', 389.

Chapter 4

Individual Burghs and Parliament

It has been said of England that, although it might be clear why the monarch called a parliament, 'the hopes and aspirations of those sending MPs to Westminster are much more difficult to ascertain', because parliamentary concerns comprised 'a minute proportion ... of local pre-occupations'.[1] The same is true for Scotland, where burgh council minutes contain a wealth of evidence relating to local concerns but frustratingly little about interactions with the centre in general or parliament in particular. Much of what burgesses did in parliament related to their whole estate, yet they were also charged to maintain 'the liberties priviledges and immunities of our ... burght' and 'our reasones and alledgeances to propone, actis, instrumentis and documentis neidfull ... to crave'.[2] A commissioner was expected to uphold and advance his burgh's interests, while ensuring that others did not secure privileges which infringed those of his own burgh. The council paid his travelling and living expenses, binding him to the corporation which he represented, and affirming the fact that he was, primarily, their delegate. These men rarely carried legislative proposals in their saddlebags but when they did they had a creditable success rate. In the sphere of parliamentary politics, the burghs rarely played a collective part, except indirectly and reactively in imposing religious and political tests on commissioners. For those commissioners, voting on issues which did not relate directly to their estate's collective agenda was explicitly left to their conscience. Councils would direct commissioners on matters of local or mercantile interest, but their instructions seldom crossed the line into political affairs. Yet parliament was not primarily a political assembly. Most of its business might not excite the scholar of high politics but examining it provides a fuller picture of what parliament was really like and what many of those who participated in it thought it was for.

Commissioners' expenses

MPs from most English boroughs ceased to be paid by their constituencies during the sixteenth century.[3] This was a stage on the journey to modern concepts of representation, where representatives are free agents, constrained by party but not

---

[1]   D. M. Dean, 'Parliament and Locality', in D. M. Dean and N. L. Jones (eds), *The Parliaments of Elizabethan England* (Oxford, 1990), 139–63, at 139; R. Tittler, 'Elizabethan Towns and the "Points of Contact": Parliament', in *PH*, 8 (1989), 275–88, at 275.

[2]   NAS, Commissions to Commissioners From Burghs, Crail, PA7/25/46/2, Haddington, PA7/25/65/1.

[3]   K. MacKenzie, *The English Parliament* (Harmondsworth, 1950), 59; M. A. R. Graves, *The Tudor Parliaments: Crown, Lords and Commons, 1485–1603* (London, 1985), 49; A. D.

meaningfully carrying the wishes of constituents to parliament.[4] Through this prism, it has been argued that parliamentary wages disappeared in England because of the significance of its parliament. In France expenses were paid to deputies in the Estates General into the seventeenth century because compensation was required for service in an inferior assembly.[5] The comparison is unhelpful because of the profound differences between the institutions. English gentlemen would represent towns for nothing because it offered the chance of political advancement. Many boroughs were happy to elect outsiders if that meant lower costs, while paying for experienced parliamentarians had other advantages. Political advancement in France did not come through service in the Estates General. Introducing the Scottish parliament into the comparison may be more instructive since, in its powers, frequency and status, it was more like the English parliament than were the French Estates General. In Scotland the payment of burgh commissioners was virtually universal, sustained by adherence to residency qualifications and a delegate theory of representation.[6] Elsewhere in Europe, towns appointed wealthy outsiders as representatives but not always to reduce costs: prestigious Castilian *procuradores* made heavy financial demands, and cities could find themselves deep in debt to them.[7] The idea that the payment of representatives indicates an assembly's weakness ignores the differences between institutions. It might be asked why English boroughs were happy to engage cut-price freelances rather than be represented by their own townsmen. Yet the key question for any town was how effective their representatives were. The English gentry's enthusiasm to represent boroughs does say something about the importance of the English parliament – they wanted to get in and were willing to pay. But that was not the concern of the boroughs. They wanted to reduce costs, create a useful relationship with a landed patron who might have connections at court, and ensure that their interests were well-served in parliament. There would have been little point in hawking a seat to a member of the gentry if the borough suffered as a result.[8]

Evidence for the payment of Scottish burgh commissioners can be found in the earliest records, and for every burgh for which financial accounts survive, but it was not regulated by parliament or even by the convention of burghs.[9] Responsibility for

---

K. Hawkyard, 'The Wages of Members of Parliament, 1509–1558', in *PH*, 6 (1987), 302–11, at 308, 310; Tittler, 'Elizabethan Towns', 276–7.

[4]   A. H. Birch, *Representation* (London, 1971), 19–21.

[5]   J. R. Major, 'The Payment of Deputies to the French National Assemblies, 1484–1627', in *The Journal of Modern History*, 27 (1955), 217–29.

[6]   Rait, *The Parliaments of Scotland*, 274.

[7]   M. A. R. Graves, *The Parliaments of Early Modern Europe* (London, 2001), 180; I. A. A. Thompson, 'Cortes, Cities and *Procuradores* in Castile', in Thompson, *Crown and Cortes: Government, Institutions and Representation in Early-Modern Castile* (Aldershot, 1993), 61.

[8]   Dean, 'Parliament and Locality', 143; Tittler, 'Elizabethan Towns', 283–6. Some English towns had one resident MP and one outsider.

[9]   ACA, Aberdeen Council Register, CR1/1, 54 (payment of expenses to their commissioner to a general council at Linlithgow, 1398); SAUL, St Andrews Treasurer's accounts, 1611–27, B65/19/1, account for 1612–13; NAS, Inverurie Burgh Court Book 1612–20, B36/6/2, 13 June 1617. These burghs have scant records for the period, yet they still contain references to parliamentary expenses.

how much was paid and how the money was raised lay with individual burghs. It might thus be regarded as surprising that commissioners were paid at all, yet they usually set out with cash in hand, a rarity in England. On their return they submitted details of expenditure, and if they were 'superexpendit' they were reimbursed or, in the unlikely event of their having under-spent, they returned the balance.[10] Shire commissioners did not represent corporations, so the crown regulated their expenses. The act of 1587 establishing shire representation stipulated that the electors were liable, without specifying how much or how the money should be raised. This resulted in occasional complaints when individual electors proved unwilling to contribute.[11] In 1633 the privy council set a flat fee of 300 merks (£200) for each shire commissioner's expenses. After 1639, longer sessions rendered the flat fee inadequate, so parliament introduced a daily rate of £5.[12]

Some burgh commissioners received a daily allowance, which varied from one burgh to another as well as over time and, as in England, was less than that paid to shire representatives.[13] Although differences in the cost of living and the widening gap between the value of the English and Scottish currencies before 1600 make direct comparisons problematic, the amount paid to burgh commissioners seems to compare favourably with that paid to their English counterparts. A statute of 1327 set 2s sterling as the daily allowance for English borough MPs but many boroughs never paid any expenses, few gave the full allowance and only 'a handful' paid more: most MPs had to pay their own way, at least in part.[14] The first explicit Scottish reference to a daily rate comes from 1563 when Haddington set an allowance of 10s; Linlithgow's commissioners received 8s, equivalent to 2s 6d and 2s sterling respectively.[15] Severe inflation meant that this did not endure; during the last quarter of the sixteenth century, £1 per day became normal, with some burghs paying even

---

[10]   Few detailed accounts survive, but records refer to payments of 'superexpenses' to commissioners 'according to his compt': AA, Montrose Council Minutes, 1617–39, M1/1/1, 29 May 1633 (undertaking to pay superexpenses); PKCA, Perth, Register of Acts of the Council 1601–22, B59/16/1, f. 80r (payment of superexpenses); DAC, Dumfries Burgh Court and Council Book 1563–64 WC4/9/2, f. 218r (a returning commissioner's account); AAC, Ayr Court and Council Records 1607–32, B6/11/4, f. 659r (a returning commissioner returns unspent money); Hawkyard, 'The Wages of Members of Parliament', 307, 309.

[11]   RPC, first series, vol. 6, 668, 687–8, vol. 7, 556–7. The rarity of these cases and the fact that they related only to one or two non-payers in a shire suggests that Rait was wrong to claim (on the basis of that evidence) that shire commissioners found it 'difficult to obtain their dues': Rait, *The Parliaments of Scotland*, 231.

[12]   RPC, second series, vol. 5, 66–7; *APS*, vol. 5, 384; Rait, *The Parliaments of Scotland*, 231.

[13]   Hawkyard, 'The Wages of Members of Parliament', 303, 305–7; J. R. Major, 'The Payment of the Deputies', 225.

[14]   Hawkyard, 'The Wages of Members of Parliament', 303, 307; Tittler, 'Elizabethan Towns', 276–7.

[15]   NAS, Haddington Burgh Registers, Council Book 1554–80, B30/13/1, f. 37r; NAS, Wallace-James Notebooks, Haddington Common Good and Treasurer's Accounts, GD1/413/4, ff. 8r, 58r; NAS, Linlithgow Burgh Court Book, 1528–65, B48/7/1, 350; A. Gibson and T. C. Smout, *Prices, Food and Wages in Scotland, 1550–1780* (Cambridge, 1995), 5–6.

more by the later 1590s.[16] From 1603, comparisons with sterling become possible again, with the exchange rate fixed at £12 Scots to £1 sterling. At the same time, there was another general increase in allowances, with Dunfermline paying £1 6s 8d (just over 2s sterling), Ayr £1 10s (2s 6d sterling), while Glasgow, Haddington and Perth paid £2 (3s 4d sterling).[17] There followed some levelling up so that, by the 1630s, most paid £2, which remained the rate paid by some during the 1640s, but continuing inflationary pressures and economic problems led to increases and fluctuations. Between 1633 and 1651 the daily rate varied from as little as £1 10s paid by Peebles, to 5 merks (£2 13s 4d) paid by Inverness, £3 paid by Kirkcudbright and £5 paid by Dumfries.[18] By the end of the 1640s, most commissioners received just under 4s sterling per day, while some got considerably more.

As well as indicating economic uncertainty, variations in expenses might relate to the commissioner's status; provosts might receive more. This was one way that some burghs chose to project their status: their provosts would dress more lavishly and spend more than ordinary commissioners. Aberdeen paid its provosts double what it gave to its other commissioners in the sixteenth century, while Dumfries, Glasgow, Haddington, Kirkcudbright and Linlithgow all paid provosts a higher rate. The 'provostis ffie' might even be paid to another commissioner. Dumfries granted it to a bailie in 1646 when he replaced the provost as the burgh's principal commissioner.[19] As with other aspects of ostentation, however, most burghs did not pay differential rates. In 1586, Ayr's commissioner was Sir William Stewart of Monkton, recently foisted on a reluctant burgh by the crown and, as commissioner to a convention of the estates, this royal client may have been specifically summoned by the king. The burgh council chose to express its disdain by slighting him, ruling 'that he be

---

[16]   NAS, Burgh Common Good Accounts, Dunbar 1578, E82/18/3; GCA, Act Book of the Burgh and City of Glasgow 1573–81, C1/1/1, ff. 85v, 87r, 243r, Glasgow Council Act Book 1594–97, C1/1/4, f. 57r; NAS, Haddington Burgh Registers, Council Book 1581–1602, B30/13/2, f. 46v; NAS, Yule Collection, Account of Andrew Kerr, Treasurer of the Burgh of Linlithgow 1592–93, GD90/2/36, ff. 9v, 10r–v.

[17]   NAS, Dunfermline Burgh Court Book 1606–13, B20/10/3, f. 92v; AAC, Ayr Court and Council Records 1596–1606, B6/11/3, ff. 334r, 381r, 636r; GCA, Glasgow Council Act Book 1605–10, C1/1/6, ff. 143v–144r, 202r; NAS, Haddington Burgh Registers, Council Book 1603–16, B30/13/3, f. 98v; PKCA, Register of Acts of the Council of Perth 1601–22, B59/16/1, f. 27r.

[18]   NAS, Peebles Council Record 1604–52, B58/13/1, 30 April 1639; DAC, Dumfries Council Minutes, 1643–50, WA2/1, f. 54r; W. MacKay and H. C. Boyd (eds), Records of Inverness, 2 vols (Aberdeen, 1911–24), vol. 2, 190; Kirkcud. Recs., vol. 2, 777.

[19]   ACA, Aberdeen Council Register, CR1/9, 418, CR1/22, 61, CR1/26, 359, 452; GCA, Glasgow Council Minutes 1648–54, C1/1/12, 7 April 1649; NAS, Haddington Burgh Registers, Council Book 1581–1602, B30/13/2, f. 131r; NAS, Linlithgow Burgh Court Book 1528–65, B48/7/1, 350; DAC, Dumfries Council Minutes 1643–50, WA2/1, ff. 46r, 47r; Kirkcud. Recs., vol. 2, 595, 598, 600, 602, 634. Different rates may have been paid more often than is recorded, for it was common for only the total sum to be accounted for, making it impossible to discern how expenditure was divided.

considerate ... in his expenses nocht according to his rank bot according as becomis commissioners that hes borne the like commissioun of befoir'.[20]

The brevity of parliamentary sessions meant that burghs rarely found themselves paying for more than three weeks' expenses before the 1640s. Yet Scottish towns, while blessed with shorter parliaments than in England, sent commissioners to conventions of burghs and general assemblies of the Church at the same daily rate, so it is unlikely that they would have had fewer days to pay for in an average year than English boroughs, where parliament was the only national assembly. That the daily rate grew with inflation in Scotland indicates that expenses were intended to cover costs, not just contribute towards them. Large sums were spent keeping commissioners at parliament during the 1640s, in spite of the financial difficulties experienced by every burgh. Aberdeen disbursed over £7,000 on travelling and living expenses for parliamentary commissioners between 1639 and 1651.[21]

There was no Scottish equivalent of the English writ *de expensis*, issued by parliament to departing MPs to prove their attendance: a returning commissioner simply submitted his account and received what was due.[22] There were, however, different ways of raising the money. Most burghs used their common good fund and parliamentary expenses were allowed by the crown's auditors.[23] Sometimes a burgh might have insufficient cash, in which case one of a number of remedies was available. A 'stent' (tax) might be imposed on burgesses, as was done in Aberdeen in 1578.[24] Another option was to borrow the money, as Stirling did in 1617.[25] Income from a particular source could be assigned to pay commissioners' expenses: in 1581, Elgin used the entry fee of a new burgess, while Aberdeen and Dundee occasionally assigned rents from burgh properties to their parliamentary commissioners.[26] English boroughs found money for parliamentary wages from similar sources, although apparently less easily.[27] In all the surviving records, only a handful of instances were found in which commissioners experienced problems securing payment.[28] The efforts to which burghs went to ensure that commissioners were paid, the advancing of money before they left, the occasional sending of money to commissioners

---

[20]   AAC, Ayr Court and Council Records 1586–89, B6/11/1/3, f. 380r. For details on status and display, see ch. 7.

[21]   This sum is derived from expenses recorded in ACA, Aberdeen Treasury Records, TA1/1–3.

[22]   Hawkyard, 'The Wages of Members of Parliament', 303, 305.

[23]   NAS, Burgh Common Good Accounts, E82.

[24]   ACA, Aberdeen Council Registers, CR 1/29, 460.

[25]   SCA, Stirling Council Minutes 1597–1619, B66/20/1, 27 Oct 1617.

[26]   *The Records of Elgin 1234–1800*, W. Cramond (ed.), 2 vols (Aberdeen, 1903–8), vol. 1, 160; ACA, Aberdeen Council Register, CR1/7, 161 (this dates from 1490; other instances of using rents can be found throughout the sixteenth century); DCA, Dundee Council Minutes, vol.1, 1553–88, 93.

[27]   Hawkyard, 'The Wages of Members of Parliament', 309–10.

[28]   ACA, Aberdeen Council Register, CR1/9, 421, CR1/22, 301, CR1/34/2, 818, CR1/53/1, 46; NAS, Burntisland Council Minutes 1646–53, B9/12/9, 147; PKCA, Register of Acts of the Council of Perth 1601–22, B59/16/1, f. 102r; R. Renwick (ed.), *Extracts from the Records of the Royal Burgh of Lanark* (Glasgow, 1893), 141–2.

during a session of parliament and the rarity of delays in reimbursing additional expenses, demonstrate that burgh councils took seriously the need to participate in parliament. They would probably have saved money by sending no one, as the fines for absence, as well as being rarely enforced, were less than most would have spent on commissioners' expenses.[29]

Although rare, some detailed breakdowns of expenditure survive, revealing what the other costs of parliamentary representation were. One of these was horse hire; even commissioners from as far away as Aberdeen and Inverness travelled on horseback rather than by sea. In 1524, Aberdeen's commissioners went 'with aucht [eight] horsis in tryne'.[30] Some burghs even made an occasion of the departure or return of their commissioners: in the 1640s, Perth's commissioners received a 'bonnarlla' (*bon aller*), with sweetened wine, while Aberdeen's returning commissioners were formally welcomed home.[31] Commissioners did not tend to travel alone; even when a burgh sent only one, he would be accompanied by 'his man' or 'his boy', who took care of his horse, carried his bags and ran errands.[32] There were various other small expenses, including courtesy payments to royal messengers who brought the precepts summoning parliament, the cost of drawing up the commission, and a fee to the clerk of parliament when the commission was handed in.[33] Accounts also reveal something of the costs associated with getting legislation through parliament.

Lobbying and legislation

Legislation, especially local issues, receives remarkably little historiographical attention, with parliamentary scholars concentrating on high politics, the mechanics of parliamentary procedure and the lives and connections of members.[34] While these are important issues, considered elsewhere in this study, the *raison d'être* of some representative assemblies (and certainly of the Scottish parliament) was to make law and, although most laws neither originated in the burghs nor related specifically to

---

[29]   Parliament set 100 merks (£66 13s 4d) as the fine for an absent burgh in 1587 and renewed this in 1617: *APS*, vol. 3, 443, vol. 4, 535. In 1610, the convention of burghs set its own fine at £40: *RCRBS*, vol. 2, 262; Rait, *The Parliaments of Scotland*, 396–8.

[30]   ACA, Aberdeen Council Register, CR 1/11, 470, Aberdeen Treasury Records, TA1/3, account for 1605–6; *Records of Inverness*, vol. 1, 147.

[31]   PKCA, Perth Accounts Charge and Discharge, B59/25/4/1/4A, account for 1645–6; ACA, Aberdeen Treasury Records, TA1/3, account for 1639–40, Aberdeen Dean of Guild Accounts 1453–1650, DGA1, account for 1640–41.

[32]   GCA, Glasgow Council Act Book, 1605–10, C1/1/6, ff. 143v–144r; NAS, Haddington Burgh Registers, Council Book 1603–16, B30/13/3, f. 98v; *Ayr Burgh Accounts*, 144; DAC, Dumfries Council Minutes 1643–50, WA2/1, f. 54r.

[33]   GCA, Glasgow Council Minutes 1636–42, C1/1/10, 9 Nov 1639 (1s at production of the commission); DCA, Dundee Treasurer's Accounts, vol. 1, account for 1592–3 (6s 8d to the messenger); *Ayr Burgh Accounts*, 148 (13s 4d for wax and parchment for the commission).

[34]   D. L. Smith, *The Stuart Parliaments, 1603–1689* (London, 1999), devotes only six pages (38–43) to legislation; Graves, *The Parliaments of Early Modern Europe*, also has six pages (195–200); I. A. A. Thompson, *Crown and Cortes: Government, Institutions and Representation in Early-Modern Castile* (Aldershot, 1993), refers to legislation only once.

them, a significant minority began in burgh council chambers. The lack of attention paid to local concerns can be attributed to two causes. Firstly, much parliamentary historiography focuses on those in government and draws primarily on the records of the institution being studied. Secondly, although few representative assemblies had no legislative powers, most had limited powers in this regard and only in Aragon, the United Provinces of the Netherlands, Poland and some Imperial states did anything comparable to the powers of the British parliaments exist; even in Aragon, towns might only submit grievances.[35] In many states, local elites could not use representative assemblies to provide solutions to their problems.

Although some burghs' petitions resulted in public general statutes, the vast majority led to private acts. The existence of the convention of burghs, where complaints and suggestions could be framed into draft statutes, is a distinction between Scotland and England which must be borne in mind in any discussion of the difference between 'private' and 'public' legislation along the lines of Geoffrey Elton's work on England: in Scotland, at least as far as the burghs were concerned, private acts rarely metamorphosed into public acts during a session, because they would already have done so in the convention of burghs.[36] Although Elton believed that the public–private distinction was 'one of the peculiarities of the English parliament', it existed in Scotland too, and of course in Ireland whose parliament was an English clone. Public statutes were printed and private ones were not: the former could be cited in court but for a private act to be used in litigation, a copy under the signature of the clerk of parliament was required.[37]

Scottish towns obtained proportionally more acts than their English counterparts. In the entire reign of Elizabeth I, 56 statutes were passed in favour of all English towns.[38] In the same period, 47 were secured for Scottish parliamentary burghs alone. Even more remarkably, 38 of the English statutes enabled boroughs to raise funds for public projects, such as roads, bridges and schools, while only six such acts were passed in Scotland.[39] Burghs seeking to undertake public works did not need a statute,

---

[35]   Graves, *The Parliaments of Early Modern Europe*, 195–7; A. R. Myers, *Parliaments and Estates in Europe to 1789* (London, 1975), 29–34; B. Kümin and A. Würgler, 'Petitions, Gravamina and the Early Modern State: Local Influence on Central Legislation in England and Germany (Hesse)', in *PER*, 17 (1997), 39–60, at 41–2, 47; P. Sanz, 'The Cities in the Aragonese Cortes in the Medieval and Early Modern Periods', in *PER*, 14 (1994), 95–108.

[36]   G. R. Elton, *The Parliament of England 1559–1581* (Cambridge, 1986), chs 3 and 12.

[37]   Elton, *The Parliament of England*, 44, 303; Graves, *The Parliaments of Early Modern Europe*, 196.

[38]   Tittler, 'Elizabethan Towns', 279–80, suggests there were 650–700 English towns, compared to no more than half that number in Scotland, even by 1650 after 50 years of rapid growth in non-parliamentary burghs of barony: see I. D. Whyte, *Scotland Before the Industrial Revolution: An Economic and Social History* (London, 1995), 179–85. By 1603, there were around 190 parliamentary boroughs in England, while in Scotland there were only 50: Smith, *The Stuart Parliaments*, 23; N. Ball, 'Representation in the English House of Commons: The New Boroughs, 1485–1640', in *PER*, 15 (1995), 117–32; and see appendix 2.

[39]   Tittler, 'Elizabethan Towns', 279; Dean, 'Parliament and Locality', 147–8. For Scotland, see *APS*, vols 3–4, *passim*. This figure excludes acts for burghs of barony which were represented by landed superiors.

nor were they hindered by the infrequency of parliaments: the approval of the crown was required but that could be applied for only with the consent of the convention of burghs.[40] Thus, far more 'imposts' were licensed in Scotland than English boroughs were able to secure.[41] A privy seal letter of 1611 in favour of Wigtown began by narrating that 'the commissionaris of the borrowis' had recognised Wigtown's need of 'ane sufficient houss waterticht for ressaving of all meill and malt ... quhairby the same micht be preserveit from the injurie of wedder and mair commodiouslie sauld'. The convention, noting that Wigtown had insufficient funds to build such a house, had granted it 'libertie and licence ... to impetrat of oure soverane Lord ane gift' of the right to take 1s for every sack of meal or malt sold, and the king and privy council were 'weill myndit and willing' to agree. Most of the privy seal letter was copied verbatim from the original act of the convention of burghs.[42]

If acts for public works are discounted, the contrast with England is striking: 41 for Scottish parliamentary burghs and only 18 for all English towns, suggesting a far more 'usable' and responsive parliament in Scotland. The 18 English acts mostly concerned 'economic privileges ... specific economic interests', and 'constitutional privilege', as did the bulk of Scottish statutes.[43] Most common in the period before the 1640s was a ratification of a burgh's charter. Although ratifications of individual charters may have been issued before the last quarter of the sixteenth century, none survives in local archives; nor do they feature in parliamentary records until that period.[44] The only extant ratifications of corporate privileges from before the later sixteenth century were granted in general to the church or the burghs. The patchy survival of the parliamentary registers before 1578 means that it is impossible to be certain whether specific ratifications were an innovation in record-keeping, or a reflection of the growing competence of parliament and the increasing esteem given to its acts.[45] The appearance in 1592 of the act 'That the ratificationis past in this present parliament sall nocht prejuge parties richtis', suggests their relatively recent appearance. It sought to ensure that ratifications were understood as valid insofar as they did not infringe the rights of others. In future parliaments, this was fulfilled by the act '*Salvo Iure Cuiuslibet*' (saving the rights of others).[46]

---

[40]   *RCRBS*, vol. 1, 440.

[41]   *RCRBS*, vols 1–3, *passim*, containing over 90 examples between 1590 and 1620 alone; RPC, first series, vol. 6, 160–61, 232, vol. 7, 335–6, 497, vol. 8, 546–7, 555–6, vol. 9, 4, 53.

[42]   NAS, Register of the Privy Seal, PS1/80; *RCRBS*, vol. 2, 149. For another example see *Aberdeen Letters*, vol. 1, 5–6.

[43]   Tittler, 'Elizabethan Towns', 280.

[44]   But see ACA, Aberdeen Council Register, CR1/22, 60–61, which is a specific instruction to Aberdeen's commissioner to get 'thair auld infeftmentis and previlegis ... ratifiit and confermit' in 1555; see *APS*, vols 2 and 3 for the absence and emergence of ratifications to individuals and corporations.

[45]   See J. Goodare, 'The Scottish Parliamentary Records, 1560–1603', in *Historical Research*, 72 (1999), 244–67, esp. at 246–7, for a discussion of the problems with the surviving parliamentary records.

[46]   *APS*, vol. 3, 561, vol. 4, 68; J. Goodare, 'Parliament and Society in Scotland 1560–1603' (Edinburgh PhD, 1989), discusses the emergence and significance of ratifications at 65,

By the end of the sixteenth century, it was accepted that a crown charter endorsed by parliament had more strength than the original grant: an extracted copy under the signature of the clerk register (the clerk of parliament) was recognised by the court of session as the strongest proof of rights that could be led as evidence. This may hint at a role for the court of session in bolstering the standing of statute in Scotland during the sixteenth century. The development may also have owed something to England, where such acts provided 'the most authoritative form of law and the one against which it was most difficult to appeal', because in England parliament was the sovereign body 'wherein all men's consents are included' in theory.[47] Too much is made of the distinctiveness of the English parliament in this respect; although conventions of the estates in Scotland issued temporary legislation, only parliament could make permanent laws, and no burgh ever got a ratification from a convention of estates.[48] Once it was obtained, the burgh's commissioner brought home an extracted copy which was put in safe storage to be brought out whenever it was needed.[49] The status of parliamentary ratifications is also demonstrated in the giving of sasine (English *seisin*), by which legal possession of properties and real rights were symbolically transferred to the grantee by a representative of the granter. In August 1601, Aberdeen obtained a new charter but did not receive sasine until after its parliamentary confirmation five years later.[50]

From the 1580s onwards, most parliaments passed a handful of acts ratifying the privileges of individual burghs. In 1633, an unprecedented 15 secured ratifications, while a number of others were unsuccessful (see below).[51] It was common throughout Europe for individuals and corporations to seek confirmation of privileges after the succession of a new ruler and, although Charles I had succeeded in 1625, this was his first parliament.[52] Charles I had also created a general climate of insecurity. The burghs were excluded from his sweeping revocation scheme, which threatened the property rights of many and was a major cause of discontent in the period leading

---

100–106. I am grateful to Dr Goodare for discussions about the problems of interpreting the apparent emergence of ratifications.

[47]   Smith, *The Stuart Parliaments*, 40, 42.

[48]   Ibid., 39, reiterates the argument; J. Goodare, *The Government of Scotland, 1567–1625* (Oxford, 2004), 86, and his 'The Scottish Parliament and its Early Modern "Rivals"', in *PER*, 24 (2004), 147–72, demonstrate Scottish parliamentary supremacy. In my own '"Tedious to rehers"? Parliament and Locality in Scotland *c.*1500–1651: The Burghs of North-East Fife', in *PER*, 20 (2000), 31–58, at 31, I erroneously implied that conventions of estates passed private acts.

[49]   NAS, Linlithgow Town Council Minute Book, B48/9/2, 37–8 (copy of an extracted ratification); NAS, Burntisland Council Minutes 1631–37, B9/12/6, f. 54r–v (extracted ratification being taken from the charter chest).

[50]   ACA, Aberdeen Council Registers, CR1/42, 1069; *APS*, vol. 4, 304. The same thing happened in 1617, with sasine following parliamentary ratification of a new charter: see ACA, Aberdeen Council Registers, CR1/48, 111–12, 169, 177–88; *APS*, vol. 4, 579–80.

[51]   *APS*, vol. 5, 86–103.

[52]   C. R. Friedrichs, *Urban Politics in Early Modern Europe* (London, 2000), 21.

up to the revolution of 1637.[53] Yet the increased desire for ratifications suggests that revocation bred a wider unease: everyone feared for their liberties. It should come as no surprise, therefore, that the demand for ratifications rose even more markedly after the revolution against Charles I. The first Covenanter parliament challenged many fundamental assumptions, wresting power from the king and abrogating it to the estates. This, along with the general insecurity created by revolution, led scores of individuals and corporations to seek the security of parliamentary ratifications: over 30 were granted to individual burghs.[54]

That ratifications in particular, and acts of parliament in general, were worth having is further attested by the lengths to which burghs went to secure them. Aberdeen's commissioners were given 200 merks (£133 6s 8d) in 1593, considerably more than their living expenses, and they secured two acts.[55] In 1633, some burghs even incurred debts to secure ratifications: Pittenweem borrowed over £350 for its commissioners' expenses and for 'perfytting ... the ratificatioun of the said burgh and erectioun of thair kirk in ane frie paroch kirk', while Aberdeen borrowed a staggering £2,000 for commissioners' expenses and 'for petitioning his majestie for ane new infeftment and ratificatioun of the tounes auld liberties'. Only 2,000 merks (£1,333 6s 8d) was actually spent, £540 of which was paid to lawyers and to the clerk register 'for passing and extracting of the act of parliament ratifieing the tounes liberties'. Although Glasgow did not need to borrow, its commissioners spent nearly £300 more than their ordinary expenses.[56] For many burghs, similar or greater expenses were incurred in the first Covenanting parliament: Glasgow paid over £700 between 1639 and 1641 for 'the ratificatioun of thair great chartour and uther writs', while Aberdeen spent 1,000 merks (£666 13s 4d) 'for expeding the tounes effaires'.[57] The comparison with England is instructive: in the late sixteenth century, Wantage spent £88 12s 6d sterling (c.£500 Scots) for just one act protecting its lands, while York had to pay £20 sterling (c.£120 Scots) merely to introduce a bill in 1572.[58]

As well as seeking legal advice and paying fees to the officers of the crown, it was in the interests of burghs to cultivate support, especially that of prominent individuals. In 1606, Perth sought to smooth the passage of the ratification of a new charter by giving half a tun of wine each to the earl of Montrose (the king's

[53]   For details of the revocation scheme, see A. I. Macinnes, *Charles I and the Making of the Covenanting Movement 1625–1641* (Edinburgh, 1991), ch. 3; A. I. Macinnes, *The British Revolution, 1629–1660* (London, 2005), 86–91; D. Stevenson, *The Scottish Revolution 1637–1644: The Triumph of the Covenanters* (Newton Abbot, 1973), 35–42.

[54]   *APS*, vol. 5, 433–571.

[55]   ACA, Aberdeen Council Registers, CR1/34/2, 796; *APS*, vol. 4, 39: one act instituted a new market day, the other confirmed the burgh's rights to ecclesiastical revenues.

[56]   SAUL, Liber Sessione et Concilii de Pettinwem 1629–1727, B60/6/1, ff. 4v–5r; GCA, Glasgow Council Minutes 1630–36, C1/1/9, 6 July 1633; ACA, Aberdeen Council Registers, CR1/52/1, 116.

[57]   GCA, Glasgow Council Minutes 1636–42, C1/1/10, 9 Nov 1639; *Glasg. Recs.*, 1630–62, 506; ACA, Aberdeen Treasury Records, TA1/3, account for 1641–2.

[58]   Dean, 'Parliament and Locality', 145, 162; Smith, *The Stuart Parliaments*, 40. Comparisons are difficult because of unstable exchange rates, so these sums are estimates; Gibson and Smout, *Prices, Food and Wages*, 5–7.

commissioner to parliament) and the earl of Dunbar.[59] In 1617, Aberdeen anticipated the need 'for gratefieing of sic of his majesties officiaris as hes greatest creditt with his hienes' and promised the clerk register 'a great reward', while in the early 1630s, it gifted barrels of salmon to Sir John Scot of Scotstarvet (head of chancery) in gratitude for his advice.[60] Burntisland, in anticipation of parliament, spent £400 in obtaining a new charter for ratification in 1633, and also gave 'thrie peices of gold' to Sir John Hay, clerk register, who had promised its confirmation.[61] As well as paying the king's advocate and others for advice, Glasgow gratified their servants in 1639, while in 1645, Perth gave gloves to the clerks of parliament.[62] Even small disbursements to fairly humble officials were an important part of the process of achieving a positive outcome.

Financial accounts and instructions to commissioners also demonstrate that, as in England, parliament provided an opportunity for a burgh to get other business done in the capital.[63] A commissioner in Edinburgh for parliament could also represent his burgh before the privy council, the exchequer or the court of session: it was common to send commissioners with the burgh's accounts for audit by the exchequer.[64] As David Dean has argued for England, this does not indicate that burghs lacked enthusiasm for parliament; they were merely maximising the opportunities that a parliament provided.[65] Many burghs had Edinburgh lawyers who were regularly consulted on a range of matters: Linlithgow paid retainers to an advocate and an ordinary lawyer.[66] These 'agents' assisted the burgh's commissioners before parliament and at any other time when the burgh had legal business in the capital. Although parliament was the only institution which could provide legislative solutions for a burgh's problems, burghs' representatives were often to be found before the court of session, where parliamentary ratifications came into their own in disputes with unfree traders, nobles, lairds and other burghs.

Ratifications were not the only acts obtained: many problems had legislative solutions. One of the earlier acts in favour of a burgh shifted the day of Irvine's weekly market; market and fair days were specified in burgh charters which could be amended only by parliament. Between 1593 and 1641, Aberdeen, Crail, Dornoch and Forfar secured similar acts.[67] In 1587, parliamentary commissions were appointed to look at bridges at Aberdeen, Ayr and Irvine to establish how much work was

---

[59]   PKCA, Register of Acts of the Council of Perth 1601–22, B59/16/1, f. 123r. One tun was roughly 1,140 litres, over 1,500 bottles.

[60]   ACA, Aberdeen Treasury Records 1578–1659, TA1/3, account for 1629–30, 1631–2; *Aberdeen Letters*, vol. 1, nos 148, 150.

[61]   NAS, Burntisland Council Minutes 1631–37, B9/12/6, ff. 38r, 54r–v.

[62]   GCA, Glasgow Council Minutes, 1636–42, C1/1/10, 9 Nov 1639; PKCA, Perth Accounts Charge and Discharge B59/25/4/1/4A, 3.

[63]   Dean, 'Parliament and Locality', 144–6; *Aberdeen Letters*, vol. 2, no. 110, vol. 3, no. 159, are examples of commissioners' reports.

[64]   *Ayr Burgh Accounts*, 264; ACA, Aberdeen Treasury Series, TA1/3, account for 1608–9.

[65]   Dean, 'Parliament and Locality', 146, 157.

[66]   NAS, Linlithgow Town Council Minute Book, B48/9/1, 257–8.

[67]   *RCRBS*, vol. 1, 333–4; Balfour, *Works*, vol. 3, 139; *APS*, vol. 4, 39, 375, vol. 5, 381; SAUL, Inventory of Charters and Other Writs, Crail, B10/13/2, no. 280.

required to maintain them.[68] Perth, Aberdeen and Dundee, not trusting the crown's financial officers, obtained acts acknowledging that they had repaid money lent to them by the king in the 1590s.[69] An impost was not enough to defend Dumbarton from inundation by the river Leven, and it secured a national tax to support the work on its flood defences in 1607.[70] In the 1640s, St Andrews successfully petitioned for the right to appoint a third minister.[71]

Further weight was lent to a burgh's cause by the support of the convention of burghs. Although its constraint on the actions of individual burghs may have made it harder for some to bring proposals before the estates, it did mean that most acts sought by individual burghs had the whole estate's backing.[72] Yet there were failures. As a result of the preservation of bills submitted to the English parliament, scholars know their success rate which, in the period of this study, was only about 30 per cent for local bills.[73] In Scotland, failed acts were discarded. The success rate of the legislative efforts of the estate of burgesses as a whole was not great, as is demonstrated in chapter three. However, the vetting of individual burghs' proposals by the convention (and their relatively uncontroversial nature) possibly led to a greater chance of success. Nevertheless, the convention's records contain so few examples of burghs' articles being approved that it is hard to judge, although only five failures have been identified: either the act of 1595 enjoining all articles to be approved by the convention in advance was ignored, or their approval was rarely minuted.[74] Other failures can be inferred from burgh records, although many of them may never have reached parliament, having fallen in the convention of burghs. In 1607, Haddington's commissioners were sent to get a ratification but none was obtained.[75] In 1633, Peebles prepared for parliament by 'seiking ... King James chartour furth of the kist [charter chest]'; the council of Montrose ordered five councillors 'to sicht the townis wreittis in the commone kist ... and ... report quhat they advise to be done'; Linlithgow appointed a subcommittee to 'advyis anent the townes evidentis and what is neidfull to be helpit be his majestie in his parliament'; Kirkcudbright planned 'to have their richtis and securities ... ratifiet in ... parliament': none secured an act.[76] Although quantification is impossible, the impression created by an examination of burgh records is that the failure rate in Scotland was much lower than in England.

The Scottish parliament seems not to have been particularly troubled with the sort of 'serious conflict between competing lobbies' which often 'spilled over into

---

68   *APS*, vol. 3, 518–20.
69   *APS*, vol. 4, 86–7, 149.
70   Ibid., 376–8.
71   *APS*, vol. 6, part 2, 151–2.
72   *RCRBS*, vol. 1, 469.
73   Elton, *The Parliament of England*, 316; Smith, *The Stuart Parliaments*, 42.
74   *RCRBS*, vol. 1, 192, 202, 329, 332, 469, vol. 2, 251.
75   NAS, Haddington Burgh Registers, Council Book 1603–16, B30/13/3.
76   NAS, Burgh of Peebles Accounts, 1623–50, B58/14/2, account for 1632–3; AA, Montrose Council Minutes 1617–39, M1/1/1, 22 May 1633; NAS, Linlithgow Town Council Minute Book 1620–40, B48/9/1, 263; *Kirkcud. Recs.*, vol. 2, 471.

Parliament' in England, although conflicts were not unknown.[77] As well as trying to block the ratifications of local rivals, burghs suffered from internal quarrels and clashed with landed neighbours. Most disputes within and between burghs were settled by the convention of burghs, but some did spill into parliament. At the beginning of the seventeenth century, Glasgow was not technically a royal burgh and the right of its pre-Reformation archbishops to appoint the magistrates had been granted to the duke of Lennox. In an attempt to free itself, Glasgow secured a new charter and obtained the king's approval for its parliamentary ratification. A group of merchants and craftsmen led by the laird of Minto, former provost and a client of Lennox, petitioned parliament in 1606 and thwarted this, a rare example of a dissident faction in a burgh appealing to parliament. It was much more common for the convention of burghs, the court of session or the privy council to deal with such divisions.[78] The subsequent unrest in the burgh gave the king second thoughts about granting Glasgow full freedom and, in 1612, parliament ratified a new charter which, although formally making Glasgow a royal burgh, restored the new Protestant archbishop's rights in the appointment of its magistrates.[79] Glasgow was again the victim of Lennox in 1641 after the abolition of episcopacy, when it was 'pitifullie crossed': an act transferred superiority of all the archbishopric's lands to the crown, but Lennox obtained an exemption recovering the right to choose the provost. The burgh's only consolation was to receive some revenues for its ministers and university.[80] Compromises were more common than overt conflicts. In 1641, in preparing for ratification of its charter, South Queensferry agreed that a neighbouring laird would retain rights to some lands and a 'loaning' (roadway) leading to them, which would be 'exceptit furth of the said ratifficatione'.[81] An act of parliament could thus amend a royal charter, demonstrating the supremacy of statute, its exclusive ability to alter existing law, and the broad acceptance of this 'modern' notion which had been expressed by Montrose in the 1620s.[82]

Securing favourable legislation was one way for a burgh to uphold and enhance its rights, but there were others. Commissioners were empowered to make 'protestations'.[83] The act *'Salvo Iure Cuiuslibet'* reserved the rights of those 'nocht

---

[77] Smith, *The Stuart Parliaments*, 41.

[78] Friedrichs, *Urban Politics in Early Modern Europe*, 33–4, 43–5; *RCRBS*, vol. 1, 312–37, 354–60, 383–6 (a dispute in Aberdeen); RPC, first series, vol. 7, 1, 12, 14–16, 31, 79, 94–100, 463, 467–8, 735–7 (a dispute in Dundee).

[79] GCA, Glasgow Council Act Book 1605–10, C1/1/6, ff. 12v, 17r, 21v, 83v, 87r–88r; *APS*, vol. 4, 484; A. S. W. Pearce, 'John Spottiswoode, Jacobean Archbishop and Statesman' (Stirling PhD, 1998), ch. 4.

[80] Baillie, *Letters and Journals*, vol. 1, 395; *APS*, vol. 5, 412–13; J. McGrath, 'The Medieval and Early Modern Burgh', in T. M. Devine and G. Jackson (eds), *Glasgow Volume 1: Beginnings to 1830* (Manchester, 1995), 17–62, at 29–31.

[81] ECA, Queensferry Council Minute Book 1634–61, SL59/1/1/1, f. 81v; *APS*, vol. 5, 570–71.

[82] Goodare, *The Government of Scotland*, 82; L. B. Taylor (ed.), *Aberdeen Council Letters*, 6 vols (Oxford, 1942–61), vol. 1, 229.

[83] For example, see NAS, Commissions to Commissioners from Burghs, PA7/25/38/1 (Anstruther Wester, 1639).

hard [heard], nor callit speciallie' to parliament.[84] If anyone present felt that their privileges were prejudiced by ratifications granted to others, they made a notarised protestation. It was common for burghs to protest against rivals' ratifications: Crail made a number of ultimately futile protestations against those obtained by new parliamentary burghs in north-east Fife.[85] In 1641, burghs made 14 protestations against ratifications to other burghs, landowners and corporations, while there were 16 protestations by others against burghs' ratifications.[86] If no protestation was entered, any future challenge to the ratified rights was seriously weakened. Although protestations indicate a burgh's failure to block an act which harmed its interests, they offered an effective compromise and can be regarded as an important conciliatory tool. They had a legal status in their own right, were included in the parliamentary record and copies under the signature of the clerk register could be obtained for use in the courts. As with other acts, burghs kept copies in their charter chests: in 1621, Aberdeen's commissioner paid 30 merks (£20) for a protestation (ten to register it and 20 to obtain a copy); in December 1641, Glasgow purchased extracts of three acts of parliament and 'the protestatiounes taine against Renfrew, Dumbartane and Rutherglen'.[87]

For most of the period, financial hardship was rarely a parliamentary issue, with the possible exception of burghs which asked for help with public works because funds could not be raised locally: Perth, Dumbarton and Irvine sought parliamentary aid for bridge-building, flood-protection and harbour repairs respectively.[88] Before the 1640s, distressed burghs resorted to their convention, seeking exemption from attendance at conventions, reduction in their share of national taxes and even exemption from their share of the fees paid to the convention's legal agent and its clerk.[89] During the 1640s, the altered role of parliament, a more intrusive and normal part of government than ever before, led to it receiving requests that would previously have been directed to the king and privy council. Coupled with this, economic dislocation caused by the wars of the 1640s and the unprecedented financial demands of the state left many burghs in such hardship that they had to turn to parliament for relief.

Although detailed work on the innovative systems for raising revenue and maintaining the army by the regimes of the 1640s is not yet complete, it seems that a disproportionate burden was borne by the parliamentary burghs.[90] From the outset they were at the forefront of buying arms and armour for the wars against Charles I: the records of almost every burgh contain references to the purchase of munitions. In the desperate preparations for war in 1638, specie flooded out of Scotland and, in

---

[84]   *APS*, vol. 4, 68.

[85]   A. R. MacDonald, 'Parliament and locality in Scotland', 41–2.

[86]   *APS*, vol. 5, 570–86.

[87]   ACA, Aberdeen Treasury Records 1559–1692, TA1/2, Aberdeen Treasurer's Accounts 1620–21; GCA, Glasgow Council Minutes 1636–42, C1/1/10, 1 Dec 1641.

[88]   *RCRBS*, vol. 2, 247; *APS*, vol. 3, 108, vol. 4, 376–8.

[89]   Pagan, *The Convention of Burghs*, 67.

[90]   D. Stevenson, 'The Financing of the Cause of the Covenants, 1638–1651', in *SHR*, 51 (1972), 89–123. Dr Laura Stewart of the Birbeck, University of London is currently working on this topic.

1639, burghs were asked to gather coin and plate from their inhabitants and send it to Edinburgh: Perth contributed over £2,500.[91] Individual merchants also lent huge sums: by 1644, William Dick of Braid was already owed 840,000 merks (£560,000) but he never received more than a fraction of it. Taxes of all sorts were levied. From 1644 the excise hit the burghs hard because of their domination of retail trade, while the monthly 'maintenance' for the army and the quartering of soldiers drained local resources. When it was considered too much to impose more taxes, 'voluntary' loans were sought and there were few years in which men were not levied for military service. Added to all this was economic dislocation resulting from the direct and indirect effects of war: thousands of lives were lost in battle; trade was disrupted; merchant shipping commandeered, captured or sunk; armies damaged property, consumed food and other supplies wherever they went, leaving dearth and disease in their wake, and the food supply was hit by disruption to agriculture.[92] In 1651, Linlithgow's estimated losses due to the wars of the previous 13 years were £20,500 sterling (£246,000 Scots), not including debts, arrears of tax and excise. Aberdeen's were £1,582,910 3s 10d in 1648.[93]

Some burghs had to borrow to pay for the state's financial demands. In 1641 Dunfermline and Kirkcudbright, among others, took out loans to cover their shares of 150,000 guilders (£162,000) borrowed by the burghs in the Low Countries to buy munitions.[94] By 1642, Linlithgow's debts were already 12,500 merks (over £8,000).[95] Some were worse off. In 1640, Burntisland's commissioner was to 'meane [i.e. declare] the pure estait of this burgh' to parliament because it was 'far superexpendit and exhaustit', while the tiny burgh of Lauder claimed that it had 'nather tread nor handling' and had been able to contribute only by accommodating 'sindrie cumpanies cuming to and from the airmie' which had 'heavielie dampnefiet' the burgh.[96] Every burgh incurred debts at some stage. By the later 1640s, many could not even afford the interest payments: from 1646, Dysart regularly borrowed to pay its interest, and in 1649 Stirling was doing the same.[97]

---

[91]   PKCA, Perth Council Minutes 1623–41, B59/16/2, 1 March 1641; NAS, Linlithgow Town Council Minute Book 1620–40, B48/9/1, 424.

[92]   D. Stevenson, 'The Burghs and the Scottish Revolution', in M. Lynch (ed.), *The Early Modern Town in Scotland* (London, 1987), 167–91.

[93]   NAS, Linlithgow Town Council Minute Book 1640–59, B48/9/2, 411; *Aberdeen Letters*, vol. 3, 134.

[94]   NAS, Burgh of Dunfermline Town Council Minutes 1638–50, B20/13/1, 98; *Kirkcud. Recs.*, vol. 2, 631; SAUL, Cupar Court and Council Records 1640–53, B13/10/3, 1 June 1641: Cupar's share of the 150,000 guilders borrowed (1,800 guilders) was £1,944.

[95]   NAS, Linlithgow Town Council Minute Book 1640–59, B48/9/2, 44.

[96]   NAS, Burntisland Council Minutes 1639–42, B9/12/7, f. 90v; NAS, 'Supplicatioun Lauder craiving exemptioun Julij 1641', Lauder Boxed Accounts 1632–1730, B46/8/5 (unnumbered bundles). Handling – commerce.

[97]   FCAC, Dysart Council Minute Book 1645–52, 1/02/01, 13 Nov 1646, 28 June 1647; SCA, Stirling Council Minutes 1619–58, B66/20/4, 20 Jan 1649. In 1649, Dysart was twelfth in terms of its share of the burghs' taxation, while Stirling was fourteenth: *RCRBS*, vol. 3, 332–3.

During the 1640s, burghs still pursued the sorts of acts that they had always sought, but they became increasingly preoccupied with money, or rather the lack of it. Numerous acts promising repayment of money lent to the state were secured, but it is not clear if any received even a fraction of what they were owed, or whether the acts were merely optimistic promissory notes. It is grimly ironic that, in the summer of 1644, Linlithgow spent nearly £600 to get an order from parliament promising repayment with interest of £2,430 that it had lent in 1642.[98] Money was repeatedly promised from the 'brotherly assistance', the huge sum (£300,000 sterling) pledged by the English parliament for Scottish support against the king, but half of it never materialised and most of what was received was immediately consumed by the army, a bottomless pit into which money constantly vanished.[99] Burghs which had lent money to buy arms in 1643 were still lobbying for payment in 1650, and asking to be allowed to keep their excise in lieu.[100] The regime was well aware that it could not get blood from a stone and exemptions from excise and maintenance were repeatedly granted. Lanark can stand as a pitiful example of the plight of many. In 1649, it petitioned for 'some effectuall meanes wherthrew [it] ... may be preserved from utter destructioune'. It had contributed £1,296 towards the purchase of arms in 1641; it was owed another £3,169 5s for quartering soldiers; its burgesses' crops had been destroyed, buildings damaged and goods stolen by passing armies to an estimated value of £1,600; £12,500 had been extorted by the Engagers for Lanark's refusal to support them. In spite of 'actis and preceptis granted be the publict' for repayment, it had received nothing. Yet its loyalty to the Covenants meant that it was content to wait until the army had been paid. Parliament could only promise not to make things worse, and Lanark was granted exemption from excise and maintenance, which it could not have paid.[101] Claims flooded into parliament, and into the committee of estates between parliamentary sessions, seeking the removal or reduction of the number of soldiers quartered on burghs and the cancellation of arrears of excise and maintenance. In 1651, Linlithgow's council was in exile at Culross because the burgh was occupied by the English. Its commissioner reported that parliament wanted voluntary contributions to support the army: he was instructed 'to use all meines ... to interceid and deall with the parliament for our exemptioun in respect of our great losses and ... the hard conditiouin we ar reducit to'. To the council's relief, he was successful.[102] The plight of the burghs and the resigned willingness of the government to grant exemptions demonstrates that, by the time of the Cromwellian invasion in 1650, burgh councils were virtually bankrupt after over a decade of expensive and destructive warfare.[103]

---

[98]   NAS, Linlithgow Treasurer's Accounts 1630–54, B48/13/1, account for 1644–5.

[99]   Stevenson, *The Scottish Revolution*, 217, 267; Stevenson, 'Financing the Cause of the Covenants'.

[100]   Balfour, Works, vol. 4, 24.

[101]   Renwick (ed.), *Extracts from the Records of the Royal Burgh of Lanark*, 136–8; *APS*, vol. 6, part 2, 313.

[102]   NAS, Linlithgow Town Council Minute Book 1640–59, B48/9/2, 390, 392.

[103]   Stevenson, 'Financing the Cause of the Covenants', 113–23, makes it clear that raising money became increasingly difficult after 1648; not that it was easy before.

Burghs usually acted alone or as a single estate but they occasionally combined to lobby parliament. Those around the Firth of Clyde, Ayrshire and possibly Galloway had a regional forum, the 'convention of the west burghs'.[104] This body can be traced from the middle of the sixteenth century and, on a number of occasions, these burghs combined to seek acts of parliament. In 1555, they obtained two acts in their favour: one against the export of victual intriguingly granted an exemption to the western burghs for their trade to the Hebrides (which are part of Scotland), while another outlawed attempts by Highlanders to charge their burgesses for fishing in Loch Fyne.[105] In 1581, an act was passed relating specifically to their exclusive rights of trade in the west, along the same lines as those obtained by the free burghs in relation to their national monopolies, while in 1584, they were unsuccessful in an attempt to gain exemption from using a new standard fish barrel 'in respect of the laik of tymmer amangis thame'.[106] The Fife burghs also worked together occasionally and held ad hoc meetings during the 1640s.[107] In 1649, Anstruther Easter and Pittenweem jointly petitioned and obtained an act to reduce the burden of soldiers quartered on them, while Kirkcaldy and Kinghorn successfully sought an exemption from a levy of soldiers, as did the burgh and university of St Andrews.[108] Co-operation between towns and shires was not uncommon in the English parliament but there is little to indicate that this was so in Scotland. The only example which has been traced comes from 1649, when Aberdeen's commissioner failed in an attempt to help Aberdeenshire secure exemption from the quartering of troops, which he had achieved for the burgh.[109]

The act of 1581 secured by the western burghs was a public statute, just as acts relating to three or more English counties were classified as public.[110] Other general statutes began life in burgh council chambers, and many for which the burghs lobbied collectively must have been raised by individual commissioners. It is seldom possible to identify the origins of proposals, although an item concerning dry-volume measures which was remitted to a parliamentary commission in 1581 had its origins in a request from Glasgow to the convention of burghs in 1579.[111] The act of 1592 giving magistrates powers over craftsmen in suburbs was instigated by Perth at the convention of burghs in 1581 and raised again by Dundee in 1587, while a number of Aberdeen's instructions to its commissioners in 1633 were explicitly to be raised at the convention of burghs, with a view to the whole estate

---

[104] AAC, Ayr Court and Council Records 1580–96, B6/11/2, f. 430v (1595); GCA, Glasgow Council Act Book 1573–81, C1/1/1, f. 206v (1577), Glasgow Council Act Book, 1598–1601, C1/1/5, f. 147r (1601).

[105] *APS*, vol. 2, 495.

[106] *APS*, vol. 3, 224–5; *RCRBS*, vol. 1, 192.

[107] SAUL, Liber Sessione et Concilii de Pettinwem 1629–1727, B60/6/1, ff. 14r, 55r; NAS, Burntisland Council Minutes 1639–42, B9/12/7, f. 82v.

[108] *APS*, vol. 6, part 2, 286, 426, 431.

[109] J. Stuart (ed.), *The Miscellany of the Spalding Club*, vol. 5 (Aberdeen, 1852), 381–2; Dean, 'Parliament and Locality', 153–6.

[110] Smith, *The Stuart Parliaments*, 40.

[111] *RCRBS*, vol. 1, 81; *APS*, vol. 3, 215.

taking them up in parliament.[112] One general statute with clear local origins (another example of co-operation between burghs in Fife) related to landing fish in the Firth of Forth. In the parliament of May 1584, Edinburgh and Crail had obtained exclusive rights to this trade, cutting out many burghs.[113] The recently-enrolled burghs of Pittenweem and Anstruther Easter had not sent commissioners to that parliament and complained that they were 'never consenting to the said act nor yet knawing of the making thairof'. It was particularly hurtful to them because they had 'litill or na uther tred'.[114] Pittenweem's commissioner raised the matter at the convention of burghs in July 1584 and it agreed to seek redress at the next session of parliament in August.[115] There was insufficient time to arrange this but when parliament next met in December 1585 the burghs requested amendment of the act of 1584: a new statute gave all free burghs on the Forth the right to land fish.[116] The issue resurfaced in 1621 after Edinburgh had obtained a new charter granting it exclusive rights to land fish in the Forth. Crail joined its erstwhile rivals, fearing a ratification of Edinburgh's charter, and parliament took the unusual step of issuing a 'Declaratioun in favouris of utheris burrowis anent the actis grantit in favoures of Edinburgh', making it clear that any ratification to Edinburgh would be 'with expres reservatioun' of the rights of other burghs on the Forth according to the act of 1585.[117] In 1594, a petition from Kinghorn led to the formulation of a public statute confirming the levy of 12d on every boat crossing the Firth of Forth for the upkeep of the harbours of the burghs on the Fife coast. Although passed as a public statute applying to nine burghs, its origin was betrayed by its title, 'Act in favour of the burgh of Kinghorne'.[118]

An overall assessment of the fortunes of the burghs in terms of legislation is positive. Of the 59 parliamentary burghs in existence by 1651, 49 (83 per cent) obtained at least one act.[119] The total (245 acts, not including protestations) works out at an average of over four for every burgh, although there were wide variations. Eight obtained just one act and only 13 managed to secure more than four. Five burghs (Edinburgh, Aberdeen, Glasgow, Dundee and Perth) accounted for over 40 per cent of the total, with Edinburgh securing 48, nearly one in five of all acts for individual burghs. It is no coincidence that these were the five wealthiest towns, nor that the ten burghs which secured no acts at all were among the poorest: although it was relatively cheap and simple to secure an act in Scotland, cost remained a factor.[120] It is also no coincidence that the five burghs which secured the most acts

---

[112]   *RCRBS*, vol. 1, 116–17, 238; *APS*, vol. 3, 579; *Aberdeen Letters*, vol. 1, 351.

[113]   *APS*, vol. 1, 302; MacDonald, 'Parliament and Locality in Scotland', 43.

[114]   NAS, Petition of the Burgesses of the Burghs on the North Coast of the Forth, Pittenweem Writs, GD62/11.

[115]   *RCRBS*, vol. 1, 191–2; NAS, Extract minute of the commissioners of burghs, July 1589 (sic, it should be 1584), Pittenweem Writs, GD62/10.

[116]   *RCRBS*, vol. 1, 204–5; *APS*, vol. 3, 378–9.

[117]   *APS*, vol. 4, 672–3.

[118]   Ibid., 80.

[119]   See *APS*, vols 2–6. All acts obtained by parliamentary burghs were included, although where petitions from more than one burgh resulted in one act (e.g. see *APS*, vol. 6, part 1, 785–6, and vol. 6, part 2, 431) each burgh was deemed to have secured an act in its favour.

[120]   See *RCRBS*, vols 1–3 for tax rolls as an indication of burghs' relative wealth.

were almost invariably represented on the committee of the articles before 1640 and, thereafter, retained that prominence on the drafting committees of the Covenanting era. Their wealth and status got them onto committees and their wealth, status and presence on the committees eased the passage of their acts.

There were also significant variations over time, with more than two-thirds of these acts being passed between 1639 and 1651. The huge increase in legislation after 1639 reflects the changing nature of parliament after the Covenanting revolution. It absorbed more and more aspects of what had previously been royal government, while extending the reach of central power into the localities in a way that James VI and Charles I could only have dreamed of. There are continuities and differences in the patterns of legislative success on either side of 1639. Edinburgh's domination was a constant, with 19 acts before 1639 and 32 thereafter. Along with Edinburgh, Aberdeen with ten and Perth with six dominated before 1639, while Glasgow and Dundee joined the leaders only afterwards. Before 1639, 15 burghs got no acts at all, a figure matched between 1639 and 1651, although not by the same burghs. Both before and after 1639, about three quarters of burghs managed to secure one or more acts of parliament. As in England the less successful burghs lay on the geographical peripheries; of the ten which secured no acts between 1550 and 1651, most were peripheral.[121] Yet too much can be made of this: Dornoch and Tain, the two most northerly parliamentary burghs, each secured three acts, while two of the failures (Inverkeithing and North Berwick) lie ten and 25 miles from Edinburgh respectively.

The number of acts obtained by the burghs certainly compares favourably with the figures available for England. Perhaps the higher Scottish success rate lay in the more straightforward legislative process.[122] An article or petition would be submitted to the clerk register before parliament, or directly to a committee once parliament had assembled. Before the 1640s, that committee would amend the submission, while also receiving input from the rest of parliament. The proposal would be amended and framed into an act which would then be voted on by the whole parliament at the end of the session. In the 1640s, the procedure became more complex; every measure was perused by each estate, as well as by a drafting committee, before being voted on by the whole house. A simpler process also meant a cheaper one and cost must have prevented many English boroughs from securing acts, for substantial fees had to be paid to the clerks and others who relied on them for a significant part of their income.[123] The clerks of the Scottish parliament were the clerk register and the clerks of the privy council, who received salaries from the crown and did not depend upon parliamentary fees, which were between 20 and 100 merks (£13 6s 8d and £66 13s 4d) for a private act in the later sixteenth century. That is equivalent to between £1

---

[121] Dean, 'Parliament and Locality', 157, 162. The ten were Annan, Dingwall, Inverurie, Kintore, Lochmaben, Rothesay and Sanquhar (peripheral) and Inverkeithing, Kilrenny and North Berwick (central).

[122] For impressions of the complexity of the English process, see Smith, *The Stuart Parliaments*, 39, and Dean, 'Parliament and Locality'.

[123] Smith, *The Stuart Parliaments*, 40; Dean, 'Parliament and Locality', 145, 162.

and £5 sterling at 1600 exchange rates, a price which every English borough would have envied.[124]

Parliamentary politics

The burghs were the least political estate in this period, as they had always been.[125] Few burgesses were to be found at court and the course of political change was driven by the greater nobles. Merchants were instinctively wary of political upheaval. It created uncertainty among consumers and might result in drastic realignments in foreign policy, causing the closure of established trading routes. They rarely became embroiled in the factional struggles which occasionally absorbed the higher nobility during the sixteenth century, tending to stand on the sidelines until disputes were over, at which point they could declare their support for the winners and carry on as before. This was epitomised in 1582 when, reluctant to endorse the Ruthven regime which had recently seized power but which did not have a firm grip on it, no burgh sent a commissioner to a convention of estates, in the knowledge that 'how soon the king obtained his liberty, he would censure and condemn the fact [i.e. the coup] as treasonable'.[126] This reluctance may have been born of experience. In the 1540s, Aberdeen had become involved in a conflict at the highest level. Its provost, Thomas Menzies of Pitfodels, allied himself with the earl of Arran (governor of Scotland for the infant Queen Mary) in a high-risk strategy to free the burgh from the earl of Huntly's influence by taking advantage of the factional conflict following James V's death in 1542. Menzies even served briefly as crown comptroller, an almost unheard-of appointment of a burgess as an officer of state. In October 1544, Aberdeen received two precepts of parliament, one from Arran and one from Mary of Guise, mother of the queen and an ally of Huntly. The council decided to acknowledge Arran's precept, against the wise advice of some who 'wald nocht consent to send ony commissaris to ony of the saidis parliamentis'. This was Arran's last throw of the dice and his failure to gain control led swiftly to the reassertion of Huntly's power over Aberdeen.[127] In the civil war of 1568–73, some burghs made a sufficiently clear commitment to the king's party (the supporters of James VI) for the queen's party (the supporters of the ousted Mary) to forfeit them, the only known attempt to strip burghs of their free status. In August 1571, the magistrates, council and communities of Dundee, Jedburgh and Glasgow were declared forfeit by a Marian parliament meeting at

---

[124] NAS, Treasurer's Accounts 1592–3, E21/68; Goodare, 'Parliament and Society', 105.

[125] See R. J. Tanner, *The Late Medieval Scottish Parliament: Politics and the Three Estates, 1424–1488* (East Linton, 2001), 268–9; Lynch, 'The Crown and the Burghs', 62.

[126] J. Spottiswoode, History of the Church of Scotland … by the Right Rev. John Spottiswoode, M. Russell and M. Napier (eds), 3 vols (Edinburgh, 1847–51), vol. 2, 295.

[127] ACA, Aberdeen Council Registers, CR1/17, 576, CR1/18, 291; *Diurnal of Occurrents*, 35; A. White, 'The Menzies Era: Sixteenth-Century Politics', in E. P. Dennison, D. Ditchburn and M. Lynch (eds), *Aberdeen Before 1800: A New History* (East Linton, 2002), 224–37, at 225–7. For the national political background, see M. Merriman, *The Rough Wooings: Mary Queen of Scots 1542–1551* (East Linton, 2000), 156–8.

Edinburgh, but it was only a symbolic gesture.[128] These forfeitures occurred in the later stages of the civil war and demonstrate the weakness of the queen's party. If it had really held power, it would simply have interfered with the election of the magistrates. No burghs were forfeited by the king's party, even though some sent commissioners to the queen's parliaments.

Although the burghs shied away from uncertain civil conflicts, whenever there was a politically significant session of parliament, they were well represented. The 22 burghs at the Reformation parliament of 1560 constituted their largest turnout in over 80 years and, contrary to recent suggestions, amounted to two-thirds of parliamentary burghs.[129] In December 1567, 28 were represented at the first parliament of the infant James VI after the overthrow of his mother, equalling the record for burgh attendance in 1479.[130] In both instances, a lack of detailed local records makes it hard to evaluate motivations for attending. The influence of powerful magnates ensuring the presence of burgh representatives cannot be discounted, particularly in the case of the more far-flung towns like Banff and Inverness in 1560, which sent their first commissioners since the fifteenth century.[131] Yet the commitment of some burghs to the Reformation must have been a factor: Ayr, Crail, Perth and Dundee had motivation enough to come out in support of religious change in 1560.[132] On the other hand, Aberdeen's conservatism is reflected in the instruction to its commissioners not to 'assent to ony ordinance ... in dirrogatioune of the quenis grace authoritie'.[133] During the later sixteenth century, the proportion of burghs attending parliament rose as the significance of parliament grew, so that large turnouts could no longer be regarded as indicative of politically significant sessions.

Despite the fact that the burghs tended to conservatism, there are no grounds to suggest, as one recent study has done, that their commissioners unfailingly followed the wishes of the government of the day because 'no royal burgh could afford to displease the king'.[134] Burghs defying the crown in parliament did not risk losing

---

[128] *Diurnal of Occurrents*, 237, 243. Dundee's provost, James Haliburton, was a privy councillor in the government of the king's party.

[129] K. M. Brown, 'The Reformation Parliament', in K. M. Brown and R. J. Tanner (eds), *The History of the Scottish Parliament, Volume 1: Parliament and Politics in Scotland, 1235–1560* (Edinburgh, 2004), 203–31, at 212, suggested that 'under one-third' of eligible burghs attended; Lynch, 'The Crown and the Burghs', 55, puts it at 'less than half'. These figures are not based on the true total of parliamentary burghs (see ch. 1 and appendix 2).

[130] *APS*, vol. 3, 3–4.

[131] Young, *The Parliaments of Scotland*, vol. 2, 769, 779.

[132] M. H. B. Sanderson, *Ayrshire and the Reformation: People and Change 1490–1600* (East Linton, 1997), 95–9, 106; M. Verschuur, 'Merchants and Craftsmen in Sixteenth-Century Perth', in Lynch (ed.), *The Early Modern Town in Scotland*; SAUL, Crail Town Clerk's Scroll Book 1554–60, B10/8/2, f. 76v; I. E. F. Flett, 'The Conflict of the Reformation and Democracy in the Geneva of Scotland, 1443–1560: An Introduction to Edited Texts of Documents Relating to the Burgh of Dundee' (St Andrews MPhil, 1981), 68.

[133] ACA, Aberdeen Council Registers, CR1/23, 319.

[134] V. T. Wells, 'Constitutional Conflict after the Union of the Crowns: Contention and Continuity in the Parliaments of 1612 and 1621', in K. M. Brown and A. J. Mann (eds), *The History of the Scottish Parliament Volume 2: Parliament and Politics in Scotland 1567–1707*

their privileges. Their rights were enshrined in statute and only parliament could amend or remove them. With the exception of the Marian parliament of August 1571, no burgh was ever forfeited. Because they were corporations, it was easier for the government, if pushed, to purge their councils. This was rarely done and there was no systematic central interference in the burghs before the later 1640s.[135] More pertinently, royal burghs frequently chose to displease the king, in parliament and elsewhere, sometimes showing a stronger inclination to do so than the other estates. Julian Goodare has shown how they were prominent in resisting and reducing the crown's demands for taxation in conventions of the estates before 1603, while in 1612, some burgh commissioners on the committee of the articles opposed the crown's taxation demands.[136] The most striking example of their failure to toe the crown's line occurred in 1621 when the king sought ratification of the five articles of Perth, designed to bring certain ecclesiastical practices in Scotland closer to those in England.[137] James VI expected urban opposition and he was right to do so: the burghs were the only estate to reject the articles, by 25 votes to 20, while they also opposed the innovative tax on interest payments. One contemporary alleged that those supporting the crown were rewarded and those voting against were penalised by the blocking of their acts and this appears to be borne out by the parliamentary record.[138] The only burghs to obtain private acts (Edinburgh and Elgin) voted with the crown, while Dumbarton opposed and failed to secure a ratification. However, Edinburgh did not manage to obtain the transfer from Aberdeen of custody of the standard salmon measure, while the act confirming the right to land fish at any port on the Forth was against Edinburgh's interests and favoured ten burghs which opposed the five articles and only two which did not. It was almost certainly promoted by the fishing ports of north-east Fife (Pittenweem, the two Anstruthers, Kilrenny and Crail), all of whom defied the crown.[139] Only one burgh, Aberdeen, had secured a ratification in 1617, so it would be rash to read too much into Dumbarton's failure.

(Edinburgh, 2005), 82–100, at 93; and see Goodare, *The Government of Scotland*, 50–51, for a better assessment of the position of the burghs.

[135] For a discussion of the notion of the never-dying urban corporation, see R. L. C. Hunter, 'Corporate Personality and the Scottish Burgh: An Historical Note', in G. W. S. Barrow (ed.), *The Scottish Tradition: Essays in Honour of Ronald Gordon Cant* (Edinburgh, 1974), 223–42.

[136] J. Goodare, 'Parliamentary Taxation in Scotland, 1560–1603', in *SHR*, 68 (1989), 23–52, at 41–5; Wells, 'Constitutional Conflict', 91–4.

[137] A. R. MacDonald, *The Jacobean Kirk 1567–1625: Sovereignty, Polity and Liturgy* (Aldershot, 1998), ch. 7.

[138] Calderwood, History, vol. 7, 492–4, 500–501, 504; M. Lynch, 'Introduction', in Lynch (ed.), *The Early Modern Town in Scotland*, 1–35, at 24.

[139] J. Goodare, 'The Scottish Parliament of 1621', in *The Historical Journal*, 38 (1995), 29–51, at 40–41; Goodare, *The Government of Scotland*, 55; F. Roberts and I. M. M. MacPhail (eds), *Dumbarton Common Good Accounts 1614–1660* (Dumbarton, 1972), 25, 27–8; ACA, Aberdeen Council Registers, CR1/50, 73; NAS, Burntisland Council Minutes 1617–23, B9/12/4, ff. 89v–90r; HMC, Report on the Manuscripts of the Earl of Mar and Kellie, 2 vols (London, 1904–30), vol. 2, 107.

While there is no explicit evidence for urban protests in 1633, 'disordoures' occurred within the estate during parliament and Aberdeen's commissioner certainly voted against the crown.[140] The burghs' solid support for the Covenants a few years later is well-attested: from the outset their councils backed the 'common cause', in contrast with their more conservative English equivalents, petitioning the privy council against the new prayer book in September 1637.[141] The convention of burghs endorsed the National Covenant in 1638, making it a test for all commissioners. The tension between 'localism' and national politics which is so prominent in English historiography is modified, at least for the burghs, by Scotland's smaller size and by the convention of burghs where urban elites met regularly to think in national terms.[142] Aberdeen refused to subscribe the National Covenant in 1638 and retained an uncertain relationship with the regime, being the only burgh to vote against the treason conviction of the marquis of Montrose in 1646.[143] Aberdeen was the exception which proved the rule of European towns tending to acquiesce in political change, suggesting that there was strong ideological opposition to the Covenant in that burgh.[144] In a number of key votes, burgesses provided decisive support for the Covenanting leadership and were enthusiastic supporters of the radical regime, led by the marquis of Argyll, which overthrew the Engagers in 1648.[145] The burghs' support for the Covenants was strong but largely tacit in parliament: they left the nobles to give the lead in the house, deferring to their social superiors in debates and decisions.[146] To be sure, individual burgesses, such as James Sword from St Andrews, Alexander Jaffray from Aberdeen, William Glendinning from Kirkcudbright and George Jamieson from Cupar were some of the most steadfast supporters of the Covenants, in terms of their

---

[140] ACA, Acts of Convention, CRB, vol. 2, 1610–36, f. 445r–v; *RCRBS*, vol. 2, 262; G. DesBrisay, "'The civill warrs did overrun all": Aberdeen 1630–1690', in Dennison et al. (eds), Aberdeen Before 1800, 238–66, at 240–41; Lee, The Road to Revolution, 133.

[141] RPC, second series, vol. 6, 554; Stevenson, 'The Burghs and the Scottish Revolution'; J. R. Young, 'The Scottish Parliament and the Covenanting Revolution: the Emergence of a Scottish Commons', in idem (ed.), Celtic Dimensions of the British Civil Wars (Edinburgh, 1997), 164–84; GCA, Glasgow Council Minutes, 1636–42, C1/1/10, 25 Aug 1638; D. Hirst, England in Conflict 1603–1660: Kingdom, Community, Commonwealth (London, 1999), 198–201. Differences between Scotland and England ran very deep: the majority of every estate in Scotland opposed the king until the later 1640s.

[142] A. Hughes, 'The King, the Parliament and the Localities During the English Civil War', in R. Cust and A. Hughes (eds), The English Civil War (London, 1997), 261–87, at 261–6.

[143] Balfour, *Works*, vol. 3, 361–2.

[144] Friedrichs, *Urban Politics in Early Modern Europe*, 21.

[145] Stevenson, 'The Burghs and the Scottish Revolution', 172–3; Young, 'The Scottish Parliament and the Covenanting Revolution'.

[146] See Balfour, *Works*, vols 3–4, for accounts of parliamentary debates; Stevenson, 'The Burghs and the Scottish Revolution', esp. 168–9, 171–2; J. Scally, 'The Rise and Fall of the Covenanter Parliaments, 1639–51', in Brown and Mann (eds), *Parliament and Politics in Scotland 1567–1707*, 138–62, at 152; Young, 'The Scottish Parliament and the Covenanting Revolution': Stevenson and Scally argue for the maintenance of the social order after 1639, while Young suggests the emergence of something more dynamic, a 'Scottish Commons'.

service on the committee of estates and other parliamentary bodies.[147] In spite of that, none of them broke through to positions of leadership; even after 1648, Scotland did not experience the same dynamic shifts in the social order that characterised the English revolution against Charles I. Good connections with the Covenanting leadership could, however, be useful. In 1649, John Jaffray, Alexander's brother and stand-in as commissioner to parliament, used his brother's connections with the most prominent members of each estate (the marquis of Argyll, Archibald Johnston of Wariston and the provost of Edinburgh), who proved to be Aberdeen's 'speciall freindis', to secure exemption from the quartering of troops.[148]

Only in the Engager parliament of 1648 is there any evidence for dynamic political behaviour by individual burghs, for the unity of their estate faltered at this point. According to one contemporary, 'almost the halfe of the burgesses' supported the Engagement, following the 'greater tounes [of] Edinburgh, Perth, Dundee, Aberdeen, St Andrews [and] Linlithgow'.[149] Although Aberdeen's support was predictable, that of others can be attributed to their tendency to acquiesce in the status quo, and to the fact that Edinburgh, with an eye to the main chance, backed the new regime.[150] Yet many burghs remained steadfast in their support for the Covenants, which had been watered down in the Engagement, and some even recorded overt political opinion in their minute books. South Queensferry instructed its commissioner to oppose the raising of troops to invade England in support of Charles I. Kirkcudbright's returning commissioner in May 1648 'declarit ... that he dissassentit to the leveying of ane armie condiscendit be the said parliament and speciallie anent the leveing of ane armie quherunto the kirk did not aggrie'. The magistrates and council 'did not onlie allow the said dissassent and proceidingis bot also gave him verie many thankis thairfore'.[151] The response of Dumfries was the most trenchant. Its commissioner reported that he was required 'to give his voice whither thair sould be a levie presently for going to England'. The council met with the other 'considerable men' of Dumfries and 'unanimouslie ... concludit ... to abyd be ther league and covenant and ... not consent to any leavy ... untill sick tyme as they have receaved satisfactioun in thair consciences annent the lauchfullnes thairoff and example of uther burrowis or ellis be compellit'. Dumfries petitioned against the levy and adopted measures to prevent anyone from sneaking off to join the Engager army.[152] Lanark's petition regarding its losses (discussed above) records its opposition to the Engagement, while Glasgow took the same stance and was summoned before parliament for its failure to levy troops.[153]

As well as the individual commissioner's actions being dictated by his conscience, it is possible that powerful nobles could rely on the votes of certain burghs.

[147] See their entries in Young, *The Parliaments of Scotland*.

[148] Stuart (ed.), *The Miscellany of the Spalding Club*, vol. 5, 381–2.

[149] Baillie, *Letters and Journals*, vol. 3, 31–42.

[150] Stevenson, 'The Burghs and the Scottish Revolution', 168–9, discusses the burghs' tendency to take the lead from the nobility.

[151] ECA, Queensferry Council Minute Book 1634–61, SL59/1/1/1, f. 178r; *Kirkcud. Recs.*, vol. 2, 820.

[152] DAC, Dumfries Council Minutes 1643–50, WA2/1, ff. 90v–93r.

[153] GCA, Glasgow Council Minutes 1642–48, C1/1/11, 25 May 1648.

Contemporary sources speak of the marquises of Hamilton and Argyll leading the votes of burghs at the time of the Engagement.[154] It could be inferred that Perth would vote with the Ruthvens during the sixteenth century, while Aberdeen might align itself with the earls of Huntly, Cupar with the earls of Rothes and Peebles with Lord Traquair. These nobles, in turn, might help the passage of legislation, although the unicameral parliament meant that burghs did not require the 'powerful sponsors' needed to steer a bill through the upper house in England.[155] If such relationships were normal, it would be nothing more than a microcosm of the tendency of the burghs not to oppose those in power nationally. There is, however, some explicit, albeit laconic, evidence for connections between burghs and individual nobles in the parliamentary context. In 1645, Linlithgow thanked the earls of Crawford and Callendar for their support of the burgh's commissioners, suspected of complicity with the marquis of Montrose.[156] Aberdeen's letter to the earl of Lothian in 1651 reminded him that he was an honorary burgess and sought his advice and assistance in helping to ease 'the distressed estait of this poor burghe' in parliament.[157] Detailed local studies of the links between nobles and burghs might provide a deeper understanding of how these relationships worked in parliament. All that can be said here with any confidence is that burghs were not dominated by landed neighbours, in parliament or outside it.

Conclusion

Parliament was not the only central body to which a burgh could turn: the privy council, the court of session, the exchequer and, of course, the convention of burghs each provided a forum in which privileges could be defended and disputes resolved. Indeed, the regular sessions of all those bodies meant that a burgh would never have to wait more than a year to be heard before any of them, whereas several years might pass between sessions of parliament.[158] In spite of this, five out of six burghs secured at least one act of parliament between 1550 and 1651. In a study of Elizabethan England, Robert Tittler questioned why English boroughs bothered to elect MPs at all, considering how rarely they were able to obtain acts. Testing Geoffrey Elton's notion that the English parliament was 'usable', an effective force which could 'satisfy legitimate ... aspirations', he looked at individual towns and found that most never submitted bills, let alone steered them to the statute book; failure was the most likely outcome for a borough's bill and parliament was thus rarely an effective 'safety valve' for local concerns.[159] The number of ratifications passed in Scotland would suggest that its parliament was more able to operate in this way. Another explanation for the relatively healthy attendance of burgh

---

[154] Baillie, *Letters and Journals*, vol. 3, 31–7; Scally, 'The Rise and Fall of the Covenanter Parliaments', 152.

[155] Smith, *The Stuart Parliaments*, 41.

[156] NAS, Linlithgow Town Council Minute Book 1640–59, B48/9/2, 166.

[157] NAS, Lothian Muniments, The provost and bailies of Aberdeen to the earl of Lothian, 31 Jan 1651, GD40/9/31. The reason for their connection is not clear.

[158] The same was true in England: Dean, 'Parliament and Locality', 157.

[159] Tittler, 'Elizabethan Towns', 280–81.

commissioners in the Scottish parliament which is absent in the English context is the solidarity engendered by the convention of burghs: even if a burgh had nothing to promote in parliament, its councillors were aware of the need for a strong urban voice. Moreover, they would have been conscious of the need to help others, even if it was just extended self-interest: if they were to submit an act to parliament, they required the same backing. Underpinning the mutual support which the convention of burghs could provide in the parliamentary context, there was a deeper solidarity which meant that if, for example, a fire destroyed large parts of a burgh, that burgh could expect financial aid from its peers. There was no such mechanism in England, so whatever misfortunes befell a borough it stood alone.[160] Most Scottish burghs sent commissioners to most parliaments in the period of this study but they rarely expected specific legislative outcomes in their favour. It was easier to obtain an act in Scotland than in England, as much because the process of legislation in Scotland was quicker and simpler than the laborious English one of multiple readings in two houses. In that sense, the Scottish parliament was a great deal more 'usable' and effective as a point of contact between the centre and the localities than its southern sister.

---

[160] Pagan, *The Convention of Burghs*, 68; *RCRBS*, vol. 2, 33–4, 53, 56–7, 62, 76, 183; Tittler, 'Elizabethan Towns', 276.

Chapter 5

Edinburgh:
The Capital and Parliament

Introduction

On Wednesday, 30 September 1579, James VI returned to Edinburgh from his childhood home at Stirling Castle to take up residence at Holyrood. The burgesses were arrayed in armour along the High Street where the king dismounted and a volley was fired from the cannons of the castle. Just over two weeks later, his attainment to adulthood and personal government was symbolised in a formal entry: the streets were decorated with tapestries and paintings and the crowds were so great that 'manie were hurt' in the crush. Edinburgh's magistrates received their thirteen-year-old king under a purple velvet canopy; he was hailed as Solomon and a boy, emerging from a descending globe, presented him with the keys of the burgh cast in silver; musicians played on viols, psalms were sung and a sermon delivered in St Giles' church. Wine was drunk at the market cross, a fanfare of trumpets greeted the recitation of the king's genealogy and, as he left the burgh to return to his palace, he beheld the good portents of the horoscope of his birth displayed upon the Netherbow port. Three days later, on 20 October, at the first parliament to meet in Edinburgh since 1573, 'the magistratis ... propynit the King with ane goldin copbuird, estimat to sex thousand merkis'.[1] The presence of the king and the agencies of central government were worth paying for handsomely and the favour of the king was worth cultivating: in 1590, Edinburgh staged a formal entry for James's queen, Anne, and in 1617 when he returned to Edinburgh after an absence of 14 years, 'ten thousand merkis in dowble angellis of gold' were presented to him in 'ane gilt baissin'.[2] The full picture of the burgh's relationship with the crown is illustrated in another incident that occurred between James's arrival in September 1579 and his formal entry on 17 October. On 7 October, he ordered the burgh to choose Alexander Clerk as provost which the council duly did, with formal protests that this 'sould not hurt thair priviledges'.[3]

James had been at Stirling since early childhood but Edinburgh remained unquestionably the capital. For over 100 years, government had maintained a

---

[1] Calderwood, *History*, vol. 3, 457–60; Moysie, Memoirs, 25–6. Propine – gift; copbuird – cupboard (literally), but here refers to the vessels held in it; 6,000 merks was £4,000.

[2] ECA, Edinburgh Council Minutes 1609–17, SL1/1/12, f. 258r. For a fuller discussion of royal pageantry see M. Lynch, 'Court Ceremony and Ritual During the Personal Reign of James VI', in J. Goodare and M. Lynch (eds), *The Reign of James VI* (East Linton, 2000), 71–92.

[3] Calderwood, *History*, vol. 3, 458. Although declared an adult, James did not begin his personal rule until 1585, after another period of factional governments ruling in his name.

virtually permanent presence there: the central courts met in Edinburgh; the crown's records and its artillery were housed in its castle; and the royal palace of Holyrood, just outside the burgh, had become the principal residence of adult monarchs. Edinburgh's status was cemented at a time when, all over Europe, peripatetic government was disappearing as growing bureaucracies became less portable.[4] Before the Stewart kings settled there, it was already the wealthiest and largest town in the kingdom and, as happened with Madrid in the later sixteenth century, its economy grew even more after it became the capital.[5] By the sixteenth century, over half of Scotland's export duties were paid by Edinburgh, with the burgh and its dependent port of Leith handling around 80 per cent of the trade in Scotland's staple exports of wool, woolfells, hides and raw cloth by the 1590s.[6] The establishment of the central civil court, the court of session, as a permanent institution in Edinburgh in the first half of the sixteenth century, combined with the growing civil service led to Edinburgh's status becoming entrenched: when Mary went on progress to the North East and when James VI left Edinburgh on hunting trips, civil servants and officers of state remained at Edinburgh, and the privy council carried on the routine business of government. When James took a prolonged holiday in Denmark-Norway from October 1589 until May 1590 to collect his bride, Anne of Denmark, government in Edinburgh continued without him (a stamp of the royal signature was even made for use on routine letters). In 1603, when he left Scotland to take up his English inheritance, Edinburgh did not share the fate of other European capitals as the result of regal unions, left with a viceroy to carry out decisions made hundreds of miles away. Nobody was in any doubt that the government of James's ancient kingdom would remain in Edinburgh.[7] Not until parliamentary union and the abolition of the privy council in the early eighteenth century did the daily business of executive government cease to be carried out there, although the continued existence of Scotland's exchequer and legal system meant that Edinburgh retained some of the trappings of a capital.

Edinburgh and the crown

Having the king on one's doorstep created a closeness which was undoubtedly an advantage to Edinburgh, giving it readier access to the corridors of power than was available to any other burgh. The crown knew that other burghs looked to Edinburgh for a lead and it was the only burgh whose magistrates were frequently appointed by the crown and the only one whose entire council was purged on a number of occasions, yet purges were rare and only the provosts tended to be courtiers: crown-

---

[4]   A. Cowan, *Urban Europe, 1500–1700* (London, 1998), 47.

[5]   Ibid., 5, 28, 47–8.

[6]   M. Lynch, 'Introduction', in idem (ed.), *The Early Modern Town in Scotland* (London, 1987), 1–35, at 8–9. Woolfells – sheepskins with wool still attached.

[7]   *RPC*, first series, vol. 4, 118–19 (instructions left for the privy council and the exchequer when James VI went to Stirling 'to mak his residence for a certane space'); J. Goodare, *The Government of Scotland, 1567–1625* (Oxford, 2004), 140–43; L. A. M. Stewart, 'Politics and Religion in Edinburgh, 1617–1653' (Edinburgh PhD, 2003), 76–7.

nominated bailies and other office-holders were always burgesses.[8] There is also no indication that courtier-provosts fed ready-made royal decisions to the burgh council, or that its commissioners in parliament acted as agents of the crown, as London's MPs often did.[9] As far as the crown was concerned, its interventions were primarily to remind those who ran the burgh that many of its advantages rested on its relationship with central government. Indeed, Edinburgh's courtier-provosts could be as much the burgh's man at court as the court's man in the burgh.[10] In the early 1590s, Sir Alexander Home of North Berwick was imposed by the crown, in spite of the burgh's complaints. He proved to be an asset, however, and when he sought to extricate himself from office in 1595, the burgh council persuaded him to continue, even seeking royal help because, according to the English ambassador, Home was 'seen to the town to be wise and conformable to them and to have such favour at the King's hands as may stead the town'.[11] Relations between Edinburgh and James VI were so positive in 1596 that it was invited to be one of the godparents for the baptism of Princess Elizabeth, the provost and bailies representing the burgh at the service.[12]

The spending power of the royal court was a great benefit to Edinburgh's merchants and craftsmen, especially because there was no Scottish equivalent of 'purveyance', by which officers of the English crown had the right to buy goods for the court at reduced prices.[13] The resident civil servants, and the judges, lawyers and advocates who made their livings in the central courts of law also provided a boost to the burgh's economy. The market for luxuries was far greater than anywhere else in Scotland: Edinburgh's skinners, tailors and goldsmiths were particularly prominent in developing their trades to suit the demands of the court and those who served it. It was the wealth and social status of Edinburgh's craft aristocracy that secured them such a favourable deal in the decreet arbitral of 1583 (an agreement between the merchants and crafts), for it included the guarantee of a seat in parliament for a craftsman. This superficially radical arrangement needs to be understood in the local context: members of those three crafts had favoured access to the burgh's merchant guild and the majority of craft commissioners to parliament would come from their ranks. All of the 20 craft commissioners to parliaments and conventions of estates in the period of this study provided goods for the wealthy: 13 were skinners, tailors and goldsmiths, two were surgeons, and the remaining five comprised two pewterers, a saddler, a bridle-maker and a pistol-maker. The big three were even more dominant than that would suggest, their members being commissioned on 41 out of the 49 occasions when a craftsman was elected to parliaments or conventions

---

[8] M. Lynch, 'The Crown and the Burghs 1500–1625', in idem (ed.), *The Early Modern Town*, 55–80, at 55, 60, 63, 65; see also ch. 2 for interference in council elections.

[9] M. A. R. Graves, *The Tudor Parliaments: Crown, Lords and Commons, 1485–1603* (Harlow, 1985), 148–9.

[10] Lynch, 'The Crown and the Burghs', 65–6.

[11] *CSP Scot*, vol. 12, 33, 41; A. L. Juhala, 'The Household and Court of James VI of Scotland, 1567–1603' (Edinburgh PhD, 2000), 252.

[12] Ibid., 279–80.

[13] P. Croft, 'Parliament, Purveyance and the City of London 1589–1608', in *PH*, 4 (1985), 9–34.

of estates.[14] These men did not represent the craftsmen in general, for most of them had 'foresworn the actual practice of their crafts'. Their interests were those of the merchant elite, because of their wealth, reliance on international trade, and membership of the merchant guild. It was the elite members of the skinners, tailors and goldsmiths, along with the wealthier surgeons, hammermen and cordiners, who sat for the crafts around Edinburgh's council table. Few acts of parliament were obtained by craft guilds, even those of Edinburgh, whose council actually protested against a ratification for its hatmakers in 1641.[15] In contrast to London, Edinburgh's council did not regard supporting its craftsmen in parliament as its responsibility and it certainly did not seek legislative proposals from them, while the craftsmen themselves did not develop effective mechanisms for lobbying parliament or central government. Although individual crafts might occasionally supplicate the convention of burghs, it represented mercantile interests and had no desire to further those of incorporated trades except against unfree craftsmen operating outside burghs.[16] This may be one explanation for the crafts' increasing recourse to the central courts during the sixteenth century, because the national and local urban authorities tended to be so biased towards the merchants.[17]

Some wealthier craftsmen, as well as some merchants, became sufficiently rich to branch out into money-lending and investment in manufactures that were beyond the means of most Scottish burgesses.[18] Edinburgh was the principal source of credit in Scotland, with people from all over the country in debt to its lenders. Monarchs were conscious of this source of specie so Edinburgh frequently found itself forced into lending money to Mary and James VI with only limited guarantees of repayment, a situation paralleled on a larger scale in London's lending to English monarchs.[19] However, the problems of being the capital were significantly outweighed by the economic advantages. Edinburgh's growth, both in terms of its economy and its population, outstripped that of other burghs because it was the capital.[20] The merchants and craft aristocracy who ran the burgh knew this well and, however

---

[14]   Lynch, 'Introduction', 9; M. Lynch, 'Continuity and Change in Urban Society, 1500–1700', in R. A. Houston and I. D. Whyte (eds), *Scottish Society, 1500–1800* (Cambridge, 1989), 85–117, at 88, 112–13; Young, *The Parliaments of Scotland*, passim.

[15]   *APS*, vol. 5, 579, and for crafts in general see vol. 12 (index); W. Makey, 'Edinburgh in Mid-Seventeenth Century', in Lynch (ed.), *The Early Modern Town*, 192–218, at 208–15.

[16]   For London, see D. M. Dean, 'Public or Private? London, Leather and Legislation in Elizabethan England', in HJ, 31 (1988), 525–48; G. Elton, *The Parliament of England 1559–1581* (Cambridge, 1986), 77–85; J. Boulton, 'London 1540–1700', in P. Clark (ed.), *The Cambridge Urban History of Britain, Volume II 1540–1840* (Cambridge, 2000), 315–46, at 341; *RCRBS*, vol. 2, 355, 487, vol. 3, 297–8; Goodare, *The Government of Scotland*, 52.

[17]   Lynch, 'The Crown and the Burghs', 66–7.

[18]   J. J. Brown, 'Merchant Princes and Mercantile Investment in Early Seventeenth Century Scotland', in Lynch (ed.), *The Early Modern Town*, 125–46, at 136–41.

[19]   ECA, Edinburgh Council Minutes 1580–83, SL1/1/6, ff. 122v, 128r (Edinburgh was asked for £20,000 but lent only 10,000 merks or £6,666 13s 4d); *Diurnal of Occurrents*, 83–4; Juhala, 'The Household and Court of James VI', 257, 260; Goodare, *The Government of Scotland*, 102, 129; Boulton, 'London 1540–1700', 341–2.

[20]   This was a pan-European phenomenon: Cowan, *Urban Europe*, 5, 9, 12, 28, 47–8.

irritating royal requests for money might be, they were determined to maintain a happy relationship with those who made them what they were. Only once was there a serious threat to Edinburgh's position and the council was quick to placate the king and recover royal favour.[21] On 17 December 1596, James VI was sitting with the court of session in the tolbooth complex in the west end of St Giles' church. Tension between the king and the Church was high because of his lenience towards recusant Catholic nobles, and some ministers and sympathetic nobles were meeting in Edinburgh to lobby the crown. When their delegation was dismissed by the king, there was an outcry which spread to a crowd outside and, amid wild rumours of a Catholic force approaching, there was a call to arms and the king perceived a threat to his person. James blamed the magistrates and council for failing to prevent the incident and left for Linlithgow, threatening the removal of the central courts. He was serious: within a few days he was seeking a new home for the court of session and in January, the courts were moved to Perth.[22] Edinburgh sprang into action, consulting with advocates regarding 'quhat cours sall be best to follow, avoyding the trubill and daynger apperand to cum upoun this burght be the indignatioun consavit be his majestie'. After three months of careful negotiation, the king and the council of Edinburgh 'drank in the counsell hous' to mark their reconciliation, the burgh having sacked its ministers, handed over their manses for the king's use, paid him 20,000 merks (£13,333 6s 8d) and presented a set of silver-gilt keys to him upon his return.[23] This was an exceptional incident. Most of the time Edinburgh was tactful in its relationships with the crown and, whatever were the consequences of the loss of the royal court in 1603, it retained its status and many of the accompanying economic benefits with the additional bonus of no longer being asked to lend money to the crown. In 1637–1638, at the outbreak of revolution, Charles I renewed the threat to move the privy council and court of session out of the burgh, but the course of events meant that Edinburgh had no need to mollify him, holding firmly to its position under the Covenanters.[24]

Parliamentary politics

Edinburgh's relationship with the crown tempered its political role. Frequent interventions in the elections of its magistrates and occasional purges of its entire council meant that those in power in the capital often owed their position to the king or his chief advisers. Even when they did not, they would have known that defying the monarch might lead swiftly to their replacement with others more willing to

---

[21] For a brief account of events see A. R. MacDonald, *The Jacobean Kirk 1567–1625: Sovereignty, Polity and Liturgy* (Aldershot, 1998), 68–70; Calderwood, *History*, vol. 5, 510ff. Julian Goodare, who is working on a detailed study of this incident, believes it was an attempted coup.

[22] GCA, Glasgow Council Act Book 1594–97, C1/1/4, f. 141r; *RPC*, first series, vol. 4, 358.

[23] ECA, Edinburgh Council Minutes 1594–1600, SL1/1/10, f. 104v; *RPC*, first series, vol. 4, 356, 374–7; Juhala, 'The Household and Court of King James VI', 254–5. The court of session eventually returned in May 1597.

[24] *RPC*, second series, vol. 6, 537, 545.

toe the king's line. The same might be said of the burgh's authorities during the Covenanting period, when shifting political fortunes at a national level could lead to significant changes of personnel around Edinburgh's council table. Its leadership of the burghs in the Reformation parliament of 1560 has to be read in the context of the conflict which had absorbed the political nation for the previous two years and was played out in a struggle for control of the capital. The magistrates and council which sought to promote 'Goddis trew ordinance for the manteinance of the trew religioun' in parliament had been foisted on the burgh in October 1559 by the Protestant Lords of the Congregation when they took control of the burgh from the forces of the regent, Mary of Guise, just days after she had rigged the elections herself.[25] During the civil war which followed the forced abdication of Queen Mary in 1567, the same see-sawing of power accompanied its occupation by one side or the other and it was repeated with monotonous regularity between 1578 and 1584 when different factions vied for control of the young king and forced their choices of magistrates, and sometimes councillors too, on the capital.[26]

The influence exercised by central government over Edinburgh must have helped the king's cause in parliament, especially if other burghs tended to follow the capital's lead. That those in power felt the need to ensure that its magistrates were friendly is proof of Edinburgh's political influence. Yet it was not slavishly acquiescent to the royal will in parliament. Even when Edinburgh's commissioners voted for the king's measures, their council might be reluctant to enforce them. This was particularly the case when it came to religious issues. In 1592, James VI, irritated by ministers' public criticism, was attempting to foist on parliament an article which would curtail their 'libertie of speeche' and empower magistrates to 'pull the ministers out of the pulpits when they speeke after that maner'. His remarks were particularly directed towards the provost of Edinburgh, William Little, whom he regarded as responsible for allowing the capital's clergy free rein to preach sedition. Little's response was remarkable: 'Sir, yee may discharge me of my office if you please, but that I cannot doe'. James asked if he would favour the ministers over the king and his reply was 'I will preferre God before man'.[27] The king had been faced down and no act resulted. Although Edinburgh voted for the five articles of Perth in the 1621 parliament (to the consternation of the radical presbyterian minister David Calderwood), the wider context suggests that its support for the crown was not unalloyed. The burgesses on the articles, where Edinburgh was always represented, were united in their resistance to the proposed tax on interest payments and annuities, which would have hit Edinburgh's moneylenders particularly hard. Edinburgh was also the centre of opposition to these religious innovations and, as parliament approached, pressure was applied to the magistrates and council to persuade them to submit an article against their ratification. The magistrates were sympathetic but no article was submitted because, in the words of one of the burgh's ministers, 'such a sute from the toun wold be prejudiciall to the rest of their sutes'. The council's subsequent reluctance

[25]   ECA, Edinburgh Council Minutes 1558–61, SL1/1/3, f. 42r–v; M. Lynch, *Edinburgh and the Reformation* (Edinburgh, 1981), 76–7.

[26]   Ibid., chs 5–8; *RPC*, first series, vol. 3, 19–20, 36–7.

[27]   Calderwood, *History*, vol. 5, 161–2.

to enforce the five articles, in spite of royal demands, indicates that its parliamentary support for them may indeed have been designed to ensure a favourable reception for its legislative programme from the crown's parliamentary managers.[28]

Edinburgh's role in the Covenanting revolution of 1637–1638 and the subsequent years of revolutionary government until 1651 has recently been the subject of detailed study, the conclusion of which is, unsurprisingly, that the priority of its ruling elite was to ensure stability by backing whoever was in power.[29] This was a common pattern throughout Europe, with towns responding pragmatically to political change, aware that, whatever the legality of the claims of new rulers, 'an army encamped before the city gates conferred legitimacy enough'.[30] In 1637, Edinburgh had better reasons than many to join the opposition, having suffered unprecedented taxes and renewed royal meddling in municipal elections. It was also struggling to cope with the financial consequences of the king's demand that St Giles' be turned into a cathedral for the new diocese of Edinburgh, with the knock-on effect that two new parish churches were required. Yet, although the burgh's authorities were probably sympathetic to those who protested against the royal imposition of a new prayer book and were reluctant to punish them in spite of royal commands to do so, the council threw its support behind the opposition only once it was clear that it was 'the only viable political power in the country' and only after other burghs had petitioned against the religious innovations. Yet Edinburgh's endorsement of the revolution appears to have persuaded the rest of the burghs to join the cause.[31] The capital's ruling elite subsequently became closely involved with the Covenanting regime, co-operating with the leading nobles, keeping the burghs in touch with what was going on and summoning their commissioners to meetings at Edinburgh. As parliamentary sessions stretched to weeks and months, the capital hosted more of the political elite than had regularly been there since the royal court had left in 1603, bringing their money with them and boosting the burgh's economy. However financially straitened burgh councils might have been by the demands of the cause of the Covenant, many in Edinburgh made a tidy profit.

Always trying to keep on the right side of the powers that be is a challenge when factional swings mean that those in power regard the previous incumbents as enemies of the nation. Edinburgh had a brush with this in 1645 when the marquis of Montrose forced it to release royalist prisoners during his rising against the Covenanting regime. The burgh was able to convince parliament and the committee

---

[28]   Stewart, 'Politics and Religion in Edinburgh', ch. 5; Lynch, 'The Crown and the Burghs', 71; J. Goodare, 'The Scottish Parliament of 1621', in The *Historical Journal*, 38 (1995), 29–51, at 33–4, 41; Calderwood, *History*, vol. 7, 460–61. I am grateful to Laura Stewart for discussions of this and for allowing me to read a draft article on the subject.

[29]   Stewart, 'Politics and Religion in Edinburgh', chs 6 and 7.

[30]   C. R. Friedrichs, *Urban Politics in Early Modern Europe* (London, 2000), 21.

[31]   Stewart, 'Politics and Religion in Edinburgh', 183; D. Stevenson, 'The Burghs and the Scottish Revolution', in Lynch (ed.), *The Early Modern Town*, 167–91, at 167, 177–8; D. Stevenson, *The Scottish Revolution 1637–1644: the Triumph of the Covenanters* (Newton Abbot, 1973), 66; John Spalding, *The History of the Troubles and Memorable Transactions in Scotland and England from 1624–1645*, J. Stuart (ed.), 2 vols (Edinburgh, 1828–9), vol. 2, 48.

of estates that it had had no option but to acquiesce in the face of insurmountable military force. To prove its case, it even sent its council minutes for inspection to St Andrews, where the estates were meeting in December 1645.[32] In 1648, a very different situation plunged Edinburgh into crisis, denting its influence among the other burghs and bringing back levels of central intervention unknown since the 1580s. When the royalist Engagers took power early in 1648, the magistrates and council of Edinburgh chose not to oppose them. In parliament, Edinburgh's example is said to have led many burghs to fall in behind the Engagement when it came to voting for a levy of troops to invade England on behalf of the king.[33] The capital itself, however, was internally divided, with its ministers and popular opinion opposed to the Engagement while its ruling elite felt compelled to acquiesce because the Engagers had taken control of the capital. The ministers and six kirk sessions of Edinburgh petitioned the council not to support the Engagement until the 'kirk and weill affected persones may be satisfied in thair consciences'.[34] In what was possibly an attempt at compromise, and well aware that the inhabitants might react violently if asked to fight for a cause which many opposed, Edinburgh agreed to contribute £40,000 to the Engagers in return for exemption from the levy.[35] The Engager regime disintegrated after the defeat of its army in England and was replaced with radical Covenanters, led by the marquis of Argyll. At the next council elections in October 1648, the new government instigated a thorough purge and the council formally disowned the Engagement.[36] Edinburgh's position was undermined and the other burghs took advantage, raising its share of taxation from 27 to 36 per cent of the burghs' total. Although falling short of Edinburgh's share of urban wealth and less than its proportion of the burghs' valued rent, it was enough to satisfy those who 'had been long grudging that Edinburgh should bear so small a proportion' and indicated the erosion of the influence which had previously kept its share of taxes artificially low.[37] Although Edinburgh was unable to overturn this decision, its parliamentary successes in 1649 (it obtained eight acts in its favour) and the return to prominence of its provost as the leader of the burgess estate suggests that it was quick to regain its former standing.[38]

---

[32]   ECA, Edinburgh Council Minutes 1644–48, SL1/1/16, ff. 69r–70r; *APS*, vol. 6, part 1, 476, 478, 502; Stewart, 'Politics and Religion in Edinburgh', ch. 7; Stevenson, 'The Burghs and the Scottish Revolution', 186.

[33]   Baillie, *Letters and Journals*, vol. 2, 31–42; Stevenson, 'The Burghs and the Scottish Revolution', 172.

[34]   ECA, Edinburgh Council Minutes 1644–48, SL1/1/16, f. 278r.

[35]   Ibid., ff. 277v, 279v–281r.

[36]   ECA, Edinburgh Council Minutes 1648–53, SL1/1/17, ff. 48v–62v.

[37]   Baillie, *Letters and Journals*, vol. 3, 98–9; Lynch, 'Continuity and Change', 101–103.

[38]   *APS*, vol. 6, part 2, 225–7, 241–2, 364–7, 416–19, 448, 491–2, 517, 723; *Spalding Miscellany*, vol. 5, 381–2; Stewart, 'Politics and Religion in Edinburgh', ch. 7.

The convention's standing committee

Edinburgh's close connections with those in government, through commerce and daily familiarity, both before and after the departure of the monarchy in 1603, meant that its council was the first to become aware of developments at the centre. If a case before the privy council or the court of session touched upon the interests of the free burghs, if a new policy initiative emerged from central government, Edinburgh might respond immediately. Consequently, the burghs saw Edinburgh as their first line of defence, the guardian of their rights and privileges, their watchtower. The crown too looked to it as a conduit into the Scottish merchant community, the first port of call whenever the views of that body were desired. Although Edinburgh's dominance of Scotland's trade goes some way to explaining this, it cannot be the entire explanation, for there is a striking parallel in the ecclesiastical sphere. First the ministers, then the kirk session and, from around 1580, the presbytery of Edinburgh served as the Church's eyes and ears, charged by the general assembly to lobby at court and call extraordinary assemblies should the need arise. But there was much more to the national role of the presbytery of Edinburgh, for it was given a range of tasks by the general assembly, including arbitration between disputing presbyteries, while other presbyteries sought its advice and guidance on various matters. The crown also recognised its status, using it as a surrogate for the Church as a whole when a quick response was required.[39] Although the role of the council of Edinburgh in the affairs of the burghs was remarkably similar to that of the presbytery in the ecclesiastical context, there were differences. The presbytery lost its remit to a general assembly commission appointed by the king in 1597 after becoming associated with the 'riot' of 1596, while the council of Edinburgh retained its standing with the crown by distancing itself from the same incident. Well aware that its primary concern was the economic interests of its merchant community, Edinburgh usually tried not to be too closely identified with the more subversive tendencies of its ministers. A brief flirtation with them in the early 1580s had led quickly to one of the crown's occasional purges of the council.[40]

The crown might remove individual magistrates and councillors but this actually served to maintain the burgh's position, while ensuring that a sympathetic ear was usually inclined towards its merchant elite. Edinburgh's huge share of the nation's trade also meant that its status was more firmly rooted than that of the presbytery of Edinburgh within the Church. It could not have been sidelined without serious inconvenience to the crown and significant disruption to Scotland's economy, whatever James VI may have threatened in 1596–1597. With more trade than the rest of the burghs put together, its interests were inseparable from those of the Scottish merchant community as a whole, indeed they might be said to have overshadowed them, for there were occasionally tensions between Edinburgh and the rest of the parliamentary burghs.

---

[39] For details of Edinburgh presbytery's role, see A. R. MacDonald, 'Ecclesiastical Politics in Scotland, 1586–1610' (Edinburgh PhD, 1995), ch. 3.

[40] M. Lynch, 'The Origins of Edinburgh's "toun college": a Revision Article', in *Innes Review*, 33 (1982), 3–14, at 4–5, 7, 9.

The crown's desire to use Edinburgh as a surrogate for urban Scotland was not commonly expressed but did occasionally manifest itself, as in 1552 when Mary of Guise and her privy council ordered that 'the Proveist and Ballies of Edinburch suld tax the haill borrowis' to finance a force of foot soldiers. Such behaviour was not to the liking of other burghs which complained that they were 'hurt be the setting ... of taxatiounis upoun thame be the toune of Edinburght' because it was 'abone [i.e. above] thair pussance and faculte' to do so.[41] The burghs soon successfully established the need for their consent to taxations, setting up in 1574 a sub-group of ten (with a quorum that must include Edinburgh) to do this on their behalf, although some continued to complain of financial demands from the capital.[42] The crown might seek the advice of Edinburgh's magistrates on specific issues (they were added to a commission of enquiry into the quality of the coinage in 1584) but nothing like the relationship between the Swedish kings and Stockholm developed, whereby the capital was expected to speak for the other towns.[43] Indeed, on two occasions in 1621 when Edinburgh was approached by agencies of central government seeking the view of the burghs, Edinburgh's response was the same: 'they wer bot ane burgh and could not do in suche a mater be thame selffis allone' for it should be 'comitted to the consideratioun of the haill burrowis'.[44]

It is hardly surprising that the crown occasionally tested the waters of burgh opinion by speaking to Edinburgh, considering how often the burghs themselves handed responsibilities to the capital.[45] The access to the monarch provided by its courtier-provosts (privy councillors like Sir Simon Preston in the 1560s or even officers of state like Alexander Seton, president of the court of session, and Sir John Arnot of Birswick, treasurer depute in the 1590s and 1600s) is part of the explanation for Edinburgh lobbying the crown in the interests of the burghs. While the written evidence suggests that it tended to resort to the privy council rather than the court, Michael Lynch has observed that, although the 'channels of communication' between the crown and the burghs are easily identified, it is hard to 'assess the instructions and expectations' passing along them. It would have been perverse had Edinburgh not used its court connections to its own advantage.[46] It also had a wealth of legal expertise on its doorstep, for the presence of the central courts, particularly the court of session, meant that the burgh had more lawyers and advocates than any other. Many of those who might provide legal counsel were members of the community

---

[41]   *RPC*, first series, vol. 1, 131; ACA, Aberdeen Council Registers, CR1/23, 319.

[42]   AAC, Ayr Court and Council Records 1580–96, B6/11/2, f. 123r; *RCRBS*, vol. 1, 33; *APS*, vol. 3, 543.

[43]   H. Schück, 'Sweden's Early Parliamentary Institutions from the Thirteenth Century to 1611', in M. F. Metcalf (ed.), *The Riksdag: A History of the Swedish Parliament* (New York, 1987), 5–60; CSP Scot, vol. 13, part 1, 136; *RPC*, first series, vol. 3, 641; Stewart, 'Politics and Religion in Edinburgh', 78–9.

[44]   *RPC*, first series, vol. 12, 84–5; *APS*, vol. 4, 590. Edinburgh responded similarly in 1633 regarding a dispute with the earl of Errol over his jurisdiction, during parliament, as high constable of Scotland: *RPC*, second series, vol. 5, 111–12.

[45]   See Edinburgh's entry in J. D. Marwick, *Index to Extracts from the Records of the Convention of the Royal Burghs of Scotland, 1295–1738* (Edinburgh, 1890), 77–80.

[46]   Goodare, *The Government of Scotland*, 36; Lynch, 'The Crown and the Burghs', 66.

of the burgh and wealthy ones too. In 1635 a tax on all householders revealed that lawyers paid more tax at the higher end of the earnings scale than all but the merchants. The lawyers' status was bound up with that of Edinburgh as the capital and they formed an important part of the burgh's ruling 'patriciate'.[47]

Without the existence of the convention of burghs, Edinburgh could not have exercised such a pivotal national role: just as the general assembly of the Church gave a peculiar national status to the presbytery of Edinburgh, so the convention of burghs granted the same status to the burgh council, commissioning it to carry out a wide range of functions. Its common seal would represent the consent of all burghs to written instructions for commissioners to the king in England at the time of his coronation in 1603.[48] In the 1580s, it was charged with keeping the records of conventions of burghs, the office of clerk of the convention usually being held by Edinburgh's own clerk.[49] It was appointed to stand as the legal representative of the burghs before the court of session in their persistent campaign to combat the encroachments of unfree traders from burghs of barony.[50] It was also commissioned to complain to the privy council about abuses of burgh privileges and the crown's failure to implement statute.[51] It was even asked to lobby the general assembly of the Church in an effort to stamp out rural Sunday markets (having already done away with them, the burghs resented the continuation of rural competition).[52] Disputes between individual burghs were referred to Edinburgh by the convention of burghs, although it was not always a willing recipient of this role, refusing outright to judge the dispute between Perth and Dundee over parliamentary precedence in 1587.[53] Edinburgh's role even extended beyond Scotland's shores. The convention of burghs had a remarkably prominent role in Scotland's international relations, participating in royal embassies and sometimes even sending independent trade delegations to foreign princes. Their ambassadors were almost always merchants from Edinburgh, which had in its archives in 1638 a collection of 39 documents relating to Scotland's trading privileges in France alone.[54] Individual burghs also

---

[47] Makey, 'Edinburgh in Mid-Seventeenth Century', 207–8; G. Donaldson, 'The Legal Profession in Scottish Society in the Sixteenth and Seventeenth Centuries', in *Juridical Review*, 21 (1976), 1–19; E. P. Dennison and M. Lynch, 'Crown, Capital, and Metropolis. Edinburgh and Canongate: the Rise of a Capital and an Urban Court', in *Journal of Urban History*, 32 (2005), 22–43, at 29.

[48] ECA, Edinburgh Council Minutes 1551–58, SL1/1/2, f. 51r; *RCRBS*, vol. 2, 163–4.

[49] *RCRBS*, vol. 1, 103, 120, 155–61, 416–17, vol. 2, 576–81; Perth Guildry Incorporation, Lockit Book 1451–1631, 594. Edinburgh was not always careful with the records, managing to lose a whole volume (covering 1631–49) between 1700 and 1878: see *RCRBS*, vol. 2, v–vii.

[50] *RCRBS*, vol. 1, 137, vol. 2, 373, 424, vol. 3, 143.

[51] *RCRBS*, vol. 1, 22, 137, 167, vol. 2, 323, 353, vol. 3, 53; *Edin. Recs.*, 1573–89, 90–91.

[52] *RCRBS*, vol. 1, 35; Goodare, *The Government of Scotland*, 190–91, notes the relative effectiveness of the burghs in implementing statute.

[53] *RCRBS*, vol. 1, 232–3, 364, 375–6 (for the dispute between Perth and Dundee see ch. 7).

[54] ACA, Aberdeen Council Registers, CR1/7, 709; *RPC*, first series, vol. 7, 377–8; *RCRBS*, vol. 1, 16, 50, 127, 140–43, 482–3, vol. 2, 39, 104, 333–5, 576–81.

looked to Edinburgh: in 1607, Perth sent a commissioner to its provost to ask for help in lobbying the government for relief from a recent parliamentary tax, while in 1637 Linlithgow engaged Edinburgh's aid in its campaign to block the erection of South Queensferry.[55]

The most important power given to Edinburgh by the convention of burghs was the summoning of extraordinary conventions. Every year, the annual general convention of burghs in July ended with the date and place of its next meeting being fixed. Well aware that matters often arose which required a response from the burghs but which might not wait until the next scheduled meeting, the convention authorised Edinburgh to summon the commissioners of burghs if, in its judgement, their deliberation and response were required. Sometimes this involved only a select group (nominated by the convention) but it could also result in a summons to all parliamentary burghs. It is not clear whether this power was first granted by the convention of burghs or whether Edinburgh took it upon itself before being explicitly authorised by the convention: Edinburgh summoned the burghs to meet as early as 1558, while the first record of the convention authorising it to do so dates from 1571.[56] These meetings covered a range of internal burgh affairs, including revision of the burghs' tax roll (by which it was laid down what proportion of parliamentary taxes each paid) and dealing with the conservator of Scottish privileges at the staple port of Veere in the Netherlands. They could also negotiate with the privy council and, during the 1640s, the committee of estates on such things as customs rates, manufactures and fisheries. Other, less prosaic matters might also give rise to an unplanned convention. In March 1603, with the departure of James VI for England imminent, Edinburgh called commissioners from all the burghs 'to consult upone sic thingis as may concerne the weill of our estait', urging that they come immediately 'in awentouris [i.e. in case] his majestie remove befor they come'.[57]

From an early stage, Edinburgh's power to summon extraordinary conventions of burghs included the specification that one should be called if a parliament 'intervened'.[58] The first record of this comes from 1560 and, four years later, Edinburgh again sent letters 'to all the burrois for convening of the commissarris

---

[55]   PKCA, Register of Acts of the Council of Perth 1601–22, B59/16/1, f. 134r–v; NAS, Linlithgow Town Council Minute Book 1620–40, B48/9/1, 368–9.

[56]   ACA, Aberdeen Council Registers, CR1/23, 26; *RCRBS*, vol. 1, 17–18, vol. 2, 6–9, 489–92, vol. 3, 219; ACA, Acts of Convention 1610–36, CRB, vol. 2, f. 433r. The patchy nature of the records of the convention before the 1580s makes it impossible make a definitive judgement on this question.

[57]   ECA, Edinburgh Council Minutes 1580–83, SL1/1/6, f. 213v (customs), Edinburgh Council Minutes 1644–48, SL1/1/16, ff. 172v, 196v (negotiations with the committee of estates); ACA, Aberdeen Council Registers, CR1/23, 26 (taxation); NAS, Burntisland Council Minutes 1639–42, B9/12/7, ff. 119r (fishing), 143v (negotiations with the privy council); DCA, Dundee Council Minutes, vol. 2, 1588–1603, 40 (conservator); NAS, Dysart Burgh Registers, Court Book 1603–50, B21/8/7, f. 264v (fishing); GCA, Glasgow Council Act Book 1598–1601, C1/1/5, f. 154r (manufactures); PKCA, Register of Acts of the Council of Perth 1601–22, B59/16/1, ff. 46v–47r (departure of the king in 1603), 333v (customs); FCAC, Kirkcaldy Burgh Court Book 1586–91, 1/06/02, f. 117r (the king's marriage).

[58]   *RCRBS*, vol. 1, 17–18, 108, vol. 2, 19–21, vol. 3, 194, 275–7.

thairof for ressonyng upoun the effairis of merchanttis before the nixt parliament'.[59] It continued to exercise this power throughout the period of this study, ensuring that the burghs had the opportunity to prepare their parliamentary agenda in advance.[60] During the 1640s, the committee of estates took advantage of Edinburgh's habit of writing to all the burghs before a parliamentary session by asking it to summon them to parliament as well as to their preparatory convention.[61] Edinburgh's co-ordinating role with regard to parliament was not confined to calling the convention of burghs. Both before and after their commissioners had gathered, the capital continued to draw upon its connections and financial resources to enhance the cause of their estate. Its records contain numerous references to payments to lawyers and advocates for legal advice and to clerks for drafting articles to be submitted to parliament on behalf of the burghs, often at the behest of the convention of burghs.[62]

The capital's leadership of the burghs continued within parliament with formal protests on behalf of the estate being made and paid for by Edinburgh's commissioners.[63] During the 1640s, this role was formalised and enhanced by the emergence of a 'speaker' for the burghs: the principal commissioner from Edinburgh, usually its provost, took on this role, protesting on their behalf against the increase in shire votes in 1640 and the admission of commissioners from the stewartry of Kirkcudbright in 1646. Edinburgh's principal commissioner was also regarded as their leader by commissioners from other burghs trying to secure an act of parliament.[64] Edinburgh's special status was recognised in 1641 when the king's list of nominees to the privy council was submitted to parliament: it included the 'provest of Edinbrughe for the tyme', which was retained by parliament while eight of the king's other nominees were removed. The provost would sit *ex officio* and, although the privy council was eclipsed by the committee of estates during the 1640s, Edinburgh was always represented on that body too.[65] Perhaps the most

---

[59] ECA, Edinburgh Council Minutes, 1558–60, SL1/1/3, f. 39r, Edinburgh Council Minutes 1561–71, SL1/1/4, f. 115r.

[60] ECA, Edinburgh Council Minutes 1594–1600, SL1/1/10, f. 155v, Edinburgh Council Minutes 1617–26, SL1/1/13, f. 148r, Edinburgh Council Minutes 1626–36, SL1/1/14, f. 266r, Edinburgh Council Minutes 1636–44, SL1/1/15, ff. 97v, 153v–154r, Edinburgh Council Minutes 1648–53, SL1/1/17, f. 82v.

[61] *Edin. Recs.*, 1626–41, 246.

[62] ECA: Edinburgh Town Treasurer's Accounts 1581–96, 707; Edinburgh Council Minutes 1580–83, SL1/1/6, ff. 163v, 166v; Edinburgh Council Minutes 1589–94, SL1/1/9, f. 254r; Edinburgh Council Minutes 1594–1600, SL1/1/20, f. 22v; Edinburgh Council Minutes 1609–17, SL1/1/12, f. 97v; *Edin. Recs.*, 1573–89, 350; *Edin. Recs.*, 1626–41, 243; *RCRBS*, vol. 1, 22, 210, 238, vol. 2, 129.

[63] ECA, Edinburgh Council Minutes 1579–83, SL1/1/6, f. 166v, Edinburgh Council Minutes 1636–44, SL1/1/15, f. 140r, Edinburgh Treasurer's Accounts 1581–96, account for 1581–2, account for 1583–4, account for 1593–4; *Edin. Recs.*, 1573–89, 350. Many protestations were not recorded in the official books of parliament.

[64] The shire commissioners also had a 'speaker': Balfour, *Works*, vol. 3, 105, 422–3; *Spalding Miscellany*, vol. 5, 381–2 (Aberdeen's commissioner named the leading noble, laird and burgess in parliament).

[65] Balfour, *Works*, vol. 3, 67–8; J. R. Young, *The Scottish Parliament 1639–1661* (Edinburgh, 1996), 163; and see Young, *Parliaments of Scotland*, vol. 2, 664–5.

remarkable aspect of Edinburgh's role as a standing committee of the burghs is that there is no evidence that it reclaimed the considerable expenses it devoted to advancing the burghs' cause, in sending letters to summon conventions, paying for legal advice, drawing up articles for submission to parliament and making formal protestations. Only when it came to lengthy cases before the court of session was there any question of financial compensation.[66] Edinburgh knew that its interests were so closely intertwined with those of the burghs as a whole that it was more than willing to shoulder the expense of promoting those interests. As with all burghs, it is reasonable to aver that local interests took precedence over national ones, yet in so many contexts, the two were the same for Edinburgh.[67]

Lobbying and legislation

The techniques employed by Edinburgh in securing legislation, for itself and for the burghs in general, had much in common with those used by others. Its accounts record payments to advocates for advice on the drafting of articles for submission to parliament and payments to clerks for writing out fair copies.[68] The quality of the legal advice available to Edinburgh was second to none; indeed, most burghs went there for counsel. During the 1580s and 1590s, Edinburgh regularly resorted to one of its resident lawyers, John Sharp, for legal advice, but it also called upon the king's advocate and the clerk register to help with drafting acts of parliament.[69] As well as using the professional services of officers of state, the burgh sought to ingratiate itself by giving gifts to powerful individuals. In 1587, John Maitland of Thirlestane, the king's secretary, was given half a tun of Bordeaux and a pipe of sack 'considerand quhow necessar and proffitabill it may be ... to bayth the generall effaires of the estaitt of burrowes and particulare effaires of this burght'.[70] The clerk register, who oversaw the clerks of parliament, was another figure whose favour was worth cultivating: in 1604, he was given £166 13s 4d 'for gud plesures and gratitudes done and to be done be him to the gude toun', and his successor in 1649 was rewarded for 'paines taken in Parliament in the touns affaires'.[71] In 1612, a debt of 4,000 merks (£2,666 13s 4d) owed by Lord Balfour of Burleigh to the burgh

---

66   *RCRBS*, vol. 1, 137, vol. 2, 424.

67   Stewart, 'Politics and Religion in Edinburgh', 58.

68   See ECA, Edinburgh Town Treasurer's Accounts 1581–96, accounts for 1581–2, 1592–3, 1593–4, Edinburgh Town Treasurer's Accounts 1636–50, accounts for 1643–4, 1646–7.

69   ECA, Edinburgh Town Treasurer's Accounts, 1612–23, 476, Edinburgh Town Treasurer's Accounts 1636–50, 22, 27. The clerk register was a trained lawyer responsible for government records.

70   ECA, Edinburgh Council Minutes 1586–89, SL1/1/8, ff. 94v–95r. Half a tun was *c.*570 litres, while a pipe was *c.*430 litres. The total (*c.*1,000 litres) is equivalent to *c.*1,333 bottles.

71   ECA, Edinburgh Council Minutes 1600–1609, SL1/1/11, f. 152r–v; *Edin. Recs.*, 1641–55, 192.

was simply written off 'for the guid offices done to the toune' by him.[72] Although Edinburgh obtained no acts specifically in its favour at that parliament, its ruling elite would have been the main beneficiaries of 'Ane act pardonying the bypast escaips of some pœnall statuts thairin mentioned', for it mitigated the punishments for those who had lent money at a higher rate of interest than the legal maximum of ten per cent.[73] It is not always possible to link specific statutes to particular acts of generosity but these gifts must have made influential individuals more disposed to look upon its requests more positively. Edinburgh's largesse was not restricted to those of high rank: it also ensured that the ordinary officers of parliament were favourable to its interests by providing occasional gratuities to the macers and clerks.[74] Geoffrey Elton has shown that London cultivated the same sorts of relationships to promote its parliamentary agenda.[75]

As well as the named recipients, many others must have received payments or gifts. In 1607 white wine, claret, ale and bread were provided for the commissioners of the burghs on the first and last days of parliament, with the bishops also benefiting on the first day.[76] In 1649, the burgh commissioners were specially convened and Edinburgh's treasurer was ordered to provide 'a sufficient deseart' for 'thair four houris' (a light afternoon refreshment) so that 'they may be spokin anent the touns affaires now presentlie passing in parliament'.[77] The burgh records are sometimes considerably more coy about who was being rewarded. In 1621, Edinburgh's commissioners were given 'such soumes ... as ar necessar for doeing of thair effaires in this parliament' without specifying to whom they were to be paid or for what.[78] In 1639, over £300 was given to 'a secreit friend to befriend our effairis in parliament' and, in a later session of the same parliament, an anonymous 'persone of creditt whom they will trust' was sent to the king 'anent such affaires as concerned the towne in privat'.[79] In 1649, having obtained a number of beneficial acts 'with a great deall of toyll, trouble and dificultie', the council thanked the provost for his efforts and agreed to refund his expenses. However, because it was deemed to be 'verie unfitt and unnecessar that the particular way of these things sould be maid knowen and manefest to everie persone', a select group of the council was empowered to 'determine quhat gratificatiouns, acknowledgmentis, allowances, debursementis or any thing else utherwayis necessarie in thair discreation sall be thoght fitt to be gevin', up to a maximum of 5,000 merks (£3,333 6s 8d). A number of acts which were vital to the burgh's ability to continue functioning had just been obtained, its entire annual income being unable even to pay the interest on its loans. Some debts

---

[72]   ECA, Edinburgh Council Minutes 1609–17, SL1/1/12, ff. 97v, 103v. Balfour was a master of the king's household and a privy councillor.

[73]   *APS*, vol. 4, 473–4.

[74]   ECA, Edinburgh Council Minutes 1573–79, SL1/1/5, f. 173v, Edinburgh Council Minutes 1589–94, SL1/1/9, f. 153v, Edinburgh Council Minutes 1600–1609, SL1/1/11, f. 147v.

[75]   Elton, *The Parliament of England 1559–1581*, 76–7.

[76]   ECA, Edinburgh Town Treasurer's Accounts 1596–1612, 851.

[77]   *Edin. Recs.*, 1641–55, 185.

[78]   ECA, Edinburgh Council Minutes 1617–26, SL1/1/13, f. 157r.

[79]   ECA, Edinburgh Council Minutes 1636–44, SL1/1/15, f. 182r.

were written off by parliament and it was granted permission to impose a levy on all sales of wine and tobacco to boost its income.[80] The bribes had been well spent.

After 1603, Edinburgh's lobbying at court becomes more visible because it required more planning and the expenses of those sent on to London had to be accounted for. On more than one occasion its clerk depute, John Hay, 'raid to London befoir the parliament'.[81] He formally became a commissioner to court for the convention of burghs in the 1620s, but as early as 1612, he was sent south for 'the commoun weill of this burgh and haill burrowes'. He was given instructions relating to the issues that he was to raise and was sent with letters addressed to named courtiers upon whom Edinburgh believed it could rely for support. Similar provisions were made in 1621.[82] Hay's instructions were drawn up by specially-appointed sub-committees of the council, a device also used to advise the burgh's parliamentary commissioners. The appointment of a sub-committee is first recorded in the council minutes in 1579 and it became a normal part of Edinburgh's parliamentary preparations for the rest of the period of this study; its remit always included the discussion of the interests of the burghs in general as well as those of Edinburgh. The council, taking advantage of the fact that parliament usually met in Edinburgh, might even instruct the sub-committee to meet 'induring the ... parliament' as well as before it, further proof of the openness of its deliberative processes after the appointment of the committee of the articles.[83]

Edinburgh's economic dominance meant that it would have been easy for it to confuse its own interests with those of the whole estate of burghs. Indeed, those interests were literally confused for they were inextricably intermingled. It is hard to imagine anything that affected the burghs as a whole that did not affect Edinburgh more than any other. That Edinburgh was well aware of this is demonstrated by its enthusiastic defence, at its own expense, of the burghs' collective privileges both within and outwith parliament. An act of 1582 which sought to ensure the proper collection of customs provides a good example. The bulk of the customs was collected as a result of the capital's export trade; the crown suspected widespread evasion and when it sought to tighten its grip on the monitoring of trade so that the customs might be gathered more effectively, Edinburgh formally protested in

[80] ECA, Edinburgh Council Minutes 1648–53, SL1/1/17, ff. 129r–131r.

[81] ECA, Edinburgh Town Treasurer's Accounts 1596–1612, account for 1611–12, Edinburgh Council Minutes 1617–26, f. 145r.

[82] ECA, Edinburgh Council Minutes 1609–17, f. 97v, Edinburgh Council Minutes 1617–26, SL1/1/13, f. 145r; *Edin. Recs.*, 1626–41, 75–6; *RCRBS*, vol. 3, 187–92, 213–17, 257–8, 263. For the origins of an agent for the burghs at court, see *RCRBS*, vol. 2, 379, 406.

[83] ECA, Edinburgh Council Minutes 1573–79, SL1/1/5, f. 169r, Edinburgh Council Minutes 1589–94, SL1/1/9, ff. 207v, 254r, Edinburgh Council Minutes 1594–1600, SL1/1/10, f. 22v, Edinburgh Council Minutes 1600–1609, SL1/1/11, f. 230r; Edinburgh Council Minutes 1609–12, SL1/1/12, f. 101r, Edinburgh Council Minutes 1617–26, SL1/1/13, f. 143v, Edinburgh Council Minutes 1626–36, SL1/1/14, f. 260v, Edinburgh Council Minutes 1636–44, SL1/1/15, f. 182r, Edinburgh Council Minutes 1644–48, SL1/1/16, ff. 31r, 249r; *Edin. Recs.*, 1626–41, 121, 222; A. R. MacDonald, 'Deliberative Processes in Parliament, c.1567–1639: Multicameralism and the Lords of the Articles', in *SHR*, 81 (2002), 23–51. No papers from these committees survive.

parliament 'in name of the burrowis'.[84] However, Edinburgh did not confuse its own interests and those of the burghs in general in the sense that it was uncertain about which was which. It had its own particular parliamentary agendas to pursue and it went about that task with as much enthusiasm and a good degree of success, judging by the number of acts of parliament it secured.

Before any other burgh secured an act in its favour, Edinburgh already had eight under its belt, apparently pioneering the private act of parliament in Scotland.[85] Acts secured by Edinburgh were not markedly different from those obtained by other burghs, for they dealt with revenues, economic privileges, public order and the jurisdiction of the burgh authorities. The difference between Edinburgh's legislative haul and that of other burghs lies in its size: between 1550 and 1651, 48 acts of parliament were passed in its favour, nearly one fifth of all acts secured by individual burghs.[86] Edinburgh's primary legislative concern (accounting for nearly one in four of its statutes) was the financial support of its ministers, charitable foundations and university. As a group, these form a useful case study of the capital's legislative agenda and achievements. Although some revenues from the pre-Reformation Church had been secured at the Reformation, these proved inadequate: they were difficult to collect, the number of ministers kept growing and so did their stipends.[87] At the Reformation, one over-burdened minister, John Knox, had a low-paid assistant, a reader who could neither preach nor administer the sacraments. Two years later, a second minister was appointed and by the 1580s there were four, then five in the 1590s, six after 1600, eight in the 1620s when the burgh was divided into four parishes and, in the later 1640s, the provision peaked at ten. Added to this, there were charitable hospitals to look after, including a new one founded by the legacy of goldsmith George Heriot in the seventeenth century, and the town's college (the University of Edinburgh) which opened its doors to its first students in 1583.[88] The burgh benefited relatively meagrely from the crown's grant of the thirds of benefices, whereby part of pre-Reformation Church livings were diverted to support the parish ministry in 1562. Although it obtained the properties of the Dominicans and Franciscans, other neighbouring ecclesiastical properties outside its walls were beyond its reach.[89] As a result, money to support the ministry, the poor hospitals and the college had to be found from other sources, including direct taxes on the burgh's inhabitants. The 12 acts of parliament ratifying Edinburgh's right to collect certain revenues between 1579 and 1649 were part of the ongoing efforts to ensure that these services were properly funded, which also involved a number

---

[84]   ECA, Edinburgh Town Treasurer's Accounts 1581–96, 7; *Edin. Recs.*, 1573–89, 232. For details of struggles between the burghs and the crown over customs, see J. Goodare, *State and Society in Early Modern Scotland* (Oxford, 1999), 113–15.

[85]   *APS*, vol. 2, 314, 374, 378, vol. 3, 59, 76, 83. The first two were obtained in 1526.

[86]   See ch. 4 for individual burghs' legislation.

[87]   For details on how Edinburgh faced the challenge of paying for its ministers, see Lynch, *Edinburgh and the Reformation*, 28, 31–5, 47n, and W. Makey, *The Church of the Covenant 1637–1651* (Edinburgh, 1979), 117–21.

[88]   Lynch, 'The Origins of Edinburgh's "toun college"'; D. B. Horn, *A Short History of the University of Edinburgh 1556–1889* (Edinburgh, 1967), 1–6.

[89]   Lynch, 'The Origins of Edinburgh's "toun college"', 6.

of cases before the court of session to secure various ecclesiastical revenues from inhabitants unwilling to part with their money.[90]

These acts indicate that Edinburgh experienced persistent problems with the collection of endowed revenues, as well as unwillingness on the part of the populace to make up the shortfall between the 'annuals' from its endowments and the needs of the burgh, which was thus prompted to reinforce its rights through statute. It would be easy, but mistaken, to assume that the repeated re-enactment of these confirmations indicates the ineffectiveness of statute as a solution to local problems. The first parliamentary ratification was secured in 1579 after a number of local solutions had been tried.[91] The confirmations of 1587 and 1592 were required to bring the town's recently-founded college and its endowments within the provisions of the legislation. There were other important legal reasons for the acts of 1587 and 1592: James VI reached his majority (21) in 1587 and the parliament of 1592 was the first after his 25th birthday, his last chance to revoke any grants made in his name during his minority. The parliaments of 1587 and 1592 therefore provided more secure confirmation than those which had preceded them, thus reducing the chance of legal challenges, and both included large numbers of other ratifications.[92] That Edinburgh was seeking a ratification of the same endowments in the very next parliament, in June 1593, is explained in a codicil added to close a loophole: any royal grants made after those to Edinburgh which appeared to run contrary to the terms of the donations to Edinburgh should not be admitted by the courts.[93] In 1606, similar provisions were added to deal with further potential conflicts, while in 1621 the ratification largely concerned new endowments to the town's college and the recent change of its name to 'king James Colledge'.[94] In 1633, now with eight ministers to support, the burgh sought from parliament the right to levy an annual tax of 12,000 merks (£8,000) on its inhabitants as the endowments were once again proving inadequate. The matter was remitted to the privy council which was empowered to reach a binding decision, which it did in 1634. As was normal in these circumstances, the beneficiary sought the security of parliamentary ratification at the first opportunity, obtaining another act of parliament in 1641.[95] Mounting economic pressures meant that Edinburgh had to return to parliament in 1647 to confirm its right to raise revenue from the inhabitants and again in 1649 when the endowments were abandoned in return for an annual levy on the burgh of 19,000 merks (£12,666 13s 4d), now intended to

[90]   *APS*, vol. 3, 169–70, 499, 582, vol. 4, 31–2, 303, 670, vol. 5, 447–50, 515, vol. 6, part 1, 258–60, 810, vol. 6, part 2, 225–7, 416–19; Lynch, 'The Origins of Edinburgh's "toun college"', 6, 8; R. D. Anderson, M. Lynch and N. Phillipson (eds), *The University of Edinburgh: An Illustrated History* (Edinburgh, 2003), 39–40.

[91]   Lynch, *Edinburgh and the Reformation*, 28, 31–5.

[92]   A. R. MacDonald, 'The Parliament of 1592: A Crisis Averted?', in K. M. Brown and A. J. Mann (eds), *The History of the Scottish Parliament Volume 2: Parliament and Politics in Scotland, 1567–1707* (Edinburgh, 2005), 57–81, at 67–8, 75.

[93]   *APS*, vol. 4, 31–2.

[94]   Ibid., 303, 670–71.

[95]   *APS*, vol. 5, 447–8.

support 12 ministers.[96] The size of the original levy had been set by statute, so any amendment required statutory approval.

It is a long-standing criticism of the Scottish parliament that repeated re-enactments demonstrate the failure of legislation to obtain the desired outcome. Julian Goodare has undermined this by suggesting that re-enactment can just as easily indicate the perceived worth of a measure.[97] Statutes were respected by the courts and what were ostensibly re-enactments often actually amended existing legislation in an attempt to improve it, while dramatically lamenting the failure of previous acts in order to ensure that parliament was convinced of the need for a new one. Whatever might be argued about re-enactments of public legislation, the numerous ratifications of Edinburgh's ecclesiastical endowments can only indicate the perceived strength of statute. Why would it have bothered to seek their confirmation if such acts were of no benefit? Just as with the apparent re-enactments of public statutes, these acts obtained by Edinburgh were each subtly different: a new act was needed when new endowments were added and there was no harm in restating pre-existing rights at the same time as confirming new ones. Statutory ratifications offered effective solutions to local problems and Edinburgh's repeated pursuit of acts relating to the same revenues is proof of that. It returned to parliament to get more acts because acts worked, not because they did not, and because new laws were now regarded as having more authority than old ones.[98] Many of the lands whose rents had been donated by the crown to support religion, poor relief and education in Edinburgh were held by people who were reluctant to pay their rents to the burgh. As a result, Edinburgh frequently found itself conducting a case before the court of session, which held parliamentary confirmations in sufficiently high regard to make acquiring them very worthwhile indeed.

It is hard to disentangle the public acts which originated around Edinburgh's council table from those which it promoted on behalf of the convention of burghs. Few general statutes which benefited Edinburgh could be distinguished from those which benefited Scotland's merchants and burgh authorities in general. Just as London's influence on the English government's social and economic legislation can only be guessed at, Edinburgh's must also remain conjectural.[99] Yet there are some instances in which it showed a particular interest in public statutes which were not obviously in the collective interests of the parliamentary burghs. In 1595, the council of Edinburgh formed a special sub-committee 'for penning ane article to be given in to the nixtt parliament or generall counsall for redressing and refrayning of the manyfauld raveshings of wemen and young damesellis, intysing thame fra thair parents be deboschet and wikket persouns'.[100] Who knows what actually prompted this, but the record noted that the problem had 'becum swa frequent within this burgh' that a legislative remedy was required. Edinburgh's efforts may have had a

---

[96]   *APS*, vol. 6, part 1, 810, vol. 6, part 2, 225–7; *Edin. Recs.*, 1641–55, 178. Only ten ministers were actually maintained from 1649.

[97]   Goodare, *The Government of Scotland*, 118–20.

[98]   Ibid., 74–5, 82–3.

[99]   Elton, *The Parliament of England*, 85.

[100]   ECA, Edinburgh Council Minutes, 1594–1600, SL1/1/10, f. 90v.

part to play in the eventual emergence, in 1612, of 'Ane act against ravischers of wemen', although it fell far short of what the burgh had sought.[101] Compromise, particularly in public legislation, was often necessary and Edinburgh was forced to back down in the later 1640s over another public statute, that abolishing ecclesiastical patronage. The radical regime which took power after the fall of the Engagers in 1648 relied heavily on the support of the Church, which was keen to abolish the right of landed patrons to appoint parish ministers. Although some in the Church had always been uneasy about this right, it was a particularly pertinent issue after so many of the nobility had supported the Engagement: the Church did not want unsympathetic royalist nobles appointing parish ministers. Parliament abolished patronage in March 1649, in the face of opposition from some nobles and lairds but with the support of others who knew that, without the Church's backing, the regime would fail.[102] Edinburgh was inclined to oppose abolition, 'it being a matter so much concerning the priviledges of this burgh', probably because of its link to the burgh's long struggle to secure ecclesiastical revenues. As well as having power to appoint the burgh's own ministers, it was the patron of a number of rural churches whose revenues had been donated to the town. It had to be careful though, for its recent support of the Engagement had not worked to its advantage. Its commissioners were therefore told to 'doe their best for the priviledge of the burgh', but if it looked like a majority would vote for abolition, 'they sould not seim singular but goe alongs with the parliament'.[103] The rest of the burghs were happy to support abolition because of the de facto power that every burgh council had over the appointment of ministers: the overlap of council and kirk session in many burghs and the power of the merchant elite as property-owners meant that they would continue to exercise effective authority over ministerial appointments, whatever the legal position. In the countryside, the abolition of patronage might have undermined the position of the nobility if it had endured. In the burghs it would change very little, but Edinburgh had to give up its rights to appoint to those rural parishes in which it had previously been patron.

   Was Edinburgh more successful in achieving legislative results than other burghs? It is no easier to judge the capital's failure rate than that of its less well-connected counterparts. Undoubtedly there were disappointments and it should come as no surprise that Edinburgh's known failures are more numerous than those of others, yet there were remarkably few. In 1617, Aberdeen's commissioner smugly reported that his burgh's success in obtaining an act in its favour had angered Edinburgh's commissioners who failed to secure any, 'notwithstanding of all thair sumptuous feastis and utheris great charges that they have bene att'.[104] In April 1633, Edinburgh was planning to submit eight articles to parliament but, remarkably, not one of them reached the statute book, although four items were remitted to the privy council

---

[101]   *APS*, vol. 4, 471; Goodare, *The Government of Scotland*, 259–60.

[102]   For background and context see D. Stevenson, *Revolution and Counter Revolution 1644–1651* (Edinburgh, 2003), 113–15.

[103]   *Edin. Recs.*, 1641–55, 190–91.

[104]   *Aberdeen Letters*, vol. 1, no. 148.

rather than being rejected outright.[105] It is not even clear if all of them ever reached parliament, for they survive only in a list of instructions carried by a commissioner sent to Charles I in advance of his coronation visit. Other solutions may have been found at court for some of the problems contained in Edinburgh's parliamentary agenda.[106] Apart from the evidence for 1633, there is very little indication that legislative failure was familiar to Edinburgh, although, before a high success rate is claimed, some caveats should be entered. First of all, the council minutes almost never provide a comprehensive parliamentary agenda, so the burgh's success rate can only be guessed at. Also, many of the articles submitted by Edinburgh were introduced on behalf of the convention of burghs, so even if failures can be identified amongst these, they were as much the convention's failures as those of Edinburgh: six of the eight items on its list of 1633 related to the burghs in general rather than Edinburgh in particular. However many failures Edinburgh had, its successes were legion and it is clear that, like London, it dominated the legislative efforts of the towns, submitting more articles and securing more acts than any other. Unlike London, however, there is no evidence that its efforts created headaches for parliamentary managers, which caused one writer in 1572 to suggest that the best way to avoid lengthy sessions would be to reduce the avalanche of bills which always descended from London.[107]

Conclusion

Edinburgh was able to provide leadership for the urban estate in parliament because of its economic power, its court connections before 1637 and its financial and political support for the Covenanting regimes thereafter. It was the convention of burghs, however, which gave legitimacy to its exercise of that role and expressed the consent of the other burghs. Without the convention of burghs, Edinburgh would have been unable to represent urban Scotland in the way that it did and would have had a role more akin to that of London in the English parliament, a dominant monster, feared and envied by the other English boroughs and an irritation to the court because of the unrestrained flood of bills which clogged up the parliamentary process.[108] Edinburgh did not always act in the interests of its fellow parliamentary burghs and occasionally clashed with them, but the mechanism provided by the convention of burghs meant that such confrontations were rare. If it can be said of London that it 'acted as a national melting pot which reduced localism and provincial insularity', in spite of its independence and power, then Edinburgh had an even more profoundly integrating effect on Scotland's merchant community, constantly

---

[105] *Edin. Recs.*, 1626–41, 316–18; *APS*, vol. 5, 447–8. The four items included three from the list of eight, plus one other.

[106] At least one other issue was also dealt with by the privy council: *RPC*, second series, vol. 5, 177–8, 185–6, 530, 535 (fishing).

[107] M. A. R. Graves, 'Managing Elizabethan Parliaments', in D. M. Dean and N. L. Jones (eds), *The Parliaments of Elizabethan England* (Oxford, 1990), 37–63, at 53; Elton, *The Parliament of England*, 77.

[108] Graves, *The Tudor Parliaments*, 31, 86, 150; Elton, *The Parliament of England*, 77.

enabling it to maintain a national understanding of its role.[109] Edinburgh was unlike every other burgh. The city fathers knew the significance of being the capital and were well aware of the lucrative presence of the court and the institutions of central government and the law. Edinburgh ostensibly saved money by rarely having to pay the expenses of parliamentary commissioners. But it more than made up for that saving by the sums spent for drafting acts for itself and on behalf of the convention of burghs and the money and gifts distributed to smooth the passage of those acts. Edinburgh shouldered an even greater expense which few other burghs ever had to consider, for it hosted parliament, a role which will be fully discussed in the next chapter.

---

[109]   Boulton, 'London 1540–1700', 343.

Chapter 6

Hosting the Estates

Parliament settles in the burghs

The physical setting of representative assemblies is a neglected area of study. Specialist and general works on the politics and procedures of parliaments in early modern Europe generally ignore it as an issue, leaving it to architectural historians as if it was of purely aesthetic interest, without political significance.[1] However, in the Scottish context, where the usual venue of parliament provides a contrast with the European norm in the early modern period, questions can be asked about the reasons for and the significance of this divergence. Until the middle of the fifteenth century, Scottish parliaments met in ecclesiastical settings, usually the Augustinian abbeys of Scone, Cambuskenneth and Holyrood, with the Dominican convent at Perth favoured in the early fifteenth century.[2] All of these had close associations with the ruling dynasty. The abbeys were twelfth-century royal foundations: Scone had the additional significance of being the royal inauguration site; Cambuskenneth was close to a prominent royal castle at Stirling; Holyrood was near Edinburgh and became one of the foremost royal residences in the fifteenth century. The Dominican convent at Perth was established by Alexander II in the thirteenth century, and its royal lodgings were a favoured residence until the assassination of James I there in 1437.[3] After that tragic event, parliaments ceased to meet in religious houses. There is some evidence in the earliest surviving parts of Linlithgow Palace that Scotland might have been going to follow the English and Continental pattern by moving its parliament into a royal palace but this did not happen, possibly because of the untimely death of the supposed architect of the scheme, James I.[4] Instead, from the middle of the fifteenth century, parliament normally convened in municipal buildings, the

---

[1] S. Kelsey, 'Introduction', in C. Jones and S. Kelsey (eds), *Housing Parliament: Dublin, Edinburgh and Westminster* (Edinburgh, 2002), 1–21, discusses this historiographical shortcoming at 1–3, while C. R. Kyle, 'Parliament and the Palace of Westminster: an exploration of public space in the early seventeenth century', in the same volume, provides interesting observations on the English parliament's physical setting.

[2] R. Oram, 'Community of the Realm: the Middle Ages', in M. Glendinning (ed.), *The Architecture of Scottish Government:From Kingship to Parliamentary Democracy* (Dundee, 2004), 15–81; Young, *Parliaments of Scotland*, vol. 2, appendix 1.

[3] J. P. Foggie, *Renaissance Religion in Urban Scotland: The Dominican Order, 1450–1560* (Leiden, 2003), 6; Oram, 'Community of the Realm', 48–9.

[4] Ibid., 50–51, 56; J. G. Dunbar, *Scottish Royal Palaces:The Architecture of the Royal Residences during the late Medieval and early Renaissance periods* (East Linton, 1999), 5–10. The size of the hall at Linlithgow and the possibility that its external statues represented the three orders of society suggest its intended use for parliament.

tolbooths of the royal burghs, with Edinburgh dominating and occasional sessions at Stirling and Perth. By 1455, the expectation was that parliament would be hosted by a burgh: a statute of that year instructed the burgh where parliament met to erect 'a seit of thre segis ilkane hear than uthir to the commissaris to sit on'.[5]

A series of royal minorities during the fifteenth and sixteenth centuries may have been partially responsible for parliament finding its home in municipal buildings rather than royal palaces. The minority of James II lasted 12 years and his personal reign only eight, followed by the eight-year minority of James III. Young monarchs began personal reigns with a lot to sort out and this bred an aggressive and assertive dynasty. Recent work has shown how parliament acted as an effective counter-weight to the first three Jameses during their adult reigns and a power for political stability during the inevitable factionalism of minorities.[6] An urban setting for parliament provided the safest option. The burghs, especially Edinburgh which never came under the influence of a prominent noble family, could provide neutral territory, an attribute also possessed by the religious houses where parliament had previously met. They were not the fortified castles of the king or the nobility which some might have been reluctant to enter for fear of arrest, imprisonment, or worse. Armed conflict in medieval and early modern Scotland, when it did not involve wars with England, consisted largely of feuds between landed families. Formal acts of reconciliation to end these feuds had to be performed in a neutral public space and the obvious location was a burgh. In 1564, the privy council ordered the earl of Cassillis and the sheriff of Ayrshire to 'assemble thair freindis, servandis, and part takeris in the burch of Air', to receive each other 'in hartlynes, tendirnes and freindschip, and to remove the rancour consavit be ony of thame ... in tymes bigane, swa that all haitrent ... salbe buryit'. In 1600, Cupar was the venue for arbitration in a feud between two Fife families, the Lundies and the Murrays.[7]

Burghs were corporations, established expressly for the purposes of trading, so they had to be open to all who might come to buy and sell. It has recently been suggested that the 'most likely' explanation for parliament's adoption of Edinburgh's tolbooth was 'opportunism on the part of the chief burgesses of Edinburgh', but there was more to it than that.[8] A powerful institution like parliament does not find a permanent home by accident. It could have moved into a royal residence, with Holyrood the obvious choice since it lay beside the burgh which was developing into a centre of government and was a prominent enough residence for James II to have been born there in 1430.[9] In the turbulent years of royal minority, towns presented to those in authority an opportunity to demonstrate that their exercise of power was open and in the interests of the whole community. Retreating into a royal palace or castle would have given out the wrong signals. Towns throughout Europe

---

[5]   *APS*, vol. 2, 43: three tiers of seats for the (burgh) commissioners.

[6]   R. Tanner, *The Late Medieval Scottish Parliament:Politics and the Three Estates, 1424–1488* (East Linton, 2001).

[7]   *RPC*, first series, vol. 1, 261, vol. 6, 83.

[8]   Oram, 'Community of the Realm', 57, also acknowledges the neutrality of the urban setting.

[9]   Dunbar, *Scottish Royal Palaces*, 55–6.

contained public spaces and acted as foci for more than just the economic life of their hinterlands. Royal proclamations were deemed to have been made to the whole of Scotland if they were read out at the market cross of each county's head burgh. As in England's county towns, head burghs also acted as a locus for royal justice, for there the sheriff's courts met and, from the early seventeenth century, so too did the quarter sessions of the commissioners for the peace.[10] Initially, sheriff courts sat in the royal castles associated with most of the king's burghs but virtually all those castles, with the exception of the few which were retained as royal residences, had vanished by the middle of the fourteenth century. In contrast to the situation in England, where separate buildings continued to be used for royal justice in the localities, sheriff courts moved into tolbooths, where burgh courts and councils met.[11] The crown's chief law-officers held justice courts in tolbooths in Edinburgh and other burghs when they went out into the localities.[12] Given their status as public buildings where local government was carried on and local as well as central justice delivered, these buildings were a logical choice for the highest court in the land.

That the openness afforded by tolbooths was regarded as a key feature of parliament is reflected in a dramatic confrontation at Stirling in 1578. In March, James Douglas, earl of Morton and regent for the young James VI since 1572, had been forced to stand down. By June, however, he was back in possession of the 'first rowme and place' on the privy council, although he could not be restored to the regency, for James VI had been formally declared an adult.[13] Morton shifted parliament from Edinburgh, whither it had been summoned originally, to Stirling, where he and the king were based. Outmanoeuvred, the opposition remained in Edinburgh, fenced (i.e. opened formally) the parliament there according to the original summons, and sent Lord Lindsay to protest formally against the change of venue. Although Lindsay's declaration was careful to acknowledge the king's right to choose where parliament met, he 'desyrit that the samyn sould be fensit and haldin within the tolbuithe [of Stirling], sua that all noblemen and utheris hafing voit mycht have frie acces therto'. The response in the king's name was that, because of 'the present estaite' of the kingdom, the 'tender yeiris' of the king and his 'many unfreindis', the safest place was Stirling Castle. Furthermore, it was pointed out that 'the tolbuithe of Sterling being ruinus', it would have been impossible to meet there. Demonstrating that those holding parliament in the castle fully accepted the normality of meeting in tolbooths, it was further stated that 'this is not meanit to induce a preparative heirefter that our

[10]   *RPC*, first series, vol. 8, 544–5; J. Schofield and G. Stell, 'The built environment 1300–1540', 371–93, at 378–9, and J. Kermode, 'The greater towns 1300–1540', 441–65, at 446, both in D. M. Palliser (ed.), *The Cambridge Urban History of Britain, Volume 1, 600–1540* (Cambridge, 2000).

[11]   M. Reed, 'The urban landscape 1540–1700', in P. Clark (ed.), *The Cambridge Urban History of Britain, Volume II, 1540–1840* (Cambridge, 2000), 289–313, at 300.

[12]   *RPC*, first series, vol. 3, 64, 245, 304, 401, 487, 643 (Edinburgh), 87, 317, 339 (Dumfries), 502 (Perth), vol. 4, 137 (Haddington).

[13]   See G. R. Hewitt, *Scotland Under Morton: 1572–1580* (Edinburgh, 1982), 44–60, for details.

parliaments salbe haldin in castellis'.[14] Stirling's tolbooth had certainly been in a dilapidated state in 1571 when parliament had last met there: the five-year-old king 'looking upward to the roofe of the hous ... saw ane holl throughe the sclaitting; he said I think ther is ane holl in this Parliament'.[15]

The appearance of armed companies from Edinburgh, Glasgow, Dundee and Perth 'to keip gairdhouse in the toun of Sterling during the tyme of the parliament ... incaice ony insurrectioun sould be' would have done nothing to mollify Morton's opponents.[16] In spite of the crown's reassurances, the earl of Montrose protested that 'quhatsoever sould be then donne sould nawayis be prejudiciall to him and the remanent lordis at Edinburgh ... in respect it was haldin within a castell, and not ane patent tolbuithe, quhair frie acces mycht be had to all the leidges'.[17] That free access was not available is proved by the difficulties experienced by some burgh commissioners. Having been refused entry, they convened in Stirling's evidently not very ruinous tolbooth to draw up a formal complaint, demanding admission. Calderwood records that 'The Erle of Morton excused himself with the ignorance of the keepers of the barr, and promised it sould be mended'. In spite of this, burgh commissioners were to gain access to parliament only by presenting their commissions to the guards at the castle's outer gate.[18]

Prompted by the opposition's complaints, the first act of this parliament was 'The declaratioun off the king and estaitis of the fredome of this parliament'. It stated that 'sum evill advisit personis' had claimed 'that thair wes na frie acces nor libertie to the ... liegeis to frelie repair and resort to our ... soverane lord his thrie estatis and lordis of articulis ... albeit the contrair thairf be notour'. To allay anxieties, the king and parliament 'declarit ... the samyn to have bene and to be ane frie and publict parliament quhair all his liegeis had and hes frie access libertie and fredome to resort and repair to the said castell ... but [i.e. without] stop, truble or interruptioun'.[19] That this incident and the rhetoric to which it gave rise resulted from fraught factional politics should not divert attention from the ideas expressed by both sides. The assertions of political rivals, whether or not they reflect sincerely held views, reveal their understanding of what was a respectable reason for doing whatever it was they were doing. The declaration of Morton's opponents and the responses in the king's name provide a rare insight into what was received wisdom about the proper place to hold a parliament, and why that was so. Parliaments should meet in tolbooths

---

[14]   For near-contemporary accounts of this parliament see Moysie, *Memoirs*, 9–12; Calderwood, *History*, vol. 3, 410–14; J. Spottiswoode, *History of the Church of Scotland ... by the Right Rev. John Spottiswoode*, M. Russell and M. Napier (eds), 3 vols (Edinburgh, 1847–51), vol. 2, 226–8.

[15]   Birrel, 'Diary', 18–19; Calderwood, *History*, vol. 3, 136.

[16]   Moysie, *Memoirs*, 11–12; *Edin. Recs.*, 1573–89, 78; GCA, Act Book of the Burgh and City of Glasgow 1573–81, C1/1/1, f. 243r.

[17]   Moysie, *Memoirs*, 12.

[18]   *RPC*, first series, vol. 3, 6; Calderwood, *History*, vol. 3, 414. The burghs were Dunbar, Haddington, Kelso, Jedburgh, Hawick, Selkirk, St Andrews and Aberdeen, and 'sindrie other burrowes'. This must be treated with caution: Kelso and Hawick were not parliamentary burghs but may have been there as petitioners.

[19]   *APS*, vol. 3, 94.

because they were 'patent'. When normality was not prevailing, a statement that it actually was had to be made by those who were violating custom.

The strongly-worded objections to holding parliament in Stirling Castle in the summer of 1578 specifically objected only to it being held in a fortress, rather than a royal residence *per se*, but they did state emphatically that a tolbooth was the proper venue. Some parliaments did meet in unfortified royal palaces without arousing any suggestions of impropriety: Holyrood Palace hosted parliament in 1573 and, in December 1585, it met in the great hall of Linlithgow Palace. These were exceptional occasions. Parliament met at Holyrood in April 1573 only because it was not safe to use Edinburgh's tolbooth. The civil war resulting from the deposition of Mary in 1567 was virtually over but Edinburgh Castle remained in the hands of the dregs of the queen's party, under siege by English forces at the invitation of the king's party. The leaders of the king's government would have put themselves at unnecessary risk by meeting in the tolbooth, well within range of the castle's artillery. They actually went there to fence parliament and elect the lords of the articles but conducted the rest of the session in the relative safety of Holyrood Palace.[20] In December 1585, Linlithgow was chosen because of an outbreak of plague in Edinburgh which had forced the fledgling university to suspend teaching, while the royal palace simultaneously provided a setting in which the 19-year-old king could symbolically demonstrate his assumption of personal rule.[21] For the next 60 years, however, parliament did not meet in a royal palace or castle and when it returned to Stirling Castle in 1645, the circumstances were very different. Parliament was controlled by the revolutionary government of the Covenanters, there was plague in Edinburgh again and the threat of royalist insurgents under the marquis of Montrose had created sufficient fear among the Covenanting leadership to prompt them to choose a defensible venue.[22] Thus, in the period of this study, parliament met only once in a royal palace during the personal rule of a king, at the very beginning of the adult reign of James VI at Linlithgow in 1585. All other instances were prompted by exceptional circumstances and occurred when people other than the king held the reins of power.

Of the 36 parliamentary sessions which met between 1550 and the Covenanting revolution in 1639, 33 met in tolbooths.[23] The comparison with conventions of the estates is striking and suggests that the differences between them and parliaments should not be downplayed, either in political or constitutional terms.[24] In the

---

[20] *Diurnal of Occurrents*, 324–5, 330–31, noted that, in January too, only the formal aspects of parliament were conducted in Edinburgh's tolbooth, and in February those in the castle had set fire to St Giles' and bombarded the town to hinder attempts to extinguish the flames.

[21] A. Grant, *The Story of the University of Edinburgh*, 2 vols (London, 1884), vol. 1, 145.

[22] D. Stevenson, *Revolution and Counter-Revolution, 1644–1651* (Edinburgh, 2003), 23, 27.

[23] Young, *Parliaments of Scotland*, vol. 2, appendix 1.

[24] J. Goodare, 'The Scottish Parliament and its Early Modern "Rivals"', in *PER*, 24 (2004), 147–72, at 149–52 and J. Goodare, *The Government of Scotland, 1560–1625* (Oxford, 2004), 47–8, discuss the differences between parliaments and conventions, putting greater emphasis on similarities and offering an alternative view of 'conventions of the nobility'.

same period, 105 conventions of the estates met whose location has been clearly identified, 57 of which met in royal palaces.[25] It was exceptional for parliament to meet in a royal palace and, although many conventions of estates met in tolbooths (at Edinburgh, Perth, St Andrews, Haddington and Dundee), more met in royal residences (at Dalkeith, Dunfermline, Falkland, Holyrood, Linlithgow and Stirling). Conventions of estates were smaller than parliaments, but that does not explain why they met in royal palaces. Linlithgow's great hall was clearly big enough to host parliament, while the 'north hall' at Holyrood, where parliament met in April 1573, was probably the room where the privy council often met. Although much smaller than the hall at Linlithgow, surviving plans suggest that it was about 15m by 7m (105m²), easily large enough for a parliament, given the numbers usually attending in this period.[26] Moreover, before the construction of the new parliament house in Edinburgh in the 1630s, the municipal venues of parliament did not afford larger rooms than were available in royal palaces.

Other reasons must be sought to explain why conventions usually met in royal palaces, sometimes even in Stirling Castle, without provoking the slightest reaction. The answer offered here is that they were, essentially, creatures of the crown: their membership was selected by the king and they usually met for one or two days and for one or two specific purposes such as the need for taxation or the passing of some emergency legislation, for they could not establish permanent laws. They were often little more than augmented meetings of the privy council, with some burgh commissioners and more than the usual number of nobles, convened at short notice to advise the king. Although a separate register for conventions of estates was begun in 1598, it was not used consistently and their records continued to be kept along with those of the privy council, the minutes of one often flowing almost imperceptibly into those of the other.[27] Parliament, on the other hand, had judicial powers, a full and open-ended agenda, a drafting committee elected from the different estates, and was open to all the lieges to receive petitions and proposals for legislation. This distinction must have been clear to contemporaries. To be sure, the date and place of parliamentary meetings were chosen by the monarch, but they belonged to the political nation in a way that conventions of the estates did not: the three estates meeting with a plenary summons were the highest court in the land and

---

[25]   It is hard to be certain about the number of conventions of estates. Being less formal, shorter and smaller than parliaments, many were not recorded officially and there is confusion between conventions 'of the estates' and 'of the nobility': the latter are usually assumed to include only peers but burghs often sent commissioners to them. See appendix 5, compiled from Young, *Parliaments of Scotland*, vol. 2, appendix 1; J. Goodare, 'Parliament and Society in Scotland, 1560–1603' (Edinburgh PhD, 1989), appendix A; and MS burgh records. Also, 57 is a minimum figure for conventions in royal palaces, as burghs used 'Edinburgh' loosely to cover Edinburgh and Holyrood.

[26]   *Diurnal of Occurrents*, 331; Dunbar, *Scottish Royal Palaces*, 5–21 (Linlithgow), 21–37 (Falkland), 60–71 (Holyrood), 87–94 (Dunfermline). Before the 17th century, less than 100 usually attended.

[27]   NAS, Register of conventions, 1598–1678, PA8/1; *RPC*, first series, passim, e.g. vol. 4, 666–8; and see J. Goodare, 'The Scottish Parliamentary Records 1560–1603', in *Bulletin of the Institute of Historical Research*, 72 (1999), 244–67, at 264.

the king, or queen, in parliament was sovereign. Conventions of the estates were more like the medieval *curia regis* where the monarch sought counsel in a relatively intimate and informal way, so they tended to meet wherever the king or queen was staying, whether that was Holyrood, Linlithgow, Stirling, Dunfermline or the royal hunting lodge at Falkland. Parliaments were more formal and much less personal, the assertion by James VI in *The Trew Law of Free Monarchies* that they were a purely advisory body notwithstanding.[28] Much of what James wrote in that work and in his *Basilikon Doron* should be seen as aspirational rather than descriptive.

The difference between parliaments and conventions of the estates can be demonstrated further by the dramatic reduction in the number of the latter after 1603. Taking the personal reign of James VI (after October 1585) as a sample, there were approximately 65 conventions of the estates before March 1603 (roughly one every three months) but only ten after James's departure for England (one every 26 months).[29] Comparing this with parliamentary sessions is revealing: the number also declined, but not as dramatically and at a different point. There were seven parliamentary sessions between November 1585 and March 1603 (on average one every 30 months) and eight between April 1603 and March 1625 (one every 33 months). The most marked decline in parliaments occurred after 1612, with only two more before 1625. This is broadly in line with the trend in England where there were nine parliamentary sessions between 1603 and 1625, but only four after 1610.[30] Whether the king was more or less in touch with the political nation after 1603 is a moot point. It is clear, however, that the means of contact between the monarch and his Scottish subjects had changed dramatically, that this resulted directly from the absence of the monarch, and that there really had been something intensely personal about the personal monarchy of James VI in Scotland before 1603.[31]

Another indication of the monarchy's lack of ownership of parliament can be found in the arrangements made for hosting it. Anyone seeking to investigate the logistics of a parliamentary session could be forgiven for making the financial accounts of the crown their first port of call. In most European countries, the prince owned the buildings in which representative assemblies met and was therefore responsible for hosting them.[32] By the fourteenth century, it was normal for English parliaments to meet in the palace of Westminster and although parliament took over much of that

---

[28]   *The Trew Law of Free Monarchies*, in N. Rhodes, J. Richards and J. Marshall (eds), *King James VI and I, Selected Writings* (Aldershot, 2003), 270.

[29]   Appendix 5; see also Young, *Parliaments of Scotland*, vol. 2, appendix 1.

[30]   D. L. Smith, *The Stuart Parliaments, 1603–1689* (London, 1999), appendix 1. Comparisons are difficult since English parliaments were longer.

[31]   Much has been written on the impact of 1603: M. Lee, *Government by Pen: Scotland under James VI and I* (Urbana, 1980); M. Lee, 'James VI's Government of Scotland after 1603', in *SHR*, 55 (1976), 41–54. Both claim continued success for James's personal role in Scottish government, while Goodare, *The Government of Scotland*, ch. 4, downplays the significance of 1603 for the way in which Scotland was governed and takes a different view of 'personal' monarchy to that offered here and in A. R. MacDonald, *The Jacobean Kirk 1567–1625: Sovereignty, Polity and Liturgy* (Aldershot, 1998), chs 5–7.

[32]   E. R. Foster, 'Staging a Parliament in early Stuart England', in P. Clark, A. G. R. Smith and N. Tyacke (eds), *The English Commonwealth 1547–1640: Essays in Politics and*

palace, it remained an occasional royal residence until the early sixteenth century.[33] The *Cortes* of Castile was paid for by the crown; in France, both the Estates General and the provincial estates met in royal buildings; plenary sessions of Sweden's *Riksdag* also met in the king's hall of state.[34] The only exception might be the United Provinces of the Netherlands, where the States General met in the Binnenhof in the Hague and provincial states met in town halls, such as the Burgerzaal at Amsterdam, built in 1648. Yet the Binnenhof was not a municipal building but the administrative centre of the county of Holland and, before the Dutch Revolt, it had been a locus of Habsburg power. Thereafter it arguably became a symbol of the dominance of Holland within the republic, and the fact that it was in a republic also renders a comparison with Scotland less meaningful.[35]

The king's treasurer and comptroller were in charge of recording the crown's incidental income and expenditure, while regular payments and earnings were accounted for annually by the exchequer. Parliaments were not a regular part of government, however frequent they may have been in some periods, so the accounts of the treasurer and comptroller would seem to be the obvious places to look. However, with the exception of the costs of fitting out the great hall at Stirling Castle in 1578 and 1645, the crown's financial records provide no clues as to what was involved in staging a parliament in early modern Scotland.[36] Yet the crown did incur a wide range of costs in relation to parliament. It issued the summonses, sending out messengers with precepts to nobles, prelates, burghs and, after 1587, to sheriffs: this cost £46 in 1578, rising to £96 by 1621. This alone shows that costs were lower than in England, where £24 sterling (£288 Scots) were spent on summoning a parliament in the early seventeenth century.[37] In addition, the privy council issued proclamations relating to parliament: all those with articles or supplications were told to submit them to the lords of the articles or the clerk register; the lieges were commanded to

Society Presented to Joel Hurstfield (Leicester, 1979), 129–46; Oram, 'Community of the Realm', 56.

[33]　　Kelsey, 'Introduction', 6.

[34]　　I. A. A. Thompson, *Crown and Cortes: Government, Institutions and Representation in Early-Modern Castile* (Aldershot, 1993), 'Cortes, Cities and *Procuradores* in Castile', 1–72, at 28–9; M. Roberts (ed.), *Sweden as a Great Power, 1611–1697: Government, Society, Foreign Policy* (London, 1968), 11–14; G. Rystad, 'The Estates of the Realm, the Monarchy, and Empire, 1611–1718', in M. F. Metcalf (ed.), *The Riksdag: A History of the Swedish Parliament* (New York, 1987), 61–108, at 69–70; Oram, 'Community of the Realm', 56.

[35]　　A. R. Myers, *Parliaments and Estates in Europe to 1789* (London, 1975), 128–30; J. I. Israel, *The Dutch Republic: Its Rise, Greatness and Fall 1477–1806* (Oxford, 1998), 293–4; A. MacKechnie, 'The Crisis of Kingship: 1603–1707', in Glendinning (ed.), *The Architecture of Scottish Government*, 82–174, at 109.

[36]　　For 1578 see *TA*, vol. 13, 210–11; for 1645, *Accounts of the Masters of Works for Building and Repairing Royal Palaces and Castles*, J. Imrie and J. G. Dunbar (eds), 2 vols (Edinburgh, 1957–), vol. 1, 445–6. For comptrollers' accounts before 1600, see *ER* and for those after that date, NAS, Comptroller's Accounts, E24. For treasurers' accounts after 1580 see NAS, Treasurer's Accounts, E21.

[37]　　*TA*, vol. 13, 201–2; NAS, Treasurer's Accounts 1621–22, E21/88, ff. 21v–22v; Foster, 'Staging a Parliament in Early Stuart England', 144.

keep the peace during parliament; at the end of the session, the acts were proclaimed by a royal herald at the market cross of the burgh in which parliament met, and the crown paid for their printing.[38] Other special items of expenditure were also recorded: in December 1585, £16 5s were spent on a new pair of stockings for the king, decorated with gold fringes and grey and black silk, while minor work was carried out on two velvet cloaks and his robe royal.[39] Occasionally, a major expense would be undertaken but that too was usually for clothing: in 1617, each of the heralds and pursuivants was given 200 merks (£133 6s 8d) 'for bying of cloathis to the Parliament', and in 1621, 1,000 merks (£666 13s 4d) was spent on the five royal trumpeters for some 'cumlie and decent clothing [for] thair attendance at the parliament'.[40]

The crown told people when to come and how to behave and it ensured that the king and his servants looked the part, but it let others deal with the logistics. It was not the host. A meeting of the parliament was a grand affair which required the streets to be prepared for the opening and closing ceremonies of riding by being fenced off and sanded to help the horses grip on the steep slope of the processional route from Holyrood Palace to the parliament house. The parliament house and the committee rooms had to be cleaned and fitted out, and furniture brought in, constructed and arranged; ceremonial guards were required and refreshments provided. To discover how all this was paid for, one must go to the records of Edinburgh, Perth and Stirling, for burghs hosted parliament and therefore paid for preparing the venue. One obvious response to this situation is that it was the result of the crown's parsimony. That is a possibility, but the other expenses shouldered by the crown were often at least as much as, and sometimes more than, those of preparing the venue. The crown saved little by not hosting parliament. It might be suggested, since royal burghs were tenants-in-chief of the crown, that tolbooths were the king's buildings anyway. However, peers were also tenants-in-chief and none would have averred that their castles actually belonged to the king, except in the sense that, in a feudal society, all heritable property ultimately did. The burghs commissioned, built and maintained their tolbooths: they owned them.

It has been argued by Richard Oram that the assassination of James I put paid to what might have been plans to make Perth the permanent seat of government, and Edinburgh came increasingly to be seen as the capital from the middle of the fifteenth century.[41] Indeed, its becoming the virtually permanent home of parliament arguably played a significant part in establishing that status. The coronation of James II at Holyrood in 1437 marked the conscious rejection of Scone as the symbolic focus of the kingdom: it would never be used again for a parliament, nor even for a coronation until 1651.[42] In the first half of the fifteenth century, 14 parliaments met at Perth, five met at Edinburgh, and a few at other venues. In the second half of the

---

[38]   See, e.g., NAS, Treasurer's Accounts 1592–93, E21/68, f. 128v, Treasurer's Accounts 1621–22, E21/88, ff. 32r–33v.

[39]   NAS, Treasurer's Accounts 1585–86, E21/64, f. 109r.

[40]   NAS, Treasurer's Accounts 1621–22, E21/88, f. 31r.

[41]   Oram, 'Community of the Realm', 48–9.

[42]   Ibid., 54–5.

century, 40 parliaments met at Edinburgh and only five elsewhere.[43] By the period under examination, not only was it normal for parliaments to meet in tolbooths, it was exceptional for them not to sit in the tolbooth of Edinburgh which, because it also hosted the central courts, had become, by the middle of the sixteenth century, the nation's legislative and judicial focus. It shared these attributes with Westminster, which serves to highlight the contrast with the English situation where both central courts and parliament met in a royal palace.[44]

The physical setting

It is remarkable, since parliament met at Edinburgh on all but 12 occasions between 1550 and 1651, that the exact location of its meetings between 1563 and 1633 remains a matter for some confusion. A number of works written over a period of more than a century have identified the venue with some accuracy, but these are contradicted by as many others, including the most recent ones.[45] Pinpointing Scotland's parliamentary chamber in this period is no mere antiquarian pursuit, for some have even used erroneous assumptions about parliament's physical context to explain its supposed political impotence.[46] The situation before 1560 is straightforward: parliaments met in Edinburgh's tolbooth at the north-west corner of the burgh's parish church of St Giles'. The precise size and appearance of the accommodation must remain uncertain, for it was demolished in 1817 and much of what then survived dated from its conversion into a gaol in the early seventeenth century. It had been the scene of parliaments for over a century when the Reformation parliament met there in 1560 for what turned out to be the old tolbooth's parliamentary swansong. Some idea of what it may have looked like can be gleaned from illustrations of what remained in the early nineteenth century (fig. 2).[47] At its eastern end was a square tower, faced

---

[43]   Young, *The Parliaments of Scotland*, vol. 2, appendix 1.

[44]   Kyle, 'Parliament and the Palace of Westminster', 86.

[45]   The following correctly placed parliament house in St Giles': P. Miller, 'The Tolbuiths of Edinburgh', in *Our Journall into Scotland Anno Domini 1629, 5th of November* from Lowther (Edinburgh, 1894), 49–56 (he believed the whole complex to be 65ft by 40ft, allowing only 15ft by 20ft for the room in which the committee of the articles, 40 people, with a clerk and tables, had to sit and deliberate); C. A. Malcolm, 'The Parliament House and its Antecedents', in G. Campbell and H. Paton (eds), *Introduction to Scottish Legal History*, (Edinburgh, 1958), 452–3. Those which failed to do so include: R. Richardson, 'The History of Parliament Square: Being an Historical Notice of the Southern Precincts of the Church of St Giles', Edinburgh', in *BOEC*, 3 (1910), 207–42, at 221; J. A. Fairley, 'The Old Tolbooth: With Extracts from the Original Records', in *BOEC*, 4 (1911), 74–113, at 88; R. K. Hannay and G. P. H. Watson, 'The Building of the Parliament House', *BOEC*, 13 (1924), 1–78, at 8, 11; Rait, *The Parliaments of Scotland*, 533; Oram, 'Community of the Realm', 65–6; MacKechnie, 'Crisis of Kingship', 84, 91. Discussions below are based on these works.

[46]   Rait, *Parliaments of Scotland*, 533; MacKechnie, 'Crisis of Kingship', 91, also hints at this. Their judgements are based on the idea that parliament met in Edinburgh's new council house.

[47]   Numerous pictorial representations of the old tolbooth survive, e.g.: D. Wilson, *Memorials of Edinburgh in the Olden Time*, 2 vols (Edinburgh, 1891), vol. 1, 238;

with ashlar and incorporating elaborately-carved statue niches, inviting comparison with London's Guildhall, and rectangular windows with hood mouldings.[48] The main block, containing more substantial rooms, probably included a large hall at first-floor level in which parliaments met. It extended to the west and may have echoed the style of the tower, faced with ashlar and embellished with carved decoration. Both the tower and the main block also had a decorative battlement: illustrations of the surviving parts of the tower show remnants of a parapet at the head of its eastern wall, while, during the demolition of the main block in the 1560s, the burgh's master of works was ordered 'to caus tak doun the battelling of the Auld Tolbuith'.[49]

By the 1550s, its fabric was in poor condition; repairs were made but these proved inadequate and, in the summer of 1560, the burgh council resolved to divide the church of St Giles' and use part of it for a tolbooth. No further action was taken at that time but in February 1562, Queen Mary wrote to the council, noting 'that the Tolbuyth of Edinburgh is ruinous, and hable haistalie to decay and fall doun'. The council was ordered to 'provide sufficient houssis and rowmes ... for the Lordis of Sessioun, Justice, and Scheref, for ministering justice to the liegis of the realme'.[50] It is at this point that confusion arises because two separate tolbooths were built to replace the one which the burgh council and the central courts vacated. The need for more space had been acknowledged in 1560 when the intention had been to maintain the old tolbooth and expand into part of the church. The new buildings were 'tolbooths' because they were used for justice and administration, but one was usually referred to as the 'counsall house' while the other tended to be called the 'tolbuith'. Instead of building both from scratch, the council, keen to maintain the presence of the central courts after a threatened move to St Andrews, quickly erected a wall cutting off the western end of St Giles' and fitted out the space as a series of courtrooms. The work started only five weeks after receipt of the queen's letter.[51] The court of session and the commissary court occupied the main floor, while the central criminal court and the burgh's own bailies' court were placed underneath, along with some prison accommodation.[52] Further evidence for the priority given to accommodating the lords of session is that work on the new chambers for the burgh council did not start until October 1562 after most of the works within the church had been completed.[53] The council must have continued to occupy part of the

---

R. Chambers, *Reekiana: Minor Antiquities of Edinburgh* (Edinburgh, 1883), 123; H. F. Kerr, 'The Old Tolbooth of Edinburgh', in *BOEC*, 14 (1925), 7–23.

[48]   Schofield and Stell, 'The Built Environment 1300–1540', 378.

[49]   Wilson, *Memorials of Edinburgh*, 123, 144.

[50]   Fairley, 'The Old Tolbooth', 85–7; R. Miller, *The Municipal Buildings of Edinburgh* (Edinburgh, 1895), 17–18; *RPC*, first series, vol. 1, 198–9.

[51]   R. Adam (ed.), *Edinburgh Records: The Burgh Accounts Volume 1* (Edinburgh, 1899), 377.

[52]   Adam, *Edinburgh Records: The Burgh Accounts Volume 1*, 387, indicates that 14 stone steps led to the upper storey; Miller, *The Municipal Buildings of Edinburgh*, 48. The upper storey would have been more spacious than the interior today suggests, for the floor has since been raised by as much as 1.5–2m. This would have allowed more height in the lower storey too, which would have been entered by a door to the south.

[53]   Adam, *Edinburgh Records: The Burgh Accounts Volume 1*, 397, refers to clearing the site in September 1562 and laying the foundations in October.

Figure 2 The old tolbooth of Edinburgh from the north-east c.1800, showing the ashlar-faced tower with statue-niches, hood mouldings over the windows, remnants of a parapet at the wallhead and, to the right, the early seventeenth-century block. Reproduced by kind permission of Edinburgh City Libraries.

old tolbooth until the completion of the new council house, outside the south-west corner of St Giles' and linked to the rooms in the west end of the church at first-floor level.

Most of the old tolbooth was demolished and the materials reused in the new buildings, leaving only the tower at the east end and the ground floor, containing shops whose lessees refused to vacate them. So it remained until the early seventeenth century, when the upper four storeys were rebuilt to serve as the burgh's gaol. The work in the 1560s, including the partial demolition of the old tolbooth, cost £4,378 16s 11½d and was finished by June 1563, just in time for parliament. But where did it meet? Just as the old tolbooth had accommodated courts, council and parliament, the new buildings were also designed as a series of flexible spaces which could be readily converted into something else. The court of session did not sit during parliamentary sessions, so the court complex in the west end of St Giles' was used for both.

Various descriptions of the setting survive and there is even a diagram of the layout of the court of session accompanying a description of 1629, although its author did not provide any scale; nor did he indicate how it fitted into the church.[54] Judging by its proportions and based on the probability that full use would have been made of the space, it occupied the whole width of the four western bays of the nave.[55] As can be seen from the early nineteenth-century plan (fig. 3), it had a central aisle with two further aisles to the north and south. It was into this space, and emphatically not the new council house outside St Giles', that the inner house of the court of session (its principal courtroom) and the outer house (for preliminary hearings) were translated.[56] Between 1563 and the construction of the new parliament house in the 1630s, parliament met in the central aisle. The space it occupied was thus about 7m by 20m ($c.140m^2$) and was lit by the great west window of the church. Although not a huge space, it did not have to accommodate many more than 100 people until after 1600. The commons chamber at Westminster, St Stephen's chapel, occupied a similar space ($c.130m^2$). Another example of a sixteenth-century conversion of an ecclesiastical space into a parliamentary chamber, it could comfortably hold about 200 people but sometimes 300 squeezed in. In the early seventeenth century, extra seats and galleries were inserted to accommodate members at busy times.[57] Whenever they were full both chambers would have been cramped, but there would have been

---

[54]   *Our Journall Into Scotland*, 26–9. For further discussion of this source, see H. L. MacQueen, 'Two Visitors in the Session, 1629 and 1636', in H. L. MacQueen (ed.), *The Stair Society Miscellany Four* (Edinburgh, 2002), 155–68.

[55]   Miller, *The Municipal Buildings of Edinburgh*, 43.

[56]   MacKechnie, 'The Crisis of Kingship', 91–2, put the court of session outside the church.

[57]   Smith, *The Stuart Parliaments*, 24; Kyle, 'Parliament and the Palace of Westminster', 87. For the dimensions of the House of Commons see N. Hawkyard, 'From Painted Chamber to St Stephen's Chapel: The Meeting Places of the House of Commons at Westminster until 1603', in Jones and Kelsey (eds), *Housing Parliament*, 62–84, at 78–9. In 1612, 109 attended the Scottish parliament. That is the first surviving sederunt since 1587 when 68 attended and, in the 1560s, 1570s and 1580s, attendances ranged from 48 (Dec 1567) to 83 (Oct 1579), see *APS*, vols 3 and 4, *passim*.

less of a crush in Scotland, where parliament had fewer members than the English House of Commons and most of the deliberations were conducted outside the main chamber, in the committee of the articles and meetings of individual estates.[58]

In preparation for a parliamentary session, there was much to be done to change the courtrooms into a parliament hall. Contemporary sources reveal that the inner house of the court of session remained intact. An account of 1612 by the king's secretary described the nobility leaving the parliament house and directly entering the 'Innerhous' to elect the ecclesiastical members of the articles. Subsequently, the same room was used by the committee itself.[59] Similarly, in 1617, Calderwood recorded that the king met with the bishops in the 'Inner Hous' to discuss an item of business and that they returned to the 'Utter Hous', in which parliament sat.[60] Hamilton's account and Calderwood's description of 1621 both show that parliament met in the space usually occupied by the outer house of the court of session. The fact that this was in the west end of St Giles' is put beyond doubt in the records of the burgh of Edinburgh for 1632. On 13 March that year, the council noted that it was a matter for regret that 'a pairt of thair grit churche ... sould be applyet to secular uses', including the court of session and parliament.[61] Another contemporary source noted that the building of the new parliament house resulted from a desire for 'another house for a Parliament House, and where actions of law may be impleaded, [rather] *than a part of the Kirk where God's word should be preached*, and whilk should be a house of prayer'.[62]

Much has been written on the construction of the new parliament house in the 1630s, so it is unnecessary to go into detail here. The consensus is that Charles I insisted that Edinburgh should provide a splendid new building.[63] Yet Edinburgh was well aware of the prestige and profit which accrued from being the seat of government and the law, as the clearing of markets from the administrative district during the 1580s and the determination to retain the status of capital in 1596 had

---

[58]   See A. R. MacDonald, 'Deliberative Processes in Parliament, *c.*1567–1639: Multicameralism and the Lords of the Articles', in *SHR*, 81 (2002), 23–51, for a discussion of deliberation before 1639.

[59]   'Memoriall anent the progres and conclusion of the Parliament haldin at Edinburgh in October 1612', in J. Dennistoun and A. MacDonald (eds), *Maitland Club Miscellany III*, (Edinburgh, 1843), 112–18. Forty people could thus meet comfortably in the inner house, further evidence that Lowther's plan covered the width of the church, otherwise those people would have squeezed into a space about 5m square.

[60]   Calderwood, *History*, vol. 7, 253.

[61]   *Edin. Recs.*, 1626–41, 103.

[62]   John Row, *History of the Kirk of Scotland from the Year 1558 to August 1637*, D. Laing (ed.), (Edinburgh, 1942), 356. The italics are mine.

[63]   Hannay and Watson, 'The Building of the Parliament House', 1–78; MacKechnie, 'The Crisis of Kingship', 94–133; D. Stevenson, *The Scottish Revolution, 1637–44: The Triumph of the Covenanters* (Newton Abbot, 1973), 51, 170; J. R. Young, 'Charles I and the 1633 Parliament', in K. M. Brown and A. J. Mann (eds), *The History of the Scottish Parliament Volume 2: Parliament and Politics in Scotland, 1567–1707* (Edinburgh, 2005), 101–37, at 103.

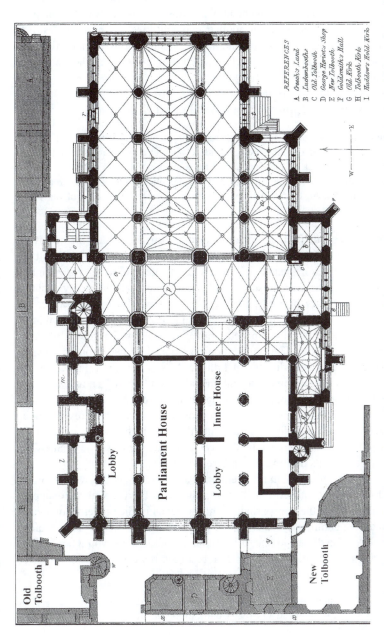

Old Tolbooth

Lobby

Parliament House

Inner House

Lobby

New Tolbooth

Figure 3   A plan of St Giles' with a conjectural reconstruction of the internal arrangements as they would have been during a parliament between 1563 and 1633. The old tolbooth is top left, the new tolbooth used by the burgh council from 1563 is bottom left. Adapted from a plan of St Giles' before 1829 in D. Wilson, *Memorials of Edinburgh in the Olden Time* (Edinburgh, 1891), vol. 2, 296.

demonstrated.[64] The magnificence of the design and the resultant expense were due to the burgh council's desire to assert Edinburgh's status as capital; it was not 'an architectural expression of [Charles I's] royalist, centralist view of government'. After all, he sought no redevelopment at Westminster, which 'was to remain a jumble of feudal palace buildings for another two centuries'.[65] Charles's desire to dispense with parliaments in both England and Scotland seriously undermines the theory that the initiative behind the building of a magnificent new house for the Scottish parliament was his.

The first notice of the proposal to remove the courts and parliament out of the church came in March 1632 when the council of Edinburgh convened

> ane gritt nomber of the honest nichtboures, regraitting that a pairt of thair grit churche whiche was apointed for divyne service sould be applyet to secular uses and withall consideering that the laick of convenient and fitt roumes within this burgh for keiping of parliament, sessioun and counsall-hous and uther publict meittings may procure the same to be abstracted furth of this burgh to the gritt lose and prejudice of the whole inhabitantis.[66]

It was resolved to erect such accommodation 'as the counsall sall designe be advyse of the maist skilfull architectouris as may with credeit and conveniencie befitt the honour of the hie estaittes of justice within this kingdome' and to raise a voluntary contribution. A week later, the magistrates and council approached the privy council for advice and support; in April the burgh appointed a treasurer for the project and by July the pledges had all been received. According to John Row, a contemporary presbyterian historian, this all happened immediately after the return of some Scottish bishops from court. The implication was that they had brought news of Charles's plan to erect a new diocese of Edinburgh, and that the ministers of the burgh had requested the vacation of the church and the building of a new parliament house.[67] Row had his own reasons for heaping blame for expensive burdens on the royalist ministers of Edinburgh and the imprecision of his account makes the dating of their alleged request impossible to pinpoint. Yet even if the construction of the new parliament house was prompted by the need to vacate the west end of St Giles', that does not make it or its design the king's responsibility.

Charles I was nothing if not an interventionist king who made his wishes known and expected them to be carried out. It would therefore be reasonable to suppose that, had the initiative for the new parliament house been his, the process would have been instigated by a command to the council of Edinburgh, or to the privy council, ordering the work to be done and that, throughout the process, he would have issued detailed instructions, but he did not. The first recorded royal intervention occurred

---

[64]   E. P. Dennison and M. Lynch, 'Crown, Capital, and Metropolis. Edinburgh and Canongate: The Rise of a Capital and an Urban Court', in Journal of Urban History, 32 (2005), 22–43, at 30; see ch. 5 for 1596.

[65]   MacKechnie, 'The Crisis of Kingship', 101–2.

[66]   *Edin. Recs.*, 1626–41, 103. The Scroll Minutes of Edinburgh Council reveal no further details as to the origin of the scheme: ECA, Scroll Minutes 1630–35, 13 March 1632.

[67]   *RPC*, second series, vol. 4, 448–9; Row, *History*, 355.

at the end of July 1632, when he asked the privy council to support the work which the burgh had 'for the honour of that our ancient kingdome so willinglie *offered* and undertaken'.[68] The first royal command to demolish the internal walls of the church came in a letter of October 1633, 19 months after the burgh's decision to vacate St Giles' but only three months after Charles's visit to Edinburgh. His priority remained the cathedral, while the resulting need for a new civic building was Edinburgh's affair. The king's only concern appears to have been swift completion, not an edifice of sumptuous grandeur to promote royal absolutism: he ordered the burgh to finish 'the new tolbuith betweene this and Lambmesse [1 August 1634]'.[69] That Charles called it a tolbooth demonstrates that it was the burgh's project, not his.

The king's deadline was missed but the new parliament house was sufficiently complete to accommodate the first Covenanter parliament in 1639. Even taking inflation into account, the costs incurred in the 1560s (less than £4,500) pale into insignificance beside the estimated £127,000 spent in the 1630s, nearly two-thirds of which had to be borrowed.[70] The cost of the parliament house tends to be added to the list of the 'causes of discontent' in Scotland in the 1630s as if it was a royal imposition.[71] However, groaning under the burden of unprecedented levels of taxation, the council of Edinburgh could have constructed something simple and relatively inexpensive without royal demur.[72] Instead, it chose to put itself under even greater financial strain by hiring the foremost Scottish architect, Sir James Murray, the king's master of works, because it wanted to build a splendid edifice to affirm its status as capital and ensure the continued presence of parliament at its heart. This may have made the strain of the tax burden harder to bear, exacerbating the irritation caused by things for which the king was responsible, but the parliament house should not be added to the list of burdens which Charles placed upon Scotland. This also means that interpretations of the building, its site and its decorative elements as symbolic of the policies of an arrogant, centralising monarch must be jettisoned.[73] Its site has been portrayed as chosen to allow the formation of an urban space reminiscent of the Roman forum, to convey royal power and to achieve a geometric relationship with other buildings by Murray, the remodelled palace block of Edinburgh Castle and Heriot's Hospital.[74] However, the choice of site makes more sense in the context of local initiative and direction. It lay at the administrative heart of the burgh, where its tolbooths had always stood. It was also the only site occupied by properties belonging to the burgh (the ministers' manses), so it was the only one which the council could

---

[68] Hannay and Watson, 'The Building of the Parliament House', 21. The italics are mine.

[69] *RPC*, second series, vol. 5, 136–7. It is clear from the context that this referred to the new parliament house.

[70] Hannay and Watson, 'The Building of the Parliament House', 77; L. A. M. Stewart, 'Politics and Religion in Edinburgh, 1617–1653', (Edinburgh PhD, 2003), 62–3, 113–14, adds further weight to the argument presented here.

[71] Stevenson, *The Scottish Revolution*, 51; M. Lynch, *Scotland: A New History* (London, 1991), 267.

[72] Hannay and Watson, 'The Building of the Parliament House', 14–16.

[73] MacKechnie, 'The Crisis of Kingship', 94, 101, 124, 134.

[74] Ibid., 101–2.

readily clear for a new building. These physical constraints render speculations as to the symbolism of the building's alignment less convincing. Edinburgh was raising a new building in its own administrative district and it chose the site. Moreover, although the building was adorned with royal symbols, the king's arms being set over the main door and thistles, roses and fleurs-de-lis used liberally in exterior decoration, the arms of the burgh (a three-towered castle) were placed above the door to the wing and on some of the corbels supporting the main hall's roof.[75]

It was essentially a successor to the tolbooth in the west end of St Giles': even the king recognised this. In the 1560s, Edinburgh had split the functions of its tolbooth, putting the central courts and parliament in one place and its own council chambers in another. In the 1630s the former was simply moved into a new building. There are thus grounds for seeing the construction of the parliament house not as a singular project peculiar to the capital but as part of the reconstruction of civic buildings across Scotland's major burghs in the first half of the seventeenth century: notable examples are Perth (finished by 1604), Aberdeen (1616–1630), Stirling (1616) and the most magnificent at Glasgow (1625–1629).[76] The reformatting of Edinburgh's tolbooths between 1562 and 1640 can even be seen as part of a wider British and European wave of construction of new civic buildings, evident in Scotland in the survival, in whole or in part, of a number of tolbooths from this era and the lack of any medieval examples.[77]

The new parliament house was built on an L-plan over under-building to compensate for the slope to the south. Viewed from the parliament close (modern Parliament Square) before it was encased in a late Georgian neoclassical facade, it had a double-height main hall approximately 37m long and 13m wide internally, on the eastern wall of which was a two-storey, two-chamber wing of approximately the same breadth and just over half the length (fig. 4). Continuity with the old tolbooth and with the accommodation in the west end of St Giles' was achieved with the names of the two chambers of the court of session, the inner and outer houses, migrating to the new building. The inner house was put in the wing and, just as when the tolbooth had occupied the west end of St Giles' and probably also in the days of the old tolbooth, the outer house shared the principal chamber with parliament.

---

[75]　Ibid., 101–27, interprets the three-towered motif as representing Heriot's Hospital. A thorough study of the corbels by art historians might shed more light on the messages in the building's design.

[76]　*Tolbooths and Town-houses: Civic Architecture in Scotland to 1833*, Royal Commission on the Ancient and Historical Monuments of Scotland (Edinburgh, 1996), 2, 24–31, 51–3, 57–8, 65–7, 71, 75–7, 78–80, 98–9, 122–6, 131, 149–50, 188, 196–7, 202, 205–6; D. Howard, *The Architectural History of Scotland: Scottish Architecture from the Reformation to the Restoration, 1560–1660* (Edinburgh, 1995), 116–29.

[77]　A. Cowan, *Urban Europe, 1500–1700* (London, 1998), 136–7; K. Giles, 'Reforming Corporate Charity: Guilds and Fraternities in Pre- and Post-Reformation York', in D. Gaimster and R. Gilchrist (eds), *The Archaeology of Reformation 1480–1580* (Leeds, 2003), 325–40; Howard, *The Architectural History of Scotland*, 116–29.

Parliament occupied about two-thirds of the hall (approximately 22m by 11m), with the dais against the south gable wall.[78]

Preparing the venue

The logistics of preparing the parliament house before 1639 were complicated by the nature of the accommodation. Edinburgh's accounts contain numerous references to the process of creating the parliament house and reconstructing the courtrooms in the aftermath of a session. In the old tolbooth, before 1560, the works and consequently the costs appear to have been limited. Only a few shillings were spent in making the bar to delineate the court of parliament and to hang tapestries.[79] After the building of the new tolbooths, costs escalated, or perhaps they were more fully recorded. Wooden partition walls had to be dismantled and others constructed to provide a space of appropriate size; a dais had to be made for the throne; as in England, tapestries were borrowed from the royal palace to line the rough deal-board walls; tables were installed to bear the honours (crown, sword and sceptre) during the session and for the clerks' use; benches for the members were moved in or constructed and fabric was provided to cover them. If parliament met in the winter, as it did in 1597, candles were also required to allow deliberations to continue when the daylight failed, 42 'walx prickettis' in this instance, at a cost to the burgh of £12 12s. Sometimes the time was tight: in 1565, the burgh paid for the breakfasts of the wrights working on the parliament house 'for haisting of the work'.[80] When it was all over, usually only about ten days after it had begun, the whole place had to be restored to its former state for the return of the court of session.[81]

For much of the period, it is hard to identify precisely which expenses applied to parliament, for the maintenance of the tolbooths was a never-ending task and the burgh council remained responsible for them at all times. In 1594, for example, it spent £13 on a cloth for the table of the court of session, a table which the burgh had undoubtedly provided. In the early seventeenth century, tapestries, green cloth bearing the royal arms and other fabrics were installed for the court of session, while in 1649 a cloth was bought for the exchequer table when the burgh also had a 'great cushion' of purple velvet with a golden fringe made for the president of the court of session.[82] The first full account for the works associated with preparing the tolbooth for parliament dates from November 1600.[83] The total cost was £191 18s 5d. This

---

[78] Chambers, *Reekiana*, illustration facing 187 (a plan of parliament house in 1779 when it retained its pre-1707 form) and 187–93, a description of the illustration.

[79] Adam (ed.), *Edinburgh Records: The Burgh Accounts Volume 1*, 136, 247, 279.

[80] Ibid., 503.

[81] Ibid., 486–7, 503–5; ECA, Town Treasurer's Accounts 1581–96, 143–4, 366–7, 710–12, 789, 881–2; ECA, Town Treasurer's Accounts 1596–1612, 118–25; Foster, 'Staging a Parliament', 135–6.

[82] ECA, Edinburgh Council Minutes 1594–1600, SL1/1/10, f. 11r; ECA, Edinburgh Council Minutes, SL1/1/17, ff. 172r, 209r; A. MacKechnie, 'Housing Scotland's Parliament, 1603–1707', in Jones and Kelsey (eds), *Housing Parliament*, 99–130, at 103–4.

[83] ECA, Town Treasurer's Accounts 1596–1612, 276–8.

Figure 4   The new parliament house, as depicted by James Gordon of Rothiemay, soon after its completion in 1639. The door to the chamber is on the right. Reproduced by kind permission of the Royal Commission on the Ancient and Historical Monuments of Scotland.

may have been exceptional because the work also involved restoring the west end of St Giles' to secular use, it having been used briefly for worship between 1598 and 1600, a period during which no parliaments met. In 1604, the costs for a curtailed session were only £87, although when parliament returned to Edinburgh in 1607 after two sessions at Perth, £241 0s 8d was spent on the necessary arrangements. By 1621 the cost of staging parliament had risen to around £400.[84]

Sadly, the separate account for the parliament of 1633 is lost, although its existence is noted in the burgh accounts for that year.[85] It is also regrettable that the records of Perth contain minimal detail of the logistics of staging a parliament outside Edinburgh. In 1604 and 1606, parliament met in Perth's tolbooth because of disease in the capital. A laconic entry in the burgh council minutes records a command to the master of works to see to 'the reparatioun of the new kirk againe the parliament', but the parliamentary record itself is clear that it met 'within the tolbuth of the said burgh of Perth', so the church may have been intended to provide accommodation for meetings of one or more of the estates during the session.[86] In the winter of 1650–1651 parliament returned to Perth as the Scots retreated in the face of an English army.[87] The impact of even very occasional visits of parliament to a burgh is demonstrated in the fact that, until its demolition in 1818, the tolbooth was known as the parliament house.[88]

Once the new parliament house was built, Edinburgh continued to pay for the hosting of the estates. The logistics of fitting out the purpose-built rooms were now more straightforward, although this did not stop costs from rising. In 1639, 254 ells of baize 'for covering the whole parliament and assemblie houses' (the general assembly of the church met in St Giles' immediately before parliament) cost £342 18s, while in June 1644, it cost 400 merks (£266 13s 4d) for the 'doun taking of the sessioun barris ... and for making ane throne and buithes for the parliament and removing of thes at the ryseing of the parliament and placeing and setting up the sessione barr againe'.[89] The parliament at Stirling in 1645 met in the castle and was paid for by the state, at a cost of nearly £250 to fit out the great hall. That which met there in 1651 sat in the burgh, as its accounts reveal that materials were actually brought 'from the castell to the parliament house'.[90] It appears to have met in Stirling's tolbooth, although the building's form and size are unknown due to its replacement

---

[84]   Ibid., 575–6, 888–9; ECA, Town Treasurer's Accounts 1612–23, 979–80.

[85]   ECA, Town Treasurer's Accounts 1623–36.

[86]   PKCA, Register of Acts of the Council 1601–22, B59/16/1, f. 84r; the 'new kirk' was the nave of the medieval church of St John, partitioned to accommodate two congregations; *APS*, vol. 4, 262. It may even be that, as in Edinburgh, Perth had a tolbooth complex, at least temporarily, which included part of the church.

[87]   *APS*, vol. 6, part 2, 608–66.

[88]   S. J. Cowan, *The Story of Perth from the Invasion of Agricola to the Passing of the Reform Bill* (London, 1904), 80–81; *Tolbooths and Townhouses*, 205–6.

[89]   ECA, Town Treasurer's Accounts 1636–50, 1638–9, discharge, 12, 1643–4, 19. 'Buithes' probably means seats like box pews.

[90]   Imrie and Dunbar (eds), *Accounts of the Masters of Works*, vol. 2, 445–6; SCA, Treasurer's Accounts 1634–1720, B66/23/1, account for 1650–51, 10.

in 1705–1706.[91] The expenses involved in buying timber, building seats, cleaning the buildings and providing light for the parliament and its committees came to nearly £200, considerably less than Edinburgh was spending by this time but sufficient to accommodate parliament in an emergency.

Comparisons between the staging of parliaments in Scotland and England seem logical but are problematic for a number of reasons. Firstly, costs in Scotland were considerably lower, whether for sending out summonses or constructing new furniture. Scottish parliaments inevitably cost less because they consisted of fewer people, with sederunts ranging between about 100 and 180 during the first half of the seventeenth century, compared to around 400 in both houses at Westminster.[92] Also, Scottish parliaments before the 1640s were cheaper to stage because they were shorter, normally lasting less than two weeks, while their English counterparts usually met for more than three months. Before 1639, had the Scottish parliament sat for as long as England's 'Short Parliament', contemporaries would have remarked on its duration. The parliaments of the Covenanters, however, matched those of England during the 1640s in sometimes meeting for months. The Scottish parliament did not have any specialist officers either, so the expenses for clerks, ushers and macers were not paid separately from their usual salaries. The clerks of the parliament, for example, were the clerks of the court of session, headed by the clerk register, while the macers who usually served the privy council also doubled up as officers of parliament.[93] In spite of these caveats, the cost of staging the English parliament in the early seventeenth century was astronomical compared to the costs in Scotland. In 1614, £1,025 11s 8d sterling (over £12,300 Scots) was spent on the relatively short, 64-day session of the English parliament.[94] Even if that sum were divided by 64 to reach a notional daily figure and then multiplied by ten to achieve a comparison with the average length of a Scottish session, it would still come to nearly £2,000 Scots, twice as much as was actually spent in Scotland.

The practicalities of preparing and maintaining the venue were not the only things that the burgh hosting parliament had to deal with, and its many other responsibilities provided opportunities for public demonstrations of urban prestige. Edinburgh was fortunate in that its role as 'the heid and principall of this kingdome'[95] and the normal venue for parliament allowed frequent public displays of status. Prosaic tasks like cleaning the streets were also necessary in any early modern town where ordure tended to accumulate. In 1606, the council of Perth ordered the 'taking away of the red [rubbish], middingis and stane aff the calsay [the paved streets]' in preparation for parliament, while in Edinburgh in 1648, the council noted with shame that the streets had 'become altogidder vile and filthie to the great disgrace of the cittie and

---

[91]   *Tolbooths and Townhouses*, 186–8.

[92]   Smith, *The Stuart Parliaments* 1603–1689, 19–26.

[93]   Rait, *Parliaments of Scotland*, 516–17; A. L. Murray, 'The Lord Clerk Register', in *SHR*, 53 (1974), 124–156, at 135.

[94]   Foster, 'Staging a Parliament', 144.

[95]   ECA, Edinburgh Council Minutes 1609–17, SL1/1/12, f. 258r.

offence both of neighbours and strangers'.[96] Although monarchs had a ceremonial guard, responsibility for policing at the time of parliament belonged to the burgh. Edinburgh expected all its able-bodied men to 'be in array agane the parliament', to line the street along the processional route from the Netherbow Port to the Stinking Stile where the members dismounted before proceeding into the parliament house. This role was taken so seriously by the burgesses that, in 1594, when the king's mounted guard 'preassed to be neerest the king, the citicens resisted, by reasoun of their priviledge to guarde the king's person in tyme of parliament till he depart the toun'. Indeed, so heated was the confrontation that 'sindrie swords were drawin' although happily without bloodshed.[97] At times of potential trouble, such as in 1592 when the forfeiture of the earl of Bothwell was anticipated, and in 1594 when the earls of Huntly, Angus and Errol were to be tried for treason, Edinburgh even mounted a watch in the steeple of St Giles' and at Holyrood Palace.[98] Public order was acknowledged by the privy council as the responsibility of the burgh and, when proclamations for keeping the peace during parliament were issued, the provost and bailies of Edinburgh were ordered to arrest any who were in breach of the peace and bring them before the privy council.[99] Crowd control was also necessary, for many people would come out to watch the riding. At Perth in 1604, 'the town mustart fourteen hundred men in armes and gude ecupage'. Two years later, the council gave ten burgesses the daunting responsibility of being 'governouris and gydaris of the multitude' during parliament, while at Edinburgh in 1633 one contemporary recorded that 'the calsey was ravelled [railed] frae the Neither Bow to the Stinking Style, with staiks of timber dung [hammered] in ... on both sydes ... so that people standing without the samen might see weill enough, and that none might hinder the king's passage'.[100]

As part of its duty to maintain public order and to ensure the timeous performance of the tasks of people with a role during parliament, the host burgh also paid extra fees and furnished new livery for their sergeants, trumpeters, drummers and pipers and might even employ some 'extraordinar drummeris' for good measure.[101] Ensign-bearers were furnished with new clothes and, to assert the burgh's visual identity,

---

[96]   PKCA, Register of Acts of the Council 1601–22, B59/16/1, f. 122r; ECA, Edinburgh Council Minutes 1648–53, SL1/1/17, ff. 92v–93r.

[97]   Adam (ed.), *Edinburgh Records: The Burgh Accounts Volume 1*, 503; Birrel, 'Diary', 44–5; Calderwood, *History*, vol. 4, 329.

[98]   ECA, Town Treasurer's Accounts 1581–96, 727; ECA, Edinburgh Council Minutes 1589–94, SL1/1/9, ff. 151r, 254v; CSP Scot, vol. 13, part 1, 135.

[99]   *RPC*, first series, vol. 4, 90–91, vol. 7, 290, 420, vol. 8, 299, vol. 12, 544–5.

[100]   PKCA, Register of Acts of the Council 1601–22, B59/16/1, f. 123r; J. Spalding, The History of the Troubles and Memorable Transactions in Scotland and England from 1624 to 1645, 2 vols, J. Stuart (ed.), (Edinburgh, 1828), vol. 2, 18; J. Maidment (ed.), *The Chronicle of Perth: A Register of Remarkable Occurrences Chiefly Connected with that City from the Year 1210 to 1688* (Edinburgh, 1831), 10.

[101]   ECA, Town Treasurer's Accounts 1581–96, 707, 784; ECA, Town Treasurer's Accounts 1596–1612, 118; ECA, Edinburgh Council Minutes 1600–1609, f. 22v; SCA, Stirling Treasurer's Accounts 1634–1720, B66/23/1, account for 1650–51, 2–7; PKCA, Register of Acts of the Council 1601–22, B59/16/1, ff. 84v, 122r.

ensigns were borne before the ceremonial guards of Edinburgh and Perth when parliament met in those burghs.[102] The burgh even paid for hanging tapestry on the market cross, and for the wine that was drunk and the glasses that were smashed there when formal proclamation of the acts took place at the end of the parliamentary session.[103] The magistrates of Edinburgh took a prominent part in the ceremonial procedures alongside the riding of parliament. It was normal for the provost, the four bailies and the dean of guild to receive new quarter-staffs to bear at 'the tyme of parliament'.[104] Edinburgh's own macer bore the burgh's mace at parliament and, in 1584, it was decided that 20 of 'the maist honest nichtbouris' from each quarter of the burgh should accompany the provost during parliament.[105] In the later 1630s, a ceremonial sword appears in the records of Edinburgh, with its own salaried sword-bearer who carried it before the magistrates at solemn occasions, including parliament.[106]

The new parliament house of the 1630s was a tremendous asset for Edinburgh, albeit that its construction placed a huge financial strain on the burgh. Like the tolbooths, it was truly a multi-purpose building which could be put to uses for which Edinburgh had not previously had adequate accommodation. In 1617, a timber banqueting house was built on the south side of St Giles' in which the king and nobility were feasted at the burgh's expense two days before the end of the parliamentary session and, on the following day, 'sundrie knights and gentlemen of good note were banketed in the same hous'. Another was constructed to feast Charles I on his visit in 1633.[107] In 1641, no such impromptu venue was required and, in the middle of the parliamentary session, on a day in which the full house did not sit, 'his Majestie with the Prince Elector [Charles Louis of Bohemia, his nephew] and quholl nobility, wes royally feasted in the grate parliament hall by the toune of Edinburgh'.[108] That the burgh used the parliament house in this way demonstrates its ownership of the building. It was used in 1640 by the burgh council to convene the 'haill nichtboures' every Tuesday to keep them informed of matters 'which concernis theme in commoun for the publict saiftie and weill of the toun' in such times of danger.[109] In 1649, Edinburgh's ownership of the building was emphasised even more strongly when the provost, dean of guild, bailies and treasurer 'sat at a

[102] ECA, Town Treasurer's Accounts 1596–1612, 845; ECA, Edinburgh Council Minutes 1609–17, SL1/1/12, f. 101v; PKCA, Register of Acts of the Council 1601–22, B59/16/1, f. 85v.

[103] Adam (ed.), *Edinburgh Records: The Burgh Accounts Volume 1*, 312–13; ECA, Town Treasurer's Accounts 1596–1612, 888; SCA, Stirling Treasurer's Accounts 1634–1720, B66/23/1, 13.

[104] ECA, Town Treasurer's Accounts 1581–96, 367, 707, 785, 874; ECA, Town Treasurer's Accounts 1596–1612.

[105] *Edin. Recs.*, 1573–98, 223, 339.

[106] ECA: Edinburgh Council Minutes 1636–44, SL1/1/15, ff. 310r–v, 314v; Edinburgh Council Minutes 1644–48, SL1/1/16, f. 178r; Town Treasurer's Accounts 1636–50, accounts for 1638–9, 1641–2.

[107] Calderwood, *History*, vol. 7, 257; Row, *History*, 363; Richardson, 'The History of Parliament Square', 216–17; Stewart, 'Politics and Religion in Edinburgh', 60.

[108] Balfour, *Works*, vol. 3, 55.

[109] *Edin. Recs.*, 1626–41, 239.

table covered with greane clothe, in the parliament house, within the inner bar, in grandeure' on the first day of a parliamentary session.[110] If they had been the real hosts of the king's parliament since the middle of the fifteenth century with quiet dignity, they were being less modest about it now.

For Edinburgh, having the officers of state, the privy council, the exchequer and the central courts of law on the doorstep and being the normal venue for parliaments brought huge advantages. For Perth, however, the coming of parliament for brief visits presented rare and precious opportunities. In 1604, the chancellor, Alexander Seton, Lord Fyvie, was gifted a tun of wine, and similar gifts were purchased in 1606 at a cost of £200 for the earl of Montrose, the king's commissioner, and the earl of Dunbar, the treasurer and the Scottish statesman most often in personal contact with the king.[111] Granting the honorary freedom of the burgh to eminent visitors at the time of parliament was also a worthwhile gesture for a burgh to make and in 1604 Perth admitted John Skene of Curriehill, clerk register, James Skene, clerk of the rolls, John's son and one of his servants, while in 1606 the burgh enrolled as burgesses four servants of the earl of Montrose, 'magni commissionarii SDN regis'.[112]

Conclusion

The question which remains is what was the wider significance of parliament meeting in civic buildings, constructed and maintained by burghs, rather than in royal palaces or properties belonging to the crown? Perhaps England can help to provide an answer. In an iconic incident in the history of the English parliamentary revolution against Charles I, on 4 January 1642 the king attempted to arrest five members of the House of Commons. He failed and this attack on the privileges of the house led to uproar. On the following day, the members of the Commons adjourned and reconvened in London's guildhall, returning to Westminster only after Charles had left London. To assert their privileges and freedom in the face of royal interference, they had withdrawn to a municipal building from a royal palace.[113] The parallel cannot be exact, but the Commons' choice of venue is striking. The fact that the English parliament usually met in a royal palace does not suggest that it was subservient to the crown in comparison to its Scottish counterpart which did not. Yet the venue of the Scottish parliament says something, surely, about how it was understood, and to whom it belonged in the minds of the political community. In a country with a relatively weak monarchy and where assertive monarchs had been only an occasional feature of political life until the later sixteenth century, sovereignty was more broadly understood. In the magnificent spectacle of the riding of parliament, even when an adult monarch was present, the crown was not worn but was carried, along with the sword of state and sceptre as part of the procession in its own right and when parliament was in session they lay on a table in the middle

---

[110] Balfour, *Works*, vol. 3, 373.

[111] PKCA, Register of Acts of the Council 1601–22, B59/16/1, ff. 81v, 123r.

[112] Perth Guildry Incorporation, Perth Guild Book, GD1/552/2, ff. 12r, 14v.

[113] D. L. Smith, *A History of the Modern British Isles 1603–1707: The Double Crown* (London, 1998), 124.

of the room. They were symbols of sovereignty: at coronations they conferred upon the monarch his or her share of sovereignty and on the table in the parliament house they denoted the fact that the king and estates in parliament were the sovereign body of the realm. It was thus entirely appropriate that the meeting itself should not take place in the king's house, but that the 'meynest of the estates' should be the host and that the king had to come to their house, not they to his. The erection of the new parliament house in the 1630s, it has been argued, reduced the neutrality of parliament's setting because it is presumed to have been done on the king's initiative. However, the burgh, which continued to use parts of the building for storage and to house the bailies' court until the end of the eighteenth century, never forgot who had built it and whose house it really was.[114]

---

[114] Glendinning, *The Architecture of Scottish Government*, 182–4.

Chapter 7

A Sense of Priority:
Status, Precedence and Display

All early modern representative assemblies included an element of ceremony and ritual but that broad commonality masks a diversity of form and symbolism. Most seem to have involved the placing of members of the assembly in order of social rank.[1] The procession which marked the opening and closing of the Scottish parliament was known as the 'riding' of parliament and it was one of the more elaborate parliamentary ceremonies in Europe. The entire membership processed (if the estates were meeting in Edinburgh) up the hill from the royal palace of Holyrood, through the Canongate, into Edinburgh through its eastern gateway, the Netherbow Port, up the High Street to the parliament house where they would dismount, enter the chamber and be seated by ushers. Although there is evidence for a ceremonial procession at the beginning of a parliamentary session as early as 1529,[2] it reached its most developed form in the early seventeenth century. The riding included a number of messages. For onlookers it emphasised the majesty of the institution of parliament and the authority of monarch and estates, the sovereign body in the realm, thus emphasising the unity of parliament and of the nation as a whole. Yet paradoxically, as in the religious processions upon which it undoubtedly drew, it also underlined social divisions, delineating the groups which were involved and their status relative to each other.[3] For those actually participating, the affirmation of the status of each group within the whole was important, as was the ranking of individuals within each estate.[4]

To medieval and early modern Europeans, 'it was a self-evident truth that peace and order could only be preserved by the maintenance of grades and distinctions'. Society was understood as being divided into 'orders' or 'estates': the way people dressed and the things to which they devoted their daily lives advertised their social

---

[1] M. A. R. Graves, *The Parliaments of Early Modern Europe* (London, 2001), 206–9; P. Cardim, 'Ceremonial and Ritual in the Cortes of Portugal (1581–1698), in *PER*, 12 (1992), 1–14; J. E. Powell and K. Wallis, The House of Lords in the Middle Ages: A History of the English House of Lords to 1540 (London, 1968), chs 30 and 31.

[2] Diurnal of Occurrents, 13.

[3] R. N. Swanson, *Religion and Devotion in Europe, c.1215–c.1515* (Cambridge, 1995), 293–4.

[4] Little has been written on this aspect of parliamentary history anywhere, but see T. Innes, 'The Scottish Parliament: Its Symbolism and its Ceremonial', in *Juridical Review*, 44 (1932), 87–124; J. Goodare, 'Parliament and Society in Scotland, 1560–1603' (Edinburgh University PhD, 1989), appendix E; Rait, *Parliaments of Scotland*, ch. 9.

positions.[5] Although such an instinctive understanding of social divisions had been a commonplace for centuries, the sixteenth century saw an intensification of concern among elites for definition and affirmation of status, between and within social orders. Unprecedented social mobility prompted the higher ranks of society to seek to bolster their status. What Lawrence Stone described as an 'inflation of honours' made those whose elevated status was of longer standing want to differentiate themselves from *arrivistes*. But the presssure came from above as well as below. As the state sought to increase its authority, nobilities felt threatened by monarchs who wanted to accord greater prestige to service to the crown. Many of the beneficiaries were 'new' noble families, previously untitled landowners whose elevation devalued the exclusiveness of noble status. The result was an increasing desire among the older nobility to define noble status more clearly and more restrictively.[6] Sumptuary laws sought to restrict, according to rank, the types of clothing people might wear, what foods they might eat, even the sorts of houses in which they might live. Indeed, the explicit purpose of an English sumptuary law of 1533 was the need to distinguish 'estates, pre-eminence, dignities and degrees'.[7]

Social divisions were made manifest in many contexts. As fixed seating emerged in churches, the prominence of nobles and urban elites was advertised by expensive pews decorated with appropriate biblical texts and heraldic badges, phenomena which were as present in Scotland as elsewhere in Europe.[8] Julian Goodare has described the 1590s in Scotland as 'a period of unprecedented aristocratic paranoia about their privileges' resulting from crown policies which, although they were 'probably not a deliberate attack on the nobility', were perceived as such by those who saw themselves as victims. Access to the monarch was restricted and the status of the senior nobles was subordinated to that of the officers of state, whether those officers held a peerage or not.[9] Between the middle of the sixteenth century and the beginning of the seventeenth, there was an unprecedented expansion of the Scottish peerage, largely resulting from the secularisation of church lands before and after the Reformation.[10]

---

[5]　L. Stone, *The Crisis of the Aristocracy, 1558–1641* (Oxford, 1965), 21; P. Burke, 'The Language of Orders in Early Modern Europe', in M. L. Bush (ed.), *Social Orders and Social Classes in Europe since 1500: Studies in Social Stratification* (Harlow, 1992), 1–12; O. Ranum, 'Courtesy, Absolutism, and the Rise of the French State', in *Journal of Modern History*, 52 (1980), 426–51.

[6]　Stone, *The Crisis of the Aristocracy*, 36–9, ch. 3; R. G. Asch, *Nobilities in Transition 1550–1700: Courtiers and Rebels in Britain and Europe* (London, 2003), 11, 14; M. L. Bush, 'An anatomy of nobility' in Bush (ed.), *Social Orders and Social Classes*, 26–46, at 28.

[7]　J. Youings, *Sixteenth-Century England* (Harmondsworth, 1984), 111.

[8]　F. Heal, *Reformation in Britain and Ireland* (Oxford, 2003), 441–3; M. L. Bush, *Noble Privilege* (New York, 1983), 146.

[9]　J. Goodare, 'The nobility and the absolutist state in Scotland, 1584–1638', in *History*, 78 (1993), 161–82, at 166; J. Goodare, *State and Society in Early Modern Scotland* (Oxford, 1999), 74; Powell and Wallis, *The House of Lords in the Middle Ages*, 581, shows that this occurred in England in 1539.

[10]　Balfour Paul, *Scots Peerage*, passim: between 1550 and 1610, 34 new peerages were created, while 8 had their peerages augmented.

Along with the inflation of honours, there was economic inflation to deal with in a period when that process really began to bite for the first time in western Europe. This was the era of the 'price revolution': prices rose but real wages failed to keep pace, leading to high levels of economic and social insecurity.[11] In Scotland, inflation struck relatively late compared to the rest of Europe but it was no less severe and was linked to a deliberate policy of the crown to devalue the coinage in a short-sighted, short-term money-making scheme.[12] The wider effect of this inflation for some was the devaluation of their landed rents. The earlier sixteenth century had seen the widespread feuing of crown and church lands, with some nobles following suit. Hereditary leases were granted for a heavy downpayment and an augmented perpetual annual feu duty. This was lucrative at first but, once inflation took hold, the value of feu duties was seriously eroded, while feudal superiors could do nothing about it unless the feuar failed to produce heirs. Although most feuing was carried out by the Church and the crown, the acquisition of former Church lands by nobles and the ennoblement of the holders of monastic properties meant that an increasing number of nobles were affected by feuing, taking on estates which had been subject to feuing by their former owners.[13] Nobles were also hit by more severe inflation in the prices of luxury commodities and, by the early seventeenth century, were increasingly living on credit, their rental incomes no longer able to keep them in the style which their social position demanded. All these factors must have contributed to noble insecurity and their desire to maintain, assert and have acknowledged what they saw as their rightful position in society. Such recognition cost nothing but its worth was beyond measure.[14]

The desire among the nobility to preserve their status in the face of an inundation of upstarts rubbed off on the rest of society. The pressures of economic flux and the inflation of honours which had affected the nobility also affected the towns, creating insecurities which were as severe there as in the countryside. Indeed, inflation had a greater impact in towns, where commerce was conducted and wages for the most part paid in coin. During the period of this study, Scotland saw the largest expansion in the number of royal burghs since the twelfth century. Between 1550 and 1651, more new royal burghs were created (17) than in any similar period since the twelfth century. An even greater number of burghs (25) sent their first recorded commissioners to parliament in this period.[15] In spite of an upswing in trade from the 1550s onwards, the expansion of the urban estate bred insecurity among pre-existing parliamentary burghs. Worried that new creations would undermine their trading privileges and erode their market share, they sought, sometimes successfully,

---

[11]   H. Kamen, *Early Modern European Society* (London, 2000), 181–2.

[12]   M. Lynch, *Scotland: A New History* (London, 1991), 183–4.

[13]   M. H. B. Sanderson, *Scottish Rural Society in the Sixteenth Century* (Edinburgh, 1982), discusses feuing in detail in chs 6 and 7.

[14]   For noble indebtedness, see K. M. Brown, *Noble Society in Scotland: Wealth, Family and Culture, from Reformation to Revolution* (Edinburgh, 2000), ch. 4.

[15]   The figures come from Pryde, *The Burghs of Scotland*. This excludes Glasgow, St Andrews and Brechin which, although not technically royal burghs until this period, were taxed and sent commissioners to parliament before 1550.

to exclude new burghs from exercising the privileges that they had been granted by the crown.[16]

Urban society was a microcosm of society as a whole, with hierarchical divisions between free and unfree, within the free between merchants and craftsmen, and between different guilds within those two groups. These distinctions were most publicly emphasised in urban processions. Before the Reformation and in the parts of Europe which remained Catholic, annual celebrations of the town's patron saint and Corpus Christi provided opportunities for the freemen to process through the streets in order of status, the lowliest craft guild at one end, the magistrates at the other, with appropriate gradations in between.[17] Townspeople knew well the importance of hierachy and fought tenaciously to maintain their places in the pecking order. In Scotland, the hierarchy of craft guilds varied from one burgh to another, depending on the importance of the occupations in the local economy.[18] Concern for precedence can be exemplified both before and after the Reformation which, while eradicating the processions associated with Catholicism, replaced them with secular occasions and new religious contexts in which rivalries could be fought out. In Aberdeen in 1538, the deacon of the hammermen 'complenit to the balyes allegiand wrang don to thame be the marenaris in usurping of thair place in the processioun on Corpus Christi day'.[19] Dundee provides an example of how inter-craft rivalry could be carried out in a religious setting after the Reformation: the baxters (bakers) erected a pew on which it was written that 'Bread is the staff of life', and the response of the fleshers (butchers) was to inscribe 'Man shall not live by bread alone' on theirs![20] The regular 'wapinschaws' (i.e. weapon-shows) involved the freemen of burghs mustering in the market place for inspection of their military preparedness. This was conducted in a hierarchy of groups, pre-eminence being given to the magistrates, council and merchants, with the crafts put firmly in their place. In Glasgow in 1583, the wapinschaw was disrupted by disputes over precedence involving both merchants and craftsmen 'concernyng thair ranking and placeing thame selfis'. In Aberdeen, the ceremonial riding of the burgh's marches was combined with a wapinschaw, thus possibly making it 'a local version' of the riding of parliament.[21]

Scottish ceremonial usually proceeded *ad seniores*: the more important one was, the closer to the rear of the procession one was placed. The hammermen of

---

[16]   See ch. 1.

[17]   Youings, *Sixteenth-Century England*, 85; E. P. Dennison, 'Power to the People? The Myth of the Medieval Burgh Community', in S. Foster, A. Macinnes and R. MacInnes (eds), *Scottish Power Centres from the Early Middle Ages to the Twentieth Century* (Glasgow, 1998), 100–131; E. Bain, *Merchant and Craft Guilds: A History of the Aberdeen Incorporated Trades* (Aberdeen, 1887), 48–61; R. Hutton, *Stations of the Sun: A History of the Ritual Year in Britain* (Oxford, 1996), 304–10.

[18]   M. Verschuur, 'Merchants and Craftsmen in Sixteenth-Century Perth', in M. Lynch (ed.), *The Early Modern Town in Scotland* (London, 1987), 36–54, at 37–8.

[19]   ACA, Council Records, CR1/15, 659.

[20]   Dennison, 'Power to the People?', 114.

[21]   Glasg. Recs., vol. 1, 102; M. Lynch and H. M. Dingwall, 'Elite Society in Town and Country', in E. P. Dennison, D. Ditchburn and M. Lynch (eds), *Aberdeen Before 1800: A New History* (East Linton, 2002), 181–200, at 184.

Aberdeen had complained because the mariners usurped their place in 'gangand behind thame aganis the commound ordinance and statutis of this nobill burght'. This appears to contrast with English and other European urban processions where 'all guild members shuffled somewhat reluctantly in due order of seniority behind the mayor and his fellow councillors', although in Ipswich and Chester's Corpus Christi processions, the tabernacle brought up the rear.[22] The riding of parliament conformed to the pattern of the lowliest at the front and the monarch or his or her representative at the rear. There may be little real significance in whether people processed *ad seniores* or *ad juniores*, as long as it adhered to a preordained order which reflected the hierachy of the participants. If the occasion demanded, it was reversed: when the nobility greeted Charles I outside Edinburgh in 1633, the most important people were, appropriately, at the front.[23] In the riding of parliament, the necessary messages were more clearly expressed in processing *ad seniores*, a pattern also used in the smaller English parliamentary procession by the seventeenth century, although not applied under Henry VIII when the prelates preceded the king in ascending order and the magnates followed in descending order, echoing the practice of religious processions in some English towns.[24] Placing the most important people and objects at the rear in Scotland provided a visual crescendo culminating in the honours (crown, sword and sceptre) and the monarch or the monarch's commissioner in his or her absence. It also meant that, once they had arrived at the parliament house, the more lowly had to wait for their social superiors. Differences in status were also made manifest in the different numbers of retainers allowed to the various ranks of parliamentary members: the higher up the social scale, the more retainers one could bring.[25]

It is not clear when the full membership began to participate in the riding of parliament, or indeed when it became a normal part of proceedings. Descriptions from the earlier sixteenth century are imprecise and the first detailed regulations were issued only in 1600. Before that time, the crown simply commanded that parliament should meet in peace, that all quarrels between members should be laid aside and that weapons and armour should not be worn (saving the swords and daggers which nobles wore as a matter of privilege), so that all the lieges wishing to petition parliament might do so 'frielie and without all perrell'.[26] In 1560, the English ambassador, Thomas Randolph, recorded that the 'lords ... assembled themselves at 10 o-clock at the Palace [of Holyrood] ... and from thence departed towards the "Tawbowth" [tolbooth] as they were in dignity',[27] suggesting that only the nobility processed, although 'lords' in this context can have a much broader meaning. The

---

[22] ACA, Council Records, CR1/15, 659; Youings, *Sixteenth-Century England*, 85; M. Rubin, *Corpus Christi: The Eucharist in Late Medieval Culture* (Cambridge, 1991), 243–71; Bain, *Merchant and Craft Guilds*, 56–8.

[23] *RPC*, second series, vol. 5, 115–16.

[24] E. R. Foster, 'Staging a Parliament in Early Stuart England', in P. Clark, A. G. R. Smith and N. Tyacke (eds), *The English Commonwealth 1547–1640: Essays on Politics and Society Presented to Joel Hurstfield* (Leicester, 1979), 129–46, at 129; Powell and Wallis, *The House of Lords in the Middle Ages*, 543, 549; Rubin, Corpus Christi, 262–3.

[25] *RPC*, first series, vol. 6, 169, vol. 7, 214.

[26] *RPC*, first series, vol. 1, 342, 596, vol. 5, 90–91.

[27] *CSP Scot.*, vol. 1, 457.

'Reformation Parliament' of 1560 is hard to evaluate in terms of the degree to which its procedures can be taken to indicate what was normal. In legislating to abrogate papal power, abolish the mass and adopt a Calvinist confession of faith, it was a revolutionary meeting.[28] However, those behind the revolution would have had compelling reasons to ensure that everything was carried out according to custom, to pre-empt allegations of invalidity which were bound to be levelled at the parliament by opponents. As late as 1578, the convention of burghs agreed that, when a parliament or convention of estates was to meet, the burgh commissioners should 'convene together and pas to the parliament or convention'.[29] This might suggest that they did not expect to be part of the formal opening procession, but it could mean that the burghs were agreeing to ensure that all commissioners participated in the riding, and did not go straight to the parliament house. As in 1560, the circumstances in July 1578 were exceptional: parliament had met in Stirling Castle, under guard and amidst a high degree of political controversy. The usual opening ceremonies were not used, save for the king walking the few yards from the palace to the great hall, accompanied by three nobles carrying the honours, but parliament was properly seated, 'Everie man being placed according to their degree'.[30]

Parliament first laid down regulations for its own conduct in 1587. Apart from a hurriedly-organised session in December 1585 at Linlithgow, the parliament at Edinburgh in July 1587 was the first since James VI had freed himself from the grip of noble factions and begun to rule in his own right; it was thus the first in his adult reign for which an eye on the longer term was possible. The ostensible purpose of the act 'Anent the Parliament' was to reverse the 'decay of the forme honour and majestie of [the] supreme court of parliament'. This sort of language reflected 'a normal intellectual assumption' of the era, that everything was subject to a cycle of decay and reform, but the regulations can be seen as part of a drive to enhance the prestige of the institutions of government after 20 years of political instability. The guidelines of 1587 went further in dating the decline of parliament to the period 'sen the deceisse of ... king James the fyft' (1542).[31] They chimed with the desire for social cohesion and clear distinctions between orders by commanding that none should represent any more than one estate, that being the one 'quhairin he commounlie professis himself to leif and quhairof he takis his styll', and ordering that every estate should have a distinctive form of dress devised by the king. Regulations for the riding were not laid down but the two following acts concerned disputes over 'prioritie of place or vote in parliament', almost certainly the result of quarrels at the beginning of the session. The first commanded members not to disrupt proceedings

---

[28] For a detailed account of this parliament see K. M. Brown, 'The Reformation Parliament', in K. M. Brown and R. J. Tanner (eds), *Parliament and Politics in Scotland, 1235–1560* (Edinburgh, 2004), 203–31.

[29] *RCRBS*, vol. 1, 70.

[30] Moysie, *Memoirs*, 9–12; Calderwood, *History*, vol. 2, 413. See also M. Lynch, 'The Great Hall in the Reigns of Mary, Queen of Scots, and James VI', in R. Fawcett (ed.), *Stirling Castle: The Restoration of the Great Hall* (York, 2001), 15–22, at 17–19.

[31] *APS*, vol. 3, 433; Goodare, 'Parliament and Society', 518; M. Roberts (ed.), *Sweden as a Great Power 1611–1697: Government, Society, Foreign Policy* (London, 1968), 11–12, reveals similar concerns there in 1617.

by disputing the position in which they were placed by the Lord Lyon King of Arms, while the second established a commission to resolve the problem. It was to meet with the Lord Lyon to decide 'how all estaitis of this realme sould ryde from the kingis palice to the parliament hous in tyme of parliament', demonstrating that the whole membership was expected to ride by this date at least. All those eligible to sit were to produce written evidence 'quhairby they clame thair dignitie prioritie and prerogative in parliament', and those failing to turn up would 'be left last in the roll'. This proved an empty threat: the commission, if it met at all, failed to resolve the matter and a similar commission established in 1592 had no more success, although the papers of Sir James Balfour of Denmilne, Lord Lyon under Charles I and Charles II, do contain a record of the ordering of the nobility at parliaments between 1592 and 1600, presumably drawn up by his predecessor Sir David Lindsay.[32]

The order of the estates

It is hard to discern the order of the procession until specific regulations were laid down in 1600. It might be assumed that the clergy, the first estate in the medieval period, processed nearest to the king. That was certainly not the case in early seventeenth-century England where the bishops processed behind the judges and privy councillors and in front of the nobility.[33] After 1560, the clerical estate in Scotland remained in flux as 'abbots' continued to sit in spite of the monasteries being defunct, while the fluctuation of the position of the episcopate meant that their numbers remained small and their status uncertain.[34] The issue was further confused by the appearance, from 1592, of shire commissioners.[35] They slotted in between the burgesses and the peers, without demur, even though the burgh commissioners thus found themselves fourth out of four estates. Not until after the abolition of the episcopate in the Covenanting revolution did the burghs protest against the status given to the shire commissioners: they objected to the shires being regarded as 'the thrid estaitt', in spite of their having clearly been an estate since the 1590s. It is hard to be certain about why the burghs feared 'the overthrow of thair estaitt' for, if the lairds were to be the third estate, then the burghs would be second. This did not happen and, for the rest of the 1640s, the burghs came last, after the lairds and nobles, as they had done before the abolition of episcopacy.[36]

---

[32] *APS*, vol. 3, 443–4, 554–5; J. Maidment (ed.), *Ancient Heraldic and Antiquarian Tracts by Sir James Balfour of Denmylne and Kinnaird, Knight and Baronet, Lord Lyon King at Arms* (Edinburgh, 1837), 60–68.

[33] Foster, 'Staging a Parliament in Early Stuart England', 129.

[34] On the clergy in parliament after 1560 see A. R. MacDonald, 'Ecclesiastical Representation in Parliament in post-Reformation Scotland: The Two Kingdoms Theory in Practice', in *Journal of Ecclesiastical History*, 50 (1999), 38–61.

[35] J. Goodare, 'The Admission of Lairds to the Scottish Parliament', in *EHR*, 116 (2001), 1103–33.

[36] ECA, Edinburgh Council Records, SL1/1/15, f. 140r. The records of the convention of burghs for this period are missing, so further investigation of this issue is difficult.

Confusion over the position of the bishops had arisen with their formal restoration in the early seventeenth century. The episcopate had been allowed to wither after 1585 and moves to revive it did not get under way until 1598.[37] The first new bishops were appointed in 1600 and an act 'Anent the restitutioun of the estate of bischoppis' was passed in 1606, by which time all 13 dioceses were filled. But where would the bishops ride? The act spoke of their 'wonted rank in parliament' but no sufficiently detailed description of the riding before this date survives to indicate what that was.[38] In 1600, bishops, 'priors' and 'abbots' rode between the lords and the earls, splitting the noble estate, raising a question about the significance of estates *per se*.[39] The nominal heads of religious houses had metamorphosed into secular landowners by the early seventeenth century, a status confirmed by the 'erection' of their holdings into temporal lordships. 'Abbots' thus vanished, the last to sit being Peter Hewat in 1617, as abbot of Crossraguel, ironically one of the few churchmen appointed to an abbacy after 1560.[40] In 1606, 'abbots' and 'priors' rode between the lairds and lords, reflecting their landed status and recent arrival, while the episcopate remained between the lords and earls. On the last day of the session, the bishops refused to ride 'becaus they gott not their old place, that is, before the erles'.[41] In the following year, they were vindicated when the privy council noted that they 'wer ever preferrit, rankit and voitit in Parliamentis and Generall Counsallis before the Lordis of the Temporall Estaite', so 'in this present sessioun of Parliament and in all tymes heirefter' they would ride 'immediatlie before the honnouris and ... be rankit before the haill Temporall Estaite'.[42] This fuelled the nobles' paranoia, making them 'take up their presuming humours, and to mislyke [the bishops] ... fearing they were sett up to cast them doun'.[43] The new bishops were not pre-Reformation prelates, many of whom had been members of noble families; they were parish ministers, the sons of lairds, burgesses and other ministers.[44] Overruling the privy council, the

---

[37]   M. Lee, 'James VI and the Revival of Episcopacy in Scotland, 1596–1600', in Church History, 43 (1974), 49–64; MacDonald, Jacobean Kirk, ch. 4.

[38]   *APS*, vol. 4, 281–4.

[39]   *RPC*, first series, vol. 4, 170–71. For the enumeration of estates and their social and political significance, see J. Goodare, 'The Estates in the Scottish Parliament, 1286–1707', in C. Jones (ed.), The Scots and Parliament (Edinburgh, 1996), 11–32.

[40]   MacDonald, 'Ecclesiastical Representation in Parliament', 40–41, 59; H. Scott (ed.), Fasti Ecclesiae Scoticanae, revised edn, 8 vols (Edinburgh, 1915–), vol. 1, 63; Hewat (appointed 1612) was the only parish minister to gain an abbacy: D. E. R. Watt and N. F. Shead (eds), *The Heads of Religious Houses in Scotland from Twelfth to Sixteenth Centuries* (Edinburgh, 2001).

[41]   *RPC*, first series, vol. 7, 221; Calderwood, *History*, vol. 6, 493–4.

[42]   *RPC*, first series, vol. 6, 221, 423. An exception was probably made for the marquises (Hamilton and Huntly) whom the bishops had recognised as having precedence in 1606 (Calderwood, *History*, vol. 6, 494) and who were given precedence in a royal letter to the privy council setting the order of processing on 24 July 1607 (*RPC*, first series, vol. 7, 533–4), a week before the privy council proclamation.

[43]   Calderwood, *History*, vol. 6, 494.

[44]   J. Wormald, 'No Bishop, No King: The Scottish Jacobean Episcopate, 1600–1625', in B. Vogler (ed.), *Bibliothèque de la Revue d'histoire ecclésiastique: Miscellania Historia Ecclesiasticae VIII* (Louvain, 1987), 259–67.

king's commissioner, the duke of Lennox, intimated that the king wanted only the archbishops placed behind the nobility, with the bishops between the earls and lords. The piqued nobles rashly suggested that all the episcopate should ride between the earls and the honours 'thinking they would not accept it', but they did and rode 'with great derisioun and detestatioun'.[45] In 1609, however, the order of procession suggested by the king was used but this time the bishops took umbrage and, on the last day, 'raid betuixt the honours and the erles', enraging some nobles who went 'on foote to the Parliament Hous, and protested against the wrong done to them'.[46] In spite of this, the episcopate rode immediately behind the nobles and in front of the honours in 1612 but, by 1633, the bishops had come to ride between the lords and the earls and the archbishops between the higher nobility and the honours.[47] The abolition of episcopacy in 1639 removed this complication temporarily but, after 1660, bishops rode between the lords and the viscounts, while the archbishops rode between the earls and the marquises.[48]

Alongside this jostling between nobles and bishops, the burgh commissioners remained firmly in their place. By leading the procession, their subordination was emphasised, and it was maintained in other formalities. Once the riding reached the parliament house and the members had dismounted, they were ushered into their places, with the lowliest sitting furthest from the throne. Even in choosing parliament's drafting committee, the lords of the articles, the nobles and prelates emphasised their superiority by leaving the house to discuss their choices in private, the commissioners waiting in the parliament house for the decision of their superiors.[49] Finally, in voting, the order of the riding was reversed to ensure the influence of the parliamentary hierarchy: the burghs' votes were called last, after their superiors had led by example, with members voting orally in descending order of precedence within each estate.[50]

Although the burghs' subordination in parliamentary ceremony and procedure was clear, the fact that they participated at all contrasts with England, where members of the Commons had no part in the procession to the Palace of Westminster. They waited until summoned to stand outwith the bar of the House of Lords to witness the opening of parliament.[51] There were different ways to emphasise the subordination of the lowlier members and it would be misleading to claim any egalitarian significance

---

[45] *RPC*, first series, vol. 7, 533–4; Calderwood, *History*, vol. 6, 669.

[46] Calderwood, *History*, vol. 7, 38.

[47] 'Memoriall anent the progres and conclusion of the parliament haldin at Edinburgh in October 1612', in J. Dennistoun and A. MacDonald (eds), *Miscellany of the Maitland Club III*, part 1 (Edinburgh, 1843), 112–18, at 114; Balfour, *Works*, vol. 4, 361–3.

[48] 'An act ... establishing the order of the ryding etc at the opening of the ensuing parliament ... 1681', in *Maitland Miscellany III*, part 1, 119–27; T. Innes, 'The Scottish Parliament: Its Symbolism and its Ceremonial', 91.

[49] A. R. MacDonald, 'Deliberative Processes in Parliament, *c*.1567–1639: Multicameralism and the Lords of the Articles', *SHR*, 81 (2002), 23–51 at 44–50; NAS, 'The method and maner of choysing the lords of the articles as the same is setled in June 1663', Cosmo Innes Transcripts, vol. 2, no. 33, RH2/2/14.

[50] Rait, *Parliaments of Scotland*, 405–7.

[51] D. L. Smith, *The Stuart Parliaments, 1603–1689* (London, 1999), 78–80.

in the Scottish procession. The evolution of the English bicameral structure lay behind the exclusion of the elected elements from the opening procession, while Scotland's single chamber was conducive to the involvement of the entire membership. It did mean that, in contrast with England, the opening ceremony of the Scottish parliament visually embodied the nation, virtually present in the three estates, which continued to embody that unity, within the bar, as parliament was fenced.[52]

The order of individuals

Although the dominant message for spectators was the majesty of parliament and the hierarchy of the estates, for participants, ranking within each estate was perhaps of greater significance and disputes led to heated confrontations, protests and even physical violence. The key indicator of status was proximity to the monarch, which applied equally to coronations and to royal banquets, where the more important you were, the closer to the monarch you sat and the sooner you were served.[53] The order of parliamentary ceremonial flowed logically from the deference due to the monarch – if he or she was placed in the procession according to his or her pre-eminence, the position of everyone else indicated their relative importance. Places were hotly contested and the criteria for judging who should go where were not always clear or consistent, even as far as the crown was concerned.

The parliamentary record contains numerous formal protests by nobles who felt that they had not been given their proper places.[54] It was bad enough that the peerage was being diluted by new creations, but the introduction of new ranks caused even greater friction as it disrupted the existing order.[55] The rapid rise to prominence between 1579 and 1581 of Esmé Stewart, Lord d'Aubigny, a Franco-Scottish cousin of James VI, created problems. He was given the vacant earldom of Lennox which soon became a duchy. Never before had Scottish ducal titles been held outwith the immediate royal family and none had ever passed through more than two generations. As the senior noble, the earl of Angus claimed the right to carry the crown (the most important of the honours) at the riding of parliament; in 1585, it was given to Lennox and Angus protested.[56] He was further disconcerted in 1599 when the earl of Huntly and Lord Hamilton were made marquises, an innovation in Scotland. Angus had previously quarreled with Huntly over precedence but now Huntly was more than a mere earl. The dispute continued until 1633 when Angus formally renounced his claim.[57]

Nobles disputing precedence sometimes refused to join the riding or even to participate in parliament at all. Occasionally they drew swords and challenged each other to mortal combat. In 1593, one dispute delayed the start of parliament for

---

[52]   Goodare, 'Parliament and Society in Scotland', appendix E.

[53]   M. Lynch, 'Queen Mary's Triumph: The Baptismal Celebrations at Stirling in December 1566', *SHR*, 81 (1990), 1–21.

[54]   See, e.g., *APS*, vol. 3, 237, 291, 375, vol. 4, 276, 594.

[55]   Asch, *Nobilities in Transition*, 14.

[56]   Calderwood, *History*, vol. 3, 465.

[57]   Calderwood, *History*, vol. 7, 452; *RPC*, first series, vol. 12, 549n; *APS*, vol. 5, 10.

five hours.[58] Before 1597, the privy council judged these disputes but, in December that year, parliament sought to do away with *ad hoc* arbitrations by establishing a commission to draw up a table of ranking. It was to meet in May 1598 and 'decyd and determinat anent the prioritie and ordour of placeis in parliament and conventionis'. All nobles and burghs 'as thay have regard to their places' were to send in evidence to support their cases, so that 'everie mannis plaice [could be] appoyntit ... according as the antiquitie of thair houses sall signifie'.[59] Although signet letters were sent to all interested parties, the commission was not fulfilled. In November 1600, another was established with the narrower remit of ranking the nobility. It compiled a 'decreet of ranking' which was printed and established as a benchmark. Anyone seeking to have it changed had to accept their existing place until they obtained a decree from the court of session by producing 'mair ancient evidentis and wreattis nor [i.e. than] hes bene produceit in the countrair'.[60] Although antiquity of title was the key, proximity to the royal family was also a factor, claimed by the Stewart earl of Arran in 1581 who demanded to carry the crown 'for he alledged his hous to be nearest to the king'. Royal blood also gave the Hamiltons an elevated position, although without an earldom until 1503.[61] Once a clear ranking was established, all those in receipt of new titles would 'tak thair placeis and rankis according to thair creationis'. Sir David Lindsay and his successor as Lord Lyon, Sir James Balfour, kept a list of the dates of ennoblements from 1596, yet disputes over precedence continued for the remainder of the life of the Scottish parliament. [62]

That burgh commissioners were also exercised by the need to have the status of their burghs recognised contrasts with the situation in England and is attributable to a number of causes. In England, borough MPs did not participate in the opening procession in which rank and precedence were articulated and contested. Also the nature of urban representation in England was diverse in the extreme, from great cities like London and York to the practically non-existent Old Sarum which, although possessing greater antiquity than most, had no residents to vaunt it. By the later sixteenth century, many borough MPs were landed clients of the nobility or carpetbaggers, representing towns for nothing in return for a parliamentary seat. Their affinity with their constituencies was much weaker than that of their Scottish counterparts who were more likely to have a real sense of civic pride. In the House of Commons, with the exception of the members for London and York, who sat at the speaker's right hand, 'everyone sitteth as he cometh, no difference being there held of any degree'.[63] Although the representatives of Portuguese towns were ranked

---

[58]   Details of such spats can be found in Calderwood, *History*, vol. 3, 417, 592–3, vol. 4, 639, vol. 6, 99, 262; CSP Scot., vol. 9, 452–5, vol. 11, 700–702; Moysie, *Memoirs*, 9–12, 65, 102.

[59]   ACA, Aberdeen Council Records, CR1/37, 309–10.

[60]   *RPC*, first series, vol. 8, 473–4.

[61]   Calderwood, *History*, vol. 3, 592–3; Balfour Paul, *Scots Peerage*, vol. 4, 397.

[62]   NLS, 'Collectanea Dominis Davidis Lindesay de Mounthe Militis Leonis Armorum Regis', ff. 98r–99r, f. 125v, Adv. MS 31.3.20, which even deals with the precedence of three earldoms created on the same day; Balfour, *Works*, vol. 4, 364–73; *RPC*, first series, vol. 11, 150–51, 535.

[63]   M. A. R. Graves, *The Tudor Parliaments: Crown, Lords and Commons, 1485–1603* (London, 1985), 22, 149; Smith, *The Stuart Parliaments*, 23.

in order of precedence, it was in relation to their personal social status, not that of their town. Only in Sweden did urban members apparently sit according to which town they represented.[64]

Some Scottish burghs were almost as concerned about their place in the pecking order as the nobles. The convention of burghs maintained the shared privileges of the burghs and heightened their awareness of that commonality; it also bolstered their consciousness of the differences in status between each other by providing another forum in which rivalries could be played out. Although there was no ceremonial opening procession, burgh commissioners sat and voted according to rank.[65] Despite the fact that the burghs were the most politically and economically weak estate, many possessed something which every noble would have envied, a pedigree dating back to the twelfth century. The vicissitudes of war and politics meant that the oldest noble titles were at least 200 years younger than those of the oldest burghs which had the advantage, as corporate entities, of never dying and the good judgement and good fortune never to find themselves sufficiently on the wrong political side to be stripped of their status. The only way for a burgh to be removed from parliament was for it to leave the country, as happened to Berwick, or cease to exist, like Roxburgh.

The most acrimonious and longest-running dispute between burghs involved Dundee and Perth. It lasted for 35 years and was reluctantly handled by the convention of burghs, the privy council, parliament, and the court of session. According to a seventeenth-century source, December 1567 saw the beginning of 'that long lasting debait betuix the tounes of Perth and Dundie anent the 2d place of precedincey amongest the burrowes'.[66] The privy council register for January 1568 recorded that, in the previous December, a 'tumult happynnit upoun the gait of Edinburgh betuix the nychtbouris [of Dundee] and the inhabitantis of Sanctjohnnestoun [Perth] in the tyme of the ... parliament'. According to David Calderwood, burgesses of the two burghs were 'striving for the neerest place to the Tolbuith' when this occurred and the Edinburgh diarist, Robert Birrell, recorded that the regent, James Stewart, earl of Moray, intervened in an attempt to reconcile the towns, perhaps because James Haliburton, provost of Dundee, was his ally.[67]

Rivalries between near neighbours are always more intense and animosity is accentuated when the two are contesting for the same thing. Work on early modern France has shown that such conflicts were most common between 'powerful families and corporations on nearly the same rungs of the social ladder', which clearly applies to the dispute between Perth and Dundee which 'raged with ludicrous vehemence on the part of the Dundonians' according to one Victorian historian of Perth.[68] It had its origins in the fourteenth century, when Dundee consolidated its lead over

[64]   Cardim, 'Ceremonial and Ritual in the Cortes of Portugal', 8; Roberts (ed.), *Sweden as a Great Power*, 11–13.

[65]   *RCRBS*, vol. 1, 230, noting that ranking applied in 'parliamentis and generall conventiouns of the Estaitis and burrowis'.

[66]   Balfour, *Works*, vol. 1, 242.

[67]   *RPC*, first series, vol. 1, 604–5; Calderwood, *History*, vol. 2, 338; Birrel, 'Diary', 13.

[68]   Ranum, 'Courtesy, Absolutism and the French State', 430; R. S. Fittis, *The Perthshire Antiquarian Miscellany* (Perth, 1875), 358.

Perth as the principal burgh on the Tay in terms of its share of international trade.[69] In 1402, it fought off Perth's attempts to assert rights over the whole river and firth and proceeded to demand exactions from Perth, whose liberties stretched to within about two miles of Dundee. Perth was vulnerable: the silting-up of the Tay and the growth in the size of trading vessels meant that, to bring imported goods to its docks and to carry exports across the North Sea, smaller boats had to ply between Perth and Dundee, so cargoes had to be trans-shipped at Dundee, where the magistrates and council demanded harbour and anchorage fees. Disputes over this rumbled on into the seventeenth century when it was finally resolved.[70] By the sixteenth century, Dundee stood in second place behind Edinburgh in terms of wealth, consistently paying the second greatest share of the burghs' slice of national taxation. Its position at the head of the Firth of Tay gave it ready access to trade with Scandinavia, the Baltic and the Low Countries. With regard to the intensification of rivalry with Perth, between 1535 and 1583 its share of urban taxation grew from 9.7 per cent to 11 per cent, while that of Perth shrank from 7.4 per cent to 6 per cent.[71] Taxes were divided by agreement among the parliamentary burghs and are therefore a reliable indicator of their fluctuating fortunes. The message from the tax record is that Perth was losing ground to Dundee.

Between 1567 and 1579, probably as a result of civil war from 1568–1573 and the lack of parliaments between 1573 and 1578, the record is quiet on the precedence dispute, yet the two continued to fight in the courts over shipping tolls.[72] However, when parliament met at Edinburgh in 1579, the dispute erupted again and the convention of burghs held at Glasgow in the following February was ordered to decide the question of priority between Perth, Dundee and Stirling 'according to the auncientie of the saidis burrowis'. The convention was also to rank the other burghs, 'swa that perpetuall ordour may be establischit amangis the saidis haill burrowis in tyme cuming'.[73] Aberdeen, on hearing of this, augmented its commission from one to three, adding the provost and the dean of guild, and providing an extra £100 for their expenses to defend 'the place of this burght in parliament, fra the quhilk Dundie, Pertht and Striviling intendit to seclud this burght to wit of the thrid place'.[74] At Glasgow, the commissioners from Dundee and Perth agreed that any 'contentioun' between burghs should be submitted to arbitrators chosen by the convention, although Perth insisted that this should not prejudice 'the prioritie of thair place'. Stirling's commissioner then intervened to ensure that 'quhatsumever

---

[69] For customs revenues, see P. G. B. McNeill and H. L. MacQueen (eds), *Atlas of Scottish History to 1707* (Edinburgh, 1996), 250–60.

[70] Detailed accounts of trade disputes between Perth and Dundee can be found in Fittis, *Perthshire Antiquarian Miscellany*, 355–64; A. Maxwell, *The History of Old Dundee* (Dundee, 1884), 114–22; E. P. D. Torrie, *Medieval Dundee: A Town and its People* (Dundee, 1990), 33.

[71] McNeill and MacQueen, *Atlas of Scottish History*, 310; M. Lynch, 'Continuity and Change in Urban Society, 1500–1700', in R. A. Houston and I. D. Whyte (eds), *Scottish Society, 1500–1800* (Cambridge, 1989), 85–117, at 115.

[72] *RPC*, first series, vol. 2, 407–8, 440.

[73] *APS*, vol. 3, 174.

[74] ACA, Aberdeen Council Records, CR1/30, 37–8.

thing beis done or decernit betuix ... Dondie and Perth tuiching the second place ... preugit nocht Striveling and the privilege it hes to the second place'.[75] To resolve the principal dispute, Dundee and Perth were each to choose three merchant burgesses to meet at the church of Rait (lying between the two burghs) and choose an 'overisman' with a casting vote. To ensure that this crucial individual was chosen fairly, a complicated process was devised: each burgh would name five burgesses of other burghs and both lists would be put into a hat (literally) on one piece of paper along with a blank piece; if Perth's representative chose the paper with the names, Dundee would choose from Perth's nominees and vice versa. After this convoluted process, the panel of seven would settle the question once and for all.[76]

It is easy to imagine the exasperation at the next convention in July 1580 when it transpired that, in spite of the effort which had gone into devising a method for reaching agreement, Perth and Dundee had not even sent representatives to Rait. The convention ruled that Dundee and Perth should 'produce and exhibit thair allegeances, defenssis and ressonis' in writing 'together with thair rychtis and titillis, writis and documentis' at a convention at Edinburgh in April 1581. In an ambitious effort to resolve the whole issue of ranking, the burghs were instructed to bring 'sure informatioun anent the ranking and placing of all uther burrowis in parliament, convention or counsall'.[77] In the following April, there was 'lang debaitt and controversie' between Perth and Dundee on the opening day and Stirling again registered its claim to second place. While the 'ranking and placing of the haill burrowes' remained on the agenda, they started by trying to resolve 'the particular debaitt betuixt ... Dundie and Perth before the generall questioun wes decydit'. Their written arguments were 'hard, red and at lenth avysitlie considerit', and remitted to the king and privy council because the dispute was 'swa debaitabill and intricate'. Indeed, they ducked the whole issue on the grounds that they could not be 'juges in thair awin caussis'. Meanwhile, Perth and Dundee would 'stand in the same estaitt as thai now presentlie remayne'. Perth's commissioner dissented, while Stirling's again asserted his burgh's right to second place. To add to the confusion, the commissioners from Aberdeen and Linlithgow protested that their right to third place must be recognised: whatever the outcome of the contest between Perth and Dundee, there were others waiting to contest it.[78]

As the convention was meeting in Edinburgh, a swift response from the privy council was obtained: it would have none of it, insisting that the burghs gave judgement as parliament had commanded, under pain of horning (outlawry). So, 'for feir of the said horning ... the maist pairt' of the convention gave Perth 'the priority ... before the burch of Dundie' until the next parliament or convention of estates, or until a judgement was made by the king and privy council. Meanwhile all burghs were to occupy 'thair awin wontit place'. The commissioners of Dundee 'alluterly dissentit', while those of Stirling, Linlithgow and Aberdeen protested again and Lanark, Haddington and Cupar 'and divers of the remanent burrowes'

---

[75]   *RCRBS*, vol. 1, 84.

[76]   Ibid., 84–5.

[77]   Ibid., 107–8.

[78]   Ibid., 114.

added their formal protests that this ruling should 'preiuge nocht thair burghis in the places quhilk thai merite as mair ancient nor the burchis contendant'.[79] So the principal criterion was antiquity, but a closer examination of the foundation dates of these burghs suggests that it was less straightforward. Cupar was clearly chancing its arm, not having been erected until 1327, later than at least 30 active parliamentary burghs, while ten were older than Linlithgow.[80] As with the nobility, other factors must have been regarded as important. With Linlithgow, the obvious one is the link to the monarchy, one of the royal palaces having been sited there since the early fifteenth century. Also, along with Lanark, which claimed fourth place, Linlithgow had replaced Berwick and Roxburgh on the court of the four burghs, the forerunner of the convention, in the 1360s. Stirling's claim to second place was, like that of Linlithgow, based on its royal associations and it could trump all but Edinburgh in having been one of the original members of the court of the four burghs.[81]

The dispute between Perth and Dundee, with interventions by Stirling, dragged on in the same vein. In November 1581, Dundee petitioned parliament for a final judgement, alleging that Perth's claim to second place was recent, and that Dundee should have priority being older, paying a higher share of taxation and being governed exclusively by merchants, while Perth had an even split of merchants and craftsmen on its council. Parliament handed the decision back to the burghs along with the ranking of all burghs 'but [i.e. without] fordar delay'.[82] The next general convention of burghs, at Perth in June 1582, judged in favour of Perth and another, immediately preceding parliament in October, followed suit.[83] The guildry book of Perth gives a full account of the events, recording the lengths to which its dean of guild, Henry Adamson, went. In June, he rode to Edinburgh to raise a letter on the act of parliament to charge the convention of burghs at Perth to resolve the dispute. He secured the signatures of the treasurer, William Ruthven, earl of Gowrie and patron of Perth, and the abbot of Dunfermline, Robert Pitcairn, but the duke of Lennox refused to subscribe. Undaunted, Adamson rode to Stirling for the king's signature, returning to Edinburgh to obtain the signet. The convention, thus formally charged, 'declarit the burgh of Perth to haif the first place afoir Dondy ... in all tym to cum'. Dundee then sought redress at parliament in October but the estates remitted the case straight back to the burghs, ordering them to make a final decision on this and 'the haill remanent burowis without delay'. The royal letter made it clear that the burghs should 'considder onlye in this cais the maist auld and ancient burgh liberties

---

[79] Ibid., 118–19.

[80] Pryde, *The Burghs of Scotland*, 21.

[81] Ibid., 4–9. It is not clear why Lanark and Linlithgow sat on the court of the four burghs for Aberdeen and Dundee were wealthier. *RCRBS*, vol. 1, 196; J. G. Dunbar, *Scottish Royal Palaces: The Architecture of the Royal Residences During the Late Medieval and Early Renaissance Periods* (East Linton, 1999), 5–10.

[82] *APS*, vol. 3, 232–3.

[83] The record of this convention of burghs is incomplete but the act is preserved in Perth: PKCA, Court Books and Court Minute Books, B59/12/1, f. 83r–v; *RCRBS*, vol. 1, 126–38; M. L. Stavert (ed.), *The Perth Guildry Book, 1452–1601* (Edinburgh, 1993), 327–8.

and previlegis', clearly indicating the expected outcome in noting 'the ancie[n]tie and antiquitie of our said burgh of Perth'. The convention of burghs duly obliged.[84]

In 1582, Gowrie's support was worth having but by 1584 the political tables had turned. A coup headed by Gowrie in August 1582 had led to the captivity of the king but a counter-coup in July 1583 overthrew his regime. He was arrested, ironically at Dundee, while trying to flee the country and was executed for treason. Dundee's reward was 'second place in voting in parliament nixt [to] Edinburgh' in May 1584, in spite of Perth's protest that the burghs had already ruled in its favour. A royal letter then charged the convention of burghs 'to rank and crave [Dundee's] voitt befoir ... Perth', previous judgements to the contrary notwithstanding.[85] In July 1587, Perth insisted on the judgements of 1581 and 1582, declaring that a 'previe letter, purchest of his Majestie' (Dundee's of 1584) could not overturn a judgement carried out on the order of parliament.[86] In exasperation, the burghs tried to remit the decision to Edinburgh, on the logical basis that its rank was the only one beyond dispute, but its commissioner 'disassentit to thatt burding'.[87] At the next parliament in December of that year, Dundee again tried to obtain a decision but parliament remitted it to the court of session.[88] Nobody wanted to make the decision and, in the meantime, the privy council and the court of session continued to wrestle with claims and counter-claims over Dundee's right to levy tolls from the merchants of Perth.[89]

In 1594, Perth was back in royal favour and the king ordered the Earl Marischal to place it second after Edinburgh at parliament in that year 'and in tyme coming', in accordance with the acts of the convention of burghs, presumably referring to the decisions of the 1580s.[90] Although this sounded like a final judgement, Dundee would not acquiesce and, seven years later, the dispute seemed no closer to resolution; if anything, relations between Perth and Dundee were deteriorating because a new royal charter to Perth ostensibly rescinded Dundee's rights over navigation on the Tay.[91] In February 1601, the king's messenger came to the cross of Dundee to proclaim royal letters, raised before the court of session by Perth, but the bailies of Dundee organised a crowd to heckle him, 'caling him knaif, lowne, and deboschit swingeour [i.e. scoundrel], casting of snaw ballis at him, and interrupting him in proclaimeing of the saidis letters, and ... schoutting and hoying of him with loud cryis throw the gait as

---

[84]   Stavert, *The Perth Guildry Book*, 328–9; the royal letter is held at Perth: PKCA, 'Letteris for Perth for the superioritie of place Perth aganis Dundie', 16 June 1582, B59/26/1/9/2; PKCA, Act of convention of burghs, 1582, B59/26/1/9/7/1 (this act is not in the records of the convention of burghs); R. Renwick (ed.), *Charters and Other Documents Relating to the Royal Burgh of Stirling AD 1124–1705* (Glasgow, 1884), no. 48, Act of Parliament 11 November 1579 (illustrating that Stirling took a copy of the act ordaining that the burghs should settle the debate between Perth, Dundee and Stirling as to their order of priority).

[85]   *APS*, vol. 3, 291; *RCRBS*, vol. 1, 175, 186–7, 195–6.

[86]   Ibid., 230–31.

[87]   Ibid., 232–3.

[88]   *APS*, vol. 3, 448.

[89]   *RPC*, first series, vol. 4, 104–5.

[90]   PKCA, James VI to the Earl Marischal, 30 May 1594, B59/26/1/9/1.

[91]   Fittis, *Perthshire Antiquarian Miscellany*, 368.

gif he haid bene a theif or malefactour'. Dundee closed ranks and the poor messenger 'failed in his proof', no Dundonians being willing to bear witness in his favour.[92]

On 1 July 1601, Perth's commissioners at the convention of burghs at St Andrews informed their council that the convention wished to resolve the dispute and that Dundee was agreeable. They had concurred, as they 'culd do na les except we suld seme unresonabill' but only on condition that the council consented. They had also told the town's representatives before the court of session at Edinburgh 'to haist ... heir and to desist fra all forder proces' and, with similar urgency, they asked the council to 'heist ane heir on the secund of this moneth althocht he suld ryd the haill nycht'. The council gave its commissioners full power to act but insisted that no infeftments dating from before the new charter of 1600 should be considered.[93] On 3 July, Perth's commissioners at Edinburgh obtained a suspension of the process on the grounds that the convention of burghs had requested them 'to submit the saidis matteris ... to the amicabill decisioun of certane uther burrowis'. Dundee protested that this was just a delaying tactic but, on the same day at St Andrews, the commissioners from Dundee and Perth agreed 'to submit thair actiouns presentle depending in the law, and all utheris thair grudgeis and controvereis' to a special convention of burghs at Edinburgh on 8 July. It duly met but, when it was resolved that the most important task was 'to tak away all grudge of the prioritie', Perth 'refuissit to submit except that particular ... war left furth' because they had not been commissioned to discuss it, insisting that the judgement of 1582 should stand.

The case was postponed yet again until the general convention in 1602.[94] However, by that time, further process before the court of session had reached such an advanced stage that it was not dealt with. At the beginning of December, the council of Perth authorised its commissioners at Edinburgh to borrow whatever sums were necessary for their case against Dundee, while its rival borrowed 5,000 merks (£3,333 6s 8d) 'in the defense of certane wrangous actionis and persuittis intendit aganes thame be the toune of Perth'.[95] On 30 December 1602, the court of session, sitting with the king, gave their final judgement.[96] Although Perth's arguments did not mention priority, its submission began with its strongest suit:

> the gryt antiquitie, gud and pleasant cituatioun of the said burgh, of auld the residence of your hienes progenitouris with thair princeis, bairnes, and fameleis, and quhair parliamentis, publict conventiounes, generall counsellis and assemblies of the esteattis of the realme wer hauldin.

---

[92]   *RPC*, first series, vol. 6, 253–4, 265.

[93]   PKCA, Register of Acts of the Council, 1601–2, B59/16/1, ff. 4r–5r.

[94]   NAS, Court of Session, Register of Acts and Decreets, Gibson's Office, CS7/195, ff. 89v–92v; *RCRBS*, vol. 2, 111, 116.

[95]   PKCA, Register of Acts of the Council, 1601–2, B59/16/1, f. 42r; DCA, Town Council Minute Book, vol. 2, 118; Maxwell, *The History of Old Dundee*, 121.

[96]   NAS, Court of Session, Register of Acts and Decreets, Gibson's Office, CS7/201, ff. 387r–393r; a copy of the decree is also in DCA, Charters and Writs, 'Decreet by King James VI and the Lords of Council deciding the dispute between the towns of Perth and Dundee respecting their privileges on the Tay and the precedence', CC1/79.

It went on to say that its new charter of 1600 had exempted its merchants from any exactions that might harm their trade, protesting that the rights obtained by Dundee over parts of the Firth of Tay were invalid because those places had already been granted to Perth. Dundee's response cited various grants from the thirteenth century onwards which had given it jurisdiction in 'all pairtis foiranent the sherefdome of Foirfair' (on the north side of the Firth of Tay east of Dundee) along with the right to insist that all ships entering the Tay had to 'break bulk' at Dundee. Furthermore, it provided a detailed account of why it should have 'the first place [after Edinburgh] in all parliamentis, assembleis, counsallis and counventiounes', along similar lines to the arguments submitted to parliament in 1580. The first was that Dundee 'is mair ancient', having existed before Perth's claim to foundation by William the Lion (1165–1214). William had indeed granted Perth its oldest extant charter, but other sources demonstrate foundation by David I (1124–1153) in the 1120s.[97] The remaining reasons reveal more about what Dundee thought were the other important criteria for precedence. The second stated that Dundee 'beiris the double of the chairgis of Perth in the subsideis of the realme, in the quhilk respect Edinburgh is preferrit to the rest of the burrowis'. Such an argument is not found anywhere else in the context of urban precedence, nor is it one that was used by nobles in their claims for precedence. If accepted, priority would have been established simply by referring to the most recent tax roll, a solution which would have led to interminable arguments involving numerous burghs. The third asserted that 'Dundie is mair civilie governit nor Perth', a reference to Dundee's two craft councillors compared to the even division of merchants and craftsmen on Perth's council. This point was suspect even in 1581, since it would have made Edinburgh no more 'civilie governit' than Dundee. After a decreet arbitral of 1583, the capital's council of 18 included six craftsmen and, like Perth, one of the four bailies was a craftsman. The variations in the merchant: craftsman ratio on burgh councils and its lack of relevance to precedence meant that Dundee's argument would not stand up. Its wealth lay principally in overseas trade, while that of Perth was more dependent on manufactures, so the crafts had a higher standing in the latter.[98] Finally, Dundee claimed that it had had priority in parliament before the burghs' judgement of 1582. It pointed out that the convention met at Perth in that year and that judgement had been obtained with the help of 'mony sinister moyenis usit be umquhile William erle of Gowrie'. This was clearly aimed at the king who would not easily forget his captivity in 1582–1583 and would still have fresh in his mind an alleged attempt on his life by Gowrie's sons at Perth in August 1600. Yet his generous charter to Perth of 1600 was evidence enough that, for James, there was nothing to forgive. The judgement clearly favoured Perth: it would have liberty of the Tay in Perthshire, on both sides of the water, while Dundee would have the same liberty in Forfarshire but would not have the right to levy tolls on Perth's ships except to pay for the upkeep of the 'tines in the watter mowthe of Tay' placed there by Dundee to guide shipping into the safe channels of the firth. Finally,

---

[97]   Pryde, *The Burghs of Scotland*, 4.

[98]   M. Lynch, *Edinburgh and the Reformation* (Edinburgh, 1981), 49–51, 63, appendix i; Verschuur, 'Merchants and Craftsmen', 38.

As to the first place and rank acclamit be ather of the saidis burrowis of Dundie and Perth in parliamentis, generall conventiounes, counsellis of the esteattis of this realme and assembleis of burrowis, Our said soverane lord findis and decernis that the said burght of Perth and thair commissioneris sall have the plaice befoir the said burght of Dundie and thair commissioneris in all the foirsaidis publict meittingis, And the said burgessis of Dundie thair saidis successouris and commissioneris sall mak na impedimentis to thame thairin in na tyme cuming.

Frustratingly, no reasons were rehearsed but the judgement in favour of Perth was just, for it had been founded before Dundee and antiquity was the most important criterion for determining rank.

The precedence of the other burghs remained on the agenda but no general decreet of ranking resulted. In 1610, the convention again asked every burgh to send commissioners 'sufficientlie instructit' to facilitate a final decision. In 1611, Linlithgow's commissioner protested that his burgh should not be prejudiced by the order in which the roll was called and in the following year those from Stirling, Linlithgow, Glasgow and St Andrews tried to push into the places they saw as their own. The convention forbade them to 'sitt doun in this present conventioun quhill [i.e. until] they be called and placed' under pain of a £10 fine. The commissioner from Linlithgow mischievously demanded the minuting of a letter from the archbishop of St Andrews 'quhairin his lordschip calles him self superior and lord of that citie', thus showing that, although St Andrews was a long-standing parliamentary burgh, it was not royal. In 1612 and 1613 a decision was again deferred and then there is silence, individual burghs being left to jostle and protest.[99] In 1633, they duly did: Glasgow, Stirling, Linlithgow and St Andrews were the contenders and Charles I, typically insensitive to proper procedure, ordered that the argument be 'desydit by the dyce'. This was done and 'Lithgow schot fyve, Stirling six, Saintandrois elevine, and Glasgow twelf ... and sa the contest endit be Glasgowes preference'.[100] Whether this worked or not is open to question, for Glasgow protested again in 1641.[101]

Dress and display

In early modern Europe, dress was a reliable indicator of rank. Sumptuary laws limited the wearing of certain luxury fabrics to the nobility and other members of the elite and, in spite of their failure to be strictly observed, the simple costs of silk and velvet meant that only the wealthy could afford them.[102] It is a cliché of modern consumerism that people express something about themselves through what they wear: it was certainly true in the early modern world and what they were saying was how wealthy they were and to what social order they belonged. Merchants were expected to dress distinctively; in 1555, the burghs declared that Scottish merchants

---

[99] *RCRBS*, vol. 2, 297–8, 314–15, 344, 401.

[100] W. Fraser (ed.), *Memoirs of the Maxwells of Pollok*, 2 vols (Edinburgh, 1863), vol. 2, 232–3.

[101] *APS*, vol. 5, 314–15, 586.

[102] Kamen, *Early Modern European Society*, 111–12; Bush, *Noble Privilege*, 128.

must be 'honnest and qualefeit men in thair abulyement and gudis' and in 1565, they ordered the conservator at Veere to fine Scottish traders who were not 'honestlie abolyiit lyke ane marchand'.[103] Individual burghs sought to ensure the proper apparel of merchants, and the dignity of the town was emphasised in the provision of uniforms for drummers, trumpeters and the armed officers who accompanied magistrates and councillors on official business and whose job it was to issue summonses from the burgh court.[104]

Scottish towns were less lavish than their English counterparts in furnishing the magistrates and councillors with gowns and robes of office, although their specific inclusion in the Scottish sumptuary laws of the later sixteenth century suggests that they did wear distinctive clothing.[105] The lack of official garb was noted by James VI after 1603 and, six years later, an act of parliament stated that, the king's international fame having spread, more foreigners were coming to visit his dominions and 'by them na doubt reporte will go throwch all the warld'. It observed that the nobility wore sufficiently grand attire at parliament but the burgh commissioners 'have nocht conformed them selffis to the lyk conveniencie'. The king was thus empowered to prescribe appropriate attire and, in 1610, magistrates and councillors were ordered to wear black gowns edged with fur at parliaments, conventions and council meetings. These were to be based on the normal gown of a burgess and a 'model' (presumably a drawing) was helpfully sent to the privy council. Separate instructions were issued for the 'principal grite burrowis' (Edinburgh, Perth, Dundee, St Andrews, Glasgow, Stirling and Aberdeen) and any others which considered themselves worthy and able. Their magistrates and councillors were to wear 'gownis of reid scarlatt cloathe, with furringis aggreable to the same' on council days, Sundays, the riding of parliament, and on 5 August and 5 November (the anniversaries of the Gowrie Conspiracy and the Gunpowder Plot), and the provost of Edinburgh was to wear a gold chain.[106] These expensive commands were to be obeyed by Michaelmas 1610, but nine years later it was noted that 'thair has bene litill or [no] obedience givin to the saidis actis'. A new deadline of 24 December 1619 was imposed, to ensure that magistrates and councillors made an impact at church on Christmas day, the celebration of which had recently and controversially been revived.[107] Tardily, obedience was achieved in at least some burghs: in 1623, Aberdeen resolved to obey; in 1627, Perth recorded the storage of the town's 'robis' in a trunk; in 1633, in preparation for the visit of Charles I, Linlithgow decided to acquire gowns for the provost, bailies and councillors; and, by 1643, Edinburgh's magistrates had red gowns, while the councillors wore black at the funeral of their provost, Sir Alexander Clerk.[108] As well as clothing their officers,

---

[103]   NLS, Fort Augustus MSS, Acc. 11218/5, ff. 331v–332r; *RCRBS*, vol. 2, 481. 'Abulyement', from the French '*habillement*', clothing.

[104]   DCA, Guildry Book GD/GRW/G1/1, f. 22v; ACA, Aberdeen Council Records, CR1/34/2, 893.

[105]   *RPC*, first series, vol. 5, 243; Youings, *Sixteenth-Century England*, 80, 85, 314.

[106]   *APS*, vol. 4, 435; *RPC*, first series, vol. 7, 613.

[107]   *RPC*, first series, vol. 12, 121, 134.

[108]   ACA, Council Records, CR1/51/1, 39; PKCA, Perth Council Minutes, B59/12/2, 31 Dec 1627; NAS, Linlithgow Town Council Minute Book, 1620–40, B48/9/1, 262–6; ECA, Council Minutes, 1636–44, SL1/1/15, f. 309v.

the burghs also displayed their shared identity with the use of flags at wapinschaws, when the men of the burgh rode out under arms, and at other occasions. The incident on the High Street of Edinburgh between representatives of Dundee and Perth in December 1567 had involved the bearer of Dundee's 'hansenye'.[109] When Edinburgh and Perth hosted parliament, their ensigns were displayed prominently, while ensigns are recorded at Dumfries, Stirling, Ayr, Glasgow, Dumbarton and Kirkcaldy. The materials for Dumfries's new ensign in 1613 suggest that it was a flag of some size, being made from over 12 yards of taffeta.[110]

The riding of parliament provided a setting in which wealth as well as rank could be displayed. Wherever one was placed in the pecking order, ostentation was an option. With the drive for greater dignity in the riding went attempts to promote the wearing of solemn dress. The act 'Anent the parliament' of 1587, in noting the decay of the majesty of parliament, perhaps had in mind an act of 1455 which had set down different coloured gowns to be worn by earls (brown), lords (red) and burgesses (blue).[111] In 1587, the king was handed responsibility for establishing appropriate forms of dress for each estate but not until 1600 were instructions issued: burgh commissoners should ride in black gowns, shire commissioners in footmantles, prelates in footmantles and silk gowns and nobles in velvet footmantles.[112] In succeeding years, the specifications became more detailed and the requirements grander. In 1605, out of concern that the 'high court of Parliament sould be honourit with all schaws of magnificence and state', dukes, marquises and earls were to wear red velvet robes lined with white ermine and taffeta and the lords robes of plain red cloth. In the following year, the king changed his mind, reserving red velvet for coronations and ordering that dukes, marquises and earls should wear the same as the lords, distinguishing 'the severall degries of honour in the copes or hoods of the same by sa mony severall gaires of quhite furring drawine athorte the same', in imitation of the English form.[113] The result was so striking that the parliament at Perth in that year was called the 'red parliament', the author of the *Chronicle of Perth* recording that the nobility were 'all in robbis of read scarlet and facit with quhyte furris'.[114]

The orders of 1610 for the apparel of magistrates and councils explicitly ordered the wearing of the new outfits at the riding of parliament and in 1617 it was laid

---

[109] *RPC*, first series, vol. 1, 605.

[110] PKCA, Register of Acts of the Council 1601–22, B59/16/1, f. 85v; ECA, Council Minutes, SL1/1/12, f. 101v; Edin. Recs., 1604–26, 3; SCA, Stirling Council Minutes, 1597–1619, B66/20/1, 6 June 1608 and Stirling Council Minutes 1619–58, B66/20/4, 24 June, 15 July 1622; AAC, Ayr Court and Council Records, B6/11/2, f. 538r; NAS, Burgh Common Good Accounts, Dumfries 1612–13, E82/17/2 and Burgh Common Good Accounts, Dundee 1575–6, E82/19/2a; GCA, Act Book of the Burgh and City of Glasgow 1573–81, C1/1/1, f. 243r; *Records of the Burgh of Dumbarton, 1627–1746* (Dumbarton, 1860), 55; L. MacBean (ed.), *The Kirkcaldy Burgh Records* (Kirkcaldy, 1908), 85.

[111] *APS*, vol. 2, 43, vol. 3, 433; Rait, Parliaments of Scotland, 429–30.

[112] *RPC*, first series, vol. 6, 170–71. Footmantles were ankle-length riding gowns.

[113] *RPC*, first series, vol. 7, 57, 160–61; Bush, *Noble Privilege*, 127.

[114] J. Maidment (ed.), *The Chronicle of Perth: A Register of Remarkable Occurrences Chiefly Connected with that City from the Year 1210 to 1668* (Edinburgh, 1831), 11.

down that those who did not come with a footmantle would be counted as absent and fined.[115] Just as magistrates and councillors were slow to adopt special gowns, their commissioners to parliament did not leap at the chance to wear footmantles for parliament. Indeed, in 1606, neither they nor the commissioners for shires participated in the riding because they had been given 'untymous warninge' of the new regulations. Lack of notice cannot have been an excuse in 1617 but so many commissioners had no footmantle that the idea of fining them and excluding them from the riding was dropped, proclamation being made that they did not have to 'address thameselves to ryde in futemantillis'.[116] The earliest mention of a footmantle in a burgh's records dates from 1617 when Ayr spent £64 on one for its provost. According to Calderwood, Edinburgh's magistrates wore footmantles in 1579, but the first mention of one it its records comes from 1621, when 'the futemantle' was spruced up for parliament. Perth's is first recorded in 1627, when arrangments were made for its safekeeping, while Aberdeen had one made in 1628 and Linlithgow in 1633.[117] The fragmentary nature of surviving records means that it is not clear whether these five footmantles represented the total or were the tip of an iceberg; after all, evidence of Ayr's and even Edinburgh's survives only in single references. The more prominent burghs probably had one and the fact that the earliest reference to Stirling's footmantle dates from 1685 should not be regarded as indicating that it did not have one before that date.[118] For others, however, it was enough to borrow one for the occasion: that commissioners from Edinburgh, Perth, Dundee, Aberdeen, Stirling and Glasgow rode in footmantles in 1617 when Aberdeen and Perth did not have one made until the later 1620s bears this out;[119] so too does a stray reference to an incident in 1621. The laird of Preston had borrowed a footmantle from the king's secretary for riding on the first day of parliament but, being expected to vote against the crown on a controversial issue, the secretary tried to stop him from riding (and therefore from voting) on the last day by demanding the garment's return. Preston cheekily countered that the secretary's plain mantle was 'not seemlie' enough, so he borrowed a velvet one from someone else. There was clearly a ready supply of footmantles in Edinburgh.[120]

For some burghs which paid for a footmantle it was no ordinary cloak. At £64, Ayr's was probably quite plain, although in 1621, 40s were spent on embellishments. Aberdeen's footmantle, on the other hand, must have been impressive: £167 17s 6d were paid for ten ells of black velvet and, by the time it was first used in 1633, a total of £323 4s 2d had been spent. The balance was devoted to decorations, including silk

---

[115] *RPC*, first series, vol. 11, 150–51.

[116] Maidment (ed.), *Ancient Heraldic Tracts*, 67; NLS, 'Collectanea Domini Davidis Lindesay', f. 98r; NAS, Treasurer's Accounts 1616–18, E21/84, f. 65r.

[117] *Ayr Burgh Accounts*, 266; Calderwood, *History*, vol. 3, 458–9; ECA, Town Treasurer's Accounts, 1612–23, 979; PKCA, Council Minutes, B59/16/2, 31 Dec 1627; ACA, Council Records, CR1/51/1, 442; NAS, Linlithgow Town Council Minute Book 1620–40, B48/9/1, 270.

[118] SCA, Treasurer's Accounts, 1634–1720, B66/23/1, account for 1685–6.

[119] NLS, 'Collectanea Domini Davidis Lindesay', f. 98r.

[120] Calderwood, *History*, vol. 7, 494.

fringes, 14 tassels, and large decorated buttons.[121] Although Linlithgow's was not as grand as Aberdeen's, it was also made of velvet and cost £266 13s 4d, including the cost of horse trappings: brass stirrups, a French brass bit and leather bridle, reins, stirrup straps and crupper all covered with velvet. Aberdeen also had horse trappings to accompany its footmantle, spending an additional £80 8s 4d on them and, by the 1680s, Perth's came with a 'bridle, stiripe leathers and uther furnitour'.[122] Thus the more prominent burghs made the regulation sober black velvet into something much more ostentatious. That they were willing to spend so much on a garment which was so rarely used demonstrates how important it was for them to assert their prestige. So precious were these mantles that considerable care was taken to ensure their preservation. In 1621, Ayr spent £3 6s 8d to transport its footmantle and the commissioner's clothes to parliament and back, while Linlithgow made special arrangments to bring its footmantle the short distance from Edinburgh in 1644. It would have been returned to the treasurer into whose care it had been committed at his election. Perth's footmantle was kept in a trunk, along with the burgh's ensign and the magistrates' and councillors' robes.[123] As well as furnishing their commissioner with a footmantle, a burgh might also provide dress for those who accompanied him to ensure an impressive entourage. In 1644, Linlithgow paid for 'ane stand of new clothes' for an officer of the town attending the provost during parliament and, in the following year, Dumfries paid £12 for 'ane stand of clothes' for a man sent to attend their parliamentary commissioner at St Andrews.[124]

Conclusion

The dispute between Dundee and Perth and its provocation of other burghs to assert their claims to places in the hierarchy reveal something important about parliament and how it was perceived. It was *the* national institution where many things were affirmed and confirmed, not least the status and position of individuals and corporations within the body politic. Yet the issue seems to have exercised some burghs more than others: most do not seem to have cared a great deal about it. Only Perth, Dundee, St Andrews, Glasgow, Aberdeen, Linlithgow, Stirling, Inverkeithing, Lanark and Cupar ever made a fuss about their ranking. A similar pattern can be seen in the interest taken in acquiring and embellishing footmantles, with only Perth, Ayr,

---

[121] AAC, Ayr Court and Council Records 1607–32, B6/11/4, f. 659r; ACA, Treasurer's Accounts, TA1/2, accounts for 1627–8 and 1631–2; ACA, Dean of Guild Accounts 1453–1650, DGA1, account for 1632–3.

[122] NAS, Linlithgow Town Council Minute Book 1620–40, B48/9/1, 270, 282; NAS, Burgh Common Good Accounts, Linlithgow, 1633–4, E82/41/7; ACA, Dean of Guild Accounts, 1453–1650, DGA1, account for 1632–3; PKCA, Perth Council Minutes 1681–93, B59/16/10, f. 11v.

[123] AAC, Ayr Court and Council Records, 1607–32, B6/11/4, f. 659r; NAS, Linlithgow Town Council Minute Book 1620–40, B48/9/1, 270, 414, and Linlithgow Accounts, 1630–54, B48/13/1, account for 1643–4; PKCA, Perth Council Minutes, B59/12/2, 31 Dec 1627.

[124] NAS, Linlithgow Town Council Minute Book, 1640–59, B48/9/2, 109; DAC, Dumfries Treasurer's Accounts, 1645–46, GC2/13/8, f. 4r.

Edinburgh, Linlithgow and Aberdeen having a clear record of one before 1660. Thus the ostentation and affirmation of hierarchy embodied in the ceremonial processions at the beginning and end of a session of parliament may have been a concern only of the greater burghs, but for them it was taken very seriously indeed and they spent considerable sums on clothing, notarised protests and, in the case of Dundee and Perth, the legal costs of a case before whatever national tribunal would hear them.

Conclusion

Parliament and the Burghs in Early Modern Scotland

In 1923, two scholars published a study of the estate of the burgesses in the Scottish parliament between 1552 and 1707. In their introduction, they stated that 'the whole position of the burghs in Parliament has necessarily been brought under review', while other incidental questions were examined. Their frank description of the results is arresting: 'In settling these side-issues ... we have found no reason to depart from the established views, and from our main line of investigation, nothing surprising has emerged.' Perhaps this was false modesty, for they did tentatively suggest that their findings were 'in some sense new'.[1] Their thinking was so constrained by the contemporary historiographical fashion, which viewed the Scottish parliament as feeble and ineffective, that they were unable to explore the implications of some of their findings. Most notably, they could not entertain the idea that the final say over whether a burgh might enter parliament or not lay with the convention of burghs, not the king.[2] Fashions have changed and, as a result, it is hoped that this study does depart from some of the established views about the Scottish parliament, how it worked, how it was perceived and how the burghs operated within it, and that some of its findings might even be regarded as surprising.

Some English historians have recently called for examination of a wider range of questions about parliament in an effort to provide a more rounded view of its history. One particular concern was that English parliamentary historiography had 'been largely written from the perspective of the centre' which produced a distorted view of parliament, whereas a study of the interaction between local communities and parliament might provide 'something closer to the contemporary perception'. [3] It has been the purpose of this study to try to address some of the questions tackled by those scholars in the English context, both implicitly and explicitly. Although it is quite impossible to know whether this has genuinely led to an understanding of parliament that is 'closer to the contemporary perception', it has shed light on aspects of parliament which have lain in the shadows for a long time.

---

[1]   J. D. Mackie and G. S. Pryde, *The Estate of the Burgesses in the Scots Parliament and its Relation to the Convention of Royal Burghs* (St Andrews, 1923), 'Introduction'.

[2]   Ibid., 5, and see ch. 1 for discussion of this issue.

[3]   D. M. Dean and N. L. Jones, 'Introduction: Representation, Ideology and Action in the Elizabethan Parliaments', in Dean and Jones (eds), *The Parliaments of Elizabethan England* (Oxford, 1990), 1–13, at 1, and D. M. Dean, 'Parliament and Locality', in the same collection, 139–62, at 139.

Another recent writer on English towns and parliament observed that when researchers go 'to the town council minute book and chamberlain's account in the borough archives', they 'do not – save for a very few of the largest towns – find anywhere near the same concern for Parliament' as the central records would lead them to expect. Parliament is found to consist of 'a minute proportion indeed of local preoccupations in the vast majority of towns'.[4] The implication is that recourse to parliament was ineffective. That was possibly the case for the average English borough but the view is certainly not universally held, for another historian urged that, 'it is important not to exaggerate boroughs' lack of enthusiasm over parliament, nor to assume ... that they did not take parliament itself seriously'.[5] It should come as no surprise that parliamentary affairs do not figure prominently in local records. Parliaments were occasional events and the men who governed early modern towns had the regular duties of magistracy and council business to attend to, ensuring that markets were properly conducted, that the council's employees fulfilled their duties, that schools, hospitals, churches and public buildings were kept in good repair, and that public order was maintained. Local issues of immediate concern inevitably fill their records: it would be astonishing for it to be otherwise. Yet when a parliament, a convention of the estates or a convention of burghs was summoned, burgh councils responded, whether or not a specific legislative outcome was sought. There is no evidence that these meetings were regarded as a burdensome inconvenience. The diligent regularity with which most burghs sent commissioners to them is evidence enough of a strong local interest in national affairs and of the view that parliamentary representation was a right which provided opportunities as much as a duty which had to be done. Their payment of real expenses to their commissioners, usually without demur, is further evidence of the value placed upon participation. To be sure, for some burghs this feeling was stronger than for others. The lengths to which the more prosperous towns went to ensure that their commissioners looked sufficiently splendid and that their rightful place in parliamentary ceremonial was acknowledged are sufficient proof of that. Yet only a small proportion of the burghs, the smallest, poorest, remotest ones, tended to avoid sending commissioners.

When a burgh did seek legislation, parliament was able to provide effective solutions to particular local problems. It was not the only body that could fulfil that role, nor was it the most common place of resort for a burgh with a problem. The privy council, the court of session and the convention of burghs all served that purpose far more commonly than parliament could, yet with regard to certain issues, parliament was the only body which could provide the desired solution, and the vast majority of burghs successfully resorted to parliament at least once. This contrasts particularly with England, where promoting a bill was expensive, time-consuming and very unlikely to succeed. The collective efforts of the parliamentary burghs, through their conventions and as an estate in parliament, are further testament to their commitment to the parliamentary process. The strategies of the convention of burghs therefore reinforce the conclusion that legislation was worth obtaining,

---

[4]   R. Tittler, 'Elizabethan Towns and the "Points of Contact": Parliament', in *PH*, 8 (1989), 275–88, at 281.

[5]   Dean, 'Parliament and Locality', 146.

amending or blocking. The convention's activities also demonstrate its effectiveness in fostering and maintaining mercantile solidarity, and channelling that solidarity into parliamentary action. The merchant elite which ran Scotland's parliamentary towns knew that parliament was neither weak nor insignificant and they were well aware of the need to use it to maintain and advance their own power within their communities, to defend against the encroachments of others and to act in concert for their collective interests.

In parliamentary politics, the burghs, collectively and individually, did not make a significant impact. The available evidence sustains the case for the burghs' lack of enthusiastic involvement at the forefront of political change. Yet John Young's argument for the emergence of a 'Scottish Commons' during the 1640s is alluring. There is no doubt that the support of the burghs was crucial to the success of both the Covenanting revolution in 1637–1638 and the subsequent government of Scotland by the Covenanters, especially after 1649. There is also evidence that the burgh and shire commissioners occasionally co-operated.[6] However, fundamental tensions existed between those two estates and the hostility of the burghs towards enhanced power for the lairds in parliament does not suggest the existence of meaningful fellow-feeling against the titled nobility. In 1640, the burghs protested against an act giving each shire commissioner a vote (previously each shire had one vote, whether it sent one or two commissioners). For the act to pass, the nobles must have supported it, so it might more easily be portrayed as a bid by the landed interest to secure control of parliament when the burgesses nearly outnumbered the votes of the other estates. This view is strengthened by the burghs' protests against the representation of the stewartry of Kirkcudbright in 1644 and 1646. They believed that it was in their interests to limit the number of shire commissioners, something they would not have done had they regarded the lairds as their allies.[7] When it came to fiscal considerations, the shire commissioners clearly had common interests with the nobility against the burgesses: they voted together in 1644 to introduce excise duties, in 1645 to levy monthly 'maintenance' for the army and in 1649 to reduce interest rates, all in the face of the burghs' protests.[8] The reduction of interest rates, as well as indicating the disproportionate burden of debt borne by the merchant community, shows that, even after the seizure of power by the radical Covenanters in 1649, the 'Scottish Commons' was at best a shaky alliance when the interests of the landed classes were at stake. After the fall of the Engagers in September 1648 and the seizure of power by the radicals under the marquis of Argyll, the role of the burgesses and lairds in parliament did become more prominent and the lairds and burgesses, egged on by the radical clergy who dominated the commission of the general assembly, did become more assertive against the powers of the nobility. Yet

---

6   J. R. Young, 'The Scottish Parliament and the Covenanting Revolution: The Emergence of a Scottish Commons', in J. R. Young (ed.), *Celtic Dimensions of the British Civil Wars* (Edinburgh, 1997), 164–84. At 166–7 he seriously overstates the shire commissioners' voting strength by giving each commissioner two votes.

7   *APS*, vol. 6, part 1, 286, 614; Balfour, *Works*, vol. 3, 247–8. For other examples of deep-seated divisions between lairds and burgesses, see *Aberdeen Letters*, vol. 2, nos 111, 112.

8   See above, Chapter 3, pp. 74–5.

noblemen still formed the political leadership: there was no Scottish equivalent of Oliver Cromwell and no real threat to the social order.[9]

Here it is possible only to scratch the surface of the period after 1660, a topic which merits a study in its own right, but a longer-term perspective provides some useful opportunities for reflection. The doubling of shire votes in 1640 marked the end of the heyday of the burghs in parliament and this was never reversed or redressed. The burgess estate, frequently the most numerous since the later sixteenth century, subsequently grew only marginally as the numbers of nobles and lairds increased significantly. After 1660, only eight burghs entered parliament for the first time and only two new royal burghs were created (Campbeltown and Dunkeld). In 1690, the number of shire commissioners was further increased, with 15 shires being granted additional commissioners.[10] Burghs of barony no longer sought entry to parliament because it had become easier to circumvent the royal burghs' monopoly on overseas trade. That the royal burghs merely pressed for the others to pay a share of direct taxation, rather than seeking the expansion of their parliamentary estate, is ostensibly puzzling.[11] Had the rising baronial burghs been granted parliamentary status it would have halted the erosion of their trading privileges and of their strength in parliament but the parliamentary burghs did not want them there. They feared the further expansion of those legally conducting international trade since it might erode their share of what they myopically saw as a finite resource. At the same time, individual royal burghs feared further loss of trade to prosperous neighbouring baronial burghs if the latter were admitted to parliament. Excessive noble influence on the recently-elevated baronial burghs may also have been a worrying prospect. This was a significant consideration after 1660 in a way in which it had not been before 1651. After the restoration of Charles II to his Scottish throne in 1660, there was a reactionary backlash by the upper echelons of society, with the reassertion of noble power.[12] The nobility were able to protect the burghs of barony, first in their breaching of the royal burghs' monopoly of overseas trade, then in securing an act to end that monopoly in 1672. Before 1651, the convention of burghs acted effectively against unfree burghs and unfree merchants but in the later seventeenth century it was no longer able to prevail against them. In spite of the partial reinstatement of their monopoly in 1690, the dam had burst and the flood was so strong that it could

---

[9]   Stevenson, 'The Burghs and the Scottish Revolution', 168–9 and, by the same author, *Revolution and Counter-Revolution 1644–1651* (Edinburgh, 2003), 196–203, generally discusses the underlying social conservatism of the Scottish revolution.

[10]   A total of 26 new shire members could be elected after 1690: Rait, *Parliaments of Scotland*, 235–6; J. R. Young, 'The Scottish Parliament in the Seventeenth Century: European Perspectives', in A. I. Macinnes, T. Rijs and F. G. Pedersen (eds), *Ships, Guns and Bibles in the North Sea and Baltic States, c.1350–c.1700* (East Linton, 2000), 139–72, at 140–41. Campbeltown took up its place in parliament but Dunkeld never did.

[11]   RCRBS, vol. 4, 139–41, 302–3, 345–6, 351–2, 356–7.

[12]   Stevenson, *Revolution and Counter-Revolution*, 203–6; K. M. Brown, *Kingdom or Province? Scotland and the Regal Union, 1603–1715* (London, 1992), ch. 6; C. Jackson, *Restoration Scotland, 1660–1690: Royalist Politics, Religion and Ideas* (Woodbridge, 2003), 18–20.

not be repaired.[13] Smaller burghs saw this and sought to leave the fellowship of the free burghs, aware that there was little advantage in remaining a member, whatever benefits it might once have brought. The wider British context of monarchs more inclined to curry favour with the nobility than the merchants may also be significant, for the admission of new parliamentary boroughs in England also ground to a halt in the later seventeenth century.[14]

The erosion of the burghs' collective strength after 1660 is also indicated by a reduced enthusiasm for the maintenance of residential qualification for parliamentary commissioners. In 1674, the burghs received a letter from Charles II noting the 'innovation' of commissioners 'who are not actuall residenters' and charging them to rectify this. The crown's desire to exclude non-residents was born out of a fear that the opposition, led by William, third duke of Hamilton, might be seeking to manipulate burgh elections.[15] The convention's reply was striking, falsely alleging that the election of non-residents had always been common.[16] In the following year, it was forced to backtrack, acts enjoining residency qualifications were reiterated and anyone participating in the election of unqualified commissioners would lose their freedom and be fined 1,000 merks (£666 13s 4d). In 1678, a non-resident commissioner was declared ineligible and, in 1681, the convention sought parliamentary ratification of their act of 1675 reaffirming the qualifications.[17] The desire of some burghs to send non-resident commissioners remained, probably because of economic difficulties, for it had been argued in 1675 that if burghs were barred from electing non-residents, it would make them 'insignificant in parliament in regard most of the burghs ... either are not able to maintain a commissioner or have not a man capable of that trust'.[18] After 1690, the election of non-residents re-emerged but now the convention of burghs stated that commissioners at conventions of burghs must be resident or 'ane member representing the said burgh in the current parliament': it was accepted that parliamentary commissioners might be outsiders, and this was reiterated in 1702.[19] The theory which underpinned the representation of the burghs before the later seventeenth century had been undermined. Before 1707, the representative system of the burghs was losing its distinctiveness and moving towards the English practice before parliamentary union. Carpetbagging and freelancing were virtually unknown before 1660, remained rare until 1690, but became significantly more common thereafter.

The failures of the parliamentary burghs after 1660 had economic causes. From the beginning of the seventeenth century, economic dynamism in Scotland was to

---

[13] W. M. MacKenzie, *The Scottish Burghs* (Edinburgh, 1949), 146–52.

[14] D. L. Smith, *The Stuart Parliaments, 1603–1689* (London, 1999), 22; A. Dyer, 'Small Market Towns, 1540–1700', in Clark (ed.), *The Cambridge Urban History of Britain, Volume II*, 425–50, at 445.

[15] G. MacIntosh, 'The Scottish Parliament in the Restoration Era, 1660–1681' (St Andrews PhD, 2002), 208–13.

[16] *RCRBS*, vol. 3, 639–42.

[17] *RCRBS*, vol. 4, 9–10, 26; NAS, Beil Muniments, Minutes of the Convention of Estates 1678, GD6/1108, f. 24. I am grateful to Gillian MacIntosh for this reference.

[18] MacIntosh, 'The Scottish Parliament in the Restoration Era', 216, n.26.

[19] *RCRBS*, vol. 4, 281–2, 305, 341.

be found elsewhere. The merchants' main priority was the import and export trade and the provision of credit. They were focused on the maintenance of privileges with respect to those activities, rather than on the longer-term goal of advancing their own economic interests and those of the kingdom as a whole. It would thus be misleading to portray their opposition to union in 1707 as representing the view of those who were most important to the Scottish economy, for that role lay largely in the hands of landowners and baronial burghs. A majority of the convention of burghs voted to oppose union in the autumn of 1706 and, although the burghs in parliament voted in favour of the first article of the treaty (on the principle of an incorporating union), they voted for it by a narrower margin than the other estates. Many of these men were representing burghs which, as a result of war and shifts in patterns of trade, were economically of no significance and could do little more than cling blindly to the remaining privileges of the parliamentary burghs.

As well as opening up the parliamentary activities of Scotland's towns, a study such as this can reveal other things about the Scottish parliament. The examination of parliamentary venues, while providing insights into the political nation's perceptions of the status of parliament within the Scottish polity, also prompts refinements of interpretations of conventions of the estates. By the middle of the sixteenth century, and probably for a significant period before that, the political community expected, even demanded, that parliament should meet in an open, unfortified municipal building. The relative insignificance of the burghs in political terms lent them the ability to provide a neutral space for the sovereign body of the realm, allowing parliament to fulfil its role as a forum in which impartial judgement could be obtained and access was available to all those with grievances and petitions. The contrast with conventions of the estates bolsters this view and serves to strengthen the argument, recently put forward by Julian Goodare, that parliament had no true rivals.[20] None questioned, let alone denied, the king's right to call conventions of the estates to his residences because they were fundamentally different from parliaments, even more different than has hitherto been acknowledged.

The emergence of the convention of burghs as a virtually autonomous national institution after 1500 was part of the process by which the localities increasingly resorted to central bodies to maintain and defend their privileges. The role of the convention of burghs in the process of admitting new parliamentary burghs has important implications for any discussion of the power of the crown. Its ability to exclude unwanted newcomers for long periods (sometimes permanently) was never specifically recognised by the crown but it was no less real. Recently-erected burghs looked to the convention of burghs to endorse their new status, while existing burghs sought to block the admission of newcomers in the same forum. The convention's ability effectively to veto decisions made by the monarch arguably classes it with the court of session, the privy council and even parliament, all of which might thwart the wishes of the king if they believed him to be in the wrong.[21] None of this

---

[20]   J. Goodare, 'The Scottish Parliament and its Early Modern "Rivals"', in *PER*, 24 (2004), 147–172, at 149–52. See ch. 6 for a discussion of the significance of the venue.

[21]   For a famous example of the court of session defying the king, see Lord Cooper, 'The King versus the Court of Session', in *Juridical Review*, 58 (1946), 83–92.

necessarily challenged the power of the crown, or the state, but it did demonstrate that the authority of the monarch was limited because of the dispersed nature of power. The convention of burghs was not the king's court and did not meet under his authority, albeit that its liberties might have been seriously curtailed had it tended to defy the king, as happened to the general assembly in the early seventeenth century.[22] It emerged by a process which looks like the seeping of power away from the centre. This points to an important aspect of the nature of state formation in Scotland: power was increasingly wielded at a national level but it was not a simple, linear process, for at least two of those national institutions, the general assembly and the convention of burghs, developed alongside the institutions of central government and it is hard to portray them as organs of the state. Although the general assembly found itself under the power of the crown between 1597 and 1638 (meeting only six times after 1602), for more than half of the period between its autogenesis in 1560 and 1651, it was effectively autonomous. So was the convention of burghs and the crown rarely interfered with it because the burghs tended not to challenge the crown's authority. Some in the Church thought in terms of 'two kingdoms' but there was no urban analogue of that vision and whenever the privy council declared that the convention of burghs had acted *ultra vires*, it was content to back down. There was 'an integrated matrix of power' covering much of Scotland by the end of the reign of James VI but it was one in which there was still a great deal of institutional autonomy, both locally and nationally.[23] The crown accepted the authority of the convention of burghs in admitting burghs to parliament, in imposing conditions on who could be elected as burgh commissioners, and in granting burghs permission to seek a licence from the crown to raise money for public works. It may have been that those at the centre were not greatly concerned that they did not exercise these powers. It might even be argued that the crown was happy to have a body like the convention of burghs to relieve the burden on its officers. Yet it could make things more complicated for the crown. In 1605, when James VI and I wanted to send an Anglo-Scottish mercantile delegation to France, the English privy council was free to choose the English members, while the Scottish privy council had to ask the convention of burghs 'whome this mater propirlie concerneth, and without whose advise no suche choise or electioun could be maid'.[24] English kings could enfranchise boroughs as a part of their prerogative and only the English parliament could set the qualifications for MPs or give a borough permission to raise money for public works. The existence of the convention of burghs was both a cause and a consequence of the limited competence of Scottish central government. Its emergence filled a vacuum in the functions of the state and its effectiveness and vitality meant that it retained independent authority.

---

[22] A. R. MacDonald, *The Jacobean Kirk 1567–1625: Sovereignty, Polity and Liturgy* (Aldershot, 1998), chs 4 and 5.

[23] Goodare, *The Government of Scotland*, esp. 304–12. The interpretation offered here differs in emphasis rather than substance, being less willing to accept the use of the word 'state' to encapsulate all organs of civil and ecclesiastical control.

[24] *RPC*, first series, vol. 7, 472–4.

In recent years, there has been an instinctive tendency among Scottish historians to look to Europe for comparative purposes.[25] This was partly a reaction against the old fashion of comparing Scottish institutions unfavourably with those of England. Now, though, the Scottish parliament can stand up to such a comparison.[26] In terms of their powers, the Scottish and English parliaments were similar and very unusual in comparison to other European representative assemblies. Most significantly, their monopoly of legislative power was not 'a characteristic common to many European assemblies'.[27] In other spheres there were parallels too, particularly in the distinction between public and private legislation. Indeed, it is hard to avoid the conclusion that Scotland was following the English lead in this respect and in the development of the sovereignty of the king in parliament. It was because of these affinities that England was able to follow Scotland in its parliamentary revolution of the 1640s. The very endurance of the Scottish and English parliaments during the seventeenth century is also unusual and is explained largely by the similarly essential constitutional roles which they had acquired. Scotland's parliament can be counted among the casualties of early modern state-building in contrast to England's. But its disappearance resulted not from weakness but strength, and the problems which that caused for the strategic interests of England and the monarchy at the beginning of the eighteenth century.[28] With regard to representation, there were also similarities between Scotland and England, with elections prior to 1637 normally involving appointment by acclamation, even when there was a degree of popular participation, and an increased incidence of contested elections after 1637. Once elected, both Scottish and English representatives possessed *plena potestas* in theory but not in practice.

Yet the differences between the two countries must not be downplayed. The delegate basis of Scottish urban representation and Scotland's adherence to the residency qualification for commissioners provide marked contrasts with England. The European dimension does provide some helpful comparisons too. Most commonly cited is the division of parliament into 'estates', another contrast with England. Yet this superficial commonality breaks down on closer examination and European parliaments, including those in Britain, are better understood as exhibiting a diversity of composition and structure: some had one chamber and many estates (as in Scotland and Naples); some had a chamber for each estate but that could mean as many as four (as in Aragon and Sweden) or as few as one (as in Castile); some had two chambers and no underpinning notion of estates at all (as in England, Ireland and Poland).[29] Even within these categories, there were variations, with sessions of the ostensibly quadricameral

---

[25]   In the context of parliament, see Young, 'The Scottish Parliament in the Seventeenth Century'.

[26]   R. J. Tanner, *The Late Medieval Scottish Parliament: Politics and the Three Estates, 1424–1488* (East Linton, 2001), 271; Goodare, 'The Scottish Parliament and its Early Modern "Rivals"', demonstrates that, by the 1560s, the monarch in parliament had the same sort of omnicompetence and sovereignty as had been achieved in England in the 1530s; see also his *State and Society in Early Modern Scotland* (Oxford, 1999), ch. 1.

[27]   M. A. R. Graves, *The Parliaments of Early Modern Europe* (Harlow, 2001), 197.

[28]   Ibid., 4, lists the parliaments which vanished and those which endured, implying that survival was related to strength.

[29]   Ibid., 162–9; Young, 'The Scottish Parliament in the Seventeenth Century'.

Swedish *riksdag* beginning in a single chamber then breaking up into separate estates never to come together again, while the supposedly unicameral Scottish parliament began in a single chamber, broke up into its estates for deliberation and reconvened to vote on the acts.[30] The Scottish electoral system, whereby commissioners were appointed by burgh councils had parallels across Europe where, unlike in England, electoral processes were more uniform. But again there were differences. In many states, the crown had much more authority over the governing bodies of towns than was exercised in Scotland; as a result it was common outwith Scotland for officers of the crown (who were often outsiders) to be appointed as parliamentary representatives. Until the later seventeenth century, the parliamentary burghs of Scotland were the nation's trading towns which shared a monopoly of privileges and a burden of responsibilities, notably paying a share of parliamentary taxation. In some European assemblies, on the other hand, the only towns to be represented were those which happened to lie within the royal demesne, regardless of their wealth, size or political power.

Whatever parallels might be identified elsewhere in Britain and Europe, early modern representative assemblies were remarkably diverse. As Michael Graves recently put it, 'the only two constants in early modern European parliamentary history are variety in kind and variability over time', which were the 'consequence[s] of circumstances peculiar to a particular society'.[31] The explanation for the nature and form of any assembly is best achieved by an examination of its native context. The Scottish parliament in general and the particular relationship between that institution and the towns which had the right to be represented in it were shaped by the nature of the development of towns in Scotland and by the kingdom's wider political culture. Although the burghs were well aware that they were the 'meynest of the estates', that does not make a study of their parliamentary activities any less valid or any less enlightening than the study of any of the other estates or any other aspect of parliament's history. The single most important reason for this is the thread which can be traced throughout this book, the role of the convention of burghs. Its existence adds an extra dimension to the study of the urban estate in Scotland, a dimension which is not available for the study of any estate in any other parliament in early modern Europe. The records of the convention of burghs make it possible to trace the development of the burghs' legislative agendas and parliamentary strategies. They provide insights into the interests of the estate as a whole and preserve numerous examples of the activities of individual burghs which are not recorded in their own records, either because those records have perished or because it was not considered appropriate to note down in burgh council minutes many of the details which historians now crave. Without the records of the convention of burghs it would have been almost impossible to write this study. Moreover, had the convention of burghs not existed it would have been an entirely different story.

---

[30]   G. Rystad, 'The Estates of the Realm, the Monarchy, and Empire, 1611–1718', in M. F. Metcalf (ed.), *The Riksdag: A History of the Swedish Parliament* (New York, 1987), 61–108, at 69; A. R. MacDonald, 'Deliberative Processes in Parliament, *c.*1567–1639: Multicameralism and the Lords of the Articles', in SHR, 81 (2002), 23–51.

[31]   Graves, *The Parliaments of Early Modern Europe*, 1, 197.

Appendix 1

Chronological Table of Events

1542	Death of James V, succession of Mary
1543	James Hamilton, earl of Arran, appointed governor of Scotland
1544–50	War with England
1548	Mary sent to France for safety
1554	Mary of Guise, mother of queen, appointed regent of Scotland
1558	Mary marries François de Valois, dauphin of France
1559–60	Rebellion by Lords of the Congregation
1560	Parliament legislates for Reformation
1561	Mary returns to Scotland after death of François II
1567	Mary forced to abdicate, James VI crowned
1568–73	Civil war between king's party and queen's party, regents rule in name of James VI
1572–8	Regency of James Douglas, earl of Morton
1579	James VI declared an adult but remains under influence of a succession of factional regimes
1585	James VI begins to rule in his own right
1603	James VI succeeds to English throne
1617	James VI makes first visit to Scotland since 1603
1618	General assembly passes 'five articles of Perth' pushing Scottish worship towards English practice
1625	Death of James VI, succession of Charles I, introduction of revocation scheme threatening all grants by the crown since 1540
1633	Charles I visits Scotland for coronation and parliament
1637	Introduction of 'Laudian' prayer book and canons for Church of Scotland, outbreak of revolution, collapse of royal power in Scotland
1638	National Covenant drawn up, protesting against civil and ecclesiastical government of Charles I, first general assembly meets since 1618, episcopacy abolished
1639	First 'Bishops' War', Charles I agrees to call parliament
1639–41	Parliament ratifies acts of 1638 general assembly and passes radical constitutional reform subordinating king to parliament
1640	Second 'Bishops' War', Newcastle occupied, Charles I forced to accept parliamentary revolution in Scotland
1642	Outbreak of civil war in England
1643	Solemn League and Covenant: Scots support English parliamentarians against Charles I in return for presbyterian reform in England and Ireland

1644–5	Royalist rebellion led by James Graham, marquis of Montrose
1647	Engagement: moderate Covenanters agree to invade England for Charles I in return for securing presbyterianism in Scotland and three-year trial of presbyterianism in England
1648	Collapse of Engagers, radical Covenanters backed by Oliver Cromwell seize power
1649	Execution of Charles I by English, Charles II proclaimed king in Scotland, England declared republic, collapse of Anglo-Scottish alliance
1650	Charles II arrives in Scotland, Covenanting army crushed at Dunbar by Cromwell
1651	Charles II crowned at Scone, collapse of Covenanter regime, conquest by Cromwellian army
1651–60	Scotland under English republican rule
1660	Restoration of Charles II

Appendix 2

Burghs' First Attendances at Parliament

The first group is presented alphabetically because deficiencies in the record make a chronological list misleading. The others are given in chronological order. The table is largely derived from Pryde, *The Burghs of Scotland*.

Burghs first recorded at parliament before 1550

Aberdeen	1357
Ayr	1429
Banff	1469
Brechin	1479
Crail	1471
Cupar	1456
Dumbarton	1471
Dumfries	1469
Dunbar	1469
Dundee	1357
Edinburgh	1357
Elgin	1469
Forfar	1471
Forres	1488
Glasgow	1546
Haddington	1367
Inverkeithing	1471
Inverness	1439
Irvine	1430
Jedburgh	1469
Kinghorn	1471
Kirkcudbright	1469
Lanark	1469
Linlithgow	1367
Montrose	1357
North Berwick	1479
Peebles	1468
Perth	1357
Renfrew	1478
Rothesay	1485
Rutherglen	1478

St Andrews	1456
Selkirk	1469
Stirling	1449
Wigtown	1469

Burghs first recorded at parliament 1550–1651

Lauder	1567
Nairn	1567
Tain	1567
Arbroath	1579
Kintore	1579
Pittenweem	1579
Auchterarder	1584[1]
Kirkcaldy	1585
Burntisland	1587[2]
Dingwall	1587
Anstruther Easter	1593
Anstruther Wester	1593
Cullen	1593
Culross	1593
Dysart	1600[3]
Dunfermline	1604[4]
Annan	1609[5]
Lochmaben	1609[6]
Sanquhar	1609[7]
Inverurie	1612
Kilrenny	1612
New Galloway	1633
Dornoch	1639
Queensferry	1639
Whithorn	1641

---

[1]   Auchterarder may have attended this parliament but it was never enrolled by the convention of burghs, nor did it send commissioners to parliament again.

[2]   Although summoned to a convention of estates in 1586, Burntisland was not represented at parliament until 1587.

[3]   Although summoned to a convention of estates in 1594, Dysart was not represented at parliament until 1600: *RCRBS*, vol. 2, 93.

[4]   Although summoned to a convention of estates in 1594, Dunfermline was not represented at parliament until 1604: *RCRBS*, vol. 2, 172.

[5]   A commissioner attended a convention of burghs at the time of parliament in 1609: *RCRBS*, vol. 2, 259.

[6]   A commissioner attended a convention of burghs at the time of parliament in 1609: *RCRBS*, vol. 2, 259.

[7]   A commissioner attended a convention of burghs at the time of parliament in 1609: *RCRBS*, vol. 2, 259.

Burghs first recorded at parliament 1661–1707

Cromarty	1661
Fortrose/Rosemarkie	1661
Inveraray	1661
Wick	1661
Inverbervie	1670
Kirkwall	1670
Stranraer	1685
Campbeltown	1700

Appendix 3

Conventions of Burghs Held at the Time of Parliaments and Conventions of Estates

All known conventions of burghs which coincided with parliaments and conventions of the estates (marked with an asterisk) in the period are shown here.

Edinburgh, May 1555[1]

Edinburgh, July 1560[2]

Edinburgh, May 1563[3]

Edinburgh, December 1564[4]

Edinburgh, April 1567[5]

Edinburgh, October 1570[6]

*Edinburgh, October 1574[7]

Stirling, July 1578[8]

Edinburgh, October 1579[9]

---

[1]   *RCRBS*, i, 12–13; ACA, Aberdeen Council Registers, CR1/22, 60–61.
[2]   Parliament met in August but this convention was specially summoned for it: ECA, Edinburgh Council Minutes 1558–61, SL1/1/3, f. 39r.
[3]   DAC, Dumfries Burgh Court and Council Book 1563–64, WC4/9/2, f. 187v; DCA, Dundee Council Minutes, vol. 1, 75.
[4]   ECA, Edinburgh Council Minutes 1561–71, SL1/1/4, f. 115r.
[5]   *RCRBS*, vol. 1, 15.
[6]   Ibid., 16.
[7]   NAS, Wallace-James Notebooks, Haddington Treasurer's Accounts 1574–5, GD1/413/4, f. 58r.
[8]   *RCRBS*, vol. 1, 53–4.
[9]   Ibid., 80; ECA, Edinburgh Council Minutes 1573–79, SL1/1/5, f. 169r, 14 Oct 1579.

Edinburgh, October 1581[10]

*Edinburgh, October 1582[11]

*St Andrews, July 1585[12]

Linlithgow, December 1585[13]

Edinburgh, July 1587[14]

Edinburgh, July 1593[15]

*Edinburgh, January 1594[16]

*Edinburgh, March 1595[17]

*Perth, February 1597[18]

Edinburgh, December 1597[19]

*Edinburgh, June 1600[20]

Edinburgh, November 1600[21]

*Edinburgh, February 1601[22]

---

[10]   *RCRBS*, vol. 1, 121–6; W. Cramond (ed.), *The Records of Elgin 1234–1800*, 2 vols (Aberdeen, 1903–8), vol. 1, 160, stating that the parliamentary commissioner is also to attend the convention of burghs.

[11]   M. L. Stavert (ed.), *The Perth Guildry Book, 1452–1601* (Edinburgh, 1993), 327–9.

[12]   ECA, Edinburgh Council Minutes May 1583–March 1585, SL1/1/7, f. 200r.

[13]   *RCRBS*, vol. 1, 200.

[14]   Ibid., 235.

[15]   Ibid., 425–6.

[16]   ACA, Aberdeen Council Registers, CR1/35, 166; DCA, Treasurer's Accounts, vol. 1, 1586–1606, account for 1593–4; ECA, Edinburgh Council Minutes 1589–94, SL1/1/9, f. 239r.

[17]   ECA, Edinburgh Council Minutes 1594–1600, SL1/1/10, f. 23v; GCA, Glasgow Council Act Book 1594–97, C1/1/4, f. 34v.

[18]   GCA, Glasgow Council Act Book 1594–97, C1/1/4, f. 150r.

[19]   ECA, Edinburgh Council Minutes September 1594–May 1600, SL1/1/10, f. 155v; *RCRBS*, vol. 2, 21.

[20]   NAS, Burntisland Burgh Court Book, 1596–1602, B9/10/1, f. 111r; GCA, Glasgow Council Act Book 1598–1601, C1/1/5, f. 83r; *RCRBS*, vol. 2, 72. The annual general convention at Kinghorn was brought forward to meet before a convention of estates at Edinburgh.

[21]   NAS, Burntisland Burgh Court Book, 1596–1602, B9/10/1, f. 113v; GCA, Glasgow Council Act Book 1598–1601, C1/1/5, f. 129v; *RCRBS*, vol. 2, 94.

[22]   Ibid., 97; ECA, Edinburgh Council Minutes 1600–1609, SL1/1/11, f. 31v.

Edinburgh, April 1604[23]

Perth, July 1604[24]

Dundee, July 1606[25]

Edinburgh, March 1607[26]

Edinburgh, June 1609[27]

Edinburgh, October 1612[28]

*Edinburgh, March 1617[29]

Edinburgh, May 1617[30]

Edinburgh, July 1621[31]

*Dundee, July 1623[32]

*Edinburgh, October 1625[33]

---

[23] *RCRBS*, vol. 2, 169; NAS, Haddington Burgh Registers, Council Book 1603–16, B30/13/3, f. 17v.

[24] ACA, Aberdeen Treasurer's Accounts, TA1/3, account for 1603–4; NAS, Burntisland Council Minutes, B9/12/1, f. 50r; DCA, Dundee Council Minutes, vol. 3, f. 24v; *RCRBS*, vol. 2, 174.

[25] NAS, Dysart Burgh Registers, Court Book 1603–10, B21/8/7, f. 109v; *RCRBS*, vol. 2, 210–23. Oddly, the burghs met at Dundee while parliament met at Perth.

[26] ECA, Edinburgh Town Treasurer's Accounts 1596–1612, account for 1606–7, 850; *RCRBS*, vol. 2, 246.

[27] Ibid., 269.

[28] PKCA, Register of Acts of the Council of Perth, 1601–22, B59/16/1, f. 201r–v; GCA, Liber Actorum Burgi et Civitas Glasguensis 1609–13, C1/1/7, 29 Sept 1612.

[29] *RCRBS*, vol. 3, 33–5.

[30] AAC, Ayr Court and Council Records, B6/11/4, 15 April 1617; SCA, Stirling Council Minutes 1597–1619, B66/20/1, 26 May 1617.

[31] NAS, Burntisland Council Minutes 1617–23, B9/12/4, ff. 87r, 88v, 89r; ACA, Aberdeen Dean of Guild Accounts, DGA1, account for 1620–21 and Aberdeen Council Registers, CR1/50, 49–50; NAS, Dunfermline Burgh Court Book 1619–32, B20/10/4, f. 60v; ECA, Edinburgh Council Minutes 1617–26, SL1/1/13, f. 148r; SCA, Stirling Council Minutes 1619–58, B66/20/4, 11 July 1621; *RCRBS*, vol. 3, 115–16, 121–4.

[32] NAS, Linlithgow Town Council Minute Book 1620–40, B48/9/1, 55: the burghs met at Dundee immediately before the convention of estates at Edinburgh, and Linlithgow sent the same commissioner to both.

[33] ACA, Aberdeen Council Registers, CR1/51/1, 204; PKCA, Perth Council Minutes 1623–41, f. 36v.

*Edinburgh, July–August 1630[34]

Edinburgh, June 1633[35]

Edinburgh, August 1639[36]

Edinburgh, November 1640[37]

Edinburgh, January 1641[38]

Edinburgh, May 1641[39]

Linlithgow, July 1641[40]

Edinburgh, December 1641[41]

*Edinburgh, June 1643[42]

*Dumbarton, July 1643[43]

*Edinburgh, January 1644[44]

Edinburgh, June 1644[45]

---

[34]   ACA, Aberdeen Council Registers, CR1/51/1, 547–8, 7 July 1630; *RCRBS*, vol. 3, 321–4.

[35]   ACA, Aberdeen Council Registers, CR1/52/1, 109; ECA, Edinburgh Council Minutes 1626–36, SL1/1/14, f. 266r; ACA, Acts of Convention, CRB, vol. 2, f. 436v.

[36]   ECA, Edinburgh Council Minutes 1636–44, SL1/1/15, ff. 91r, 97v; GCA, Glasgow Council Minutes 1636–42, C1/1/10, 31 July 1639.

[37]   ACA, Aberdeen Council Registers, CR1/52/1, 591–3; NAS, Dunfermline Town Council Minutes 1638–50, B20/13/1, 80; *Edin. Recs.*, 1626–41, 243.

[38]   NAS, Burntisland Council Minutes 1631–37, B9/12/6, ff. 114v, 115r; ECA, Edinburgh Council Minutes 1636–44, SL1/1/15, f. 178v.

[39]   *Edin. Recs.*, 1626–41, 246–7; GCA, Glasgow Council Minutes 1636–42, C1/1/10, 3 April, 12 and 24 May 1641.

[40]   ACA, Council Records, CR1/52/1, 643; NAS, Dysart Burgh Registers, Court Book 1623–45, B21/10/1, f. 40v; GCA, Glasgow Council Minutes 1636–42, C1/1/10, 24 June 1641. The annual general convention of burghs met immediately before parliament.

[41]   ACA, Aberdeen Council Registers, CR1/52/1, 689.

[42]   SCA, Stirling Council Minutes, B66/20/4, 29 May 1643.

[43]   ACA, Council Records, CR1/52/1, 802. The annual general convention of burghs coincided with the convention of estates.

[44]   SAUL, Cupar Court and Council Records 1640–53, B13/10/3, 24 Jan 1644; ECA, Edinburgh Council Minutes 1636–44, SL1/1/15, ff. 331v–332r.

[45]   ACA, Aberdeen Council Registers, CR1/52/1, 834.

Edinburgh, December 1644–Jan 1645[46]

Edinburgh, May 1645[47]

Perth, July 1645[48]

St Andrews, November 1645[49]

Edinburgh, November 1646[50]

Edinburgh, January 1648[51]

Edinburgh, January 1649[52]

Edinburgh, June 1649[53]

Edinburgh, March 1650[54]

Edinburgh, May–June 1650[55]

---

[46] ACA, Aberdeen Council Registers, CR1/53/1, 29; DCA, Dundee Council Minutes, vol. 4, f. 185v; ECA, Edinburgh Council Minutes 1644–48, SL1/1/16, f. 28v.

[47] ACA, Aberdeen Treasurer's Accounts, TA1/3, account for 1644–5.

[48] FCAC, Dysart Council Minute Book 1/02/01, 23 June 1645.

[49] ACA, Aberdeen Council Registers, CR1/53/1, 67, Aberdeen Treasurer's Accounts, TA1/3, account for 1645–6.

[50] ECA, Edinburgh Council Minutes 1644–48, SL1/1/16, ff. 141v–142r; ACA, Aberdeen Council Registers, CR1/53/1, 86–7.

[51] Ibid., 194, 198.

[52] DCA, Dundee Council Records, vol. 4, f. 216r; ECA, Edinburgh Council Minutes 1648–53, SL1/1/17, f. 82v.

[53] *Kirkcud. Recs.*, vol. 2, 858. Kirkcudbright's commissioner was sent to parliament and a convention of burghs, although there is no indication of the timing or location of the latter.

[54] ACA, Aberdeen Council Registers, CR1/53/1, 260; SAUL, Cupar Court and Council Records 1640–53, B13/10/3, 1 March 1650; ECA, Edinburgh Council Minutes 1648–53, SL1/1/17, f. 233v.

[55] *RCRBS*, vol. 3, 355.

Appendix 4

The Proportion of Eligible Burghs at Parliament, 1542–1651

Some early creations were ineffective until the sixteenth century, so burghs are included only once they are known to have sent a commissioner to parliament, the method by which the figure for earlier attenders was derived in the past.[1] Auchterarder has been excluded because if it sent a commissioner to parliament it did so only once (in 1584) and was never enrolled by the convention of burghs. Whithorn is excluded until 1641 because, although it was on the burghs' tax roll of 1535 and attended the convention of burghs from 1574, it was excluded from parliament until 1641 due to resistance from neighbouring Wigtown.

Parliaments without surviving sederunts have been excluded. Estimates for the parliaments of 1594–1609 have been derived from surviving sederunts of conventions of burghs at the time of parliaments. These should be treated with caution, however: in 1593, 36 burghs were represented in parliament, but only 28 at the convention of burghs immediately before, while in 1612, 46 were represented at parliament but 47 at the convention of burghs.[2] Those dates marked (CE) were conventions of the estates to which all those normally called to parliament were summoned.

Mary (1542–67)	Parliamentary Burghs	Number and Percentage at Parliament
March 1543	34	13 (38%)
Dec 1543	34	10 (29%)
Nov 1544	34	8 (24%)
Sept 1545	34	7 (21%)
Aug 1546	35	6 (17%)
Nov 1558	35	10 (28%)
Aug 1560	35	22 (63%)
April 1567	35	8 (23%)

[1]   J. D. Mackie and G. S. Pryde, *The Estate of the Burgesses in the Scots Parliament and its Relation to the Convention of Royal Burghs* (St Andrews, 1923), 3–4.

[2]   *APS*, vol. 4, 423, 468; *RCRBS*, vol. 1, 423, vol. 2, 377–8. The 'odd' burgh in 1612 was Rothesay.

James VI (1567–1625)

Dec 1567	38	28 (74%)
Aug 1568	38	19 (50%)
Oct 1579	41	35 (85%)
Oct 1581	41	15 (37%)
May 1584	41	22 (54%)
Aug 1584	41	15 (37%)
Dec 1585	42	19 (45%)
July 1587	44	30 (68%)
July 1593	48	36 (75%)
July 1594	48	28 (58%)[3]
Nov 1600	49	31 (63%)[4]
July 1604	50	35 (70%)[5]
Aug 1607	50	25 (50%)[6]
June 1609	53	40 (75%)[7]
Oct 1612	55	46 (84%)
May 1617	55	45 (82%)
July 1621	55	49 (89%)

Charles I (1625–49)

June 1633	56	50 (89%)
Aug 1639	58	51 (88%)
June 1640	58	51 (88%)
Nov 1640	58	34 (59%)
April 1641	59	05 (08%)
May 1641	59	21 (36%)
July 1641	59	56 (95%)
Aug 1641	59	56 (95%)
Nov 1641	59	56 (95%)
June 1643(CE)	59	53 (90%)
Jan 1644(CE)	59	25 (42%)
April 1644(CE)	59	20 (34%)
May 1644(CE)	59	10 (17%)
June 1644	59	42 (71%)
Jan 1645	59	46 (78%)
July 1645	59	19 (32%)
July 1645	59	33 (56%)
Nov 1645	59	32 (54%)

---

[3] *RCRBS*, vol. 1, 423.
[4] *RCRBS*, vol. 2, 93.
[5] *RCRBS*, vol. 2, 171–2.
[6] *RCRBS*, vol. 2, 246.
[7] *RCRBS*, vol. 2, 269.

Nov 1646	59	48 (81%)
March 1648	59	48 (81%)
Jan 1649	59	51 (86%)

Charles II (1649–51)

May 1649	59	50 (85%)
March 1650	59	25 (42%)
Nov 1650	59	19 (32%)[8]
March 1651	59	21 (36%)[9]

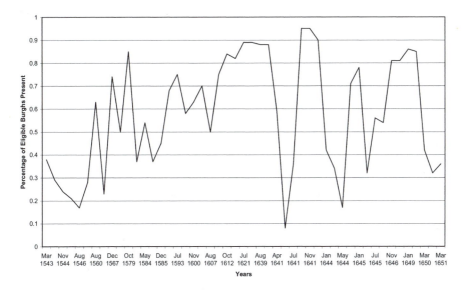

Figure 5   Percentage of Eligible Burghs at Parliament, 1543–1651[10]

---

[8]   The sederunt comes from Balfour, *Works*, vol. 4, 179–82.

[9]   The sederunt comes from Balfour, *Works*, vol. 4, 258–62.

[10]   Forty-nine sederunts were entered, although not every session is listed on the horizontal axis.

Appendix 5

Locations of Conventions of Estates 1561–1630[1]

Conventions listed in Young, *The Parliaments of Scotland*, are marked with an asterisk, while those in J. Goodare, 'Parliament and Society in Scotland, 1560–1603', (Edinburgh PhD, 1989), Appendix A, are marked with a hash. The latter designated meetings at Edinburgh and Holyrood as 'Edinburgh' but here a distinction is made to illustrate how frequently they met in the palace. The existence of the others is derived from burgh records and referenced in footnotes.

*Edinburgh, 22 December 1561

#Edinburgh, 28 September 1564

#Stirling, 15 May 1565

#Edinburgh, 9 July 1565

*Edinburgh, 6 October 1566

#Edinburgh, July 1567

#Stirling, 29 July 1567

#Edinburgh, 22 August 1567

#Stirling, 12 February 1569

*Perth, 28 July and 1 August 1569

#Edinburgh, 14 February 1570

#Edinburgh, 4 March 1570

---

[1] Conventions of estates in 1643 and 1644 have excluded been because the triennial act of 1640 fixed the next meeting of parliament for summer 1644 unless the king called one sooner, preventing the Covenanters from calling a parliament. To circumvent this, they called conventions, summoning everyone entitled to attend parliament. They were thus fundamentally different from previous conventions of estates.

*Edinburgh, 12 and 17 July 1570

*Stirling, 5 and 7 September 1571

*Edinburgh, 24–25 November 1572

Edinburgh/Holyrood, October 1574[2]

*Holyrood, 5 March 1575

Holyrood, 28 October 1575[3]

*Stirling, 8 March 1578

*Stirling, 12 June 1578

*Stirling, 16 July 1578

*Stirling, 15 November 1578

*Stirling, 15 and 25 January 1579

*Stirling, 12 March 1579

*Stirling, 7 August 1579

Stirling, March 1579–80[4]

*Holyrood, 26 February 1581

*Perth, 11 July 1582

*Holyrood, 19 October 1582

*Holyrood, 19 April 1583

*Holyrood, 7 December 1583

Perth, July 1583[5]

---

[2]   NAS, Wallace-James Notebooks, Haddington Treasurer's Accounts 1574–5, GD1/413/4, f. 58r, expenses paid to returning commissioner.

[3]   *RPC*, first series, vol. 2, 467.

[4]   ACA, Aberdeen Council Records, CR1/30, 25, 3 Feb 1579: 'conventioun of the nobilite'.

[5]   *Edin. Recs.*, 1573–89, 284, 23 July 1583: 'generall conventioun of the realme'.

St Andrews, August 1583[6]

Holyrood, April–May 1585[7]

*St Andrews, 31 July 1585

*Holyrood, April 1586

St Andrews, 31 August 1586[8]

St Andrews, 15 September 1586[9]

*Holyrood, 18 September 1586[10]

*Holyrood, 20 December 1586

Holyrood, 20 April 1587[11]

*Holyrood, May 1587

*Holyrood, 4 April 1588

Edinburgh, 20 May 1588[12]

*Holyrood, 27 July 1588

---

[6]   ECA, Edinburgh Council Minutes, SL1/1/7, f. 13r, 16 Aug 1583: 'conventioun of the estaitts'.

[7]   NAS, Haddington Burgh Registers, Council Book 1581–1602, B30/13/2, f. 23v, 27 April 1585: 'conventioun of the estatis'.

[8]   ACA, Aberdeen Council Records, CR1/32, 93, 22 Aug 1586: 'conventioun to be haldin ... according to the kingis majesteis missive'.

[9]   AAC, Ayr Court and Council Records, B6/11/1/3, f. 380r, 7 Sept 1586.

[10]   Young, vol. 2, 754; ECA, Edinburgh Council Minutes, SL1/1/8, f. 43v, 16 Sept 1586: 'conventioun of the estaits ... at this burght'; NAS, Haddington Burgh Registers, Council Book 1581–1602, B30/13/2, f. 36r: 'conventioun of the nobilitie ... at Halierudhous'; RPC, first series, vol. 4, 104.

[11]   ACA, Aberdeen Council Records, CR 1/32, 185, 14 April 1587: 'conventioun of the nobilitey and thre estaitis ... at Edinburght'; AAC, Ayr Court and Council Records, B6/11/1/2, f. 425r, 16 April 1587: says it was at Holyrood; NAS, Haddington Burgh Registers, Council Book 1581–1602, B30/13/2, f. 41r, 2 April 1587: 'convention of the nobility' at Holyrood.

[12]   *RPC*, first series, vol. 4, 284; DCA, Dundee Treasurer's Accounts, vol. 1, account for 1587–8: expenses paid 20 May 1588 to someone 'to pas to ... the conventione off the estaitis'.

Edinburgh, 24 November 1588[13]

Holyrood, 10 February 1588–9[14]

Holyrood, 24 April 1589[15]

*Edinburgh, 21 May 1589

*Stirling, August 1589

#Edinburgh/Holyrood, January–February 1590[16]

*Holyrood, 15 May 1590

*Holyrood, 12 June 1590

*Holyrood, 29 July 1590

*Edinburgh, 6 May 1591

*Edinburgh, 6 August 1591

Edinburgh, 20 April 1592[17]

Edinburgh, 24 May 1592[18]

*Stirling, 11–12 September 1593

*Linlithgow, 31 October 1593

*Edinburgh, 12 November 1593

*Holyrood, 23 and 26 November 1593

*Holyrood, 27 December 1593

---

[13]   ACA, Aberdeen Council Records, CR1/32, 431, 20 Nov 1588: 'conventioun of the estatis'.
[14]   AAC, Ayr Court and Council Records, B6/11/1/3, f. 502r, 5 Feb 1588/9.
[15]   ACA, Aberdeen Council Records, CR1/32, 489–90, 11 April 1589: 'conventioun of ... nobilitie baronis and utheris estaittis'.
[16]   *CSP Scot*, vol. 10, 837: although written in Edinburgh, the source gives no location for the convention.
[17]   *Edin. Recs.*, 1589–1603, 63, 14 April 1592 (Young, vol. 2, 754, no place of meeting given).
[18]   *CSP Scot*, vol. 10, 676–7.

*Holyrood/Edinburgh, 17 and 21 January 1594

*Edinburgh, 29 April 1594

Edinburgh, 25 May 1594[19]

*Holyrood, 10 September 1594

*Holyrood, 28–29 November 1594

*Holyrood, 15 March 1595

#Edinburgh/Holyrood, 24 November 1595[20]

*Holyrood, 22–25 May 1596

*Falkland, August 1596

*Dunfermline, 29 September 1596

*Edinburgh, 30 November 1596

*Edinburgh, 13 December 1596

*Linlithgow, 21–22 December 1596

*Edinburgh, 1 January 1597

*Holyrood, 6–8 January 1597

*Perth, 3–5 March 1597

*Dundee, 13 May 1597

*Linlithgow, 28 October 1597

*Edinburgh, 1 November 1597

*Holyrood, 29–30 June 1598

---

[19] ACA, Aberdeen Council Records, CR1/35, 312, 6 May 1594; ECA, Edinburgh Council Minutes, SL1/1/9, f. 253r, 15 May 1594; *CSP Scot*, vol. 11, 343–4.

[20] *CSP Scot*, vol. 12, 54, 78–9: although written in Edinburgh, the source gives no location for the convention.

Holyrood, 7 July 1598[21]

*Dalkeith, 17 August 1598

*Unknown location, 30 October 1598

*Holyrood, 14 December 1598

*Holyrood, 1 February 1599

*Holyrood, 2 March 1599

*Holyrood, 17 May 1599[22]

*Falkland, 31 July 1599

*Holyrood, 11 and 14 December 1599

*Perth, 27 March 1600

Edinburgh, 20 June 1600[23]

*Holyrood, 10 February 1601

*Perth, 11 September 1601

*Holyrood, 2 February 1602

*Perth, June 1602

#St Andrews, 8 July 1602

Edinburgh, 15 July 1602[24]

*Haddington, 5 July 1603

---

[21]   *RPC*, first series, vol. 5, 467.

[22]   *Edin. Recs.*, 1589–1603, 248, 16 May 1599: dates it to 17 May while Young, vol. 2, 755, has '(?)' beside 18 May.

[23]   ACA, Aberdeen Council Records, CR1/39, 348, 21 May 1600; AAC, Ayr Court and Council Records, B6/11/3, f. 319r, 19 May 1600; NAS, Burntisland Court Book, B9/10/1, f. 111r, 10 June 1600; GCA, Glasgow Burgh Act Book, 1598–1601, C1/1/5, f. 83r, 20 May 1600; NAS, Haddington Burgh Registers, Council Book 1581–1602, B30/13/2, f. 121v, 4 June 1600; SCA, Stirling Council Minutes 1597–1619, B66/20/1, 5 June 1600.

[24]   NAS, Burntisland Council Minutes, B9/12/1, f. 11v, 13 July 1602; PKCA, Perth, Register of Acts of the Council 1601–22, B59/16/1, f. 32v, 12 July 1602; SCA, Stirling Council Minutes 1597–1619, B66/20/1, 9 July 1602.

Perth, 2 November 1603 [25]

*Edinburgh, 6–7 June 1605[26]

Unknown location, 8 August 1605[27]

*Edinburgh, 20 May 1608

*Edinburgh, 26–27 January 1609

*Edinburgh, 30 April 1616

*Unknown location, 22 May 1616

*Edinburgh, 7 March 1617

*Edinburgh, 26–27 June 1621

*Edinburgh, 27 October–2 November 1625

*Holyrood, 28 July–7 August 1630

Numerical Analysis

A total of 112 meetings: 48 in burghs (Edinburgh (33), Dundee (1), Haddington (1), Perth (8) and St Andrews (5)); 57 in royal residences (Holyrood (36), Stirling (14), Linlithgow (3), Falkland (2), Dalkeith (1) and Dunfermline (1)). Of the remaining seven, three met at unknown locations while four met at Edinburgh or Holyrood but the record is not clear which.

---

[25]   PKCA, Perth, Register of Acts of the Council, 1601–22, f. 63r–v, 31 Oct and 7 Nov 1603: dean of guild to 'furneis all necessaris to the conventioun haldin at this burght', while a bailie was paid for refreshments given at 'this last conventioun to certane of the lordis'.

[26]   ACA, Aberdeen Treasurer's Accounts, TA1/1, account for 1604–5, dates it to 6 June, so it may have met on both days.

[27]   PKCA, Perth, Register of Acts of the Council, 1601–22, f. 103v, 9 July 1605: a letter from the crown for keeping 8 Aug 'with remanent commissionaris of burrowis the nobilitie'.

Bibliography

N.B. Individual essays in edited collections are not cited separately in the bibliography, only in footnotes.

Primary Sources

Manuscripts

Aberdeen City Archives
Acts of the Convention of Burghs, CRB.
Council Records, CR1.
Dean of Guild Accounts, DGA1.
Treasurer's Accounts, TA1.

Angus Archives
Montrose Council Minutes, M1/1.

Ayrshire Archives Centre
Ayr Court and Council Records, B6/11.

Dumfries Archives Centre
Act of the Parliament of the Four Burghs, 1500, RG2/2/4A.
Council Minutes, WA2/1.
Court and Council Records, WC4/9–10.
Treasurer's Accounts, GC2/13.

Dundee City Archives and Records Centre
Charters and Writs, CC1.
Council Minutes.
Guildry Book, GD/GRW/G1/1.
Treasurer's Accounts.

Edinburgh City Archives
Convention of Royal Burghs Papers, SL30/8/14.
Edinburgh Council Minutes, SL1/1.
Edinburgh Council Scroll Minutes, 1630–35.
Edinburgh Town Treasurer's Accounts.
Moses Bundles.
South Queensferry Council Minutes, SL59/1/1/1.

Fife Council Archive Centre
Culross Town Council Minutes, B/CUL1/1/1.
Dysart Council Minutes, 1/02.
Kirkcaldy Burgh Court Records, 1/06.

Glasgow City Archives
Glasgow Council Minutes (including accounts), C1/1.

National Archives of Scotland
Burgh Records:
Burntisland Council Minutes, B9/12.
Burntisland Court Books, B9/10.
Dunfermline Court Records, B20/10.
Dysart Court Books, B21/8 and 10.
Haddington Council Records, B30/13.
Haddington Court Records, B30/12.
Inverurie Burgh Court Books, B36/6.
Lauder Boxed Accounts 1632–1730, B46/8/5.
Linlithgow Council Minutes, B48/9.
Linlithgow Court Book, B48/7.
Linlithgow Treasurer's Accounts, B48/13.
North Berwick Burgh Records, B56/16/6.
Peebles Council Records, B58/13.
Peebles Court and Council Records, B58/8.
Peebles Treasurer's Accounts, B58/14.

Government Records:
Burgh Common Good Accounts, E82.
Comptroller's Accounts, E24.
Court of Session, General Minute Books, CS8.
Court of Session, Register of Acts and Decreets, CS7.
Parliamentary Commissions, PA7/25.
Register of Conventions of Estates, 1598–1678, PA8/1.
Register of the Privy Seal, PS1/80.
Supplementary Parliamentary Papers, PA7/23.
Treasurer's Accounts, E21.

Other Manuscripts:
Cosmo Innes Transcripts, RH2/2/14.
Cunningham Grahame Manuscripts, GD22
Dalhousie Papers, GD45.
Dundas of Dundas Muniments, GD75.
Lothian Muniments, GD40.
Pittenweem Writs, GD62.
Wallace-James Notebooks, GD1/413.
Yule Collection, GD90.

National Library of Scotland
'Collectanea Dominis Davidis Lindesay de Mounthe Militis Leonis Armorum Regis', Adv MS 31.3.20.
Denmilne Papers, Adv MS 33.7.11.
Fort Augustus MSS, Acc.11218.
Marquis of Hamilton's parliamentary diary, 1648, MS 8482.

Perth and Kinross Council Archives
Charter by James VI to Perth, 1600, B59/23/27.
Papers relating to disputes between Perth and Dundee, B59/26/1/9.
Perth Council Minutes, B59/16.
Perth Court Records, B59/12.
Perth Treasurer's Accounts, B59/25.

Perth Guildry Incorporation
Lockit Book 1451–1631.
Perth Guild Book, GD1/552/2.

St Andrews University Library, Manuscripts and Muniments
Crail Town Clerk's Scroll Book 1554–60, B10/8/2.
Cupar Court and Council Records, B13/10.
Inventory of Charters and Other Writs, Crail, B10/13/2.
Liber Sessione et Concilii de Pettinwem 1629–1727, B60/6/1.
St Andrews Treasurer's Accounts, 1611–27, B65/19/1.

Stirling Council Archives
Council Minutes, B66/20.
Fragmentary Records 1561–97, B66/15/5.
Treasurer's Accounts, B66/23.

Printed Primary Sources

Accounts of the Lord High Treasurer of Scotland, T. Dickson and J. Balfour Paul (eds), 13 vols (Edinburgh, 1877–).
Accounts of the Masters of Works for Building and Repairing Royal Palaces and Castles, J. Imrie and J. G. Dunbar (eds), 2 vols (Edinburgh, 1957–).
Acts of the Parliaments of Scotland, T. Thomson and C. Innes (eds), 12 vols (Edinburgh, 1814–75).
Adam, R. (ed.), *Edinburgh Records: The Burgh Accounts Volume 1* (Edinburgh, 1899).
Botfield, B. (ed.), *Original Letters Relating to the Ecclesiastical Affairs of Scotland*, 2 vols (Edinburgh, 1851).
Calderwood, David, *History of the Kirk of Scotland*, T. Thomson and D. Laing (eds), 8 vols (Edinburgh, 1843–9).

Calendar of the State Papers Relating to Scotland and Mary Queen of Scots, 1547–1603, J. Bain et al. (eds), 13 vols (London, 1898–1969).

Dalyell, J. G. (ed.), *Fragments of Scottish History* (Edinburgh, 1798).

Dennistoun, J. and MacDonald, A. (eds), *Maitland Club Miscellany III*, part 1 (Edinburgh, 1843).

Diurnal of Remarkable Occurrents That Have Passed Within the Country of Scotland Since the Death of King James the Fourth Till the Year MDLXXV, T. Thomson (ed.), (Edinburgh, 1833).

Dumbarton Common Good Accounts 1614–1660, F. Roberts and I. M. M. MacPhail (eds), (Dumbarton, 1972).

Duncan, A. A. M. (ed.), *Regesta Regum Scottorum*, vol. 5, *Robert I* (Edinburgh, 1988).

Exchequer Rolls of Scotland, The, J. Stuart et al. (eds), 23 vols (Edinburgh, 1878–).

Extracts from the Council Register of the Burgh of Aberdeen, J. Stuart (ed.), 4 vols (Aberdeen, 1844–72).

Extracts from the Records of the Burgh of Edinburgh, J. D. Marwick et al. (eds), 13 vols (Edinburgh, 1869–1967).

Extracts from the Records of the Burgh of Glasgow, J. D. Marwick et al. (eds), 11 vols (Glasgow, 1876–1916).

Extracts from the Records of the Royal Burgh of Lanark, R. Renwick (ed.), (Glasgow, 1893).

Fraser, W. (ed.), *Memoirs of the Maxwells of Pollok*, 2 vols (Edinburgh, 1863).

Galloway, B. and Levack, B. P. (eds), *The Jacobean Union: Six Tracts of 1604* (Edinburgh, 1985).

Haig, J. (ed.), *The Historical Works of Sir James Balfour*, 4 vols (Edinburgh, 1824).

Innes, C. (ed.), *Ancient Laws and Customs of the Burghs of Scotland*, vol. 1 (Edinburgh, 1868), 156.

HMC, *Report on the Manuscripts of the Earl of Mar and Kellie*, 2 vols (London, 1904–30).

Kirkcudbright Town Council Records 1606–1658, John, IV Marquis of Bute and C. M. Armet (eds), 2 vols (Edinburgh, 1958).

Laing, D. (ed.), *The Letters and Journals of Robert Baillie, A.M. Principal of the University of Glasgow, 1637–1662*, 3 vols (Edinburgh, 1841–2).

MacBean, L. (ed.), *The Kirkcaldy Burgh Records* (Kirkcaldy, 1908).

Maidment, J. (ed.), *Ancient Heraldic and Antiquarian Tracts by Sir James Balfour of Denmylne and Kinnaird, Knight and Baronet, Lord Lyon King at Arms* (Edinburgh, 1837).

——, *The Chronicle of Perth: A Register of Remarkable Occurrences Chiefly Connected with that City from the Year 1210 to 1668* (Edinburgh, 1831).

1629, 5th of November from Lowther (Edinburgh, 1894), 49–56.

Moysie, David, *Memoirs of the Affairs of Scotland, 1577–1603*, J. Dennistoun (ed.), (Edinburgh, 1830).

Murray, A. L. (ed.), 'A Memorandum on the Customs, 1597', in *Miscellany of the Scottish History Society, Vol. XIII* (Edinburgh, 2005), 66–82.

Pryde, G. S. (ed.), *Ayr Burgh Accounts 1534–1624* (Edinburgh, 1937).

Records of Elgin 1234–1800, The, W. Cramond (ed.), 2 vols (Aberdeen, 1903–8).

Records of Inverness, W. MacKay and H. C. Boyd (eds), 2 vols (Aberdeen, 1911–24).

Records of the Burgh of Dumbarton, 1627–1746 (Dumbarton, 1860).

Records of the Convention of the Royal Burghs of Scotland, J. D. Marwick and T. Hunter (eds), 7 vols (Edinburgh, 1866–1918).

Register of the Privy Council of Scotland, J. H. Burton et al. (eds), 37 vols (Edinburgh, 1877–).

Registrum magni sigilli regum scotorum, Register of the Great Seal of Scotland, 11 vols, J. Thomson et al. (eds), (Edinburgh, 1882–1914).

Registrum secreti sigilli regum scotorum, Register of the Privy Seal of Scotland, 8 vols, M. Livingstone et al. (eds), (Edinburgh, 1908–82).

Renwick, R. (ed.), *Charters and other Documents relating to the Royal Burgh of Stirling AD 1124–1705* (Glasgow, 1884).

Rhodes, N., Richards, J. and Marshall, J. (eds), *King James VI and I, Selected Writings* (Aldershot, 2003).

Roberts, M. (ed.), *Sweden as a Great Power 1611–1697: Government, Society, Foreign Policy* (London, 1968).

Robertson, J. and Grubb, G. (eds), *History of Scots Affairs, from MDCXXXVII to MDCXLI, by James Gordon, Parson of Rothiemay,* 3 vols (Aberdeen, 1841).

Row, John, *History of the Kirk of Scotland from the Year 1558 to August 1637,* D. Laing (ed.), (Edinburgh, 1842).

Spalding, John, *The History of the Troubles and Memorable Transactions in Scotland and England from 1624 to 1645,* J. Stuart (ed.), 2 vols (Edinburgh, 1828).

Spottiswoode, John, *History of the Church of Scotland ... by the Right Rev. John Spottiswoode,* M. Russell and M. Napier (eds), 3 vols (Edinburgh, 1847–51).

Stavert, M. L. (ed.), *The Perth Guildry Book, 1452–1601* (Edinburgh, 1993).

Stuart, J. (ed.), *The Miscellany of the Spalding Club,* vol. 5 (Aberdeen, 1852).

Taylor, L. B. (ed.), *Aberdeen Council Letters,* 6 vols (Oxford, 1942–61).

Terry, C. S. (ed.), *The Cromwellian Union: Papers Relating to the Negotiations for an Incorporating Union Between England and Scotland 1651–52* (Edinburgh, 1902).

Webster, B. (ed.), *Regesta Regum Scottorum Volume VI: The Acts of David II, King of Scots 1239–1371* (Edinburgh, 1982).

Reference Works

Balfour Paul, J. (ed.), *The Scots Peerage,* 9 vols (Edinburgh, 1904–14).

McNeill, P. G. B. and MacQueen, H. L. (eds), *Atlas of Scottish History to 1707* (Edinburgh, 1996).

McNeill, P. and Nicholson, R. *An Historical Atlas of Scotland c.400–c.1600* (St Andrews, 1975).

Matthew, H. C. G. and Harrison, B. (eds), *Oxford Dictionary of National Biography,* 60 vols (Oxford, 2004).

Pryde, G. S., *The Burghs of Scotland: A Critical List* (Oxford, 1965).

Scott, H. (ed.), *Fasti Ecclesiae Scoticanae*, revised edn, 8 vols (Edinburgh, 1915–).

Watt, D. E. R. and Shead, N. F. (eds), *The Heads of Religious Houses in Scotland from Twelfth to Sixteenth Centuries* (Edinburgh, 2001).

Young, M. D. (ed.), *The Parliaments of Scotland: Burgh and Shire Commissioners*, 2 vols (Edinburgh, 1992–3).

Secondary Sources

Anderson, R. D., Lynch, M. and Phillipson, N. (eds), *The University of Edinburgh: An Illustrated History* (Edinburgh, 2003).

Asch, R. G., *Nobilities in Transition 1550–1700: Courtiers and Rebels in Britain and Europe* (London, 2003).

Bain, E., *Merchant and Craft Guilds: A History of the Aberdeen Incorporated Trades* (Aberdeen, 1887).

Balfour Melville, E. W. M., 'Burgh Representation in Early Scottish Parliaments', in *EHR*, 59 (1944), 79–87.

Ball, N., 'Representation in the English House of Commons: The New Boroughs, 1485–1640', in *PER*, 15 (1995), 117–24.

Barrow, G. W. S., *Robert Bruce and the Community of the Realm of Scotland*, 3rd edn (Edinburgh, 1988).

—— (ed.), *The Scottish Tradition: Essays in Honour of Ronald Gordon Cant* (Edinburgh, 1974).

Birch, A. H., *Representation* (London, 1971).

Brown, K. M., 'Parliament, Crown and Nobility in Late Medieval and Early Modern Scotland, *c.*1250–1707', in *Rapprasentanze e Territori. Parlamento Friulano e Istituzioni Rappresentative Territoriali nell'Europa Moderna* (Udine, 2003), 119–39.

——, *Noble Society in Scotland: Wealth, Family and Culture, from Reformation to Revolution* (Edinburgh, 2000).

——, *Kingdom or Province? Scotland and the Regal Union, 1603–1707* (London, 1992).

Brown, K. M. and MacDonald, A. R. (eds), *The History of the Scottish Parliament, Volume 3: The Scottish Parliament, A Thematic History* (Edinburgh, forthcoming).

Brown, K. M. and Mann, A. J. (eds), *The History of the Scottish Parliament, Volume 2: Parliament and Politics in Scotland, 1567–1707* (Edinburgh, 2005).

Brown, K. M. and Tanner, R. J. (eds), *The History of the Scottish Parliament, Volume 1: Parliament and Politics in Scotland, 1235–1560* (Edinburgh, 2004).

Brown, L. F., 'Ideas of Representation from Elizabeth to Charles II', in *The Journal of Modern History*, 11 (1939), 23–40.

Bush, M. L. (ed.), *Social Orders and Social Classes in Europe since 1500: Studies in Social Stratification* (Harlow, 1992).

——, *Noble Privilege* (New York, 1983).

Campbell, G. and Paton, H. (eds), *An Introduction to Scottish Legal History* (Edinburgh, 1958).

Cardim, P., 'Ceremonial and ritual in the Cortes of Portugal (1581–1698)', in *PER*, 12 (1992), 1–14.

Chambers, R., *Reekiana: Minor Antiquities of Edinburgh* (Edinburgh, 1883).

Clark, P. (ed.), *The Cambridge Urban History of Britain, Volume II, 1540–1840* (Cambridge, 2000).

Clark, P., Smith, A. G. R. and Tyacke, N. (eds), *The English Commonwealth 1547–1640: Essays in Politics and Society Presented to Joel Hurstfield* (Leicester, 1979).

Connor, R. D. and Simpson, A. D. C., *Weights and Measures in Scotland: A European Perspective*, Morrison-Low, A. D. (ed.), (Edinburgh and East Linton, 2004).

Cooper, Lord, 'The King *versus* the Court of Session', in *Juridical Review*, 58, (1946), 83–92.

Cosgrove, A. and McGuire, J. I. (eds), *Parliament and Community* (Belfast, 1983).

Cowan, A., *Urban Europe, 1500–1700* (London, 1998).

Cowan, S. J., *The Story of Perth from the Invasion of Agricola to the Passing of the Reform Bill* (London, 1904).

Croft, P., 'Parliament, Purveyance and the City of London 1589–1608', in *PH*, 4 (1985), 9–34.

Cruickshank, C. G., 'Parliamentary Representation of Tournai', in *EHR*, 83 (1968), 775–6.

Cust, R., 'Parliamentary Elections in the 1620s: The Case of Great Yarmouth', in *PER*, 11 (1992), 179–91.

Cust, R. and Hughes, A. (eds), *The English Civil War* (London, 1997).

Dean, D. M., 'Public or Private? London, Leather and Legislation in Elizabethan England', in *HJ*, 31 (1988), 525–48.

Dean, D. M. and Jones, N. L. (eds), *Parliament and Locality, 1660–1939* (Edinburgh, 1998).

——, *The Parliaments of Elizabethan England* (Oxford, 1990).

Dennison, E. P., Ditchburn, D. and Lynch, M. (eds), *Aberdeen Before 1800: A New History* (East Linton, 2002).

Dennison, E. P. and Lynch, M., 'Crown, Capital, and Metropolis. Edinburgh and Canongate: The Rise of a Capital and an Urban Court', in *Journal of Urban History*, 32 (2005), 22–43.

Devine, T. M. and Jackson, G. (eds), *Glasgow Volume 1: Beginnings to 1830* (Manchester, 1995).

Dickinson, W. C., 'Burgh Commissioners to Parliament', in *SHR*, 34 (1955), 92–5.

Dillon, J., *King and Estates in the Bohemian Lands 1526–1564* (Brussels, 1976).

Donaldson, G., 'The Legal Profession in Scottish Society in the Sixteenth and Seventeenth Centuries', in *Juridical Review*, 21 (1976), 1–19.

——, *Scotland: the Shaping of a Nation* (Newton Abbot, 1974).

Dunbar, J. G., *Scottish Royal Palaces: The Architecture of the Royal Residences during the Late Medieval and Early Renaissance Periods* (East Linton, 1999).

Duncan, A. A. M., 'The Early Parliaments of Scotland', in *SHR*, 45 (1966), 36–58.

Elton, G. R., *The Parliament of England 1559–1581* (Cambridge, 1986).

——, 'Tudor Government: The Points of Contact I, The Parliament', in *Transactions of the Royal Historical Society*, fifth series, 24 (1974), 183–200.

Evans, R. J. W. and Thomas, T. V. (eds), *Crown, Church and Estates: Central European Politics in the Sixteenth and Seventeenth Centuries* (London, 1991).

Ewan, E., *Townlife in Fourteenth-Century Scotland* (Edinburgh, 1990).

Fairley, J. A., 'The Old Tolbooth: With Extracts from the Original Records', in *BOEC*, 4 (1911), 74–113.

Fawcett, R. (ed.), *Stirling Castle: The Restoration of the Great Hall* (York, 2001).

Ferguson, W., 'The Reform Act (Scotland) of 1832: Intention and Effect', in *SHR*, 45 (1966), 105–14.

——, *Scotland's Relations with England: A Survey to 1707* (Edinburgh, 1977).

Finer, S. E., *The History of Government*, 3 vols (Oxford, 1997).

Fittis, R. S., *The Perthshire Antiquarian Miscellany* (Perth, 1875).

Flett, I. E. F., 'The Conflict of the Reformation and Democracy in the Geneva of Scotland, 1443–1560: An Introduction to Edited Texts of Documents Relating to the Burgh of Dundee' (St Andrews MPhil, 1981).

Foggie, J. P., *Renaissance Religion in Urban Scotland: The Dominican order, 1450–1560* (Leiden, 2003).

Foster, S., Macinnes, A. and MacInnes, R. (eds), *Scottish Power Centres from the Early Middle Ages to the Twentieth Century* (Glasgow, 1998).

Friedrichs, C. R., *Urban Politics in Early Modern Europe* (London, 2000).

Gaimster, D. and Gilchrist, R. (eds), *The Archaeology of Reformation 1480–1580* (Leeds, 2003).

Galloway, B., *The Union of England and Scotland 1603–1608* (Edinburgh, 1986).

Gibson, A. and Smout, T. C., *Prices, Food and Wages in Scotland, 1550–1780* (Cambridge, 1995).

Gil, X., 'Parliamentary Life in the Crown of Aragon: Cortes, *Juntas de Brazos*, and Other Corporate Bodies', in *Journal of Early Modern History*, 6 (2002), 362–95.

Glendinning, M., *The Architecture of Scottish Government: From Kingship to Parliamentary Democracy* (Dundee, 2004).

Goodare, J., 'The Scottish Parliament and its Early Modern "Rivals"', in *PER*, 24 (2004), 147–72.

——, *The Government of Scotland, 1560–1625* (Oxford, 2004).

——, 'The Scottish Political Community and the Parliament of 1563', in *Albion*, 35 (2003), 373–97.

——'The Admission of Lairds to the Scottish Parliament', in *EHR*, 116 (2001), 1103–33.

——, 'The Scottish Parliamentary Records 1560–1603', in *Bulletin of the Institute of Historical Research*, 72 (1999), 244–67.

——, *State and Society in Early Modern Scotland* (Oxford, 1999).

——, 'The Scottish Parliament of 1621', in *The Historical Journal*, 38 (1995), 29–51.

——, 'Who was the Scottish Parliament?', in *PH*, 14 (1995), 173–8.

——, 'The Nobility and the Absolutist State in Scotland, 1584–1638', in *History*, 78 (1993), 161–82.

——, 'Parliamentary Taxation in Scotland, 1560–1603', in *SHR*, 68 (1989), 23–52.

——, 'Parliament and Society in Scotland, 1560–1603' (Edinburgh PhD, 1989).

Goodare, J. and Lynch, M. (eds), *The Reign of James VI* (East Linton, 2000).

Gouldesbrough, P., *Formulary of Old Scots Legal Documents*, Stair Society (Edinburgh, 1985).

Grant, A., *The Story of the University of Edinburgh*, 2 vols (London, 1884).

Graves, M. A. R., *The Parliaments of Early Modern Europe* (London, 2001).

——, *The Tudor Parliaments: Crown, Lords and Commons, 1485–1603* (London, 1985).

Grever, J. H., 'The Impact of the City Councils of Holland on Foreign Policy Decisions (1660–1668)', in *PER*, 14 (1994), 31–46.

——, 'The Municipal Level of Decision-Making in Holland (1660–1668)', in *PER*, 13 (1993), 17–27.

Griffiths, G., *Representative Government in Western Europe in the Sixteenth Century* (Oxford, 1968).

Hannay, R. K. and Watson, G. P. H., 'The Building of the Parliament House', in *BOEC*, 13 (1924), 1–78.

Hawkyard, A. D., 'The Enfranchisement of Constituencies 1509–1558', in *PH*, 10 (1991), 1–25.

——, 'The Wages of Members of Parliament, 1509–1558', in *PH*, 6 (1987), 302–11.

Hayden, J. M., 'Deputies and Qualities: The Estates General of 1614', in *French Historical Studies*, 3 (1964), 507–24.

Heal, F., *Reformation in Britain and Ireland* (Oxford, 2003).

Hewitt, G. R., *Scotland Under Morton: 1572–1580* (Edinburgh, 1982).

Hirst, D., *England in Conflict 1603–1660: Kingdom, Community, Commonwealth* (London, 1999).

——, *The Representative of the People? Voters and Voting in England Under the Early Stuarts* (Cambridge, 1975).

Horn, D. B., *A Short History of the University of Edinburgh 1556–1889* (Edinburgh, 1967).

Houston, R. A. and Whyte, I. D. (eds), *Scottish Society, 1500–1800* (Cambridge, 1989).

Howard, D., *The Architectural History of Scotland: Scottish Architecture from the Reformation to the Restoration, 1560–1660* (Edinburgh, 1995).

Hutton, R., *The Stations of the Sun: A History of the Ritual Year in Britain* (Oxford, 1996).

Innes, T., 'The Scottish Parliament: Its Symbolism and its Ceremonial', in *Juridical Review*, 44 (1932), 87–124.

Israel, J. I., *The Dutch Republic: Its Rise, Greatness and Fall 1477–1806* (Oxford, 1998).

Jackson, C., *Restoration Scotland, 1660–1690: Royalist Politics, Religion and Ideas* (Woodbridge, 2003).

Jones, C. (ed.), *The Scots and Parliament* (Edinburgh, 1996).

Jones, C. and Kelsey, S. (eds), *Housing Parliament: Dublin, Edinburgh and Westminster* (Edinburgh, 2002).

Juhala, A. L., 'The Household and Court of James VI of Scotland, 1567–1603', (Edinburgh PhD, 2000).

Kamen, H., *Early Modern European Society* (London, 2000).

Keith, T., 'Municipal Elections in the Royal Burghs of Scotland: I. Prior to the Union', in *SHR*, 13 (1915-16), 111–25.

——, The Origin of the Convention of the Royal Burghs of Scotland, with a Note on the Connection of the Chamberlain with the Burghs', in *SHR*, 10 (1913), 384–402.

Kerr, H. F., 'The Old Tolbooth of Edinburgh', in *BOEC*, 14 (1925), 7–23.

Kidd, C., *British Identities Before Nationalism: Ethnicity and Nationhood in the Atlantic World* (Cambridge, 1999).

Kishlansky, M., *Parliamentary Selection: Social and Political Choice in Early Modern England* (Cambridge, 1986).

Koenigsberger, H. G., *Estates and Revolutions: Essays in Early Modern European History* (New York, 1971).

Kümin, B. and Würgler, A., 'Petitions, *Gravamina* and the Early Modern State: Local Influence on Central Legislation in England and Germany (Hesse)', in *PER*, 17 (1997), 39–60.

Law, G., 'The Earl's Ferry', in *SHR*, 2 (1905), 14–29.

Lee, M., *The Road to Revolution: Scotland under Charles I, 1625–1637* (Urbana, 1985).

——, *Government by Pen: Scotland under James VI and I* (Urbana, 1980).

——, 'James VI's Government of Scotland after 1603', in *SHR*, 55 (1976), 41–54.

——'James VI and the Revival of Episcopacy in Scotland, 1596–1600', in *Church History*, 43 (1974), 49–64.

Lindsay, Alexander Lord, *Lives of the Lindsays*, 3 vols (London, 1858).

Lynch, M., *Scotland: A New History* (London, 1991).

——, 'Queen Mary's Triumph: The Baptismal Celebrations at Stirling in December 1566', in *SHR*, 81 (1990), 1–21.

——, (ed.), *The Early Modern Town in Scotland* (London, 1987).

——, 'The Origins of Edinburgh's "Toun College": A Revision Article', in *Innes Review*, 33 (1982), 3–14.

——, *Edinburgh and the Reformation* (Edinburgh, 1981).

Lynch, M., Spearman, M. and Stell, G. (eds), *The Scottish Medieval Town* (Edinburgh, 1988).

MacDonald, A. R., 'Deliberative Processes in Parliament, *c.*1567–1639: Multicameralism and the Lords of the Articles', in *SHR*, 81 (2002), 23–51.

——, '"Tedious to Rehers"? Parliament and Locality in Scotland *c.*1500–1651: The Burghs of North-East Fife', in *PER*, 20 (2000), 31–58.

——, 'Ecclesiastical Representation in Parliament in post-Reformation Scotland: The Two Kingdoms Theory in Practice', in *Journal of Ecclesiastical History*, 50 (1999), 38–61.

——, *The Jacobean Kirk 1567–1625: Sovereignty, Polity and Liturgy* (Aldershot, 1998).

——, 'Ecclesiastical Politics in Scotland, 1586–1610' (Edinburgh PhD, 1995).

——, 'The Subscription Crisis and Church-State Relations, 1584–1586', in *Records of the Scottish Church History Society*, 25 (1994), 222–55.

Macdougall, N. A. T., *An Antidote to the English: The Auld Alliance, 1295–1560* (East Linton, 2001).

——, (ed.), *Church, Politics and Society: Scotland 1408–1929* (Edinburgh, 1983).

Macinnes, A. I., *The British Revolution, 1629–1660* (London, 2005).

——, *Clanship, Commerce and the House of Stewart, 1603–1788* (East Linton, 1996).

——, *Charles I and the Making of the Covenanting Movement 1625–1641* (Edinburgh, 1991).

——, T. Rijs and F. G. Pedersen (eds), *Ships, Guns and Bibles in the North Sea and Baltic States* (East Linton, 2000), 139–72, at 140–41.

MacIntosh, G., 'The Scottish Parliament in the Restoration Era, 1660–1681' (St Andrews PhD, 2002), 208–13.

Mackenzie, K., *The English Parliament* (Harmondsworth, 1950).

MacKenzie, W. M., *The Scottish Burghs* (Edinburgh, 1949).

Mackie, J. D. and Pryde, G. S., *The Estate of the Burgesses in the Scots Parliament and its Relation to the Convention of Royal Burghs* (St Andrews, 1923).

McQueen, A. A. B., 'The Origins and Development of the Scottish Parliament, 1249–1329' (St Andrews PhD, 2002).

MacQueen, H. L. (ed.), *The Stair Society Miscellany Four* (Edinburgh, 2002).

Major, J. R., 'The Payment of Deputies to the French National Assemblies, 1484–1627', in *The Journal of Modern History*, 27 (1955), 217–29.

Makey, W., *The Church of the Covenant 1637–1651* (Edinburgh, 1979).

Marongiu, A., *Medieval Parliaments:A Comparative Study* (London, 1968).

Maxwell, A., *The History of Old Dundee* (Dundee, 1884).

Merriman, M., *The Rough Wooings: Mary Queen of Scots 1542–1551* (East Linton, 2000).

Metcalf, M. F. (ed.), *The Riksdag:A History of the Swedish Parliament* (New York, 1987).

Miller, J., 'Representatives and Represented in England 1660–1698', in *PER*, 15 (1995), 125–32.

Miller, P., 'The Tolbuiths of Edinburgh', in *Our Journall into Scotland Anno Domini 5th of November from Lowther* (Edinburgh, 1894).

Miller, R., *The Municipal Buildings of Edinburgh* (Edinburgh, 1895).

Mitchison, R., *The Old Poor Law in Scotland: The Experience of Poverty, 1574–1845* (Edinburgh, 2000).

Muir, A. G., 'The Covenanters in Fife, *c*.1610–1689' (St Andrews PhD, 2001).

Murray, A. L., 'The Lord Clerk Register', in *SHR*, 53 (1974), 124–56.

——, 'The Last Chamberlain Ayre', in *SHR*, 39 (1960), 85.

Myers, A. R., *Parliaments and Estates in Europe to 1789* (London, 1975).

O'Brien, I. E. , 'The Scottish Parliament in the 15th and 16th Centuries' (Glasgow PhD, 1980).

O'Callaghan, J. F., 'The Beginnings of the Cortes of Leon-Castile', in *The American Historical Review*, 74 (1969), 1503–37.

Pagan, T., *The Convention of the Royal Burghs of Scotland* (Glasgow, 1926).

Palliser, D. M. (ed.), *The Cambridge Urban History of Britain, Volume 1, 600–1540* (Cambridge, 2000).

Patrick, D. J., 'People and Parliament in Scotland 1689–1702' (St Andrews PhD, 2002).

Pearce, A. S. W., 'John Spottiswoode, Jacobean Archbishop and Statesman' (Stirling PhD, 1998).

Powell, J. E. and Wallis, K., *The House of Lords in the Middle Ages: A History of the English House of Lords to 1540* (London, 1968).

Rait, R. S., *The Parliaments of Scotland* (Glasgow, 1924).

——, 'Parliamentary Representation in Scotland', in *SHR*, 12 (1914), 115–34.

——, *The Scottish Parliament Before the Union of the Crowns* (London, 1901).

Ranum, O., 'Courtesy, Absolutism, and the Rise of the French State', in *Journal of Modern History*, 52 (1980), 426–51.

Richardson, R., 'The History of Parliament Square: Being an Historical Notice of the Southern Precincts of the Church of St Giles', Edinburgh', in *BOEC*, 3 (1910), 207–42.

Royal Commission on the Ancient and Historical Monuments of Scotland, *Tolbooths and Town-houses: Civic Architecture in Scotland to 1833* (Edinburgh, 1996).

Rubin, M., *Corpus Christi: The Eucharist in Late Medieval Culture* (Cambridge, 1991).

Russell Major, J., 'The Third Estate in the Estates General of Pontoise, 1561', in *Speculum*, 28 (1954), 460–76.

Sanderson, M. H. B., *Ayrshire and the Reformation: People and Change 1490–1600* (East Linton, 1997).

——, *Scottish Rural Society in the Sixteenth Century* (Edinburgh, 1982).

Sanz, P., 'The Cities in the Aragonese Cortes in the Medieval and Early Modern Periods', in *PER*, 14 (1994), 95–108.

Sharpe, K., 'Crown, Parliament and Locality: Government and Communication in Early Stuart England', in *EHR*, 101, (1986), 321–50.

Smith, D. L., *The Stuart Parliaments 1603–1689* (London, 1999).

——, *A History of the Modern British Isles 1603–1707: The Double Crown* (London, 1998).

Smout, T. C., *Scottish Trade on the Eve of Union 1660–1707* (Edinburgh, 1963).

Stevenson, D., *Revolution and Counter-Revolution, 1644–51* (Edinburgh, 2003).

——, *The Scottish Revolution, 1637–1644: The Triumph of the Covenanters* (Newton Abbot, 1973).

——, 'The Financing of the Cause of the Covenants, 1638–1651', in *SHR*, 51 (1972), 89–123.

Stewart, L. A. M., 'Politics and Religion in Edinburgh, 1617–1653' (Edinburgh PhD, 2003).

Stone, L., *The Crisis of the Aristocracy, 1558–1641* (Oxford, 1965).

Swanson, R. N., *Religion and Devotion in Europe, c.1215–c.1515* (Cambridge,1995).

Tanner, R. J., *The Late Medieval Scottish Parliament: Politics and the Three Estates, 1424–1488* (East Linton, 2001).

——, 'The Political Role of the Three Estates in Parliament and General Council in Scotland' (St Andrews PhD, 1999).

Terry, C. S., *The Scottish Parliament: Its Constitution and Procedure* (Glasgow, 1905).

Thompson, I. A. A., *Crown and Cortes: Government, Institutions and Representation in Early-Modern Castile* (Aldershot, 1993).

Tittler, R., 'Elizabethan Towns and the "Points of Contact": Parliament', in *PH*, 8 (1989), 275–88.

Torrie, E. P. D., *Medieval Dundee: A Town and its People* (Dundee, 1990).

Ulph, O., 'The Mandate System and Representation to the Estates General under the Old Regime', in *The Journal of Modern History*, 23 (1951), 225–31.

Vogler, B. (ed.), *Bibliothèque de la Revue d'histoire ecclésiastique: Miscellania Historia Ecclesiasticae VIII* (Louvain, 1987).

Whyte, I. D., *Scotland Before the Industrial Revolution: An Economic and Social History, c.1050–c.1750* (London, 1995).

Wilson, D., *Memorials of Edinburgh in the Olden Time*, 2 vols (Edinburgh, 1891).

Youings, J., *Sixteenth-Century England* (Harmondsworth, 1984).

Young, J. R., (ed.), *Celtic Dimensions of the British Civil Wars* (Edinburgh, 1997).

——, *The Scottish Parliament 1639–1661: A Political and Constitutional Analysis* (Edinburgh, 1996).

——, 'Scottish Covenanting Radicalism, the Commission of the Kirk and the Establishment of the Parliamentary Radical Regime of 1648–49', in *Records of the Scottish Church History Society*, 25 (1995), 342–75.

Index